MODERN CABINET WORK

A COMPREHENSIVE TREATISE ON MAKING FINE FURNITURE

MODERN CABINET WORK
FURNITURE & FITMENTS

An account of the theory & practice in the production of all kinds of cabinetwork & furniture with chapters on the growth and progress of design and construction illustrated by over 1,000 practical workshop drawings, photographs & original designs

PERCY A. WELLS

Head of Cabinet Department, L.C.C. Shoreditch Technical Inst.
Silver Medalist, Royal Society of Arts

& JOHN HOOPER, M.B.E.

Honors Silver Medalist, City & Guilds of London Institute.
Silver Medal, Carpenters' Company, Cabinet Section

Third Edition Revised

Fox Chapel Publishing

CAMBIUM PRESS

Modern Cabinet Work

© 2006 by Cambium Books
All Rights Reserved

ISBN-13: 978–1–892836–28–1
ISBN-10: 1–892836–28–9

First printing: July 2006

A Cambium Press Title
John Kelsey, Editor

Cambium Press books are published by
Fox Chapel Publishing
1970 Broad Street
East Petersburg PA 17520
www.FoxChapelPublishing.com

Publisher's Cataloging-in-Publication Data

Wells, Percy A.
Modern cabinet work : a comprehensive treatise on making fine furniture / Percy A. Wells & John Hooper. -- 3rd ed., rev. -- East Petersburg, PA : Cambium Press, c2006.

p. ; cm.
ISBN-13: 978-1-892836-28-1
ISBN-10: 1-892836-28-9
Originally published as: Modern cabinet work, furniture & fitments : an account of the theory & practice in the production of all kinds of cabinet work & furniture with chapters on the growth and progress of design and construction ; illustrated by over 1000 practical workshop drawings, photographs & original designs. Philadelphia : Lippincott, 1922, 3rd ed., rev.
Includes index.

1. Cabinetwork. 2. Furniture design. 3. Woodwork. I. Hooper, John. II. Title. III. Modern cabinet work, furniture & fitments.

TT197 .W45 2006
684.1/04--dc22   0607

Printed in the United States of America
10 9 8 7 6 5 4 3 2 1

FOREWORD

First published in London in 1908, "Modern Cabinet Work" remains the most comprehensive and complete treatise for the woodworker and furniture maker in the English language. Known worldwide as "the cabinet-maker's Bible," it enjoyed robust sales in at least six editions throughout the first half of the twentieth century. The last edition, the sixth of 1952, regrettably underwent such extensive revision that the character of the original work was lost, with much valuable information replaced by an inconsequential overview of post-WWII production methods. Perhaps as a result, the work soon went out of print, to be supplanted during the 1970s by "The Encyclopedia of Furniture Making," by Ernest Joyce, which, as the astute reader will detect, owes much to "Modern Cabinet Work."

The third edition of 1922, reprinted here, was written at a time when powered machinery had taken its rightful place in the workshop, but when hand tools and skills had not yet been discarded. As a result, the authors of Modern Cabinet Work were able to present the two approaches side-by-side, in a happy synthesis that uses machinery for the hard and repetitive work that it does best, while reserving hand skills for the detail work that gives character to fine furniture and built-ins (here called "fitments").

The 1922 edition featured many fold-out double-page drawings, which have been preserved at their original scale by division into two and sometimes three parts, which now appear on successive pages. These inserted pages have been given the same number as the original page they follow, with the addition of the letters A, B, C, et cetera. This maneuver preserves the original pagination, cross-referencing, and indexing in this facsimile volume.

Furniture aficionados and furniture makers in the 21st century will find much to admire and much to learn in this fine book, and we are delighted to give it new life.

May 2006   JOHN KELSEY, EDITOR

PREFACE

CONSIDERING the importance of the Craft of Cabinetmaking, it is surprising that no work has been published dealing fully with its modern developments and progress. During the last twenty-five years remarkable changes have taken place in methods of production as well as in taste and fashion as they affect house furnishing, and to-day the term "Cabinetmaking" covers a much wider scope in craftsmanship than it did formerly. It has been the aim of the authors to produce a book which illustrates step by step the practice of the craft in all its applications, from the making of a joint, to the preparation, setting out, and complete construction of the numerous and various types of furniture and woodwork which the Cabinetmaker is called upon to make. They have also endeavoured to combine essential features in good design and construction with modern processes and materials.

It is hoped that the book will meet the needs of the Craftsman and others engaged in the trade, as well as a numerous and increasing public interested in furniture. Much of the material has been prepared in connection with lectures given during the past few years at the L.C.C. Shoreditch Technical Institute.

PERCY A. WELLS.
JOHN HOOPER.

August 1909.

————————

NOTE TO THIRD EDITION.

THE rapid sale of the second, and a call for a third edition of "Modern Cabinet Work" is particularly gratifying to the Authors, and is a further proof of its appreciation by Designers, Craftsmen, and the Furniture Trade generally, both at home and abroad.

This new edition has been brought up to date by the inclusion of fresh text and plates illustrating some recent developments in modern furniture. It is hoped that the book will continue to enhance the prestige of an ancient and interesting craft.

PERCY A. WELLS.
JOHN HOOPER.

May 1922.

NOTE OF ACKNOWLEDGMENT

THANKS are sincerely tendered to the following gentlemen for the use of designs, photographs, or drawings:—The Right Hon. the Earl of Dysart; Lieut.-Col. G. B. Croft-Lyons; Mr J. S. Henry; Mr Ambrose Heal (Heal & Son, Ltd.); Messrs Geo. Trollope & Sons; Mr Harry Hems, Exeter; Mr Frank Stuart Murray; Mr H. E. Marillier (Morris & Co.); Mr George Jack; Mr E. R. Gimson; Mr Charles Spooner; Mr S. Hicks, Principal of the Shoreditch Technical Institute; Mr W. B. Dalton; Mr R. Waterer, Jun. (Waterer & Son, Chertsey); Mr J. P. White, Bedford; Mr E. J. Minihane; Messrs Wilson Bros., Leeds; Mr Fred Skull, High Wycombe; Mr D. Richter, The Bath Cabinet Makers Co.; Mr W. Willingale; Mr A. Gregory; Messrs Oetzmann & Co.; Mr Park (London and North-Western Railway Company); Mr Gordon Russell; and Mr J. H. Sellers. Thanks are also due to Messrs A. J. Shirley & Co. for the loan of examples of metalwork, and to Mr Thomas Johnson, Mr Edward Pite, and Mr E. Newbery Flashman for special designs they have prepared. The Authors are also indebted to Mr A. Carr for photographs of workshop processes; and to Mr G. Gummer and Mr A. Jessop for assistance with drawings; to Mr John Dunkin for kindly reading proofs; to Mr Percy J. Smith for the lettering of the cover and title-page; and to Messrs Batsford for lightening a heavy task with much help and consideration.

PERCY A. WELLS.
JOHN HOOPER.

CONTENTS

I. INTRODUCTION.

II. TOOLS, APPLIANCES, MATERIALS.

III. DRAWING, GEOMETRY, DESIGN: TECHNICAL TERMS.

IV. JOINTS AND THEIR APPLICATION.

V. WORKSHOP PRACTICE.

VI. FRAMED-UP WORK, TABLES, &c.

VII. CARCASE WORK.

VIII. BEDSTEADS AND MISCELLANEOUS FURNITURE.

IX. VENEERS AND VENEERING, MARQUETRY AND INLAYING.

LIST OF DOUBLE-PAGE DRAWINGS AND PHOTOGRAPHIC PLATES

Double-page drawings in in the 1922 edition have been converted into single pages that appear successively. They are numbered with the suffix A, B, C, etc., so as to preserve the original indexing and internal references.

(Single-page drawings are included in the general index.)

LIST OF PLATES

MODERN CABINETWORK, FURNITURE, AND FITMENTS

[*NOTE.—Throughout this work the letters "f." signify figure, and "p." page. When the figure referred to is on the same page, no page number is given. When the same or several figures on the same page are referred to close together, the page number is given only with the first reference.*

The figures of each illustration, where it consists of several, are separately numbered, and where there is more than one block on each page the numbering is continued throughout that page. References to illustrations are made primarily to the pages on which the figures occur, and in no case is the numbering continued beyond each separate page, with the exception of the photographic and double plates, which it will be found are numbered continuously in Roman numerals.]

CHAPTER I.

INTRODUCTION.

CABINETMAKING—ANCIENT AND MODERN.

Origin of Cabinetmaking—Development of Furniture—The Cabinetmaker, Old and New—Division of Labour—Present-Day Requirements and Prospects.

IT is a long stretch from the fifteenth to the twentieth century, but it covers a period that embraces the beginning and gradual rise of a craft which has taken a place in the front rank of skilled trades. No one engaged in it, whether apprentice or journeyman, salesman or designer, manager or master, can afford to ignore its historical side, when at any time he may be called upon either to design, make, or sell a piece of furniture which directly or indirectly bears some relation to the fashions of bygone periods. Having to face this fact, we may briefly refer to the development of cabinetmaking, and to changes at different periods, before turning to the practical reasons for which this book is written, viz., to explain the actual making of furniture of all kinds.

Cabinetmaking grew out of the needs and necessities of the times, as ideas of household comfort and taste grew and improved. Even the furniture of the fifteenth century—rude as it appears to us—was an advance on that of the thirteenth, when goods and chattels were preserved in "dug outs," or chests roughly hewn out of the solid, and chairs were luxuries for kings

alone.   As domestic life improved, and housekeeping articles increased, it
became necessary to "cabin" or enclose them, and the "joyner" who made
the "cabins" or "cupboards" gradually developed into the cabinetmaker.
How and when the separation took place it is impossible to say, as the transition was a slow one, but the earliest records we have of it are in the doings of
a "Guild of Cofferers," a society of craftsmen in the fifteenth century who made
a specialty of the construction of chests, "coffers," or "hutches" as they were
named, and it is reasonable to suppose that they also made other articles of
household use.   From the chest—which for a long time served as cupboard,
seat, table, and bed—we can trace the development of much of our modern
furniture.   It improved in construction as time went on, and was panelled and
framed into legs.   It was an easy and natural thing to lengthen the legs
and add another "cabin" or drawer as seen in the fifteenth century Gothic
cabinet illustrated in Plate II.   Shelves were fixed on the top, or another cupboard with a cornice supported by pillars was added, and the old chest became a
"buffet," or "court," and "cheese" cupboard, and from this it is not such a big
jump to the Yorkshire "dresser," or to the nineteenth century sideboard with
cupboards, drawers, and a back.   Again, the chest with back and arms became a
"settle," the forerunner of our settee and sofa.   Out of it, too, grew the "almery,"
"armoire," "press," and the chest of drawers.   A fine example of a "press" is
illustrated on p. 3; it may be compared with a modern wardrobe.

Much has been said in praise of the old cabinetmakers, and deservedly so,
for we can learn a great deal from their work, but the conditions of labour and
living are changed, and the cabinetmaker of to-day is called upon to show a
finer skill and larger resource than were ever exhibited by the craftsmen of the
ancient guilds.   The demands upon his craftsmanship vary from making the
daintiest articles for the boudoir, to the massive furnishings of a Town Hall.
He must be equally ready to repair an umbrella stand or fit up a royal saloon, a
yacht, or an office; to tackle any job that comes along in any style or material,
or to cheerfully pack up his tools when there is none.   When so much praise
is given to the old cabinetmakers, equal recognition is due to their successors in
modern times.

The introduction of flats; the increase of luxurious hotels; the changes
and improvements in house building which have brought the "fitment" and
the "ingle nook," have all tended to widen the scope of the cabinetmaker's
craft.   But his work is not confined to domestic furnishings only.   Special
furniture is made for ships, yachts, trains, schools, hospitals, sanatoria, museums,
offices, municipal buildings, libraries, and reading rooms.   Photography has
created a demand for minute but skilled work; the increasing use of stationery,
and the manufacture of surgical and scientific apparatus, have brought about the
"case-maker," whilst the theatre, the garden, and various sports all call for work
of a specialised character.

On the other hand, the decline of the apprenticeship system, and the increasing division of labour, tend to produce a specialist in one branch of the trade
only, as against an all-round workman, and it is more difficult for a lad to get a
thorough training than in former years.   Any decline in the standard of workmanship must end in disastrous results for all concerned, and beginners in

PLATE II.

2A

GOTHIC CABINET, FIFTEENTH CENTURY, AN EARLY DEVELOPMENT OF THE DRAWER AND UPPER CUPBOARDS.

PLATE III.

DAY COMPARTMENT IN THE ROYAL TRAIN FOR HER MAJESTY QUEEN ALEXANDRA,

PLATE IV.

2C

JACOBEAN DINING ROOM. DESIGNED BY MR. THOMAS JOHNSON.

Oak Furniture Designed by C. Spooner and A. J. Penty.

Satinwood Bedroom Furniture. By J. S. Henry Ltd.

the trade who seriously wish to master their craft will not be satisfied at learning one part of it only. As fashions change, there must ever be a demand for good and resourceful cabinetmakers, and although it may be necessary to specialise

Seventeenth Century Oak Press, in the Strangers' Hall, Norwich.

for a time, there are numerous means whereby a man may study various sides of his craft. It is hoped that this book may serve a useful purpose in giving a practical insight into some of these branches.

The furniture designers and cabinetmakers of to-day have to show the public that they can design and make furniture equal to if not surpassing the antique specimens for which there is such an increasing craze. It is only by showing the public that well-designed and soundly-made furniture can be produced at moderate prices that a demand for such will be established and increased.

In looking ahead, it is safe to say that the future of the English furniture and cabinetmaking trade generally must depend upon the quality of the work put upon the market. The combination of designer, maker, and machine should produce a type which can hold its own against all comers, and appeal to all buyers. There is a growing desire for good furniture, and it behoves the cabinetmaker to be ready for these changes, and well equip himself for fresh demands upon his intelligence and labour.

Cabinetmaking is a craft which must always be closely allied to the great mother art of architecture. It embodies some of the finest traditions of English craftsmanship, and whatever changes have taken place or may come, these traditions must continue to hold the imagination of the workers in it, whether individual or collective. If these traditions are carried on, we should then have English furniture what it has been in the past—good to make and pleasant to live with.

CHAPTER II.

TOOLS—APPLIANCES—MATERIALS.

Hand Tools—Planes—Chisels—Saws—Files, &c.—Their Construction, Cutting Action, Selection, and Care of—A Cabinetmaker's Kit and Tool Chest—Special and Shop Tools—Workshop Appliances and Materials.

PLANES.

CABINETMAKERS do not require so many tools as they did fifty years ago, but it is still as necessary to have a good "kit," and to know how to take care of it. A thorough knowledge of tools is only obtained by long practice, but there are certain mechanical principles underlying their construction which should be understood from the beginning.

The most prominent of all the tools is the plane, in its many and various

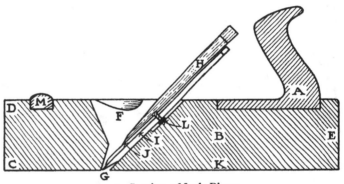

1. Section of Jack Plane.

shapes, sizes, and uses. Its size, in any particular work, has been settled by long usage and proof. Although the machine has saved much laborious labour, the hand plane must always remain an indispensable tool. Fig. 1 above shows a sectional side view of an ordinary jack plane. The names of its parts are as follows :—A, toat or handle; B, body or stock; C, toe; D, nose; E, heel; F, escapement; G, mouth, on one side nearly vertical, on the other at 45 deg.; H, wedge; I, cutting iron; J, cap or back iron; K, sole; L, screw. These names apply more or less to planes of all descriptions, varying only in those

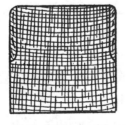

3. End of Plane, showing Rays in Wrong Direction.

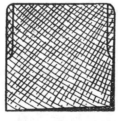

2. End of Plane, with Rays in Right Direction.

where a screw is used in place of the wedge. Sometimes a button, M, of boxwood is sunk in near the nose to take the hammer marks.

English wooden planes are made of beech, which should always be well seasoned and straight grained. It should also be cut so that the sole is as near as possible at right angles to the medullary rays, to allow for a uniform shrinkage. A stock which has been "cleft" from the raw timber is more likely to remain true than a sawn one, but, as this is an expensive method, only the best planes are made from cleft wood. In buying a plane it is important to examine the end of the stock. Fig. 2, p. 5, shows the rays in a jack plane as near right as they can be, whilst f. 3 illustrates the result of irregular cutting when shrinkage takes place, the diagram being somewhat exaggerated to show it. A stock which has been cut from the outside portion of the tree is far better than one cut near the heart, and the sole of a plane should not be on the heart side.

For finishing purposes iron planes are used. Those of English make are heavy and solid, with rosewood mountings, the stock being made either of cast or malleable iron, or gunmetal. The American planes are lighter, and flimsy in construction compared with those of English make, and are consequently cheaper, but they do not produce such a fine surface, nor last as long. French planes are sometimes preferred, but the choice of tools is a matter of individual experience.

The cutting action of such tools as planes, chisels, and spokeshaves is similar to that of the wedge. The bevelled edge of the plane iron lifts or splits the fibres of the wood and produces a shaving, the thickness of which is determined by the depth of the iron's edge protruding beyond the sole of the plane. In a like manner a paring chisel is forced under the fibres, and separates them as a wedge does. A saw crushes the fibres, whilst a file, rasp, or glass-paper reduces the surface of the wood to powder by continuous friction.

1. Cutting and Cap Iron.

Action of Back Iron.—Fig. 1 shows a cutting iron with the "back" or "cap" iron fixed. This back iron breaks the shaving as it passes into the mouth, as shown in f. 2A, whilst f. 2B illustrates the action of the single iron tearing the fibres. The edge of the back iron is set close to the cutting edge of the other, the distance varying slightly in different planes. In the "jack" it would be a full $\frac{1}{16}$ in., and less in

2A.   2B.

Cutting Action of Plane with and without Back Iron.

trying and iron planes. The cap iron should "bed" down quite flat to the surface of the cutting iron, or shavings will be forced between them, and the mouth become choked. The best plane irons are "gauged" to equal thickness from end to end, and those not gauged get thinner towards the top, and as the iron wears away the cutting space in the mouth is widened, which prevents fine work being done. The "pitch" of a plane iron is the angle at which it is set in the stock, and 45 deg. is known as the cabinet "pitch" in a trying plane. There are, however, other planes which have no back iron at all, but their cutting irons are set at a much lower pitch, and their edges are much closer to the mouth, whilst in the "bull nose," "chariot," and "shoulder" planes, the bevels of the cutting irons are also reversed. Fig. 1 below shows the angle of the iron in a trying plane, and if 10 deg. are taken off for the "basil" or grinding slope, the actual cutting angle is 35 deg., which is made less in sharpening. Fig. 2 shows the "smoothing" plane iron at an angle of 50 deg., which is lessened as in the last named. The higher the pitch the nearer to a scraping action, as in the "toothing" plane, with a single iron at an angle of 80 deg. Fig. 3 is the "shoulder" plane, with

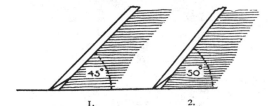

1.   2.

Angles of Trying and Smoothing Planes.

3.

Angle of Shoulder Plane.

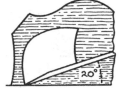

4. Angle of Chariot Plane.

5. Angle of Bull Nose Plane.

6. Angle of Wood Rebate Plane.

an iron sloping at 20 deg., and as the basil is reversed the cutting angle is from 25 deg. to 30 deg. Fig. 4, the "chariot," and f. 5, the "bull nose" planes, whilst f. 6 shows the wooden "rebate" plane, with a slope of 50 deg., and the basil set in the usual way, giving a cutting angle of about 40 deg. The escapement in this plane is inclined to the face of the iron, a provision which takes the place of a back iron, and breaks the shaving. In the iron rebate plane the angle is lowered to 30 deg., and time and long usage have proved that these angles are the best for the special work which the plane has to do.

Following the above details it is only necessary to give a brief description of the planes as they are shown on next page.

Jointer Plane, f. 1, 26 to 30 in. long, 3 in. sole. Used to shoot long joints, dining-table tops, &c. Also made in iron up to 24½ in.

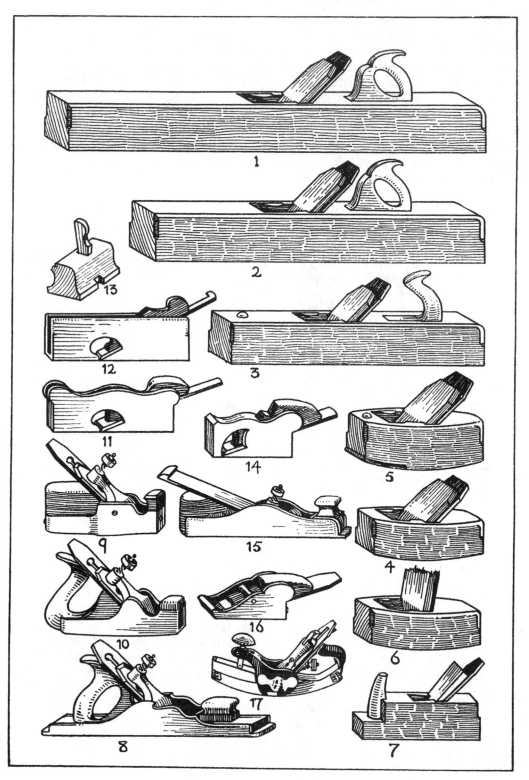

VARIOUS PLANES.

Trying, or **Trueing-up Plane,** f. 2, usual size 22 by 3¼ in. taking in 2½-in. iron. Used for all purposes in trueing-up and preparation work. Shorter ones are also known as "panel planes," some of which have a removable slip, so that the edge of the iron can be worked close in for sunk bevels on panels.

Jack Plane, f. 3, 17 by 2¼ in., and smaller with 2¼-in. iron, used in "jacking-up" stuff, or roughly preparing for the try plane.

Smoothing Plane, f. 4, usual size 8 by 3 in., with 2¼-in. iron, but varying in smaller sizes. Its name implies its use, that of smoothing and finishing. These planes are sometimes faced with steel, or have steel fronts as in f. 5.

Toothing Plane, f. 6, with a single iron, milled so that the edge resembles saw teeth. Used for toothing surfaces in preparation for veneering. Also useful for cleaning off, previous to scraping.

Bismarck, or **Roughing Plane,** f. 7, a single iron plane for taking off the dirt and first rough surface of boards.

Iron Panel, or **Jointer Plane,** f. 8, from 13½ to 26½ in. English make with rosewood fittings. Can be used for joints or finishing. An extremely useful plane for all types of work.

Iron Smoothing Plane, f. 9, with block fitting, and f. 10, with a handle. These iron planes are fitted with a screw in place of the wooden wedge for fixing the irons.

Iron Shoulder Plane, f. 11, of malleable iron or gun-metal, 8 in. long, from 1 to 1½ in. wide. Always a handy plane to cabinetmakers for shooting shoulders, short veneer joints, &c. It is made with square or skew mouth, and single iron.

Iron Rebate Plane, f. 12, from 6 to 9 in. long, ½ to 1½ in. wide, and fitted with one or two single irons.

Router, or "**Old Woman's Tooth,**" f. 13, usually made of beech with a mouth to take a plough iron. Used for routing out grooves across the grain in wide stuff.

Bull Nose Plane, f. 14, iron or gun-metal, 1 to 1¼ in. wide, for finishing off stopped rebates and angles where other planes could not be worked. Single iron.

Mitre Plane, f. 15, also made in wood, with low pitch and single iron for shooting mitres.

Chariot Plane, f. 16.—A small thumb plane with single iron and mouth near the front as in the "bull nose," but the sides are not open. Used for smoothing and finishing small work.

Compass Plane, f. 17.—The sketch shows the American patent with a thin steel sole which can be adjusted by a screw to any curve, either convex or concave. This is one of the many patents known as "Stanley" planes. "**Wooden Compass**" are similar to smoothing planes, but have a curved sole, and a brass or iron stop in the front to vary the curve.

The Plough, f. 11, p. 16, is an expensive tool, but with care will last a lifetime. It is really an adjustable plane for grooving, and should have a set of eight irons.

Wooden Rebate Plane, f. 10, p. 16, with single iron from ¾ to 1¾ in. wide, and made with box sole or slip

Side Rebate Planes are made in wood or iron in right and left pairs, and are used for trimming the sides of rebates and grooves.

Moulding Planes, such as "ogee," "ovolo," and hollows and rounds are supplemental tools, some of which a cabinetmaker should possess. Hollows and rounds are numbered in pairs, of which eighteen pairs make a full set. Moulding planes go by widths. Other pairs are the "rule joint," "hook joint," "groove and tongue, or matching" planes. **Bead** planes are sold singly.

The Side Fillister is a rebating plane with a movable fence on the sole and a screw stop for depth, as well as a spur for cutting the wood in advance of the iron. A "Trenching" or Dado Grooving Plane is of a somewhat similar make. Chamfer planes are also made in wood and iron. The "Stanley" group of planes include patent combinations of the moulding, grooving, ploughing, and other tools, as well as the ordinary try, jack, and smoothing planes.

SAWS.

HAND, BACK, AND FRAME SAWS.

Hand Saw, f. 1 opposite. In grade, known as "Rip," "Half Rip," "Hand," and "Panel," with straight or skew backs. Blades from 20 to 28 in. long, and handles of apple or beech. A good blade will be thinner at the back than in the front for easy working. The "Rip" has coarse teeth numbering four to the inch, and getting wider nearer the handle ; angle of teeth 90 and 30 deg. ; the Half Rip is not quite so coarse, and, as their name indicates, they are used for ripping down thick stuff in the direction of the grain. The **Hand Saw** proper is of more general use for cutting both ways—blade about 26 in. and teeth six to the inch, or the number may vary in all saws. The **Panel Saw** is shorter, thinner, and finer, and is used for cutting thinner stuff. The **Compass Saw** has a narrow tapering blade, for work which a wider one could not do.

Bow, or Frame Saw, f. 2, for cutting curves and shaped work. A thin blade 10, 12, or 14 in. long, $\frac{1}{8}$ and $\frac{1}{4}$ in. wide, fixed between two uprights and pulled taut by the string and bar. The blade can be turned to any angle by twisting the handle at both ends. Foreign workmen use frame saws with wide blades, and chairmakers also cut their curves with double handed frames held upright. **Fret** and **Marquetry Saw Frames** are much slighter and narrower, and are usually made of steel. The blades are very fine and are sold in bundles of a dozen.

Keyhole, or Pad Saw, f. 3, from the pad or socket which also serves as a handle into which the blade passes when not in use. The blade, which tapers, is fixed by two screws at the nozzle of the pad.

Back Saws.—These are used for finer work, and can only penetrate the wood to a given depth owing to the ridge of iron, or brass, which runs along the top of the blade and is known as the "back." In section, this "back" is split and tapers slightly from the top, thus forming a spring to hold the blade and keep it flat and rigid. When the blade works loose it

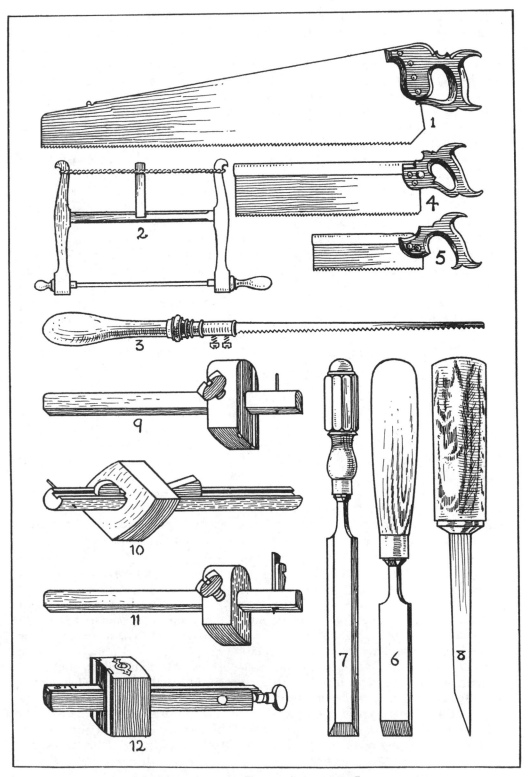

HAND, BACK AND FRAME SAWS AND CHISELS.

is liable to buckle, and can be set right again by a careful and gradual adjustment of the back by tapping it on the top edge until its increased grip has restiffened the blade. The brass backs are superior to the iron, as they give an additional weight to the saw. These saws vary in length from 8 to 14 in. on blade. The longest is commonly known as the **Tenon Saw**, f. 4, p. 11, from its use in cabinet work for cutting tenons and shoulders. The teeth are usually placed twelve to the inch and $\frac{1}{16}$ deep, but, as in all saws, this depends entirely on the type of work to be done, but twelve to an inch is coarse enough for general use. The smaller "back" saws are better known as **Dovetail Saws**, f. 5, used, as their name implies, in cutting the finer joints. The construction is the same as in the tenon saw, but the blade is thinner and not so deep, and the teeth are cut about fifteen to the inch and more, as the fineness of the work requires. For exceptionally small and fine work these saws are made with 4 or 6 in. blades and a turned handle.

Saw Sets.—To make a clear entry for a saw it is necessary that its teeth should cut a passage wider than the thickness of the blade. This is done by "setting" or bending the teeth alternately to the right and left with a tool known as a "saw set," which is cut to take various thicknesses and has an adjustable gauge to prevent an over set. The setting is done by inserting the tooth in the cut and pressing the handle downwards. Care must be taken

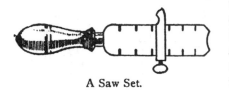

A Saw Set.

that there is not too much set and that it is equal on both sides, or the saw will run. Setting is also done with a hammer by striking the teeth on a vice or anvil made for the purpose, but the gauge method is the safest. In sharpening a saw, the edges of the teeth are slightly bevelled alternately in opposite directions, and the set should be put on after the sharpening. Saws often work loose at the handle, and a forked turnscrew, f. 7, p. 14, is used to tighten them up.

Chisels.—For all ordinary purposes a **Firmer Chisel**, f. 6, p. 11, is used. As its name denotes, it is shorter, thicker, and so firmer than the long paring chisel, f. 7, and which generally has a bevelled edge. Handles for chisels are usually made of ash, hornbeam, beech, or box, and are round or octagonal. The latter is better for the grip, and is least likely to roll off the bench. Chisels are made in sets of twelve from $\frac{1}{16}$ to 2 in. wide, but can be bought in half sets or singly, with or without handles.

Mortise Chisels, f. 8, with beech handle. A thick leather washer should be inserted at the joint where the tang enters the wood to prevent splitting.

Gauges.—Fig. 9 is a **Marking Gauge**, made of beech, with box screw or wedge, f. 10, and a steel pin for the marker.

The Cutting Gauge, f. 11, is of the same shape and wood, but with a brass wedge and steel blade for the cutter. This cutter is bevelled with a slightly rounded face, which is always placed inside near the stock, to ensure a clean cut. As the pressure on the gauge is in a forward direction, there would be a tendency for the cutter to run inwards if the bevel were on the outside, and so spoil or injure the work in hand. **Mortise Gauge**, f. 12, p. 11.—This gauge has double markers, and is more elaborately made. The inside point is fixed to a brass bar which is grooved into the stem, and is flush with its surface. At the end of the stem a thumb-screw is attached to the bar which enables the point to be adjusted to any width required, after the screw in the stock has been loosened. These gauges are usually made of rosewood or ebony, but the cheaper ones have no thumb-screw attachment. **Panel Gauge**, f. 1, with a long stem and wide fence, which has a rebate on the inside under edge, and a **Tee Gauge**, f. 2,

which has a length-
ened fence to clear
any projections,
and can be fitted
with a long point or
pencil for gauging
in grooves or panels
below the working
surface. These two
gauges can be

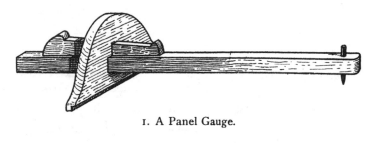

1. A Panel Gauge.

bought, but they are mostly made by the workman, and are best in hardwood.

BORING TOOLS.

The Brace, f. 14 & 15, p. 14, sometimes called a "stock," is used for boring purposes, and is made with expanding jaws to take any "bit." The most service-able brace is of American pattern and English make. Some are fitted with a ratchet for reverse action, by which a hole can be bored near the floor or in a position where it is not possible to take the whole sweep. The best in quality have ball bearings, and are nickel-plated. The width of sweep varies from 6, 8, and 10 in., the 6 in. being the one generally used for ordinary work.

Bits are made with square and tapering shanks to fit the jaws of a brace, whilst the boring points are of many and differing shapes. Fig. 1, p. 14, is a Centre Bit, made in all sizes up to 2 in. Fig. 2, Spoon or Pin Bit; f. 3, Shell Bit, and f. 4, the Nose Bit; all of which are used for boring across the grain. Fig. 5, the Gimlet or Swiss Bit for quick

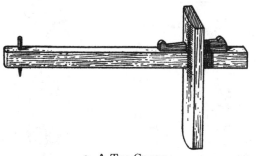

2. A Tee Gauge.

boring in soft woods. Fig. 6, Screwdriver, or Turnscrew Bit, used in a brace for driving screws home; and f. 7 is the Split Turnscrew for tightening up screws in saw handles. Fig. 8, the Twist or Jenning's Bit, a quick, clean borer both ways of the grain. Those with short twists are known as Dowel Bits. Fig. 9 is the Rose Countersink for enlarging the splay in a hole to take the head of a screw. Though specially made for brass, it can be used for metal or wood. Fig. 10, one for iron, and f. 11, the Snail Countersink for wood. For very large holes, there are patent bits with expanding cutters boring up to 5 in. dia-

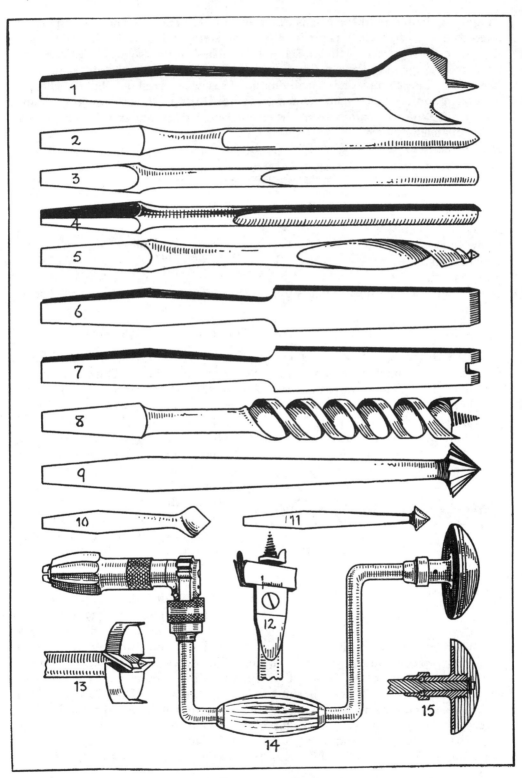

BRACE AND BITS.

meter, see f. 12 opposite. A patent cylindrical centre bit with four cutters is shown in f. 13; it bores clean, and can be obtained from ⅜ up to 1⅜ in. in width. **Rimers** are bits for enlarging holes, and are square or half round in section, and tapering to a point. The Shell Rimer is half round but hollow, whilst the others are solid, and are used chiefly for metal. **Drills**, with an Archimedean stock, are often used for small holes in very fine work. **Stock Drills** are usually preferred for boring in hard woods, as they do not drift in boring. They are fixed in an ordinary brace, and can be obtained in the usual sizes. A **Brace Bit Holder** is a handy substitute for the brace when it cannot be used. It is a box or hardwood handle similar to that on a gimlet, with a square tapering hole to take the shank of the bit, and is very useful for riming. **Bradawls** and **Gimlets** are hand-boring tools which need no illustration. They are really bits fixed in a handle, and are useful where the brace is not necessary or where a hole is required to start a nail. A **Marking Awl** is a thin steel pointer fixed in a handle, and is used for setting or " marking " out. It is often combined with a **Marking Knife** at the other end, and both are used for the same purpose, the knife chiefly for soft, and the marker for hard woods.

A **Sliding Bevel**, f. 4, p. 16, and a 6-in. **Square**, f. 8 & 9, are indispensable tools, and are made of rosewood or ebony, with a steel blade and a brass plate on the inside edge. Larger squares for carcase work can be bought, but are usually made in the workshop, and are best in mahogany. This also applies to **Set Squares** for testing inside angles.

Spokeshaves are made of wood, box, or beech, f. 6, p. 16, and iron, f. 7. They are a form of plane with a single blade, and a cutting angle of 10 deg. The face of the blade is slightly concave, whilst the stock can be rounded on the face to suit any curve. In wooden shaves the blade is sprung into the stock and held by the two ends or tangs, which enter a tapering hole. The American iron shaves have a small iron similar to a plane which is held in place by a thumb-screw. The sizes of spokeshaves go according to length of blade, from 1½ to 4 in., and it is important to remember that the burr is not rubbed off the face of the blade in sharpening.

Screwdrivers are made in various sizes and shapes, the " London " pattern having a broad flat blade and flat handle, and those known as " cabinet " drivers a round blade and oval handle. Thumb drivers 1 to 2 in. on the blade are extremely handy where a longer blade cannot be used.

Oilstones are of various quality and manufacture. The " Washita " is a good one for all-round use, and the " Turkey " for a keen finished edge. " Charnley Forest " is a slow cutter, but is also good for finishing, and " Arkansas " is a first-class satisfactory stone. All the above are natural stones, whilst the one known as " India Oilstone " is a composition, light brown in colour, and has the advantage of not being so liable to break if knocked down. It is also a fast cutter, and does not wear down as much as the others. Slip stones for gouges can be obtained in all the above qualities. Oilstones should be cased in wood, set in plaster of Paris, and covered with a lid. They need to be frequently rubbed down, either on a flat stone with sand, or on a sheet of emery cloth. Sweet oil with a little paraffin is the best for sharpening purposes. In choosing an oilstone it is as well to remember

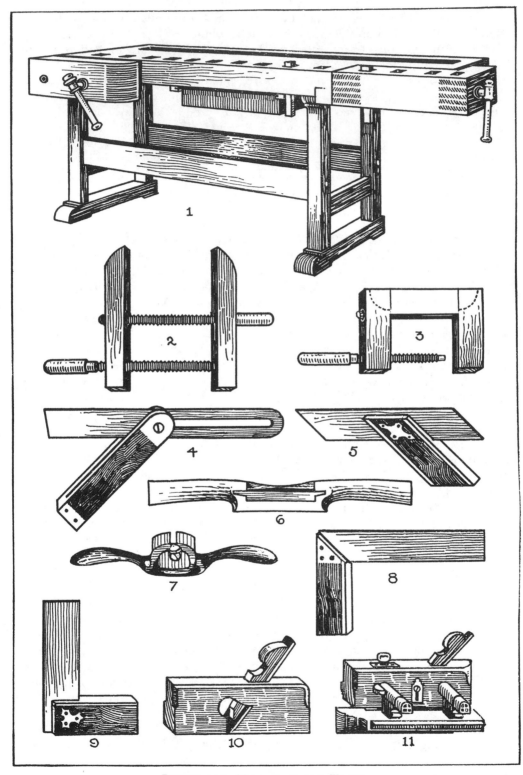

BENCH AND MISCELLANEOUS TOOLS.

that there are good and bad qualities in all kinds, but the cutting power of a stone can be tested by rubbing the thumb nail on it, and if it grips the nail it can safely be chosen as a fast cutter.

Files are made in various sections, as flat, half round, round (known as rat tail), square, and three-cornered (known as saw files), all cut for wood or metal. The cuts are known as "single" and "double" for saw files, "bastard" for wood, and "smooth" for metal. Flat files are made with one "safe" or smooth edge, as those for making keys, known as "warding" files.

Rasps are made in similar sections to files, but instead of cuts across the surface, they are chipped all over in such a way as to raise coarse cutting points. Rifflers are curved files and rasps.

Many **Mitre Cutting Tools** are made in the shop, such as the **Mitre Block**, for small work; the **Mitre Box**, for cornice mouldings; the **Mitre Shooting Board**, a combination with the ordinary shooting board; the improved **Mitre Shooting Block**, with wood or iron screw, see sketch; and the "**Donkey's Ear**," for shooting mitres from the inside of upright mouldings; the **Mitre Template**, in wood or metal, all of which are illustrated in

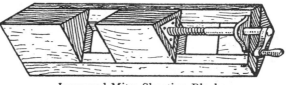

Improved Mitre Shooting Block.

the chapter on "Workshop Practice." **Mitre Cramps** are patent tools used by picture frame makers.

Cramps are usually supplied by the shop, and are made both in wood and iron, the best make having a bar with a T section, to which a lengthening bar can be attached for a long job. Small G-shaped cramps or **Thumb-Screws** are always useful.

Hand-Screws are generally found by the shop, but most cabinetmakers like to have a few of their own, especially small ones. The **Hand-Screw**, f. 2 opposite, with two screws made of beech, which if black leaded will work sweeter, is bought in sizes from 4 to 18 in. measured along the chop, and sold at one penny per inch. The **Hand-Screw**, f. 3 opposite, with single screw, has a more direct pressure, but cannot be used in as many ways as p. 2. The strongest make has a bolt right through to strengthen the joints, and the screws work sweeter if black leaded. Very small hand-screws are useful for fixing fine mouldings, but a good substitute for them is the wire "dog" or split chair spring, and the patent spring clothes' peg is very handy for similar purposes.

The Bench, shown in f. 1 opposite, with beech or birch top, in sizes from 4 to 8 ft., is fitted with vice and tail screws in wood or iron according to price. An all-round useful size is 5 ft. 6 in., which with iron screws will cost seventy-five shillings, and with wood screws sixty shillings. It is fitted with drawer, trough, and two iron stops, which with the tail screw make a convenient cramp for holding stuff and glueing up. A hole can be bored through the top to take an iron **Holdfast**. To make the bench more useful, holes can be bored down the leg, into which a pin can be placed at convenient heights for supporting long stuff when being worked in the vice, or the bottoms can be boarded in as a shelf. A grease box can be fixed on the end, as well as a stop for cutting against. For home use the cabinetmaker will find the English-made bench with double wood screw, 4 ft. 6 in. long, at twenty-one shillings, both serviceable and cheap, whilst the patent iron grip vices can be fixed to any bench.

There are many tools, such as the hammer, mallet, pincers, &c., which need no special description, but they are named in the following list, which is given as a specimen "kit" for a cabinetmaker. The sizes are suggested, with their cost price. The figures have been supplied by Messrs Tyzack & Sons, Old Street, E.C., but they are subject to fluctuation.

A KIT OF TOOLS.

	£	s.	d.
Trying plane, 22 in., gauged iron	0	7	0
Jack plane, 17 in., gauged iron	0	5	0
Smoothing plane, gauged iron	0	4	3
Bismarck (roughing), single iron	0	1	9
Toothing plane	0	3	3
Circular (compass) plane, adjustable, Stanley	0	10	3
Rebate plane, 1 in., skew mouth	0	2	4
Side rebate planes, one pair	0	5	6
Iron shoulder plane, $1\frac{1}{4}$ in., malleable	0	14	0
Iron rebate plane, $\frac{3}{4}$ in., malleable	0	10	6
Iron panel plane, $12\frac{1}{2}$ in., English make	1	7	6
Iron smoother plane, English make	0	18	6
Iron bull nose plane, $1\frac{1}{8}$ in.	0	7	0
Chariot plane, $1\frac{1}{4}$ in.	0	7	0
Hollows and rounds, half a set, nine pairs	1	19	6
Bead planes, $\frac{1}{4}$ and $\frac{1}{8}$ in.	0	5	0
Firmer chisels, eight, $\frac{1}{16}$ up to 1 in.	0	5	0
Bevelled edge paring chisels, $\frac{1}{4}$ in., $\frac{1}{2}$ in., and $\frac{3}{4}$ in.	0	3	10
Mortise chisels, $\frac{1}{8}$ in., $\frac{1}{4}$ in., $\frac{3}{8}$ in.	0	4	10
Squares, 6 in., 12 in. (20 in. wood, for carcase work, home made)	0	4	10
Set mitre, 10 in.	0	2	4
Sliding bevel, 9 in.	0	2	0
Striking knife and marking awl	0	0	4
Hammers, two	0	2	2
Pincers and cutting nippers	0	1	10
Oilstone (India), slips, and can	0	7	6
Screwdrivers (two), and one "thumb" driver	0	2	6
Mallet, 5-in. head	0	1	2
Hand saw, 26 or 28 in.	0	5	6
Panel saw, 24 in.	0	4	6
Tenon saw, 14 in., brass back	0	6	6
Dovetail saw, 10 in.	0	5	0
Bow saw, 12 in.	0	3	9
Pad, or keyhole saw	0	1	4
Small steel frame saw	0	1	6
Rule, 2 or 3 ft., four fold	0	1	0
Scraper, 5 by 3 in. and sharpener	0	0	11
Cork rubber	0	0	2
Files, various, wood and metal	0	4	0
Rasps, various	0	1	6
Mortise gauge, with set screw	0	4	0

	£	s	d
Cutting gauge - - - - - - -	£0	0	10
Marking gauge - - - - - - -	0	0	8
Panel gauge, home made - - - - - -		...	
Ratchet brace, English made - - - -	0	5	3
Twist bits, $\frac{1}{8}$ in., $\frac{1}{4}$ in., $\frac{3}{8}$ in., $\frac{1}{2}$ in., " Jenning's dowel " -	0	4	9
Spoon bits, $\frac{3}{32}$ in., $\frac{1}{8}$ in., $\frac{3}{16}$ in., $\frac{1}{4}$ in. - - -	0	1	2
Centre bits (black), $1\frac{1}{4}$ in., 1 in., $\frac{7}{8}$ in., $\frac{3}{4}$ in., $\frac{1}{2}$ in. - - -	0	1	$10\frac{1}{2}$
Countersinks (rose), $\frac{1}{4}$ in., $\frac{1}{2}$ in. - - - -	0	0	8
Turnscrew and forked turnscrew bits - - -	0	0	$7\frac{1}{2}$
Dowel rounder - - - - - - -	0	1	0
Bench holdfast - - - - - - -	0	4	6
Compasses, one pair - - - - - -	0	1	0
Thumb-screws (six), **G** pattern - - - -	0	10	0
Dowel plate, four holes - - - - -	0	1	1
Mitre shooting block, with iron screw - - -	0	12	6
Mitre cut, home made - - - - - -		...	
Mitre template, brass - - - - - -	0	1	6
Firmer gouges, $\frac{1}{4}$ in., $\frac{1}{2}$ in., $\frac{3}{4}$ in. - - - -	0	2	1
Scribing gouges, $\frac{1}{4}$ in., $\frac{1}{2}$ in. - - - - -	0	1	7
Carving gouges, straight, $\frac{1}{4}$ in., $\frac{3}{8}$ in., $\frac{1}{2}$ in. - -	0	1	9
Bradawls, six assorted - - - - -	0	1	0
Gimlets, three assorted - - - - -	0	1	0
Veneering hammer (home made) - - - -		...	
String gauge (home made) - - - - -		...	
Scratch stock (home made) - - - - -		...	
Punches (two) - - - - - - -	0	0	4
Small glue-pot - - - - - - -	0	1	6
Router (old woman's tooth) - - - - -	0	2	3
Plough with irons - - - - - -	1	1	0
Tongueing and grooving planes, one pair - - -	0	6	6
Bolting iron for shooting locks - - - -	0	1	0
Spokeshave, wood - - - - - - -	0	0	11

In many instances such a kit of tools **may** take years to collect, but an apprentice or beginner should commence early and buy good ones. A start can be made with just the necessary tools as follows :—Trying, jack, and smoothing planes, hand, tenon, and dovetail saws, oilstone, hammer, rule, screwdriver, square, oilcan, two gauges, mallet, pincers, and three firmer chisels, at a cost of £2. 7s. A brace and bits, scraper, rebate plane, spokeshave, mortise chisel and gauge should be got as time goes on and as the need arises. Such a "kit" must of necessity be kept in a chest. A handy size is 3 ft. 3 in. by 21 in. by 21 in. deep, made of good yellow deal or pine, dovetailed together, and painted black or dark green. It should have a small plinth piece planted round, and the lid can be made to lap over the front and ends. The chest will need a good spring lock and two strong handles. Fig. 1, p. 20, shows an arrangement for inside drawers and trays, of oak or mahogany, which should be made to half the width and slide from back to front. At the bottom of these is a sliding panel to enclose the lower space in which moulding planes can stand upright against the front and be easily recognised. The lid can be recessed, if desired, as a suitable place for saws and squares, and either enclosed or left open. Fig. 2, p. 20, shows the plan of the chest open. The top could be divided into three boxes with flaps, as shown, or made with drawers like the section. Another arrangement would be to make a case and fit it with drawers, but in the former suggestion the trays can be divided up to take the tools as required. There are many "extras" which a cabinetmaker soon collects, such as bench brush, set squares, grease box, tape and sponge, &c., which take up room and need their proper places, and to provide them is a task which becomes a pleasure to a craftsman interested in his tools.

Stoves for heating glue and providing a "hot plate" vary according to the size of the shop. The enclosed stove for coal, with chimney pipe attached, is effective for all small purposes, and serves as a good warming table. Gas and oil stoves are also made both for glue and hot plates, but steam tables and stoves are in general use in larger shops, and have the advantage of always being ready and also of warming the shop. Patent stoves are now made, either fixed or portable, to which can be attached either gas or electric heating power. Veneer presses are necessary in shops where any large veneers are laid, and where steam is used there is an iron press with heater underneath. The other forms of presses are given in the chapter on Veneering.

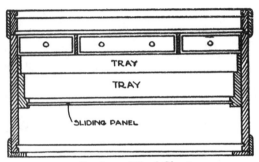

1. Section of Tool Chest.

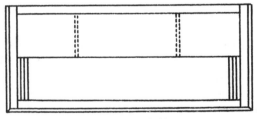

2. Plan of Tool Chest.

Glue is made from hides, intestines, and hoofs of animals, and the skins and refuse of fishes. These substances are boiled and filtered into cooling troughs, where they thicken to a jelly in suitable blocks from which the cakes are cut. These cakes are then stamped, scored, and hung out to dry, during which time they lose about half their bulk. They are then ready for the market. Good glue should be clear and transparent, not muddy, and should break brittle and clean. In qualities, the Scotch is the best for general purposes, the commoner kind being known as Town glue. Salisbury glue is a specially good quality, and is sold in thinner and smaller cakes than the Scotch. Liquid fish glue has the advantage of being ready for use, not needing to be made hot, but it takes longer to dry. Russian glue is made up in small white cakes ; and what is known as marine or waterproof glue is run into boxes, but it is extremely doubtful if any glue can be made quite waterproof. In large shops glue is put into cold water to soak until it becomes a thick jelly ; it is then boiled off and strained into a pan from which, when cold, it can be cut and put into the pots and heated off for the workshop. If left too long in the pan it will decompose and become unfit for use. In an ordinary way the cake is broken up—between a piece of sacking—into small pieces, put into the pot until three parts full, and then well covered with water.

The boiling off should be gradual. A white froth will appear on the top, which is the lime in the glue, and should be skimmed off. Care should be taken that the water in the outside pot does not boil away or the glue will burn and lose its quality, and that pots are free from dirt and grease. On no account should glue be used which is not thoroughly boiled off, and it is better to strain it, if possible, before a final heating.

Nails, screws, and glass-paper are described in Chapter V.

THE CARE OF TOOLS.

With a little care, tools will work the sweeter and last the longer. When new planes are bought they should be well soaked with linseed oil by filling up the mouth with a wedge of soft wood and then pouring the oil into the escapement. The oil will soak through the pores and help to set the wood, but it must not be overdone. After the week's work, planes should be rubbed over with the oil rag. A sheath for the saws—just a kerf in the edge of a bit of ⅜-in. stuff— will save the teeth. Bits are best kept in a baize bag, with a division for each one, and iron planes are safer if treated in the same way, or kept in wood cases with a piece of baize at the bottom. Chisels in a drawer should lie alternate ways, and it is economical never to put them away blunt. Oilstones should be kept covered, and too much oil left on tends to harden the stone. When planes wear down they need remouthing. The diagram shows how this may be done, and if a bit of good dry beech is not available, rosewood or box is the best to use. New planes sometimes choke and the mouth may need filing back, or the edge of the back iron is too thick, or does not bed well. "Chatter" in a plane is also due to the irons not bedding properly. The soles of wood planes wear irregularly and need shooting with an iron one, and care must be taken to get the sole true in the length. If tools are kept in good order they save labour and make work easier.

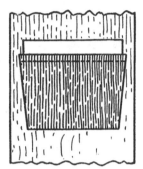

Remouthing a Plane.

CHAPTER III.

DRAWING—GEOMETRY—PERSPECTIVE—DESIGN— TECHNICAL TERMS.

Value of Drawing—How to begin—Instruments—How to make and use them—
Materials—Geometry: Plane and Solid—Its necessity and use in Practical Work
—Scales—Figures—Projection—Perspective—Technical and Workshop Terms.

A KNOWLEDGE of drawing is essential to a good craftsman and especially
to a cabinetmaker. In ordinary work he must be able to read a scale or
full-size drawing and interpret a plan or a section. A foreman or "setter
out" must be capable of translating one from the other, and know enough
of detail and construction to draw them in a practical and legible manner.
To a young beginner the best thing to do is to attend an evening class and
accept the course of work advised by the instructor, and also to practise at
home. The latter is possible to all, and a good beginning is to measure up
a table or chest of drawers and draw it to a convenient scale in front and end
elevation, plan and section. Details such as mould-
ings, carving, or turning, should be carefully studied
and drawn full size if possible. By close attention
and frequent practice the difficulties of first attempts
should be overcome, and the necessity for continued
effort in the early years of their career cannot be
too strongly urged upon all who wish to excel in the
various branches of their craft. This chapter will
deal with elementary principles and practical methods
applied to drawing for cabinetmakers in a general
way.

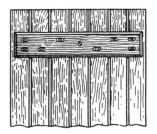

A Braced Drawing Board.

INSTRUMENTS.—The most serviceable **Drawing
Board** is one made of pine, well braced at the back with mahogany, which is slot
screwed to allow for shrinkage (see sketch). For all-round purposes an imperial
size, 30 by 22 in., is the most useful, but the board should be made a little larger.
It can be bought for 5s., or, if made, there must be a careful selection of first
quality pine, dry and free from shakes. To secure the least amount of warpage,
cut the 11-in. boards into two or three strips and rejoint them after reversing
the edges. Then plane them carefully flat and square, gauge to thickness, and
finish the face side with glass-paper, rubbing both ways. The pieces to brace
the back should be of 1-in. stuff about 3½ in. wide, and straight grained with
brass slots inserted for the screws in the position shown.

Tee Square.—To suit the board a 30-in. blade is necessary, and one that tapers, as in f. below, is the best to have. Those sold are usually made of pearwood, and cost about 2s. 6d., whilst the more expensive ones are of mahogany with an ebony edge. If made, mahogany is the best wood to use, and the stuff must be carefully selected. The thickness of the blade should not be less than $\frac{1}{8}$ in., and the taper from 4 to 2 in. with a slight bevel on the top of the straightedge. The headpiece for a 30-in. blade should be 12 in. long, 2 in. wide, and $\frac{1}{2}$ in. thick, with a small bevel on the inside top edge, to clear any slight abrasion on the corner of the board. The

Tee and Set Squares.

blade is fixed to the headpiece with a little thin glue and .brass screws, whilst two hardwood dowels give an added security. The square is best kept hung up by a hole bored in the blade.

Set Squares.—These are made in pearwood, mahogany, vulcanite, or gelatine, the latter being transparent. Handy sizes are 6 in. for 45 degs. and 8 in. for 60 degs. The solid ones, f. 3, p. 24, can be bought from 6d. upwards, but these are liable to warp. A better form is shown above, keyed at the joints and edged with ebony or pearwood.

Instruments are sold separately or in complete sets. A small set can be bought from 15s., but a start can be made with the following single pieces :— A pencil compass with an adjustable pen, a pair of dividers, an upright ruling pen, and a metal or boxwood protractor used for obtaining angles.

Pencils are graded as follows :—Very soft, BB ; medium, B—these are best for freehand drawing ; HB, a little harder for general use ; F, a grade harder ; and H, hard enough for geometrical drawing ; whilst HH is suitable for very fine lines. For line work a pencil should be sharpened to a chisel point, but for freehand or sketching a round one is best.

Paper.—Imperial cartridge 30 by 22 in. is a useful quality and size for ordinary purposes, but for pen and more finished work Whatman's hot pressed sheets are used. For working drawings use good lining paper or continuous roll cartridge in varying qualities. It must be noted that there is a face side to paper, *i.e.*, the smoothest. A moderately soft rubber should be used for cleaning out. To fix the paper on the board insert a pin at one of the top corners, then pass the hand over the surface diagonally to the opposite corner and fix another pin, repeating the process across the other diagonal. The paper should be fixed clear of the left hand and bottom edges of the board. For water-colour and special work the paper is stretched. This is done by well damping it in clean water and then pasting the edges to the board. In drying, the paper will become taut and ready for use.

The Tee Square is held by the left hand, and the headpiece must be kept tight up to the board. Fig. above shows the tee and set squares in position. With practice it will be quite easy to slide the set square along whilst the tee square is held rigid and straight. A scale rule is useful, and can be bought from a shilling upwards, or a packet of single cardboard scales are obtainable.

For "**inking in**," the liquid Indian ink as sold in 6d and 1s. bottles is the best to use. This process requires practice and care. To fill the drawing pen, dip an ordinary pen into the ink, and insert the nib into the opening, drawing it back carefully against the edge, or a fine brush can be used in the same way. The screw will tighten or loosen the point according to the thickness of the line required, and the pen should be tried on an odd piece of paper first. Before commencing to use the pen, see that there are no loose ink spots on the outside, then hold it upright against the tee or set square edge, and carefully draw it from left to right. Curved lines should be drawn first, and straight ones carried into them; where they cannot be done with a compass, the ordinary French curves are used. Some tee squares are bevelled on the under edge to prevent a blot if the ink happens to run, but this is not necessary if the pen is filled and used properly. All the diagrams in this book were drawn in the manner described above, and with a square edge. The pen should be carefully wiped when done with.

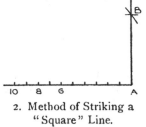

1. Method of Striking a Perpendicular Line.

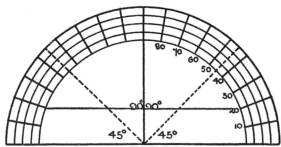

2. Method of Striking a "Square" Line.

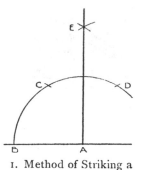

3. Drawing Parallel Lines with Set Squares.

In pencil drawings, the lines should be put in lightly at first, and thickened when all details are drawn. For full-size working drawings a blue pencil is used for the sections, and red for the plans, or the section is outlined with a thin wash of colour. Sections are also shown by straight crossed lines, called "hatchings," and the outline of the moulding in a thick line, as seen in the sections of mouldings throughout the book. Separate portions in the construction are distinguished by hatching in opposite directions.

It is sometimes necessary to "fix" or "set" a charcoal or pencil drawing to prevent its being rubbed out, and to make it partially permanent. This is done with a liquid called "fixative," which is really a solution of shellac and methylated spirit. It is sprinkled on to the drawing through a blow-pipe.

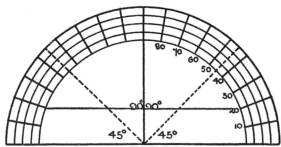

4. A Metal or Horn Protractor.

Tracing is done through a specially prepared thin paper, which is nearly transparent, and can be bought from a penny a sheet upwards, according to quality. It is excellent practice for a young beginner as an aid to neat and quick work. The tracing paper must be carefully stretched and pinned over the drawing, and the tracing commenced from the top downwards. Upright lines should be drawn first, and an F pencil is the best grade for ordinary work. A drawing can be transferred to another sheet by placing it flat on to the paper, and rubbing all over the back of it with a pencil. Patterns of fretwork, flat carving, or pierced work, such as chair backs, &c.,

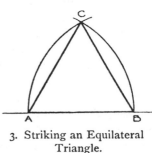

1. Dividing a Circle.

are "rubbed" off by placing the paper on the pattern and rubbing all over it with black heel-ball. The holes will be left white, and the design shown where the heel-ball has touched the wood.

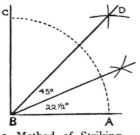

2. Method of Striking Mitres and Half Mitres.

To colour or "wash" in a drawing of any size, a large camel-hair brush called a "mop" is used. It must be kept fairly full of wash and passed quickly over the drawing, commencing at the top and working downwards from and to left and right alternately. To secure a flat even tone and surface, the brush must not be passed over twice until the first coat is quite dry. For detail work a hair brush is used, and in all instances the brushes should be well washed and cleaned, and left in shape when put away.

Suitable colours for woods are as follows, but, of course, they must vary according to the wood and the tints required :—**Rosewood**, vandyke brown and rose madder with little yellow ; **Oak**, vandyke brown and little yellow ochre ; **Mahogany**, vandyke brown, lake and yellow ochre, with a little burnt sienna ; **Satinwood**, gamboge, yellow ochre, little vandyke brown ; **Walnut**, vandyke brown, Prussian blue, and a little crimson lake; **Pine**, yellow and a little brown.

GEOMETRY.—It is only intended to give a few elementary examples which can be applied to practical and workshop needs. These may be supplemented by reference to a good text-book on the subject. To begin with lines. The tee square and set square are used in drawing horizontal and vertical lines respectively, but it might happen that a vertical line had to be drawn where these instruments were not available.

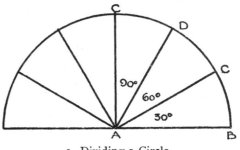

3. Striking an Equilateral Triangle.

In this case the methods shown in f. 1 opposite can be adopted, and failing a compass, a piece of string and a bradawl will do it. From point A strike a semicircle, cutting line in B ; with same radius strike off from B the points c and d ; from c and d strike arcs at e. From a draw a line through the intersection of the arcs. This will be the vertical or square line. As a second handy method, f. 2, p. 24, suppose it was desired to cross cut a board at right

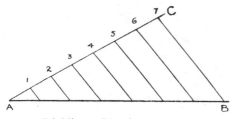

1. Dividing a Line in Equal Parts.

angles without the aid of a square. From the point a mark off 10 in. along the edge of the board ; take six of the inches and mark from a the arc at b ; then take the length of 10 in., and from number 8 mark another arc, cutting the first one at b. Through the intersection draw a line to point a, and the board can be cut off square. All this can be done with a two-foot rule. Geometri-

cally this method is known as a scale of equal parts, and it can be used in other ways, *e.g.*, to test the angle of the room.

Parallel lines—other than horizontal—are drawn with the two set squares.

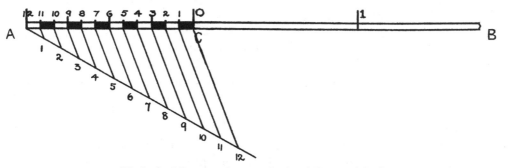

2. Method of Constructing any Scale of Feet and Inches.

Holding one firmly, the other is moved up or down, and lines drawn as shown in f. 3, p. 24. Lines at any angle are usually drawn with the aid of a protractor, a small rectangular instrument made of boxwood, or in metal, or horn, as a semicircle, upon which is marked the number of degrees contained in half a circle, of which there are 180. From this it is possible to mark off from a given spot a line at any angle. Fig. 4 shows the metal or horn protractor. Apart from the use of the protractor, it is useful to remember that the radius of a circle steps round its circumference exactly six times, so that a circle or semicircle can be easily divided up into twelve or six equal parts, as in f. 1, p. 25. This would be handy in setting out tops for veneering. As the angle b a c is 90 degs.,

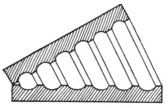

3. Method of Dividing Fluted Pilasters in Equal Proportions.

or a right angle, d would be a line at 60 degs., and c one at 30 degs. A mitre, or line at 45 degs., usually the pitch of a cornice, is obtained by bisecting or halving a right angle, as in f. 2, p. 25. Draw the angle a b c, strike an arc from b, cutting both lines at a and c. With the same radius strike two more arcs from A and C, cutting each other in D.   Through D draw a line into the corner at B, which will be the mitre line.   The "half mitre" is obtained by bisecting the lower portion.   Again, a line at 60 degs. can be easily obtained by the following method :—Supposing that on a given line at point A, f. 3, p. 25, the line is required, from A with any radius describe an arc cutting the line at B, from B strike a similar arc, cutting the other in C, a line through C to A is the one required at 60 degs.   If C also be joined

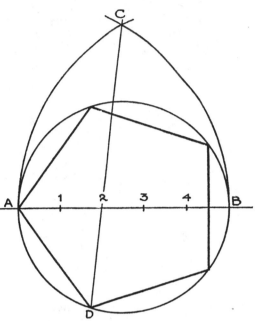

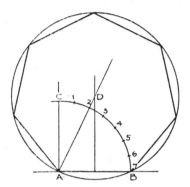

1. Method of Constructing a Polygon on a Given Side.

2. Method of Constructing a Polygon in a Given Circle.

to B we get an equilateral or equal-sided triangle, or the sixth part of a hexagon.

Problems which can be turned to practical account are those relating to proportion and the equal division of lines, by which scales are constructed.

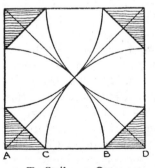

3. To Strike an Octagon in a Square.

As a first example, take a line A B, 3 in. long, f. 1, p. 26, which has to be divided into seven equal parts.   From A draw a line A C, at any angle, above or below, 30 degs. being the most convenient.   From A cut off seven equal parts along A C, join number 7 to B, and from each of the other points draw parallel lines to it until they cut the line A B.   A B will then be equally divided.   This is easily applied to constructing a

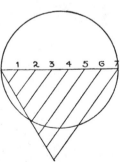

4. To Obtain Approximate Circumference of a Circle.

scale of feet and inches to any proportion.   Fig. 2 shows how such a scale is made.   Draw a line of indefinite length, A B.   Suppose the scale is 2 in. to represent 1 ft., and feet and inches are to be shown.   From A mark off lengths of 2 in.   Draw a line at any angle from A as before, and mark off twelve equal divisions on it.   From the twelfth draw a line to C, and complete the parallel lines as in the previous diagram.   A C will then be divided into twelve parts for the inches, add as many 2-in. divisions along the line A B as you require feet, with numbers as shown, and the scale is complete.   The inches must be numbered from right to left, an advantage easily seen if a length of 1 ft. 3 in. is wanted and taken off with the dividers.   A double line gives a breadth to the scale, and enables the inches to be made plainer by alternate shading.

1. A Trammel.

This can also be applied in many ways to bench work.   Suppose a frieze or gallery has to be divided into a given number of parts ; instead of wasting time with compass or rule, reduce the rail to a convenient scale, treat it as a line A B, and divide it as described above.   Or again, when a smaller or larger pilaster has to be fluted, reeded, or moulded in proportion to another, it can be quickly set out by this method, see f. 3, p. 26, treating the given pilaster as the angle line A C in f. 1, and the one to be divided equally to it as A B.   A further development of this principle applied to mouldings is seen in Chapter X.   Coming now to the construction of the figures known as polygons, or many-sided figures, the pentagon has five sides; hexagon, six ; heptagon, seven ; octagon, eight ; nonagon, nine ; and decagon, ten, &c.   These are frequently occurring in cabinet work.   Fig. 1, p. 27, shows a general method of constructing any polygon when the length of the side is given.   Let A B be

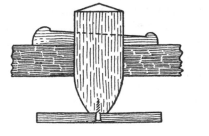

2. Section of Bar and Head   3. Side View of
   of a Trammel.   f. 2, p. 28.

the given side of a heptagon.   At A erect a perpendicular, and with A B as radius strike an arc, cutting it in C.   Divide this arc into seven equal parts, numbering from C.   From A draw a line through number 2.   Bisect A B, and draw a perpendicular, cutting the line at D, which is the centre of a circle, with DA as radius, in which the sides of the heptagon can be divided off and drawn. Fig. 2 illustrates the method of constructing any regular polygon within a given circle, a problem sometimes occurring in veneered work, and in setting out columns, &c.   Strike the circle and the diameter A B.   Divide into the same number of parts as sides in the polygon, say five, and with A and B as centres, and radius A B, describe arcs meeting in C. From C, and through the second

division, draw a line cutting the circle at D. The line A D is one side of the pentagon. The two methods described above apply to the making of any of the regular polygons, but there are quick and ready ways for drawing a hexagon or an octagon, forms which are often used for table tops, *e.g.*, the sides of a hexagon are at an angle of 60 degs., and can be quickly drawn with the set square, and in a like manner the octagon, with an

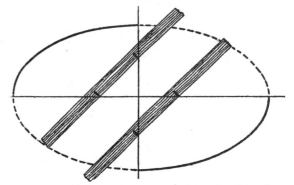

1. Method of Striking an Ellipse with a Straightedge.

angle of 45 degs. But suppose a square table has to be converted into an

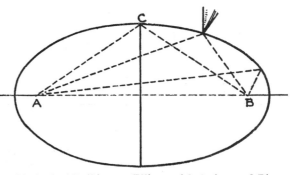

2. Method of Striking an Ellipse with String and Pins.

octagonal one, it can be set out with a pencil and rule, as in f. 3, p. 27. Draw the diagonals, and from each corner mark off a distance equal to half the diagonal, as at A B and C D. Repeat this all round, and join the points for the octagon. There are many other methods, but those described are the most practicable in their application to cabinet work.

It is often necessary to measure the circumference of a circle or the length of a curve and to reduce it to a straight or "stretch" out line for setting out purposes. The string does not always serve, but the circumference of a circle is approximately $3\frac{1}{7}$ times its diameter. The diagram f. 4 shows a quick way of obtaining this. Draw the circle and its diameter, which is divided into seven equal parts ; three times the diameter and one part equals (approximately) the circumference. An approximate length of any curve or serpentine line can be obtained by drawing a straight line on a piece of tracing paper,

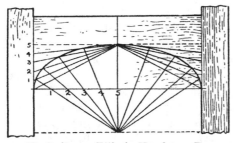

3. To Strike an Elliptic Head to a Door.

and holding the line on the curve as near as possible, tick off lengths at short intervals whilst turning the straight line in the direction of the curve. Any kind of curve can be quickly measured in this way.

The construction of "ovals" or, strictly speaking, ellipses, is a very important part of geometry for a cabinetmaker. The two best-known workshop methods are (1) by the use of an instrument called a trammel, and (2) by the aid of pins and string. The trammel is usually made by the cabinetmaker himself, and is shown in f. 1, p. 28. The base, out of ½-in. Cuba mahogany, is halved together and grooved, the grooves being about $\frac{3}{16}$ in. deep. The ends are halved off to take a screw as shown if wanted for fixing. The bar should be made of good hard wood, rose, or satinwood, and into this are screwed two sliders to fit the groove, and these are left loose enough to allow the bar to revolve. The end of the bar is bored to take a pencil, with a small wedge to secure it. To set the trammel for working order, mark off from the pencil point to the centre of head half the short axis or width of the required ellipse, and set with wedges; then from same point mark off half the long axis,

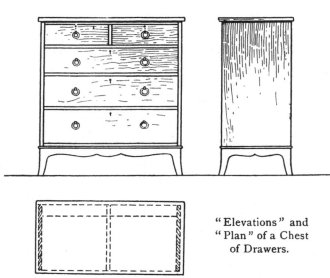

"Elevations" and "Plan" of a Chest of Drawers.

or length, and fix the second head. The sliders should work easily up and down the groove. The base must be fixed or held firmly when the bar is moved round to complete the ellipse. Fig. 1 shows the trammel in the position of describing an ellipse, and f. 2 is a section of bar and head, and f. 3 a side view of the sliding piece, but a more elaborate one can be constructed with metal heads through which the bar is passed, with a thumb-screw to adjust the points.

Failing a trammel the same principle can be applied with a straightedge, f. 1, p. 29, or narrow piece of cardboard. Draw the long and short axes of the required ellipse, and from one end of the straightedge mark off half the short axis and also half the long one. These two points must be kept on the two lines as seen in diagram f. 1, and moved round slowly, as pencil marks are made at the end of the straightedge at short distances. On completing the four quarters, the ellipse can be finished freehand. This is a handy method, and another one well known in workshops is by using a piece of string and three pins as follows (see f. 2):—Set out the long and short axes. From C mark off the length of half the long axis cutting it in A and B, at the points A, B, C, drive in three panel pins, and tightly tie a piece of thin twine around them as shown. Then pull out the pin at C, and firmly hold the pencil point in its place and move it round with the twine taut until the ellipse is complete. This method can only be used where it will not injure the wood to knock in the pins, and where this objection arises either the last-named trammel method must be adopted, or a template of the ellipse prepared and the line marked from that.   There is also another way which is sometimes used to set out an elliptic head to a door by intersecting lines (see f. 3, p. 29). This shows the top rail of the door, and the dotted line on it the height of the curve, whilst the middle line is the inside edge or rail, and represents the long axis of the ellipse.   Below it draw another dotted line the same distance as the top one (this can be done by fitting a piece of pine in the same thickness as the rail), then draw the centre line or short axis. Divide the angles into five equal parts and carry the division across to the opposite one as shown.   Draw lines through, and from the numbers as shown, and where they intersect the lines at corresponding numbers, the points are given to join up the ellipse freehand.   A complete ellipse can be constructed by this method when others are not possible.

All the above problems are known as plane geometry, or the treatment of flat surfaces.   Other problems applied to practical work will be found in Chapter X., but when we come to the drawing of solids— such as a chest of drawers would be—other principles are necessary.   When a scale drawing of a job is required, three views of it are usually given, i.e., the front, end, and plan, and in most instances all these are necessary. The elevation stands on a ground line and in the vertical plane.   The plan should be drawn underneath—and a little below—the front view, and will rest in the horizontal plane. This is what is known as the orthographic projection, or right projection, as it gives correct views of an object, and is the method adopted in all drawings and designs of a prac- tical nature when real dimensions are neces-

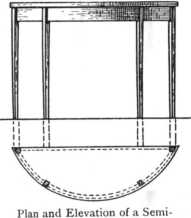

Plan and Elevation of a Semi- circular Table.

sary.   The sketch opposite shows a chest of drawers drawn in this way, and to a young beginner the best illustration of the principle involved is to look at a chest standing against the wall.   If the outline could be drawn on the wall and the bearers and fronts put in, we should then get a front elevation on the vertical plane represented by the wall.   In the same way an end view would be shown, or projected on to, the right hand wall, another vertical plane.   To get the plan, an exact outline of the top would be marked on the floor, which is the horizontal plane, and the intersecting line between the wall and the floor is shown on the paper as the ground line on which the chest is standing, so that the student must imagine the wall as lying flat on the paper, and the floor below the ground line, or as it is technically known, the X Y line.   This the student can easily illus- trate for himself by folding the paper up to form a right angle, and holding a note- book at one end, when the three planes are exhibited, then by turning the book into the vertical plane as though it were hinged on its inner edge, and laying the paper flat again, the position of the two elevations should be understood.

These views are essential if the correct shape of a job is to be known, *e.g.*, of a semicircular or elliptic table, see p. 31.   The elevations are straight while the plans give the real shape, as in f. 1 below, which shows a three-corner cabinet in a similar position.   The true length and shape of the curved rails of the table and the sloping sides of the cabinet can only be shown on the plan.   It is often necessary to give two, three, or more elevations, as in the case of fitments, and it is from these scale views that the foreman sets out the full-size working drawings and adds the details.   The actual method adopted is given in the chapter on "Foreman's Work."

1. Elevation and Plan of a Three-cornered Cabinet.

For the simple or pictorial illustration of square and rectangular objects such as joints and parts of work, an easy method is by oblique projection.   In this, one face is always parallel to the V.P., and the lines of the other faces are drawn at any convenient angle, as in f. 2.   In isometric projection, which is also used, the horizontal lines are drawn at an angle of 30 degs., as in f. 3, and in both methods a 30-deg. set square can be used rapidly, whilst real measurements are struck off along the lines which are parallel to each other.   Most of the joints in this book are drawn in oblique projection, but it must be clearly understood that these methods are only applicable to such small things, neither must they be confused with perspective.

Perspective is a branch of drawing mostly used by draughtsmen, designers, and salesmen, and needs some hard study and continued practice to become efficient in it.   The student should well master the principles of solid geometry first, and if possible attend a class where he can learn perspective drawing step by step.   Failing this, he might begin by sketching simple objects, being above all careful to get a good view rather than a showy one.   Continual practice alone can train the eye to correct views and quick drawing, whilst experience will soon show the best methods, and it is recognised that draughtsmen as a rule make their own.   On the other hand, principles cannot be ignored, and it is necessary to understand them before striking an individual line.   These principles are illustrated on p. 33, where the "setting up" of a table, chest, and room is briefly outlined.

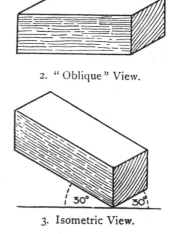

2. "Oblique" View.

3. Isometric View.

Several methods are adopted, and men specialise in perspective as in other branches.   That termed "parallel perspective," f. 1, is often utilised, but its principles, if applied to the

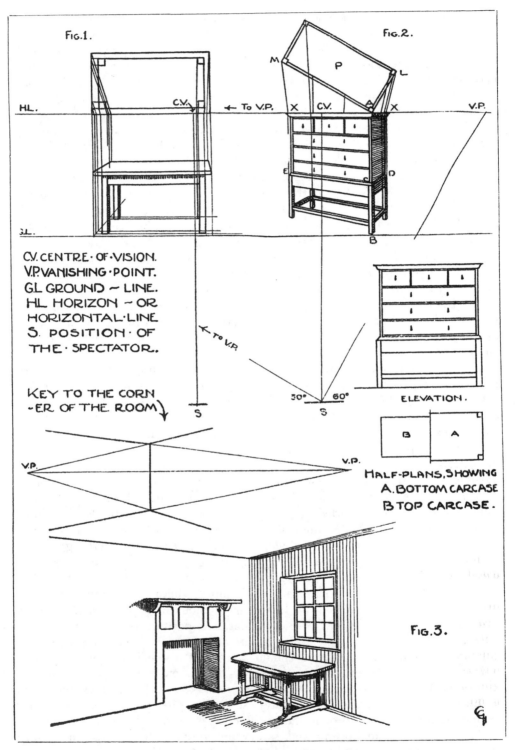

METHODS OF DRAWING IN PERSPECTIVE.

representation of certain objects such as the table shown, do not succeed in producing a satisfactory view. An adaptation of "architects' perspective" is generally used, as being more correct and suitable for its purpose; though a rule-of-thumb method, it is most effective in the hands of a good draughtsman. See f. 2 & 3, p. 33. Lines above the eye—or higher than 5 ft.—appear to come down, and those below to rise up. All these lines would meet at one point known as the vanishing point or V.P. The diagram explains how this point is found.

Fig. 2 shows the elevation and plan of a chest of drawers. Plan P is placed anglewise, one side making, say, 30 degs. with a horizontal drawn through A. S is suitably placed below the plan, so that the best view is obtained. G.L. is ruled parallel to H.L.—5 ft. in this instance—below. The V.P.'s are found by ruling lines from S parallel to the sides of P. Drop perpendicular A B to G.L. Draw from B to each V.P. From B cut off B C, the height of the table part on B A. From C rule to each V.P., draw lines from L and M, in direction of S to X X. From X X drop perpendiculars cutting the vanishing lines. The method of finding the legs is shown at L. The chest is found by repeating the necessary part of the process, and the positions of the divisions, handles, &c., by marking them on the plan and projecting. The important decorative features are introduced by hand. The drawing is transferred to the paper for finished work, and completed either by firm outlining, shading, or colouring, according to the capacity of the draughtsman. This problem forms the key by which a great number may be drawn. Most tables, cabinets, &c., in their *main* lines are rectangular in form, or deviate very little from it. Dimensions vary; parts project; some pieces have shaped or curved work; but the underlying principle is there. These difficulties can only be overcome by experience. When dealing with work above the eye, f. 3, with key, draw the plan on a separate slip of paper, and pin in position until all points X X have been marked on H.L. Then remove the slip and proceed as in f. 2.

Design.—Without some knowledge of the principles of design it is not possible to build up a good piece of furniture. Good proportion, good colour, and the right use of materials and ornaments are essentials in fine cabinetwork. There must also be a knowledge of construction and of the methods of building up, with all their possibilities and limitations. Added to these are certain forms and sizes which long usage has fixed, such as the height of a writing table, a chair, or a sideboard. There are differences to remember when designing a wardrobe and a china cabinet; for in the one it is carcase work with flat surfaces to cover, and in the other it is principally framing where the harmony of many lines has to be considered. The treatment of mouldings and their relation to position in projecting, receding, or on the flat, is important, as well as the proper placing of ornament. The metal fittings are a feature which must not be under-estimated, and in all work there should be a right appreciation of their value and position in a design. A careful study of old examples should prove of real practical value to designers and cabinetmakers alike, and especially in obtaining good proportion. For heavy, solid furniture, such as is needed for the hall, library, or dining-room, the best Jacobean period affords some excellent models, whilst the mahogany and satinwood work of the eighteenth century supplies many useful suggestions for lighter cabinetmaking.

Technical and Workshop Terms.—The names of the principal parts of furniture are taken from architecture, as in plinth (the base) ; surbase (table part or half base); pilaster cornice, and pediment. The names of mouldings are similar, as in ogee, ovolo, and dentil (see chapter on "Mouldings"), and a box cornice which consists of top or cornice moulding, frieze and neck moulding—or architrave—is known as an "entablature." The term "carcase" is applied to the body of a job, and "in the white" refers to work in any wood when it is unpolished. The parts of a door are known as the "stiles," which are the uprights, the "rails," which are horizontal, and the centre uprights are called "muntins." "Chamfer," "splay," "bevel," and "cant," are terms of similar meaning applied to equal or unequal ("splay") slopes planed off the "arris" or corner. When boards or panels have twisted out of the flat they are said to have "cast," or are in "winding." Other terms are given with the work to which they apply, and a larger list will be found in the Glossary.

CHAPTER IV.

JOINTS AND THEIR APPLICATION.

Pilaster Hingeing—Dustproof Joint—Centre Hung Door—Rebated Edge Joint—Centre Hinged Bureau Face—Bevel Rebated Joint—Secretaire Face Front.

Miscellaneous Joints. Plate XIII.

Pocket Screwing—Handrail Joint—Cleating—Dovetail Cleating—Buttoning—Dovetail Keying—Slot Screwing.

Joints Connecting Movable Parts of Furniture. Plate XIV.

Plain Hinged Joint—Rule Joint—Knuckle Screen Hinge Joint—Revolving Bracket—Hinged Bracket—Finger Joint—Knuckle Joint—Slide Supports.

THIS chapter describes and illustrates most of the joints used in cabinetwork, and to render the explanations more explicit, diagrams are introduced showing the applications of many of the joints, and their places in actual portions of completed work.

GLUED JOINTS.

Rubbed Joints, f. 1.—These are the simplest kind of joints to make, and are rubbed into position when glueing. They are the most suitable for thin boards or wood of fairly open texture. They are sometimes cramped if the stuff is crooked. An application of this joint is illustrated in f. 10.

Ploughed and Tongue Jointing, f. 2, is the commonest method of jointing. Either one or two cross tongues are used, according to the thickness of stuff, and the additional glueing surface afforded by the tongues increases the strength of the joint. Feather tongues are not nearly so strong as cross tongues, which are cut across the grain. Both tongues prevent the passage of light and air should the joint part in the course of time, but feather tongues are generally used for dry jointing only. Cross-tongued joints are used in nearly all cases where a strong joint is required, such as f. 16.

Matched Joints, illustrated in f. 3, are generally used for dry jointing, but may be used also in glued joints. The difference between a "tongued" and a "matched" joint is that the former has a loose tongue inserted in the groove, whilst the latter consists of a tongue worked upon the solid and fitted into a corresponding groove. An application of this joint to a division rail is shown in f. 15.

Secret Slot Screwed Joints, f. 4, are not much used for glued joints in furniture, but they are especially useful for jointing stuff, such as shelves, &c., which are required almost immediately after glueing. The secret screwing permits of planing and fitting if carefully handled whilst the glue is drying, but its most useful application is in the fixing of shelves and brackets, as shown in f. 11, pilasters in f. 13, and to almost every kind of fitting required to be firmly but secretly fixed, ranging from panelling to the pediment or gallery on a sideboard.

Dowelled Joints, f. 7.—Dowels are cylindrical pieces of wood about 2 in. long—beech for preference—inserted into holes which are bored into the jointed

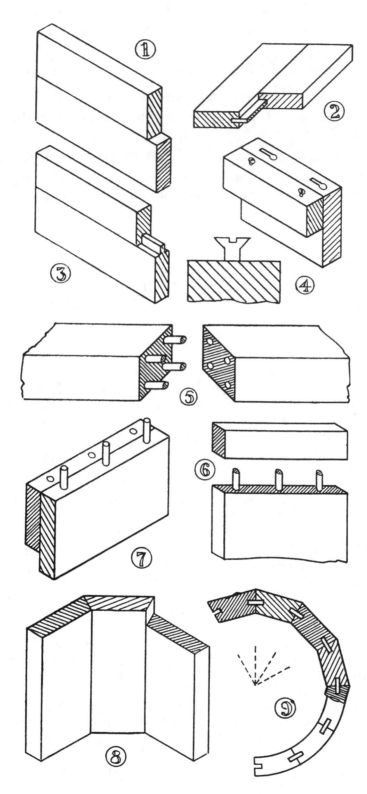

GLUED JONTS.

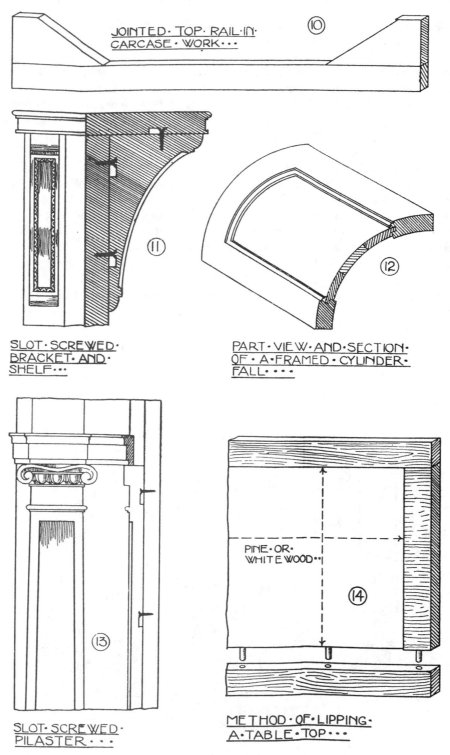

JOINTED·TOP·RAIL·IN·
CARCASE·WORK··· ⑩

⑪ ⑫

SLOT·SCREWED·
BRACKET·AND·
SHELF···

PART·VIEW·AND·SECTION·
OF·A·FRAMED·CYLINDER·
FALL····

⑬

PINE·OR·
WHITE WOOD··

⑭

SLOT·SCREWED·
PILASTER···

METHOD·OF·LIPPING·
A·TABLE·TOP···

GLUED JOINTS (CONTINUED OVERLEAF).

edges of stuff. They may be used in nearly every instance for strengthening joints. Applications are shown in f. 12 & 14.

Dowelled Butt Jointing, f. 5, is used for lengthening timber, such as large cornice mouldings and casings round girders for beam ceilings. This joint is also used in work where cross grain prevents tenoning.

Dowelled Clamping, f. 6, is a variation of dowelled jointing proper. The diagram shows long grain jointing to end grain, but it is also used for jointing end grains together. The application of both types is shown in f. 14, which is a writing table top.

Bevelled Jointing, f. 8, consists of making joints between pieces of stuff to form various angles or corners. It is a variation of "rubbed jointing," but cramping is usually required. This is effected by glueing blocks on the pieces and pulling together with hand-screws. The applications of this joint—f. 16 & 17—are in commode carcases, but the joint is used in practically every instance where bevelled or rounded corners are required. Occasionally the joints are tongued as shown, or blocked if possible.

Coopered Joints.—This term is applied to the jointing shown in f. 9, used for connecting pieces to form various curves, as, for instance, a cylinder table fall—f. 12—curved panels in framing, and circular or kidney-shaped carcases and pedestals.

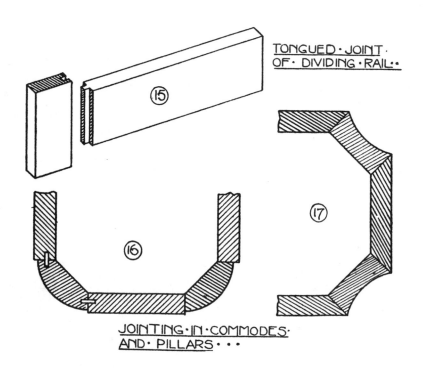

TONGUED · JOINT ·
OF · DIVIDING · RAIL · ·

JOINTING · IN · COMMODES ·
AND · PILLARS · · ·

PLATE VIc. GLUED JOINTS.

HALVED AND BRIDLE JOINTS.

The diagrams f. 1 to 4 show various **halved joints.** These are the simplest connecting joints in cabinetwork, and are used for a variety of purposes. Where two pieces of wood form a **X** shape, such as the illustration f. 19, the halved joint effects the strongest connection, whereas tenoning or dovetailing would considerably decrease its bearing strength. Similarly to mortising and tenoning, halved jointing is used in conjunction with mitreing in moulded work, especially in connecting shaped forms in the underrailing of tables, cabinets, and sideboards, dealt with in their respective chapters. The chief uses of these joints, however, are in faced-up grounds for doors, and skeleton grounds for fixing, being both economical and strong. **Dovetail Halved Joints,** f. 5 to 8, are used to resist an outward strain, such as would occur in the strengthening pieces halved into very large frames. **Bridle Joints,** f. 9 to 12, in their various forms may be used in most of the instances enumerated above, where a stronger joint having a neater appearance is required.

Halved Angle Joint, f. 1. — The end of each piece is halved and shouldered on opposite sides, fitting into each other. This is the commonest form of halving, and most used, on account of its simplicity and strength. The outside angles in the frames illustrated in f. 13, 14, & 17, show its use, and it is very effective for connecting battens to form skeleton grounds for stretching material upon, or for fixing to rough walls where a true and secure ground is required for panelling or fitments.

Halved Tee Joint, f. 2.—This is of similar construction to the above joint, and is used for connecting cross pieces in framing to act as stretchers or cross rails and muntings, as in f. 14. This illustration refers to a halved-up frame or ground, to receive "mitred" and "butted and mitred" facing, which are glued down, and allowed to project beyond the inside edge, forming a rebate to receive the panel.

Oblique Halving, f. 3.—A variation of the above for oblique connections, such as in f. 15. Similar pieces are occasionally dovetail halved across the angles of large frames to act as strengthening braces.

Mitred Halving, f. 4.—This is the weakest form of halving, due to decreased glueing surface, caused by mitre, and indicated by mitre and dotted line. Its use is rendered necessary when the face side of frame is moulded, and is restricted to very light frames.

Dovetail Halving, f. 5, 6, & 7.—These are effective joints for connecting cross rails in framing, where an outside strain occurs. The application, f. 15, refers to a gallows bracket used for supporting fixed shelves, or hinged for collapsible wall flaps.

Stopped Dovetail Halving, f. 8.—This is similar to the three previous joints, and is used where the edge of a framing is seen, or an ordinary halved joint is unsightly.

Angle Bridle Joint, f. 9.—A very strong joint, used for similar work to

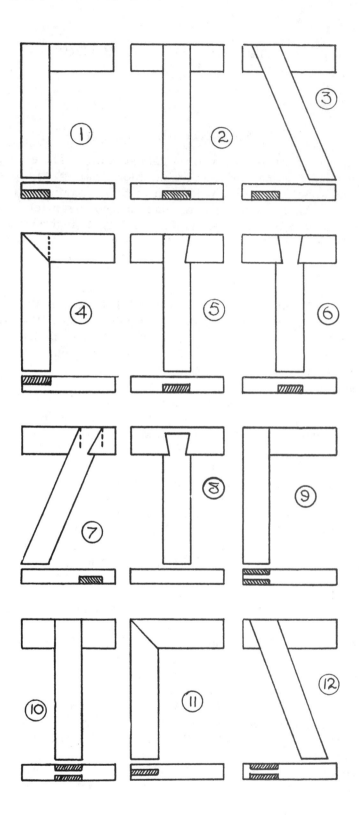

HALVED AND BRIDLE JOINTS.

⑬

HALVED·
JOINTS·IN·
FACED·UP·
DOORS···

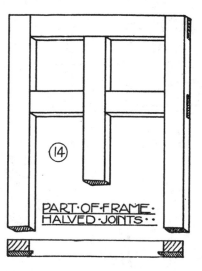

⑭

PART·OF·FRAME·
HALVED·JOINTS···

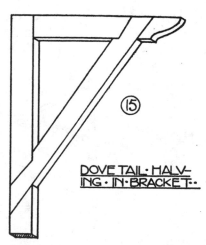

⑮

DOVE TAIL·HALV-
ING·IN·BRACKET··

Halved and Bridle Joints (continued overleaf).

previous examples. It is an excellent joint for connecting segments in curved rims and frames. The glass frame, f. 18, *a*, shows its use as a substitute for mortising and tenoning.

Tee Bridle Joint, f. 10.—Used for connections where a stronger joint than lapped halving is required. Fig. 17, *a*, shows its application to a framed groundwork, which is afterwards faced up, with the glass frame pivoted at its centre, forming a dressing-table top part. This is a suitable method of construction for enamelled work, where the end grain of joints is concealed.

Mitred Bridle Joint, f. 11.—Suitable for both flat and moulded frames, as in f. 18, *b*, &c.

Oblique Bridle Joint, f. 12.—This is used for connecting the inside member of framing.

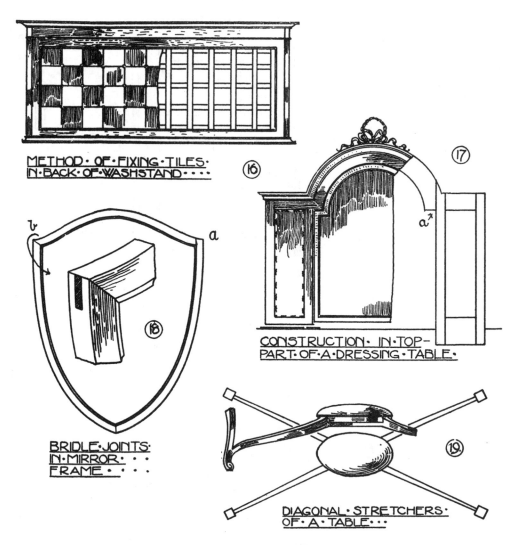

METHOD·OF·FIXING·TILES· IN·BACK·OF·WASHSTAND···· ⑯

⑰

⑱ BRIDLE·JOINTS· IN·MIRROR··· FRAME····

CONSTRUCTION·IN·TOP- PART·OF·A·DRESSING·TABLE·

⑲ DIAGONAL·STRETCHERS· OF·A·TABLE···

PLATE VIIc. HALVED AND BRIDLE JOINTS.

MORTISE AND TENON JOINTS.

Stub Mortise and Tenon.—Fig. 1 illustrates the type of mortising and tenoning mostly used in doors and framing of furniture. It consists of a rectangular solid projection formed on the ends of rails, fitting into a corresponding cavity cut into the stile called a mortise, and secured with glue. When used in doors, the tenon is reduced in width as shown in diagram, thus allowing sufficient wood to remain on the stile to afford the necessary strength in resisting a lengthwise strain. Inside members of framing, as cross rails, muntings, &c., are either tenoned in full width or reduced on both sides, according to the size of tenon, and arrangement of grooves or rebates to receive the panel. Applications shown in f. 11, 13, & 20.

Haunched Mortise and Tenon, f. 2.—This has similar uses to above, but additional strength is obtained by the formation of a haunch, which fits into a small adjoining stub mortise, the centre groove to receive the panel being usually enlarged to receive the haunch. Applications shown in f. 11.

Through Mortise and Tenon, f. 4.—These are either tenoned, or haunched and tenoned as diagram, and pass right through the stuff. The outside of the mortise is made rather larger than the inside, thus permitting the entry of wedges when glueing; these are driven home, and form a very strong kind of dovetailing. This joint is not largely used in furniture, but is especially useful for heavy framing, f. 15, and groundworks as in f. 16.

Foxtail Wedging, f. 5, consists of an ordinary stub tenon, the mortise being cut larger at the bottom. Saw cuts are made down the tenon, and wedges inserted just before glueing up; these when driven home cause the tenon to spread, thus forming a fox or dovetail type of joint.

Barefaced Mortise and Tenon, f. 6.—This is used when the rail is thinner than the stile, or when shouldering both sides of the tenon would tend to decrease the strength of joint. The tenon can be the full width of rail, or haunched on either side to suit particular circumstances.

Long and Short Shoulder Mortise and Tenon.—Fig. 7 shows one shoulder of rail cut back to fill the space caused by rebating the framing. This joint has many variations, being used as shown, or in combination with mitred mouldings (see f. 17). Its chief use, however, is with grooved or rebated frames and doors with the moulding planted in afterwards (see f. 14).

Pinning, f. 8, is a variation of through mortising and tenoning applied to carcase work. The diagram shows a division mortised into a carcase top or bottom. It is afterwards wedged diagonally, or across the tenon, when the carcase is glued up (see carcase division in f. 19).

Tongued Shoulder Mortise and Tenon, f. 9.—An ordinary mortise and tenoned joint with cross tongues inserted in the shoulders. The tongued joint prevents the shoulder springing by affording additional glueing surface. Chiefly used in vestibule and lobby doors, and for thick framed groundworks as in f. 16.

Double Mortise and Tenons, f. 10, is really a stub mortise and tenon joint

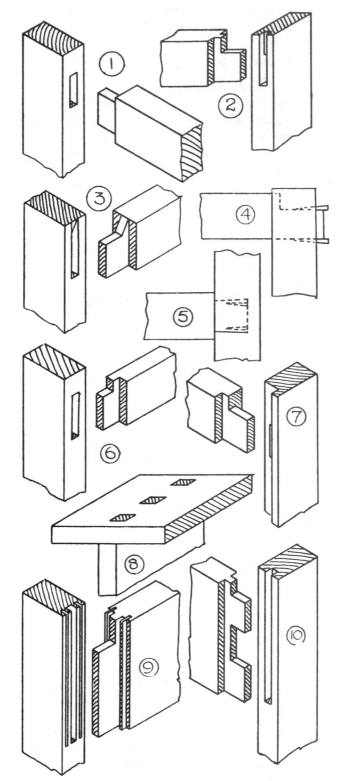

MORTISE AND TENON JOINTS.

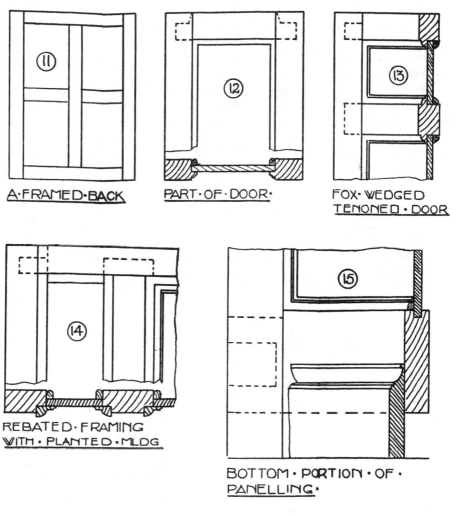

⑪

A·FRAMED·BACK

⑫

PART·OF·DOOR·

⑬

FOX·WEDGED
TENONED·DOOR

⑭

REBATED·FRAMING
WITH·PLANTED·MLDG

⑮

BOTTOM·PORTION·OF·
PANELLING·

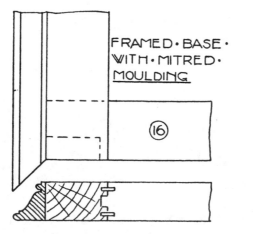

FRAMED·BASE·
WITH·MITRED·
MOULDING

⑯

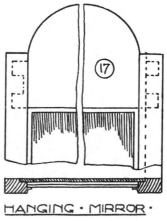

⑰

HANGING·MIRROR·

MORTISE AND TENON JOINTS.

haunched out to form two tenons, thus increasing the lateral strength of stile. It also applies to haunched-through mortising and tenoning. Sideboard ends are frequently naunched to form four or more tenons, a method which effects a stronger connection than dowelling.

Twin Mortise and Tenons are used in very thick stuff, and consist of two tenons placed side by side, occasionally haunched to form double twin tenons. They are used chiefly for lock rails of doors, with a wide haunching between, thus allowing the removal of wood to receive the mortise lock, without weakening the joint. Further uses of this joint are dealt with in chapter on "Air-tight Work."

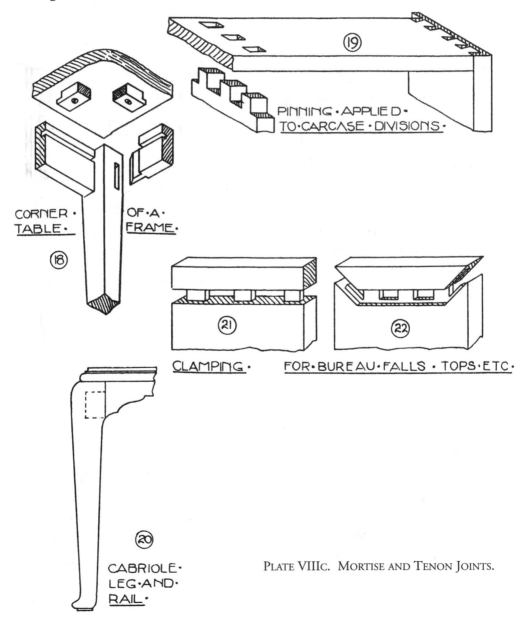

⑲ PINNING·APPLIED· TO·CARCASE·DIVISIONS·

CORNER· TABLE· ⑱

OF·A· FRAME·

CLAMPING· FOR·BUREAU·FALLS·TOPS·ETC· ㉑ ㉒

⑳ CABRIOLE· LEG·AND· RAIL·

PLATE VIIIc. MORTISE AND TENON JOINTS.

DOVETAIL JOINTS.

Through Dovetailing, f. 1.—This is the strongest form of dovetailing— sometimes called common dovetailing—the end grain showing on both sides of the angle formed. It is generally used for boxes, cases, pedestals, plinths, &c., that are usually faced up afterwards, thus concealing the joint. Exceptional instances occur in scientific instrument cases, the dovetails being visible. Application f. 12 applies to carcase work, and f. 21 shows a bevelled dovetail hopper. For angles and proportions of dovetailing refer to chapter on "Workshop Practice and Construction."

Lapped or Stopped Dovetailing, f. 2, is so called because a lap is left upon the pin piece; it is used in carcases, drawers, and similar settings, proportions varying according to the work. The applications f. 13, 15, 16, &c., show various forms of ordinary lapped dovetailing applied to carcases of furniture, the joint being concealed with top, plinth, or cornice, &c.

Secret Lapped Dovetailing, f. 3, is somewhat similar to above, two laps are formed, and the joint, when glued up, only shows the end grain of lap in pin piece. This joint is generally used in boxes and plinth frames, which are afterwards rounded off, the radius of quadrant equalling width of lap.

Mitred Secret Dovetailing, f. 4, is the neatest type of dovetailing; pieces are really dovetailed together, the laps being mitred. This joint is always used for bases, plinths, &c., in solid work where an invisible dovetail joint is required, and is also the best joint for connecting groundworks before veneering. Application in f. 24, *a* and *b*.

Cistern Dovetailing, f. 5.—So called because of its almost exclusive use in cisterns and hot-water tank casings. The pins and dovetails are spaced equally to ensure proportionate shrinkage, but it is occasionally used for ordinary carcase and box work.

Keying, f. 6.—This is called German dovetailing and also finger-jointing. It is shown here as a machine dovetail joint, and is largely used on the Continent; it is, however, quite unsuitable for making by hand.

A Common Dovetail, shown in f. 8, is used chiefly for dovetailing brackets together, and also for frames, which are required to resist a heavy downward pull. Several variations of this joint occur, including the four following :—

Common Lapped Dovetail, f. 7.—For similar uses to the above, also in light doors, and connecting curved rails of frames, where mortise and tenon joints cannot be effectively employed, f. 17.

Common Housed Dovetailing, f. 9.—When shouldered and dovetailed on one side only, it is called bareface dovetail housing. These types are the simplest form of housed dovetailing, and the dovetailing is parallel throughout its length. Used in connecting rails of plinths, stretcher frames, &c. Application shown in f. 24 and 20, *b*.

Shouldered Dovetail Housing, f. 10.—Like the above joint, this is

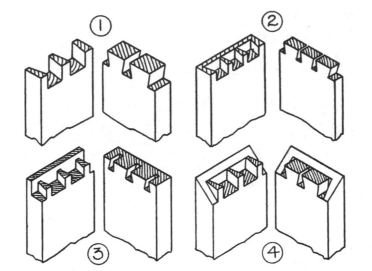

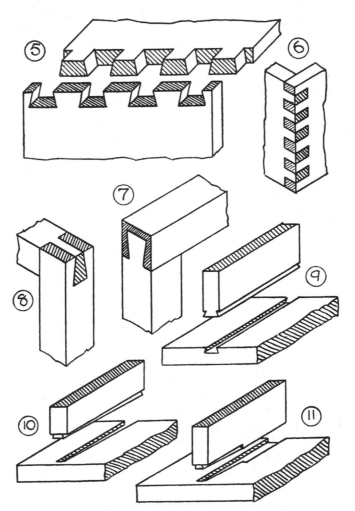

DOVETAIL JOINTS.

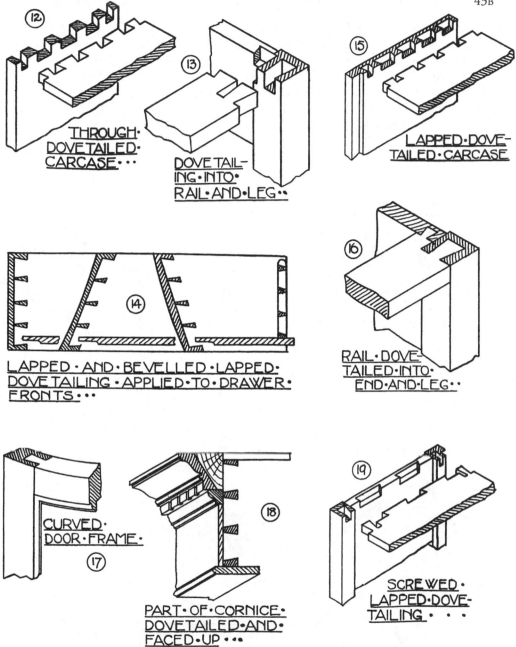

⑫ THROUGH·
DOVETAILED·
CARCASE···

⑬ DOVETAIL-
ING·INTO·
RAIL·AND·LEG··

⑮ LAPPED·DOVE-
TAILED·CARCASE

⑭ LAPPED·AND·BEVELLED·LAPPED·
DOVETAILING·APPLIED·TO·DRAWER·
FRONTS···

⑯ RAIL·DOVE-
TAILED·INTO·
END·AND·LEG··

⑰ CURVED·
DOOR·FRAME·

⑱ PART·OF·CORNICE·
DOVETAILED·AND·
FACED·UP···

⑲ SCREWED·
LAPPED·DOVE-
TAILING····

DOVETAIL JOINTS (CONTINUED OVERLEAF).

shouldered on one or both sides, but the dovetail tapers in its length also. Used for similar purposes to above, and also for connecting fixed shelves to divisions, false bottoms and in carcases (see f. 20, *a* and *c*).

Dovetailed and Housed, f. 11.—Another variation of the above joints, and used for comparatively small carcase work, where the length of an end does not demand a dovetail right through the stuff in order to prevent it sagging or bending.   Application in f. 23.

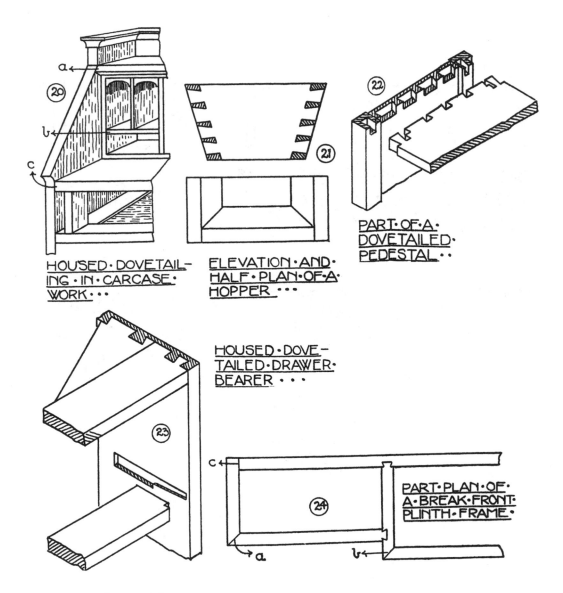

HOUSED·DOVETAIL— ING·IN·CARCASE· WORK··•

ELEVATION·AND· HALF·PLAN·OF·A· HOPPER·•••

PART·OF·A· DOVETAILED· PEDESTAL··•

HOUSED·DOVE— TAILED·DRAWER· BEARER·•••

PART·PLAN·OF· A·BREAK·FRONT· PLINTH·FRAME·

PLATE IXc. DOVETAIL JOINTS.

MITRED JOINTS.

Plain Mitre, f. 1.—This is the simplest method of connecting end grain pieces in plinths, skirtings, &c. Blocks are glued in the internal angle, thus strengthening the joint. Although this joint is frequently used for end grain mitreing, it is most suitable for mitreing with the grain, a variation of which is shown in f. 3, *a*. For application of plain mitreing, refer to f. 12.

Tongued Mitre, f. 2.—This is similar to f. 1, with the addition of a cross tongue inserted at right angles between the mitre. It is chiefly used for end grain mitreing, and forms a very strong joint, if strengthened with angle block, when the internal angle is not seen. Application in f. 12.

Veneer Keyed Mitre, f. 3, consists of a plain mitre, which, when glued up, is strengthened by kerfing the angle with a saw, and glueing hardwood veneers into the cuts. Chiefly used in cases and boxes, where both sides of the angle are seen, and is especially suitable for connecting thin wood, which would not permit of mitre dovetailing. Applications shown in f. 14, A.

Dovetail Keyed Mitre, f. 4.—This has similar uses to former joint. Hardwood slips are prepared, dovetailed in section, and slightly tapered in length, glued into corresponding sockets, and levelled off when dry. See f. 14, B.

Rebate and Mitred Joint, f. 3, *a*.—Used for connecting varying angles in framing, casings, &c., chiefly in painted work. The rebate strengthens the joint, and also prevents the mitres slipping when glueing and nailing.

Bolted Mitreing, f. 5.—A plain mitre, fixed together with a hand rail bolt. Short dowels are inserted to prevent working. It is used for heavy work, such as wooden fender curbs and moulded openings of fireplaces. Application shown in f. 15.

Screwed Mitreing, f. 6.—A plain mitre, strengthened by screwing through outside of frame. Variations of this joint are the plain mitre, and dowelled or pinned. All are used in light moulded frames.

Mason's Mitre Joint, f. 7.—An ordinary mortise and tenon joint, with the moulding worked right through the muntings, and on the rail as shown. The corners are then carved to form a mitre on the moulding. It is used chiefly in mediæval furniture and fittings. See f. 17.

Mitred Stuck Moulding.—Fig. 9 is a mitred stuck moulding used for connecting mouldings in framing to form various angles. This is the most common joint used in moulded framing and doors.

Tongued Mitre Joint, f. 8.—The diagram shows a sectional view of the joint, which is a variation of plain mitreing, and is nearly always used for end grain jointing. The tongue should be about one-third thickness of stuff, and may run right through the mitre or stop as shown. It is an especially useful joint for mitreing mouldings round groundwork, connecting double bolection mouldings, as in f. 18, quartering stuff for tops and panels, mitreing stuff round tops which project slightly above the surface to receive

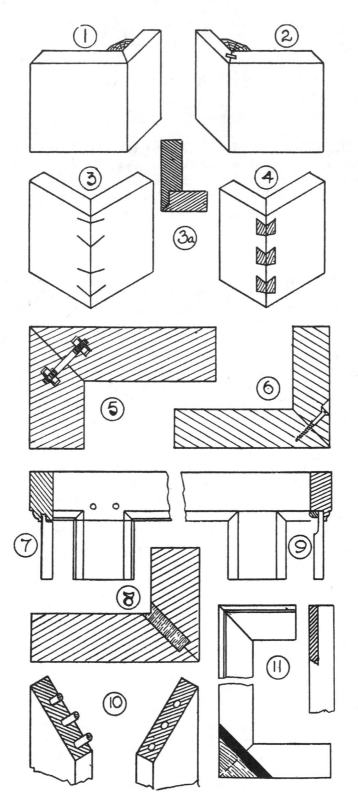

MITRED JOINTS.

A·PLINTH·FRAME·SHEWING·APPLICATION·
OF·BLOCKED·AND·TONGUED·MITRE·JOINTS···

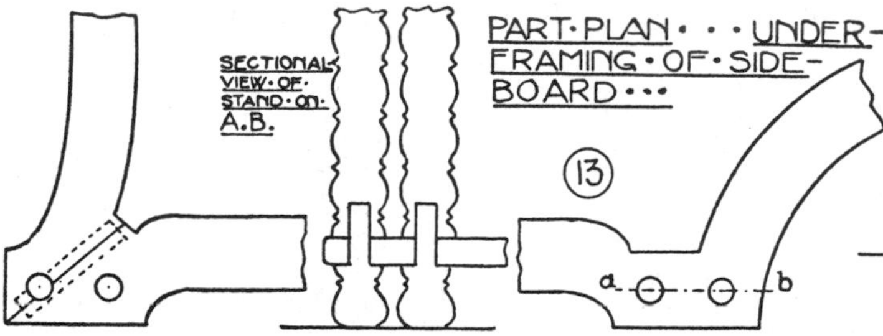

12

SECTIONAL·
VIEW·OF·
STAND·ON·
A.B.

PART·PLAN··· UNDER-
FRAMING·OF·SIDE-
BOARD···

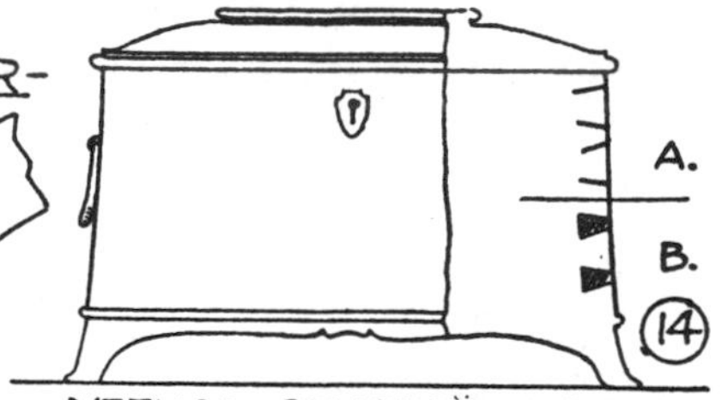

13

a — b

METHOD·OF·KEYING·ANGLES·
IN·BOXES·AND·CASKETS···

A.

B.

14

MOULDED·OPEN
ING·OF·MANTEL
PIECE···

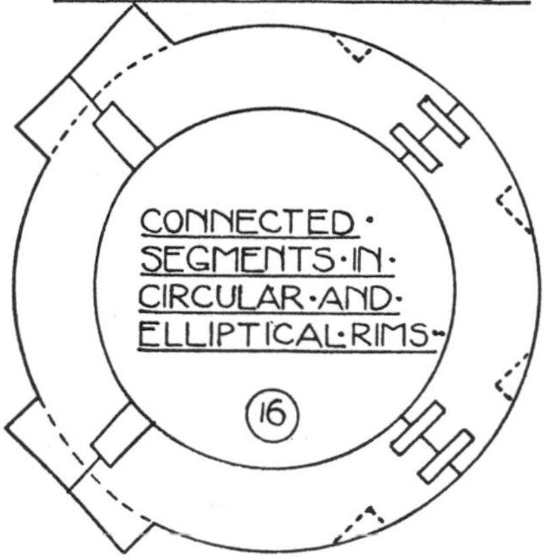

15

CONNECTED·
SEGMENTS·IN·
CIRCULAR·AND·
ELLIPTICAL·RIMS·

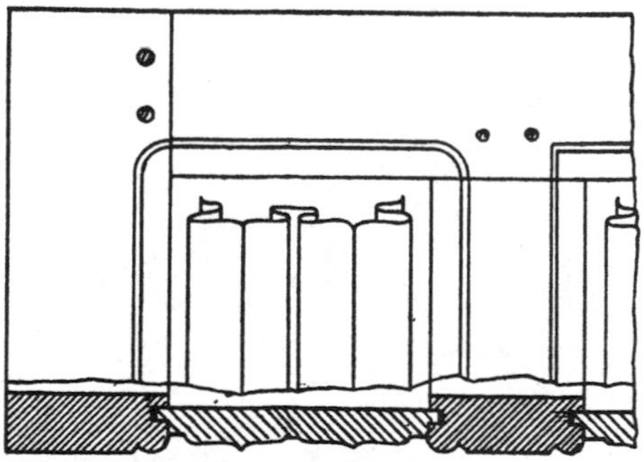

16

FRAMING·WITH·MASONS·
JOINTS·AND·MITRE···

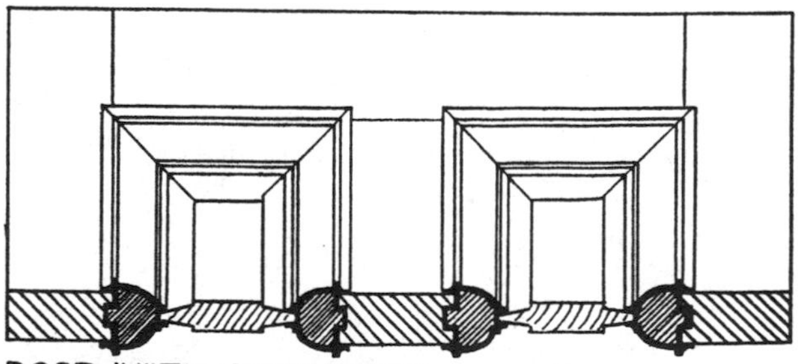

17

DOOR·WITH·MOULDINGS·
MITRED·AND·TONGUED···

18

MITRED JOINTS.

leather linings, and also for connecting segments in curved work; see f. 13, or with dowels, as shown in f. 16.

Dowelled Mitre, f. 10.—This has similar uses to the above, where both sides of the angle are seen, and secret fixing required.

Braced Mitre, f. 11.—This is used chiefly for strengthening plain mitres in framings, such as moulded panel openings which are occasionally separated from the main framework. The black portion also shows a slip dovetailed in section, known as a dovetail key, used to brace the backs of frames at the joint.

FRAMING JOINTS.

A Butt or Square Joint, f. 1, is usually secured by glueing and nailing. This joint when used as an external angle in framing would be secret-screwed or screw-nailed if for painted work.

A Tongued Joint, f. 2, is chiefly used for connecting external and internal angles of framing, building up pedestals and pilasters. Application shown in f. 22, *a*.

The Barefaced Tongued Joint, f. 3, is shouldered on one side only, and is used for internal and external angles, with a bead worked upon the tongued piece to hide the joint. It is also used for external angles, omitting the bead (see f. 21).

Tongue and Ovolo, f. 4.—A variation of above joint, and used for external angles, the ovolo forming an alternative method of finishing corner (see f. 22, *b*).

The Return Bead and Butt, f. 5, consists of a plain butt joint with a "return" or "staff bead" worked upon the through piece. Application shown in f. 22, *c*.

Rebate and Ovolo, f. 6.—A variation of the butt joint, suitable for painted work, and secured by nailing.

Bead and Rebate, f. 7.—A rebated joint, with a bead to hide the joint. Secured by nailing or secret screwing. Also used for connecting framed and munted backs to carcase ends (see f. 26, *b*, when it is screwed in position).

Rebate and Mitre, f. 8.—A very useful joint in connecting framing at any angle. The rebate acts as a guide or stop when fixing, which is generally nailed or screwed, and pelleted in painted work. Application shown in f. 22, *d*.

Rebate and Round, f. 9.—An ordinary rebated joint, glued together, with the corner rounded off. Chiefly used in nursery fittings.

Hollow Corner Jointing, f. 10, shows a method of forming hollow angles or corners. Groove and tongue joints are used, and glued into position when fixing.

Splayed Corner Jointing.—Fig. 11 is an example of a splayed pilaster, with the method adopted in joining the ends or frames. The application in f. 24 refers to a wardrobe with splayed pilaster corners.

Fluted Corners, f. 12.—The fluted piece is shaped as shown in diagram, in order to facilitate fixing, by clearing any projections or irregularities in the corner of a wall. A similar joint is largely used for external angles in Chippendale hollow cornered pedestal tables, these corners being fluted, carved, or reeded.

Matched Joint, f. 13.—So called, because the tongue is worked upon the solid, differing from a tongued joint, when a loose tongue is inserted. It is used for connecting boards to form matched backs, partitions, munted backs, &c. (see f. 25, *a*).

Beaded Matching, f. 14.—The former joint elaborated by the addition of a bead on the tongued piece, nearly always used dry for similar purposes as above (see f. 25, *b*).

V-Matching, f. 15.—A variation of the above joint. The edges of each piece are chamfered, thus forming a V joint (see also f. 25, *c*).

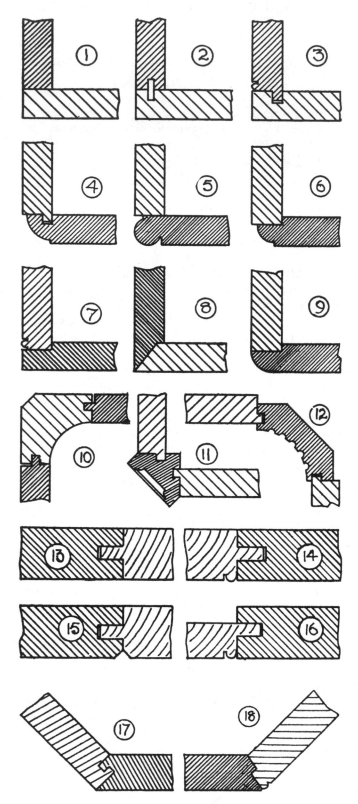

FRAMING JOINTS.

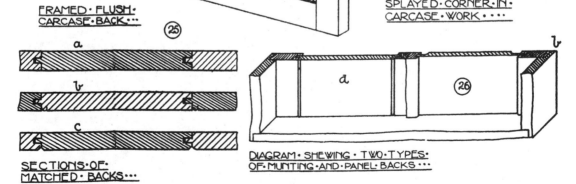

CONSTRUCTION · OF ·
CHIMNEY · BREAST ·
AND · PILASTER · · · ·
20

MARBLE ·
SLIP.

SECTIONAL · PLAN ·
FRONT · CORNER · OF ·
A WARDROBE · · · ·
21

a

22

d   c   b

VARIOUS · METHODS · OF · CONNECTING ·
ANGLES · OF · PANELLING · · · ·

A · BEAD · AND · BUTT · PANEL ·
B · BEAD · AND · FLUSH · Dº · ·
23

A

B

24

SPLAYED · CORNER · IN ·
CARCASE · WORK · · · ·

FRAMED · FLUSH ·
CARCASE · BACK · · ·
25

a

b

c

SECTIONS · OF ·
MATCHED · BACKS · · ·

b

d   26

DIAGRAM · SHEWING · TWO · TYPES ·
OF · MUNTING · AND · PANEL · BACKS · · ·

FRAMING JOINTS.

Barefaced Tongue Groove and Bead Joint, f. 16.—This is used chiefly in munted backs, the panel being thinner than the munting (see f. 26, *a*). In the framing at f. 23, A, it will be noticed that the panel is beaded lengthways only in the "bead and butt." The "bead and flush" framing has the head moulding returned at both ends. This is effected by scratching the moulding across the grain, or by the cleaner and more usual method of rebating the stuff away and mitreing a piece of moulding in the rebate thus formed between the mitres (see f. 23, B).

Double Tongued Mitre Joint, f. 17.—A variation of the rebate and mitre joint, used for external angles. It is very strong, and made secure by nailing.

Double Rebate and Bead, f. 18—Of similar uses to the above, and secured by nailing.

HINGEING AND SHUTTING JOINTS.

The diagrams on the opposite page illustrate in section the most important methods of arranging hinged parts of furniture. The exact position of pin centre, either of butt or pivoted centre hinge, is indicated by a small black circle, but where centre hinges are used, they will be noted in the following text. The methods of fixing the various hinges is described in Chapter XII.

Fig. 1, *a*, shows a **Butted Hinged Joint**, the commonest method of hanging doors. The entire hinge is sunk flush into the hanging stile. *b*, **Rebated Astragal Shutting Joint**. The astragal is glued to the stile, and rebated to form a projection, which conceals any shrinkage in the adjoining stile. Brass astragal mouldings are frequently used with this joint, with a flange rebated and screwed into the stile. *c*, **Rebated Hinge Joint**, of similar uses to the butted hinged joint, but is more dustproof. Fig. 2, *a*, **Rebated Dustproof Joint**, is similar to the preceding joint, with a dust bead glued into the carcase end, and fitting into a corresponding groove in door stile. These beads are sometimes covered with felt or rubber, and form an absolutely dust and airproof connection. *b*, Similar to astragal shutting joint, f. 1, but rebated into the meeting stile. *c*, A simple dustproof joint, but very effective. Fig. 3, *a*, shows the position of stiles when the doors are hung over the carcase. *b*, A rebated astragal joint, stronger than previous types of wood astragals, but has the disadvantage of showing a space if either of the stiles shrink. It is most suitable for flush or laminated doors. *c*, A dustproof joint with bead worked upon the end. Beads are also inserted in carcase top and bottom. Fig. 4, *a*, a **Centre Hung Door**. Centre hingeing is used for very heavy work, such as glazed wardrobe doors. It is much stronger than butt hingeing, is neater in appearance, and the centre pivots are invisible. *b* shows the shutting stile of the door against a stop bead screwed to the end. **Rebated Shutting Joint**, *c*. **Rebated Pilaster Hingeing**, *d*, suitable for Tallboy chests, cabinets, &c., which have drawers enclosed by doors. The projection portion enables the drawers to pull out when the door is open, without the addition of false ends to permit the drawers clearing the edge of door. **Dustproof Joint**, f. 5, *a*, suitable for single door carcases, rendering the locking stile dustproof; and *b*, detail for the hingeing stile. Fig. 6, *a* and *b*, are details for a single door fitted between the carcase ends. **Centre Hung Door**, f. 7, shows a hollowed pilaster and stop bead. The false end is inserted to allow trays or drawers to pull out beyond the edge of door, which only swings in an angle of 90 deg. Fig. 8 shows an alternative arrangement for a similar purpose, the door in this case passing through an angle of about 130 deg. **Rebated Edge Joint**, f. 8, is used in drawers of the Queen Anne and William and Mary periods, having a neat appearance, and concealing any shrinkage which might occur in the drawer. Fig. 10 shows its application to a cabinet door. The diagram, f. 12, indicates a **Centre Hinged Bureau Fall**, with stop rebates. Quadrants or stays are fixed to the ends for support when in a horizontal position. **Bevel Rebated**

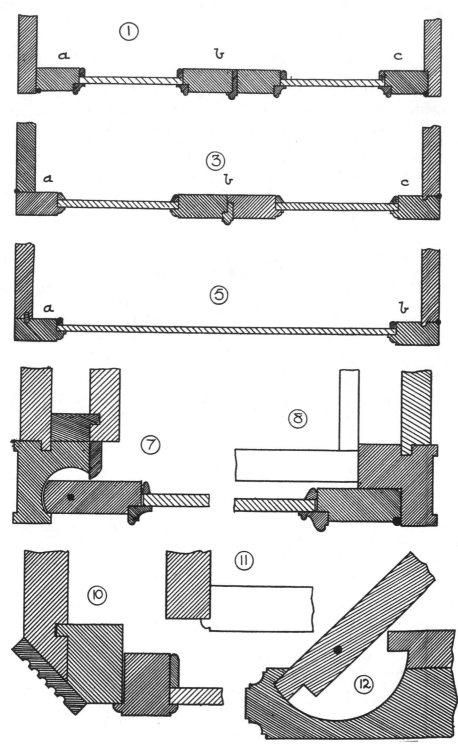

HINGEING AND SHUTTING JOINTS.

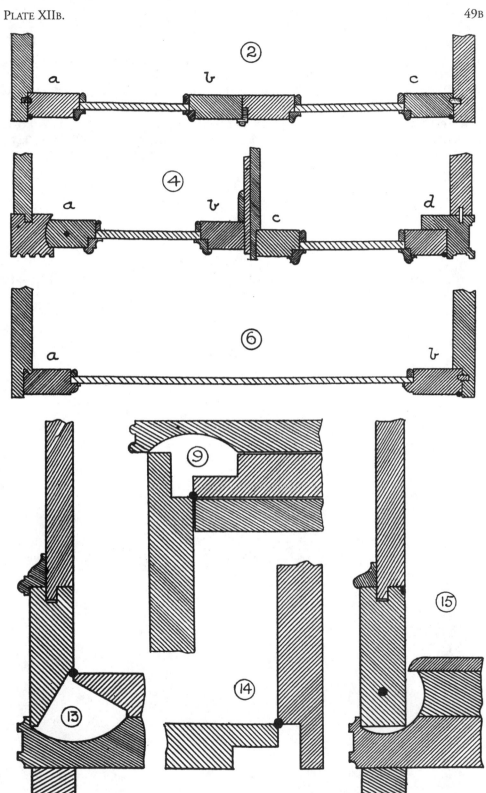

Hingeing and Shutting Joints.

Joint, f. 13, is largely used for secretaire flaps and falls, which are also supported with quadrant stays. Fig. 9 is another application of this joint to a sliding and falling leaf in a liqueur cabinet. When brought to a horizontal position it is pushed home between the divisions. Fig. 14 shows this joint applied to a secretaire drop front drawer in a bookcase bottom part. The drawer is partly withdrawn before the front is released. **Secretaire Fall Joint**, f. 15, has similar uses to f. 13.

MISCELLANEOUS JOINTS.

Pocket Screwing.—Figs. 1 and 2 show, in elevation and section, two methods of pocket screwing. The first consists of boring holes obliquely from the top edge of a rail or rim, then gauging a pocket as shown. The second example *b* has a ½-in. hole bored in the rim to admit a screwdriver, and then a smaller hole is bored to take a screw, and a button glued into the hole under rim when finishing. Both these methods are largely used for fixing table tops (see f. 9), and for work of a similar character.

The Handrail or Dowel Screw Joint, f. 3, is not used to any great extent in furniture, but is occasionally useful for connecting segments of curved work, chair rails, serpentine curves, and butt joints. Its chief recommendation is its simplicity, and the fact that it is a secret fixing. Fig. 12 gives an example of its use in connecting the curved segments of a semi-head frame, but a dowelled joint in this case would be equally effective.

Cleating, f. 4, consists of screwing cleats or clamps across boards to hold them quite straight. It will be noticed that the screw holes are slotted. This is to allow the stuff to move if either contraction or expansion occurs.

Dovetail Cleating, f. 5, is a variation of the above, the cleat being dovetailed both in section and lengthwise. This joint acts similarly to f. 4, for which it is substituted when the thickness of stuff permits of grooving.

Buttoning, f. 6.—A method of fixing the wide tops of counters, bank desks, and tables (see also f. 9). A rectangular block of wood is rebated to fit a corresponding groove on inside of rail, then screwed securely to top, allowing a small space to remain between the butt of the button and the rail, this permitting contraction and expansion. Buttoning is undoubtedly the best kind of fixing for almost every kind of top; but laminated and small work, where shrinkage is scarcely perceptible, does not demand this provision. The use of buttons applied to T iron cleating is shown in f. 11, and f. 10 applies to wooden cleats buttoned down. Georgian panelling frequently contains panels 8 to 12 ft. wide. The shrinkage is, of course, proportionately large, and if the panels were not treated in this way, buckling would ensue if there were any dampness.

Dovetail Keying, f. 8.—Hardwood keys about ½ in. thick, double dovetailed as shown, are inlaid into wide surfaces to increase the strength of joint; their use is almost restricted to repair work, such as shakes or splits which are first glued and then keyed. The diagram f. 13 illustrates their use in joints placed at intervals of about 15 in.

Slot Screwing, f. 7, indicates the method of forming this joint, which is always used to secure a drawer bottom at the back, ensuring a close joint inside, and yet allowing for shrinkage to occur in the bottom. The front edge is glued into groove, so that any shrinkage which takes place is towards the front. Its application is shown in f. 11 for fixing T iron cleats, and in f. 14 the munted bottom of a drawer.

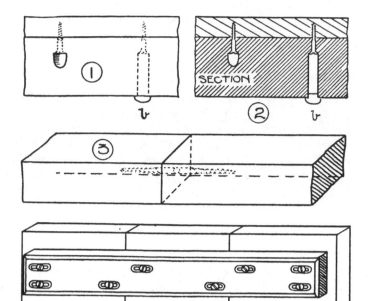

SECTION

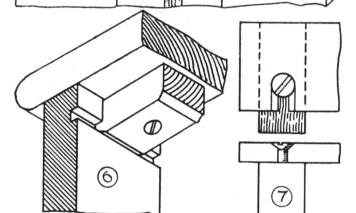

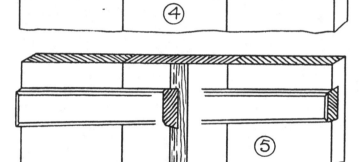

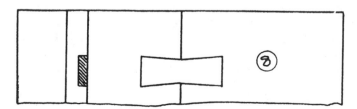

Miscellaneous Joints.

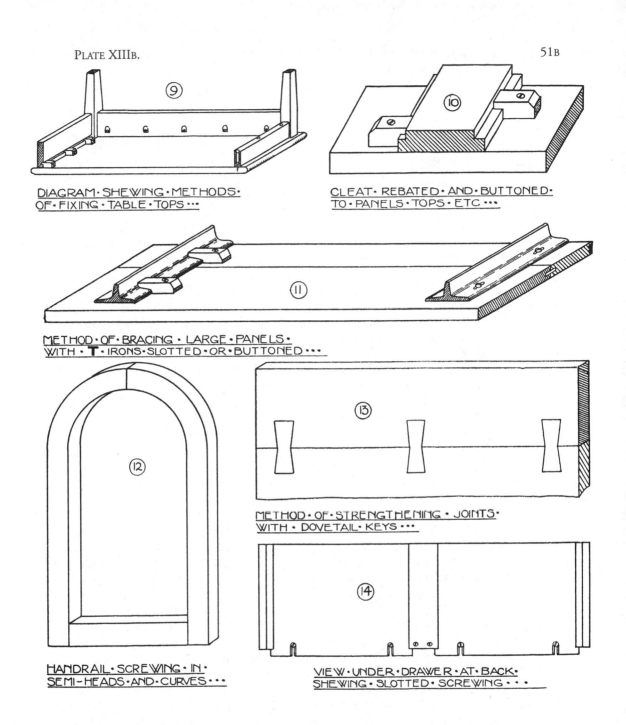

DIAGRAM·SHEWING·METHODS·
OF·FIXING·TABLE·TOPS···

CLEAT·REBATED·AND·BUTTONED·
TO·PANELS·TOPS·ETC···

METHOD·OF·BRACING·LARGE·PANELS·
WITH·**T**·IRONS·SLOTTED·OR·BUTTONED···

HANDRAIL·SCREWING·IN·
SEMI-HEADS·AND·CURVES···

METHOD·OF·STRENGTHENING·JOINTS·
WITH·DOVETAIL·KEYS···

VIEW·UNDER·DRAWER·AT·BACK·
SHEWING·SLOTTED·SCREWING···

MISCELLANEOUS JOINTS.

JOINTS CONNECTING MOVABLE PARTS OF FURNITURE.

Plain Hinged Joint.—Fig. 1 is an ordinary butt or back flap hinged joint used for connecting the drop leaves of tables. Its use is confined to inferior work, but it could be applied to any of the tables shown in f. 12, 13, 14, &c. When the leaf is raised the top is quite flush, but it has an unsightly appearance when lowered, a small space showing at the joint, as well as the knuckles of the hinges.

The **Rule Joint,** f. 2, consists of an ovolo worked upon the fixed edge of a top, with a corresponding hollow on the leaf. Special rule joint hinges or back flaps are used to connect them. When setting out the joint, the distance from the flat side of hinge to centre of pin or knuckle must be gauged from under side of top, see f. 3. The stop square, shown by continuation of dotted line, is placed directly above the centre, and the centre of pin is also the point for striking moulded section. The hinges are sunk flush underneath, and as the leaf swings up or down, the moulded edges fit close and conceal the housing of hinges. This is used for connecting hinged leaves to table tops. See examples opposite, and patent rule joint hinge in Chapter XII.

Knuckle Screen Hinge Joint, f. 4.—The meeting joints of the wings are shaped to section as seen in the diagram, with a moulded piece fitting between them. Hinges are fixed at top and bottom as shown, with a centre hinge for long joints. This connection is used in first-class screen work, and is quite draught-proof. Application shown in f. 14.

Revolving Bracket, f. 5.—This consists of a piece of wood about $1\frac{1}{2}$ in. wide fitting into the end, and pinned as shown. It can only be used in conjunction with a false top, such as in f. 18, the dotted line indicating a false top framing, which receives one end of the iron pin. It is used chiefly in well top work and Pembroke tables.

Hinged Bracket, f. 6.—This is an ordinary shaped bracket hinged to the ends of carcases and tables to support small leaves. When the leaf is lowered the bracket is invisible. Used as in application f. 16.

Finger Joint, f. 7 & 9.—The elevation and plan of a movable interlocking joint is shown swinging in an angle of 90 deg. The bracket is hinged to a piece fixed to the rail, an iron pin acting as centre. It is used chiefly for brackets, as shown in f. 15, and for fly rails, as f. 12, 13, & 19.

Knuckle Joint, f. 8 & 11.—This is another method of interlocking movable rails, shown in elevation and plan, neater in appearance than the former joint, and used for similar purposes. This joint, if made as diagrams, opens at right angles. Fig. 11 shows a method of making to swing in an angle of 180 deg., the mitre lines acting as stops in both cases. Both finger and knuckle joints are used for brackets, and for connecting legs on fly rails, which give more stability to a table than brackets. Application shown in f. 13, 15, &c.

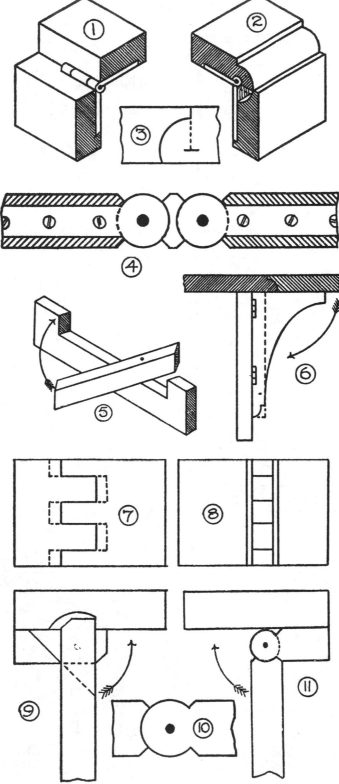

Joints Connecting Movable Parts of Furniture (continued overleaf).

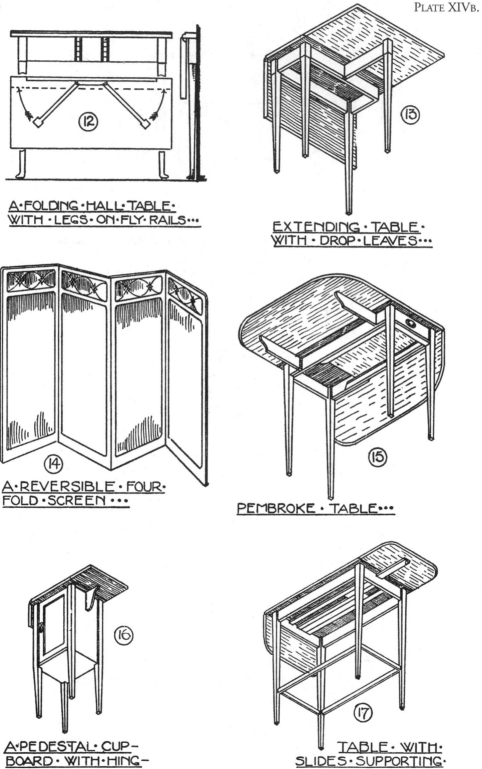

A·FOLDING·HALL·TABLE·
WITH·LEGS·ON·FLY·RAILS···

EXTENDING·TABLE·
WITH·DROP·LEAVES···

A·REVERSIBLE·FOUR·
FOLD·SCREEN···

PEMBROKE·TABLE···

A·PEDESTAL·CUP-
BOARD·WITH·HING-
ED·BRACKETS···

TABLE·WITH·
SLIDES·SUPPORTING·
FLAPS····

JOINTS CONNECTING MOVABLE PARTS OF FURNITURE.

Slide Supports.—Fig. 17 shows another method of supporting leaves. Slides are inserted under the top, dovetailed or grooved in section, and corresponding bearers are fixed to the framing and top. The diagram shows a pair of slides acting parallel to each other, but they may also be arranged to butt at the centre, according to available space and required projection of slide when extended.

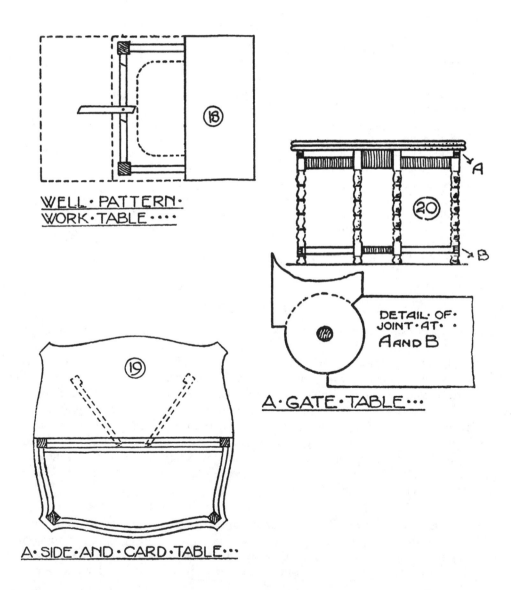

WELL·PATTERN· WORK·TABLE·····

A·GATE·TABLE···

A·SIDE·AND·CARD·TABLE···

PLATE XIVc. JOINTS CONNECTING MOVABLE PARTS OF FURNITURE.

CHAPTER V.

WORKSHOP PRACTICE AND CONSTRUCTION.

GENERAL WORKSHOP PRACTICE.

Procedure in Hand and Machine Shops—Marking out—Sharpening Saws—**Sawing** — Ripping—Cross-cutting—Tenoning — Shouldering—**Planing**—Use of Winding Strips—Squaring Edges—Jointing Joints in Winding—Jointing Thin Boards—Glueing Rubbed Joints—Cramping up—Dowelled Joints—**Ploughing**—Tongueing—Rebating—**Mortising and Tenoning**—Proportions for Tenons—Setting Mortise Gauge—Clearing out Mortises—Necessity for Upright Mortising—Dowelling a Butt Joint—Dowelling Rails—**Dovetailing**—Setting out Angle for Dovetailing—Correct and Incorrect Angle—Dovetail Template—Spacing—**Mitreing**—Mitreing Mouldings—Panel Mouldings—Mitreing Breaks—Stuck Mouldings—Use of Templates—**Scribing Mouldings**—Application of Scribing—Sharpening Gouges—Use of Slip Stones—**Working Mouldings**—Stuck-planed and Scratched Mouldings—Setting out for Working—Use of Rubbers—Toothing—Sharpening and Using—**Glass-papering**—Grades and Sizes—Cleaning off Doors and Framing—**Nailing**—Bradding—Pinning—Descriptions and Uses of ditto—**Preparing Surfaces**—Stopping—Wood Inlays—Composition — Removing Stains — Raising Bruises.

INTRODUCTION.

THIS chapter consists of brief explanatory descriptions of methods in general use for making the various joints, and in the manipulation of tools and material. When the work is of such a character as to need special appliances and processes, such as veneering and marquetry, they are dealt with in a separate chapter. The methods illustrated and described are those generally used in good class work, but it must be pointed out that they vary somewhat according to the training, shop, and individual experience of the worker. At the same time they are essential beginnings in the production of sound, clean fitted, and substantial furniture The chapter is in sections, as follows :— (*a*) General Workshop Practice, (*b*) Carcase Construction, (*c*) Door Making, (*d*) Drawer Work, (*e*) Curved Work.

Remarks on Procedure in Hand and Machine Shops.—Commencing with the design of a piece of furniture, the foreman or draughtsman "sets out," *i.e.*, makes a drawing of the job, either on stiff paper, or upon a ½-in. pine board, called a "rod." This "setting out," together with a "cutting list," viz., a list of material required in making the job—all sizes full to allow for working and fitting—are handed to the "marker out," who selects and cuts out the "stuff," which is then given to the cabinetmaker to proceed with the work. Each piece is marked to correspond with the numbers on the cutting list, and the section of each piece is numbered upon the drawing. In machine shops the cutting list is given to a "marker out," who chalks out all the stuff upon the boards and planks, numbering each piece to correspond with list. The stuff is then taken in hand by the machine foreman, who superintends the cutting out and planing

up. A "setter out" is employed who marks the prepared material to length, and also gauges mortises, tenons, &c., according to the machine capacity of the shop; and when the machining is completed, the material, drawing, and cutting list are placed in the cabinet-maker's hands to complete the job.

1. Marking out with Thumb and Rule.

Marking Out.—The preliminary chalking or marking out of material needs very careful attention, regarding economical arrangement, suitability as to soundness, uniformity in colour between the pieces of stuff, and the direction of grain and figure. When large boards are to be marked, they should first be roughed over with a smoother or "Bismarck" plane, carefully faced, and the cutting lines produced in the following manner:—First, with a piece of whitened whipcord or twine, held on the mark at each end, and quite taut, and then gripped about the centre with finger and thumb, raised 1 or 2 in. and then released. This gives a perfectly straight and clear white line. Second, if the boards have a straight sawn edge, a rule held between the thumb and fingers of left hand may be used as a gauge, and lines drawn with a pencil parallel to the edge,

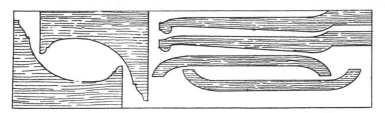

2. Marking out Shapes.

see f. 1. The third method is to mark points upon the stuff, and connect them with lines drawn with a straightedge and pencil.

Allowances for Working and Fitting.—The allowance for working when marking out for machine cutting and planing should be $\frac{1}{8}$ in. full extra width. This is allowed for the saw cut, and an additional $\frac{1}{8}$ in. for planing and fitting; thus a door stile set out 2 in. wide, would be marked out $2\frac{1}{4}$ in. All stuff should be marked, as rail, cross rail, drawer front, &c., or numbered to correspond with the cutting list and drawing. When marking shapes and brackets, cabriole and other curved legs, they should be marked out from a template, as shown in f. 2, called in workshop language "one in the other."

Sharpening and Setting Saws.—A full description of saws is given in the chapter on "Tools." Although the spacing and pitch of the teeth vary in different types, sharpening and setting is exactly similar. The following description of a hand-saw, for instance, will therefore be sufficient for all purposes. The blade should be fixed in a saw filer's vice, *i.e.*, one with extra long jaws, the teeth just projecting above the edge. A three-cornered saw file is then inserted between two teeth, and pressed lightly but firmly forward once or twice, taking care not to alter the pitch or angle of the teeth. The spaces are filed alternately from one side, and then the saw is reversed, and the remaining spaces also filed. To obtain the set, alternate teeth are bent outwards by tapping with the hammer and punch, or with a "saw set." The amount of set varies according to the type of saw. Hand and panel saws which diminish in section towards the back, require less set than a blade of equal thickness throughout.

1. Ripping Stuff on Bench.

2. Ripping Stuff on Stool.

Sawing.—The tool used by cabinetmakers for cutting stuff lengthwise is usually a hand-saw, the joiner's rip-saw only being needed for exceptionally thick stuff, or where it is more convenient to use stools than a bench. The method generally employed is to fix the stuff firmly to the bench with a hand-screw or holdfast, f. 1. The cut is then commenced by making a short kerf with the saw held handle downwards, about three or four strokes being necessary, then the position of the saw is reversed, drawn lightly upwards for a short distance, and then pressed downwards in an almost upright direction ; the length of stroke is increased as the blade enters the wood, until two-thirds of its length is employed. Care must be taken not to exert much pressure on the downward stroke, as the saw is liable to buckle and jar the hands on to the teeth. The saw must be occasionally looked at from behind, to judge whether the cut is square and free from winding. Should the sawn edges press together and bind the saw blade, a chisel or wedge must be inserted. The saw must be properly sharpened and set, or it will have a tendency to draw away from the line. Ripping stuff on stool is illustrated in f. 2, p. 56.

Cross-Cutting.—The stuff is placed upon stools or bench, and held firmly with knee or holdfast respectively. Commence a cut by placing the heel of the saw close to the edge, then draw the saw upwards for a short distance, and push down very lightly, care being taken not to withdraw the saw when it is brought into cutting position

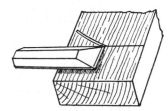

1. Commencing a Tenon Cut.

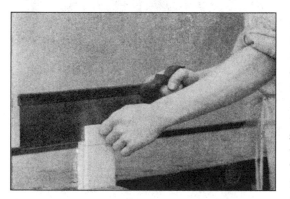

2. Finishing a Tenon.

again ; it should be held at an angle of about 45 deg. to surface of board. Sometimes when cross-cutting, the board will commence to split close to the cut with a loud report ; this is generally due to forced seasoning of the wood, but sometimes indicates branch stuff, which has considerably more "spring" or "life" than boards from the trunk of a tree. To prevent further splitting, well cramp the board near the cut, and then shear or cut the fibres altogether, by holding the saw horizontally.

Cutting Tenons.—The tenon saw is used for general tenoning, but where large tenons have to be made, a hand-saw is preferred. The pieces must be held firmly in the bench vice, and the cut commenced on the end grain ; then saw diagonally towards the shoulder line (see f. 1 above), afterwards reversing stuff, and cutting downwards square with the face edge (see f. 2). By this method the first saw cut acts as a guide, and ensures greater accuracy than when cut square right down. Very small tenons are cut with a dovetail saw.

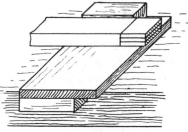

3. Use of Shoulder Board.

Shoulder Cutting.—After the tenon cuts are made, the beginner experiences some difficulty in cutting the shoulders. To reduce this difficulty with shoulder line, he should place the piece on the shoulder board (see f. 3), and carefully chisel a **V** shaped cut against the line, as shown in f. 4. The saw may then be placed in the channel formed,

4. Commencing a Shoulder Cut.

and drawn backward, afterwards pushing forward with a light stroke. The thumb placed against the blade assists to keep the saw upright (see f. 1 below); the handle should be gripped firmly but not tightly, or the hand will shake, thus preventing a clean cut. In wide shoulders, place a straightedge against the

1. Cutting a Shoulder.

2. Sharpening on Oilstone.

line, and use it as a guide when making the cut. This method should not be practised long, or efficient mastery of the tool will not be obtained. Very wide tenons and shoulders are worked with rebate and shoulder plane only, the straightedge acting as a guide for rebate plane.

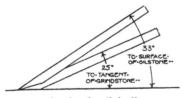

3. Angles for Grinding.

Planing may be roughly divided into four sections. First, Roughing up stuff with a "Bismarck" before marking out. Second, Jack planing, used after roughing to reduce stuff in width or thickness with a greater degree of accuracy before trying up. Third, Try planing, for finishing surfaces and edges perfectly straight and true, and general fitting and jointing. Fourth, Smooth planing, before finishing with scraper and glass-paper. The scientific principles of cutting action, slope of handles, and pitch of irons vary according to the particular uses of the plane, but the general methods of grinding and sharpening are common to all.

To Sharp and Set Plane Irons.—The jack or trying plane is firmly

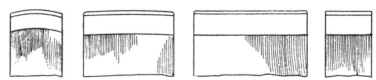

4. Cutting Edge Shapes.

grasped with the fingers on the sole of the plane, the thumb pressing against wedge in the throat, then struck sharply with the hammer upon the button. This loosens the wedge, and the iron can be easily removed, the thumb preventing it slipping through the mouth. Smoothing planes should be struck upon the heel against the top of bench. The cap iron is unloosened by holding top end of irons in left hand, and resting it upon the forepart of bench, then turning the screw with a wide screwdriver. Apply a few drops of oil to the oilstone, and grasp the iron, bevel downwards, with the right hand, assisting with the left hand, f. 2 opposite. Then apply the iron to the stone, and rub to and fro nearly the whole length. The iron is kept as far as possible moving in a parallel direction, at an angle of about 33 deg. to oilstone surface ; an undulating motion, which causes a round bevel, and necessitates frequent grinding, is thus avoided. Fig. 3 illustrates the angles at which the iron is held when grinding and sharpening ; the grindstone should revolve in a direction away from the operator when grinding irons or chisels. A slight burr is caused by the rubbing of iron upon oilstone,

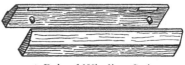

1. A Pair of Winding Strips.

and the iron should be turned over, held quite flat upon the stone, and rubbed slightly to remove the " true " or wire edge. Then wipe with shavings or cotton waste, and whet the iron by drawing it across the palm of hand, each side alternately, or upon a buff strop. To test for a keen edge lightly slide the ball of the thumb along, and it will be found to grip smoothly.

Convexity of Cutting Edge.—Jack plane irons are sharpened slightly convex. Bismarck and roughing planes more convex. Trying, smoothing, compass,

2. Testing a Board with Winding Strips.

and panel planes almost perfectly straight, with the corners rubbed off (see f. 4). Bullnose, shoulder, rebate, fillister, and plough irons are sharpened quite straight care being taken to produce sharp, square corners, which ensure easy working.

Set of Irons.—The amount of iron projecting beyond the cap iron is said to be coarse or fine, according to the distance between, which varies according to the texture of the wood.

To Set the Iron.—The screw should be placed in the hole and drawn along the slot, tightened with thumb and finger, and adjusted close to cutting edge (the distance varying from $\frac{1}{64}$ to $\frac{1}{16}$ in., thus reducing the splitting action of the iron upon the wood, the greater distance for soft woods), and finally the screw tightened.

1. A Face Mark.

Setting the Plane.—Place the heel of plane on forepart of bench, the left hand holding the plane in a sloping direction, insert plane iron, pressing it with thumb against throat, adjust for set or projection of iron beyond sole, and judge by glancing along the sole, then place wedge in position, and tap home with a hammer; the wedge must not be driven too tightly or it will force the plane hollow. Should the rim project too much, tap the button and then wedge again.

2. Use of a Cramp Rack Support.

Planing Up.—To plane true and out of winding, called "trueing up," proceed as follows:—First remove rough surface with jack plane and "traverse" (i.e., plane across the board, if it exceeds 15 in.), then plane lengthwise, testing it with edge of plane across the board; if either hollow or round, light will be visible at the centre or edges accordingly, indicating the high parts. The trying plane is then worked in the direction of grain, removing the superfluous wood, until a flat surface is produced, which is tested with winding strips, f. 1, p. 59. Winding strips are pieces of hard wood planed quite parallel, with white sights let into one piece. Place one at each end of the board; then, standing about a foot away from the near piece, lower the head until the eye is level with the edge of strip, f. 2, p. 59, and observe whether both edges

3. Marking Stuff for Jointing.

lie in the same plane; if this is the case the lines are parallel. When the stuff is twisted, opposite corners of the strips appear high, indicating that more planing is required diagonally to produce a flat true surface. After planing diagonally, finish with strokes right through the board, which, if quite true, will allow the iron to bite or grip throughout the whole length. A mark is then applied, f. 1 above, called a face mark, which suffices to show the face side, and also indicates the "trued" or "shot" edge.

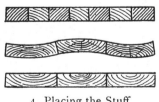

4. Placing the Stuff.

Squaring the Edge.—Shooting and squaring the edge usually follows the "facing up," a straightedge square with face side being produced. The stuff is fixed in bench vice, supported with a rack, f. 2, a few shavings are removed with jack plane, and the trying plane is placed on the edge, the left hand grasping fore front and fingers on sole, acting as a guide which prevents the plane slipping off the edge. Slightly raise the heel of plane, and draw backwards

1. Testing a Joint with Straightedge.

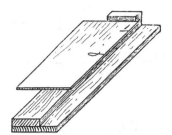

2. Shooting Joints on Thin Stuff.

until the cutting iron is behind the end, then press forward the whole length of joint. If the edge is round, commence planing at the centre; if hollow, remove stuff from each end, and then in both cases take off fine shavings the whole length. Edges above 4 ft. in length are tested for accuracy with a long straight-edge, and also with try square on the face side.

Jointing.—When jointing, the pieces are arranged on the bench in order, bearing in mind position of heart side, direction of figure and grain, and uniformity in colour between them. Fig. 3 opposite illustrates the correct arrangement of stuff with heart grain in same direction, and also the method of marking cross lines below numbers, to show position when glueing up. Fig. 4 opposite indicates position of heart grain in jointing. Proceed to shoot face

3. Position for Glueing.

edge of piece marked 1, then insert the second piece in vice, and shoot the edge, place both edges together, and test across face sides at both ends, with a straightedge. Any irregularities in the joint will be at once apparent, and may be rectified by taking fine shavings from the high side of edge. Cramped joints should be shot slightly hollow.

Winding Joints.—Sometimes the jointing stuff is in winding, and when this is the case, test with a straight-edge about the centre of boards only (f. 1 above), planing joints until both faces are in line. It will be observed that one end of the board is hollow, and the other end round.

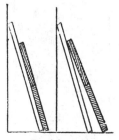

4. Position when Drying.

When glueing up, hand-screw a cleat at each end, then cramp in centre first, and then at each end, when the joint should pull up quite flat.

Jointing Thin Boards.—After marking as described previously, place one piece on shooting board, f. 2, number upwards. Shoot the edge with the plane on its side. The second piece is then shot number downwards. This is called "under and over." The bevel formed on each piece, due to unequal projection of plane iron, and inaccurate shooting board, thus counteract each other.

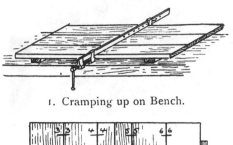

1. Cramping up on Bench.

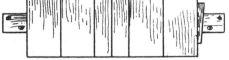

2. Jointing up Thin Stuff.

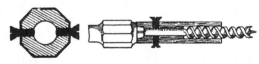

3. Method of Marking for Dowels.

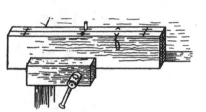

4. Stop Gauge on Dowel Bit.

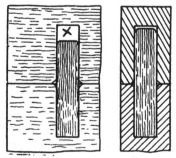

5. Correct and Incorrect Length of Dowels.

Glueing Rubbed Joints.—To glue up rubbed joints, secure one piece firmly in bench vice, and lay the other edge against it, forming a blunt V (see f. 3, p. 61). The glue should be thoroughly heated, and of such consistency as will prevent it breaking quickly into bead-like drops as it falls from the brush. Well brush the glue over joints, and bring the stuff into position again. Grasp the top piece at each end, and rub to and fro steadily. The strokes will gradually shorten as the air and glue are expelled, and finally cease as soon as the lines coincide, as when first marked. They can be placed against bearers until dry (see f. 4, p. 61, which illustrates correct and incorrect position of boards against bearers when drying), the weight of boards in the second diagram partially opening and breaking the joint.

Cramping Joints.—Place two bearers across the bench, well glue joints, and fold over in position ; a cramp is then applied at centre, f. 1 above. If the joint is shot slightly hollow, one cramp is sufficient. Tap the joint with a hammer until both pieces are quite flush or level. Thin stuff is planed slightly hollow, and cramped between iron stops of bench, with a weight on them to prevent springing, or, if a large number of joints require glueing, improvised cramps as in f. 2, small pins preventing buckling.

Dowelled Joints.—Fix both pieces as in f. 3, square lines across at intervals of about 9 in., then gauge lines in centre of edges, the intersections being pierced with a marking awl, and then bored with a dowel bit. The stop gauge fixed to dowel bit, f. 4, determines the depth of dowel hole, which should be about 1 in. Should the dowel fit tightly, reduce by driving through a dowel plate, or tooth with plane. The dowels are glued into one piece, and cut off to length, filling the holes as shown in f. 5.

Badly fitting dowels cause indentations to appear on the wood, by the contraction of air and glue. They are especially noticeable when the material is polished.

Ploughing a Tongued Joint.—The main parts of a plough are the "skate," "fence," and stop. Set the plough with the iron projecting about $\frac{1}{32}$ in. below the edge of skate, and turn the thumb-screw to regulate depth of groove, tightening the side set screws to prevent it working loose. The wedges are then slackened, and the stem tapped at either end until the distance required between fence and cutter is

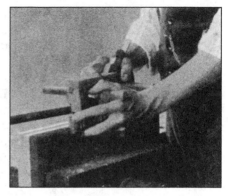

1. Method of Holding a Plough.

obtained, then tighten wedges and again test carefully. The plough is held as in f. 1 above, with wood fixed as shown, the driving power is obtained with the

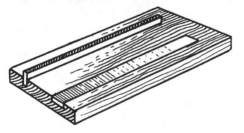

3. Board for Planing Tongues.

2. Cross Grained Tongue.

4. Feather Tongue.

right hand, steadying the tool with the left. Ploughing commences at the front, and working backwards, and then right through to finish. The plough must be held quite steady during this operation, or a rolling motion will occur, and the groove be irregular.

Tongued Joints.— Cross tongues, f. 2, are made by shooting the end of a thin board of hardwood, then gauging off pieces about $\frac{3}{4}$ in. wide, which are reduced to thickness in the tongueing board, f. 3. Feather tongues, f. 4, are cut lengthway of the grain, and are seldom used in cabinet work. Proceed to shoot joint as previously explained for rubbed joints. Plough the grooves, as described from face side.

5. Commencing a Rebate.

6. Ploughing a Large Rebate.

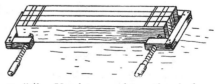

7. Stiles Hand-screwed together before Marking Mortises.

Glue cross tongues into one piece, finish glueing, and cramp together. All joints should be warmed before glueing, ensuring close joints, and more rapid drying. Badly fitted tongues have a similar effect to bad dowelling, particularly in thin stuff, and are also unsightly on the end view.

Rebating.—Rebates are formed by gauging lines upon face side and edge of stuff, and chamfering away the corner, f. 5, p. 63, then a shoulder is cut with chisel, which enables the rebate plane to obtain a start, finally rebating to the dotted lines. Very large rebates are ploughed, f. 6, and finished with rebate plane. A side fillister is used when a number of similar rebates require working. This is set with screws and fence upon the side and bottom, a spur attachment on the side facilitating cross-grain cutting. This spur must project slightly beyond the corner of the iron, or a ragged edge will result.

1. Setting a Mortise Gauge.

Mortising and Tenoning Proportions.—Stub and through mortises and tenons are about one-third the thickness of stuff, or rather more than under if the mortise chisel is not exactly one-third the thickness of wood. The stiles should be hand-screwed together, f. 7, and mortise lines squared across the edges in pencil. Shoulder lines on rails are marked with striking knife or chisel, returning the lines all round the rails. Through mortise lines are returned on the face side and back edge.

Setting the Gauge.—The mortise chisel may fit easily between the points, f. 1 above; loosen set screw of head, and tap the gauge stick until the points coincide with a chisel mark previously made in centre of edge, tighten the set screw, and gauge between the mortise lines. A stile is then fixed in bench stops, f. 2. Commence the cut at centre of mortise, working towards the near end, removing the core as you go, then reverse the chisel and

2. Mortising and Testing with Square.

cut to far end of mortise. If through mortising is being executed, cut half way through from one side, and then reverse the stuff. The core is removed with a core driver, viz., a piece of hard wood 9 in. long, rather smaller than the mortise, driven through the hole.

Clearing out Stub Mortises.—Stub mortises are gauged for depth by glueing a piece of paper on the side of the chisel, f. 3, which indicates when the proper depth is reached. Stub mortises are cleared out with a small firmer chisel. It is essential for well-fitting work that the

3. Paper Gauge for Depth.

4. A Float.

mortise should be upright.   Fig. 2 opposite shows how to test with a try square, but it is usually sufficient to view the relative position of chisel and material when standing at the near end.

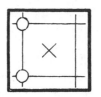

1. Marking Dowels in a Butt Joint.

Necessity for Upright Mortising.—Badly cut mortises prevent the rail lining up with the stile, necessitating paring the mortise, and glueing a veneer on the opposite cheek.   Unless through mortises are cut vertically from either edge, a shelf or

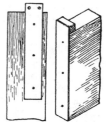

2. A Dowel Rounder.

ridge is formed, which must be removed with a float.   A cavity is thus formed between the opposite cheek and the tenon, which considerably lessens the strength of the joint.   A float may be made with an old file, softened in the fire, and serrations or teeth filed up, and afterwards hardened again, f. 4 opposite.   When mortising very heavy timber, it should be placed on saw stools, the workman either sitting astride or sideways whilst working, to keep it steady.

3. Templates for Dowelling Rails.

Dowelling a Butt Joint.—To dowel a butt joint, f. 1 above shows the position of dowels for material 3 in. square. Mark diagonals with a marking awl, intersecting in centre of stuff, gauge lines from face sides only, $\frac{3}{4}$ in. and $2\frac{1}{4}$ in. respectively from the edge, and where they intersect is the centre for boring holes.   Glue the dowels into one piece, cut to length, and round off ends with dowel rounder, f. 2.   A V-shaped groove cut along dowel with chisel, allows glue and air to escape, and prevents the joint splitting.   To cramp together long pieces of stuff, use iron cramps with lengthening bar, or a piece of quartering with cleats and folding wedges.

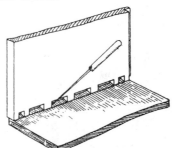

4. Marking Dovetails from Pins.

Dowelling Rails into Legs.—Fix the legs together, and set out lines showing position of rails, prepare a zinc or veneer template to section of rail, f. 3, gauge centre line for boring points on end of rail, alter gauge, adding the amount of square required to be left on leg when the rails are glued in, and gauge legs between rail lines.   Prick position of points through the template, and transfer to rail, pricking through with a marking awl, then lay the template on leg, the gauge line in centre of template corresponding with gauge line on leg, and prick through, then bore for dowels, which are glued into rails first, and finally knock together.

5. Cutting Dovetails in Vice.

Dovetailing is executed by two distinct methods.   The first consists of cutting the pins first, f. 4, and in marking the dovetails with an awl.   This is a general rule in Continental workshops, but where a large number of pieces require dovetailing, it will be found quicker to hand-screw them together, as in f. 5, previous page, and cut the dovetails first.

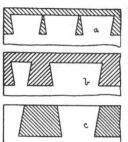

1. Proportions for Dove-tailing.

Secret dovetail joints, which cannot be marked by this system, are executed by cutting pins first, and this method will also be found more convenient when handling very large carcase work.

Setting out Dovetails.—The ratio between dovetail and pin varies according to the work in hand. Thus, in drawer work, the pins are very narrow, and the dovetail large, f. 1, *a*. This makes a strong joint, and is not unsightly or cumbersome. Carcase dovetails that are concealed by plinth or cornice have the pins cut larger, the ratio of pin and dovetail being 1 : 3, f. 1, *b*. Again, cistern dovetailing required to resist the heat generated when soldering the lead lining, have both pin and dovetail equal; any shrinkage which may then occur is evenly distributed throughout the whole case, f. 1, *c*.

Angle of Dovetails.—The angle for cutting dovetails to obtain the maximum amount of strength from the joint may be either 1 in 6 or 1 in 8. It will be found advantageous to cut exterior dovetailing, such as drawers, instrument cases, &c., where they must have a neat appearance, 1 in 8, and the heavier types for carcases, bases, and chests, 1 in 6. To obtain the bevel, set out a line square with the edge of a board, divide into six or eight parts as required, erect a perpendicular one division long, and set the bevel as shown in f. 2, or make a dovetail template to both angles, f. 3.

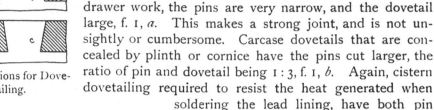

2. Obtaining the Slope.

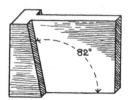

3. A Dovetail Template.

Incorrect Angles for Dovetailing are illustrated in

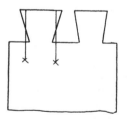

4. Incorrect Angle for Dovetailing.

5. Marking Dovetails with Saw

f. 4, where it will be noticed that a sharp angle considerably lessens the strength of the joint, due to the short grain. To execute the joint prepare the stuff to width and thickness, shoot one end of each quite square, and gauge the thickness of each piece on to both sides of the other piece. Set out dovetails, cut with saw, and to mark the dovetails fix as shown in f. 5 opposite, then draw a dovetail saw through the cuts, pressing the teeth against the end grain. When the dovetailed piece is removed, the saw marks show exact position of pins, which are then cut, care being taken to just leave the mark upon the wood. Cut the shoulders with dovetail saw, and with a bevelled firmer chisel chop away the waste, cutting half-way through from either side and slightly inwards, thus ensuring a close joint when dovetails are put together.

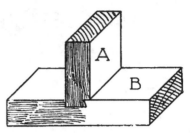

Housed Dovetails.—Dovetail housed joints may be shouldered on one side only or both. To make the joint, f. 1, set out thickness of stuff on A, and gauge ¼ in. per depth of dovetail. Gauge depth also on B. Mark dovetail on B, tapering slightly in its length. Cut with dovetail saw to gauge line, and remove core with chisel, finishing the depth with a router or "old woman's tooth," as in f. 2. Mark on each edge of B the width of dovetail, cut the shoulder, and chisel or plane down to line, fitting and casing as required. This joint should fit hand tight. Very tightly fitting joints curve the housed piece.

1. A Housed Joint.

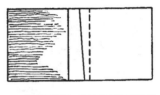

2. Cutting Housed Joints.

Mitreing.—This is the joint formed between two pieces of wood or moulding. Thus the bisection between any of the angles in f. 3 are mitres, although the number of degrees in the angles vary. The term "right" mitre is applied when the angle formed by the mouldings is 90 degs. "Internal" and "external" mitres are the terms applied when the moulding meets in an angle or corner, and at a salient angle respectively. Fig. 3, A, B, and C, shows "internal" and "external" mitres. To find the angle of intersection between two straight lengths of moulding, place a piece of moulding close to the edge of framing, and draw a pencil along the edge, then repeat with adjoining edge, and the point of intersection joined to the corner of frame gives the correct angle for cutting. Where curved mouldings intersect with straight lengths, a curved mitre is necessary, or a straight mitre is obtained by

3. Diagram showing Various Mitres.

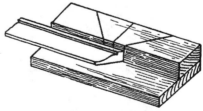

4. Use of a Mitre Cut.

obtaining geometrically a moulding section that will unite in a straight line. See chapter on "Practical Geometry and Setting Out."

Mitreing Mouldings.—Mouldings must be well damped before cleaning up, thus swelling the minute ridges or bruises caused by spindle cutter or scratch stock. The longest lengths possible should be used, and all pieces must "follow on," *i.e.*, be mitred in the same order as when in the length ; this avoids any possibility of faulty mitres, owing to slight differences in sections.

1. A " Mitre " Shooting Board Attachment.

Mitreing Panel Mouldings.—Cut one end of length in mitre cut (see f. 4, previous page), and then plane the mitre on shooting board, f. 1 on this page. This represents an ordinary shooting board with a hardwood block dry dowelled, having its edges at an angle of 45 degs. with the edge of board. Place the trying plane on its side, and hold the moulding firmly against the edges of block, then plane the mitre, mark moulding to length, and shoot off to the mark. Large mouldings for cornices, bases, and double bolection mouldings cannot be planed on the shooting board, and are held in mitre block, cut with block saw, f. 2, and planed down level with the surface. It is necessary with large mouldings to have a very accurate mitreing box. Fig. 3 illustrates one for this purpose, and it is a very effectual guide for a fine panel saw. The "donkey ear shoot" is used for mitreing long edges of boards which cannot be held in a mitre block, f. 4. When mitreing "bolection" mouldings, a hardwood slip should be fixed on board to prevent the edge splitting away during planing, f. 1 opposite.

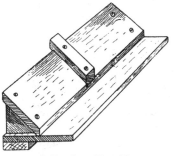

2. A Mitre Block Saw.

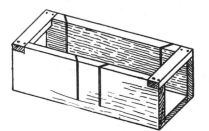

3. Mitre Box for Large Mouldings.

Mitreing Breaks.—When mitreing round small breaks in cornices, pilasters, plinths, &c., a length of moulding, sometimes not exceeding $\frac{1}{4}$ in. long, cannot be held conveniently in block, because of the differences between length, breadth, and thickness. A board is then prepared by screwing a piece of hardwood planed to angle of 45 degs. at one end, and a correspondingly thick piece to act as a rest for plane (see f. 2 opposite). Pins are driven in until their heads project $\frac{3}{16}$ in. from the

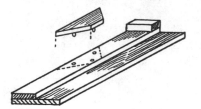

4. A Donkey Ear Shoot.

board, and are filed to a sharp point. The moulding is pressed on to these points, close to the stop, and the moulding can be planed to the desired thickness, that is, level with both pieces.

Mitreing Stuck Mouldings.—"Stuck" mouldings on doors, framing, &c., require a mitre template, which is either of brass or wood. Fig. 3 below illustrates a brass combination template, and the wood template illustrated in f. 4 consists of a rectangular block, rebated and then planed to angles of 45 degs. at each end. Fig. 5 illustrates a panel mitre template used for cutting the internal mitres of moulded panels. Fig. 1, p. 70, shows the stile of a door, with a stuck moulding, which also forms the rebate to receive the panel.

1. Shooting a Bolection Moulding.

Use of Template.—Fix the stile in stops or vice, and cut away the moulding from mortise line. Then apply the template with its square edge against the right or mitre line, and fix with **G** cramp. A paring chisel is used to cut the mitre, and must be pressed firmly on the template, and the shoulders thrust forward.

2. Shooting a Moulding Break.

Scribing.—The term "scribing" applies to two different methods of fitting joints. In the first case it is used to counteract the effects of shrinkage in the mouldings of doors and screens, when a mitred moulding would show an unsightly gap between the mitres. The rail moulding is cut and scribed to fit the stile, and in the event of shrinkage taking place, its effect is not apparent, the moulded rail shrinking along the stile, and, when the moulding is polished previous to scribing the joints, no unsightly mark is perceptible. Scribing in conjunction with mortising and tenoning effects a stronger joint than mitreing, especially when used for connecting moulded rails in screens, &c. A simple illustration is the solid bar of a sash frame, f. 2, next page, where mitred joints are impossible, owing to their weakening effect; other suitable applications are in connection with fitment cornices and dados, where a better fitting joint is obtained more rapidly than mitreing (f. 3, next page) and having the same appearance. The possibility of scribing mouldings is determined by the profile or section; speaking generally, bold sections are most suitable, but it is difficult to make a clean scribe if the members are of slight curvature. Undercut mouldings of the Louis period, for instance, cannot be scribed. The second kind of scribing consists of fitting boards, furniture, or framing to irregular surfaces, and is accomplished by wedging the work in position, and setting it true to marks or with a spirit level. A pair of dividers is set to the greatest space between the job and the floor or wall, as the case may be, and is then drawn along the surfaces, one leg following the irregularities of floor, and the other making a line on the stuff, which is cut with bow saw

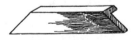

3. A Brass Combination Mitre Template.

4. Wooden Mitre Template.

5. Panel Mitre Template.

and finished with spokeshave. The edges should be slightly bevelled from the outside face, ensuring a close fit, and the work will then stand as previously wedged in a relatively level position.

1. Application of a Mitre Template.

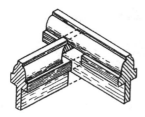

2. A "Scribed" Solid Sash Bar.

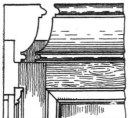

3. Scribing a Dado Moulding.

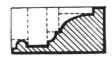

4. Working a Moulding.

Sharpening Gouges.—Gouges are divided into two groups, " Firmer " and " Scribing." The "firmer" type have the ground bevel outside and are sharpened upon an oilstone, similarly to an ordinary chisel, with a revolving motion to suit the curve, and the " burr " is then removed with a slip stone fitting into the inside curve and held quite flat upon it. Unless the slip is bedded firmly inside the curve, a small bevel will result, which affects the cutting action. Scribing gouges are ground upon the inside, and sharpened by rubbing a slip stone moistened with oil along the bevel, until a slight burr is obtained ; this is removed by laying the gouge upon an oilstone, and rubbing lightly with a revolving action. Both kinds may be "stropped" upon a piece of hide to obtain a keener cutting edge.

Working Mouldings with "hollows and rounds."—When a large quantity of mouldings are to be worked, it is usual to have them done on a spindle machine, but a knowledge of handwork mouldings is invaluable when short lengths are required with little delay. To work the moulding, f. 4 below, gauge the stuff to width and thickness, and gauge lines coinciding with dotted lines in diagram, the portions marked can then be ploughed from the edge and the rebate worked. Complete the small hollow by chamfering away and hollowing out with a small round, and the astragal with rebate and hollow plane. Hardwood mouldings, containing a number of small members, should be first worked as described, and finished off with a steel cutter fixed in a scratch stock.

5. Using a Moulding Plane.

Stuck Mouldings are worked with a moulding plane, the sole and cutter shaped conversely to the section required. The English pattern moulding plane is held at an angle indicated by lines on the forepart of plane, shown in f. 5, and must be held quite steady, or varying sections will result. French pattern moulding planes are held quite upright, and are recommended. The use of these planes is restricted to small ogees, ovolos, hollows, and broken ogees, seldom exceeding $\frac{3}{8}$ in. wide, but with repetition work planes of much larger sections may be made to advantage. Fig. 1 illustrates the method of scratching small mouldings when planes are not available, but its use is practically confined to very hard, crisp wood, which lends itself readily to a scraping action. Fig. 2 is the section of a pilaster, showing scratch stock in position and the moulding formed. Curved mouldings are worked in a similar way, the butt of the scratch stock being curved to fit the sweep or shape.

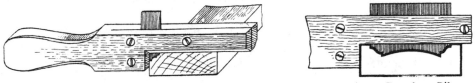

<table>
<tr><td>1. Scratching a Small Moulding.</td><td>2. Scratching a Panel on Pilaster.</td></tr>
</table>

Use of Rubbers.—To finish straight lengths of moulding with glass-paper, prepare wood rubbers (see f. 3) shaped a little quicker than the various members of moulding section. The glass paper is then held firmly round them, and rubbed to and fro along the length, using finer glass-paper as the marks left by the plane are removed. All rubbers should be made 4 in. long, and kept in a prepared box, ensuring a quick selection of rubbers to fit any section. Curved lengths are cleaned up with small cork rubbers, such as are illustrated in f. 3, *a*, *b*, and *c*.

Toothing.—A toothing plane is used for roughening groundworks before veneering, and also for removing inequalities in veneer, due chiefly to faulty cutting. The iron is fixed almost perpendicularly in the plane stock, and has a number of minute serrations on the flat side, which, when the iron is ground and sharpened, form a saw-like cutting edge.

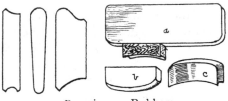

3. Papering up Rubbers.

The iron is sharpened in the ordinary way, but the burr is not removed on the oilstone, instead of which it is driven into the end grain of a very hard block of wood, this sufficing to remove the burr.

When toothing a groundwork or panel for veneering, the strokes are first taken in diagonal directions from corner to corner, and straight strokes right through the board to finish; this removes the ridges left by the trying plane, and the roughened surface materially assists the cohesion of veneer. Toothing is also useful for flatting a veneered surface before scraping, especially when the surface is composed of various veneers, differing in thickness; this applies, of course, only to saw-cut stuff.

Scraping is the process immediately following the "smoothing up" of material, previous to glass-papering. A scraper is a thin, flat piece of steel 4 in. by 3 in. and $\frac{1}{16}$ thick. To sharpen it, first file both edges quite square. Rub down the edges on oilstone until all file marks are removed, leaving a perfectly smooth edge. Then lay the scraper upon the stone, and rub the burr off the flat sides. Transfer to bench as in f. 1, and rub down with a scraper sharpener, afterwards holding it vertical, f. 2, with the sharpener held at an angle of 85 degs. with surface. Take a sharp stroke upwards, thus making a slight burr or cutting edge with each successive resharpening. The angle at which sharpener is held is reduced slightly. A carefully sharpened scraper frequently permits of about twelve resharpenings in all, then refiling, &c., is repeated. Scraper shavings are very fine, and give a finely finished surface before glass-papering.

Hard woods only are scraped, but oak, having a prominent silver grain figure, must be papered up after smoothing. A scraper removes the softer material, and leaves the silver grain above the surface, which is very unsightly when polished.

1. Use of Scraper Sharpener.   2. Vertical Sharpening of Scraper.

Glass-paper is made in seven grades or sizes, ranging from 2½ to 000 Flour glass-paper, but cabinetmakers rarely use a stronger size than M. 2. The purpose of glass-paper is to produce a perfectly flat surface after scraping, but it should be very sparingly used, good cabinetmakers seldom using stronger than F. 2. Glass-paper is manufactured by covering a sheet of coarse paper on one side with thin glue, and sprinkling with minute particles of sand and glass. It must be used quite dry, as when in a limp condition the glue is damp, which causes the glass-paper to clog. To clean off pine or white wood for a painted surface F. 2 is used, and rubbed diagonally and across the grain ; but for polished surfaces in any wood all strokes must be in the direction of the grain. First scour the stuff with a piece of F. 2 placed round a cork rubber, size 4 by 3 by 1 in., taking care that no loose ends are left, which scratch the surface and round off the sharp edges, then rub down with 1½, finishing with No. 1 or Flour paper. In framing and doors the muntings are papered right through, then the rails, and finally the stiles, afterwards rubbing with a circular motion over the shoulders, and finishing with straight strokes until all marks are removed. Very soft or spongy material should be sized first, thus securing the loose fibres which would otherwise rise up and tear, but the rubber should not be moved too rapidly, or the glue will become softened in the glass-paper, and cause it to clog. The special treatment of inlaying in pearl, ivory, metal, &c., will be dealt with in a succeeding chapter.

Screwing and Nailing.—Screws are used in cabinetwork for fastening the various parts of work together—carcases, fittings, &c., and are made of both iron and brass, with round and flat heads. For fixing locks, hinges, &c., brass screws are usual, but oak work demands the use of brass screws, owing to the secretion of an acid which corrodes iron, and causes a black stain to appear in the surrounding wood. When boring to receive screws, a nose-shell or gimlet bit is used, boring in the case of a 2-in. screw about $1\frac{1}{2}$ in. deep, but, of course, no hard or fast rule can be laid down for timber of varying texture. To fix metal plates to wood, bore the entire length of shank, and the screw will worm its way into the side of the hole securely; round-headed screws are generally used for fixing metal work.

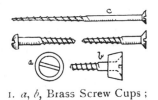

1. *a*, *b*, Brass Screw Cups; *c*, Lath Screws.

To obtain a flush surface the material is countersunk to receive the screw head, which, when driven home, is quite flush with material. Brass cups are used in work that is required to be detached frequently, such as fillets, beads, &c. (see f. 1, *a* and *b*). Lath screws, as the name suggests, f. 1, *c*, are for screwing into the laths of plaster partitions where ordinary screws would split the laths and prevent a secure fixing.

Bradding and Pinning.—Although nails and brads are not used to any extent in good cabinetwork, their use is sometimes applied to various jobs outside furniture production, executed by cabinetmakers. The various kinds are French nails, round, square, and elliptic in section, f. 2, A, B, C. They may be driven in almost any direction without previous boring and without splitting the wood, unless near the edge of a board; the head ends are roughened for greater holding power, and they are used chiefly in rough case work. Sizes vary from 1 to 4 in. long, but cast and wrought nails, f. 2, D, E, F, may also be driven without boring; their use is chiefly for fixing skeleton framings, &c., to receive fittings or panelling. These nails are rather wedge-shape in section as well as tapering in length, and have a tendency to "draw" or "drift" towards

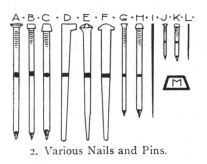

2. Various Nails and Pins.

the wide edge, f. 2, M; this is counteracted by inclining the nail in the opposite direction before driving. When nailing the ends of boards together, the nail points should incline towards each other in pairs, thus forming a kind of dovetailed joint. French panel pins are both round and elliptic in section, f. 2, G, H. Although the latter type are not much used, sizes range from $\frac{3}{4}$ to 2 in., used for fixing mouldings to painted works; they do not require boring, unless in hardwood, when a hole is made with bradawl about three-fourths of their length. French brads, f. 2, J, K, vary from $\frac{1}{2}$ to $\frac{3}{4}$ in.; similar uses to panel pins. Veneer pins, f. 2, L, are really thin pieces of wire pointed at one end, used for securing veneer during the process of laying with cauls ; they are left projecting about ⅛ in. from stuff, and withdrawn after the veneer is laid. Needle points, f. 2, I, previous page, are for fixing enamelled and gilt mouldings, they are driven in without previous boring, and snapped off level with surface.

Preparing Surfaces consists of filling any cavities or imperfections in the wood, such as are caused by the removal of loose knots, &c., before veneering, painting, or polishing. A stopping composed of litharge and glue is best, but a mixture of glue and whiting, or glue and plaster, is effective ; either should be well pressed into the hole whilst hot, and allowed to project beyond the surface to allow for shrinkage whilst drying, and then levelled down. These mixtures apply only to veneered or painted work ; polished work must have any holes filled with inlays of a similar wood, but it must be clearly understood that stopping of any kind is unsatisfactory in polished work, and should only be resorted to when rendered absolutely necessary by such circumstances as the concealment of screws for fixing, and then only in inconspicuous positions. Pelleting is an effective method ; a piece of wood, with the direction of grain as indicated in sketch, is turned to the given shape ; the screw is sunk below the surface, and the pellet glued in and levelled off when dry. For larger holes diamond-shaped inlays are necessary. Cut to shape, lay over hole, mark round with awl and mortise to depth, glue the inlay in position and level off when dry, a bevelled edge ensuring a close joint.

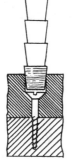

Method of Pelleting a Hole.

Removing Stains.—Oak and mahogany which have been stained with ink or by contact with iron can be cleaned by the application of a solution of oxalic acid. The crystals are allowed to dissolve in warm water, to which is afterwards added a few drops of spirits of nitre ; this preparation applied to a stain will remove it almost instantly. The surface should then be cleansed with water.

Raising Bruises.—Bruises in furniture or boards can be raised by applying a wet rag to them, which is heated by the application of warm irons, thus causing the fibres to swell into position again.

CARCASE CONSTRUCTION.

Definition of Carcase—Procedure in Making—Setting out Carcase and Housed Dovetails —Cutting ditto—Glueing up and Testing—Construction of Plinths and Cornices— Varieties of ditto—Faced up and Veneered Frames—Making a Mitred Frame —Cutting Grooves for Tongues—Glueing up—Blocking Testing for Squareness— Mitreing Mouldings—Cornice Frames—Mitreing Facings—Cornice Mouldings —Glueing ditto—Margin Gauges.

Definition of Carcase.—A "carcase" consists of a "box" which may be divided with partitions to receive doors, drawers, &c., as in wardrobes, cabinets, chests of drawers, and stationery cases. The example illustrated in f. I opposite shows a carcase used in combination with a plinth and cornice, door and drawer, forming a hanging wardrobe, but large work, such as dwarf bookcases, library break-front cases, and winged wardrobes, are composed of three or more carcases,

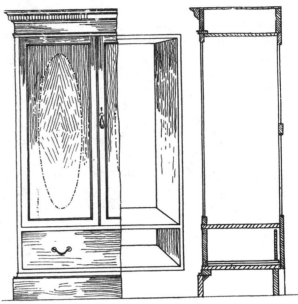

1. A Wardrobe Carcase.

the number and size being determined by the design, size of available material, and adaptation to easy handling during packing and transport. So that in the execution of a complete wall case or similar fitting for a building abroad, all the conditions stated above are considered. Similar construction, however, with but slight variations is applied to all carcase work.

To Make a Carcase.— The stuff is first planed up, gauged to width and thickness, and the ends hand-screwed together. The lengths and division are then squared across the edges with a try square, and a large wooden square, f. 2, is used to return the lines on both sides. The top and bottom of carcase are set out similarly, and the division, which is shorter, by the difference in length between housed and lapped dovetails. All pieces are then planed to width, rebating ends to receive the back, as shown in the working drawing, and the inside surfaces are cleaned up before gauging for dovetails.

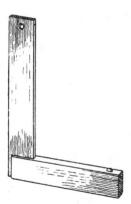

2. A Wooden Square.

3. Cutting a Diminished Dovetail.

Setting out Dovetails.—Gauge the length of dovetail on the ends, and also across the ends of both top and bottom, then gauge their thickness on to the insides of ends. Square division lines across carcase ends and set out the diminished dovetails as follows :—Gauge lines $\frac{3}{8}$ and $4\frac{1}{2}$ in. from front edge between division lines, this space representing the length of actual dovetail, the remainder of division simply being housed into end; this forms a strong joint, but frequently divisions, &c., are dovetailed the whole width. Set out dovetail as in f. 3, removing the darkened portion with a chisel, undercutting side *a* to form a dovetail; a tenon saw can then be inserted and the cuts made right across ends; pare away core with a "firmer" chisel and finish to depth by routering away with an "old woman's tooth." Gauge and cut the dovetails on division ends, carefully test sockets, and fit until the division drives home hand tight. Set out the dovetails on carcase ends, with a small dovetail back and front (refer to f. 1, *b*, p. 66), thus securing a close joint at shoulder should the ends have a tendency to work hollow on the outsides. Place ends on bench and saw dovetails, chopping away the sockets. To mark the top and bottom, either is laid on bench, inside face upwards, and the end is placed exactly on gauge line, marking with awl as shown in f. 4, p. 65. The lines of dovetails are left on the stuff after

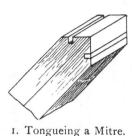

sawing. This method also applies to secret lapped and mitred dovetail joints which cannot be marked by drawing the saw through dovetail cuts. After marking cut the shoulders with saw and remove waste between dovetails, then knock carcase together dry, and if satisfactory proceed to glue together as follows :—

1. Tongueing a Mitre.

Glueing up.—An assistant should hold the ends upon the bench face, edges down, with the division glued into position; the top and bottom are then glued and driven home by striking with a hammer a hardwood block placed across the dovetails. To test for squareness measure diagonally with a thin lath or rod; when the lengths between opposite corners, *i.e.*, diagonals, are equal, the case is quite square.

Construction of Plinths.—So many and various methods are in vogue for constructing plinth and cornice frames, that only two can be dealt with in this chapter; these are characteristic types, and reference to the chapter on "Carcase Work" will show the reader a great number of varied examples. Plinth frames are constructed either of (*a*) solid wood, (*b*) groundwork dovetailed and faced up, or (*c*) dovetailed and veneered. Where a solid plinth is required the joints at front corners are either plain mitred and blocked secret mitre, dovetailed, or tongued mitred and blocked. Plinths that are faced up are usually dovetailed, and a thin ¼-in. facing of figured wood is mitred round the pine or whitewood groundwork; through dovetails are used which, though shrinking somewhat after glueing, do not affect the outside appearance, such as would be the case in a veneered groundwork; the contraction causing the veneer to show distinctly the shape of dove-

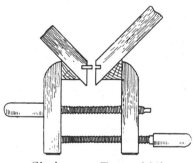

2. Glueing up a Tongued Mitre.

tails when polished. For veneered plinths the joints must be similar to those used for a solid plinth frame.

To Make a Mitred Plinth Frame.—Plane up all stuff true, and gauge to width and thickness. Set out full length of front plinth rail and also one end of side rails with a set mitre. Square across the length of side rails and shoot to mark. Square back rail to length for diminished dovetail, making the width equal to width of side rail plus moulding thickness ; this obviates the necessity of glueing a filling piece at back between the plinth moulding. Fix one end of front rail in mitre block, cut with block saw, and shoot down level with block, and repeat with the remaining mitres ; then place two mitres together (see f. 1 opposite) forming a right angle, permitting the use of a marking gauge to mark position of tongues which are cut with dovetail saw and chiselled to depth if the rails do not exceed 6 in. in width, but if above that width a plough can be used. Set out diminished dovetail for the back and fit together ; this should set back about $1\frac{1}{2}$ ft. from ends of rails, to permit of scribing over skirting, if necessary. Blocks are then glued as shown in f. 2 opposite, which when dry are hand-screwed together with mahogany or oak cross tongues inserted in the grooves, then glue the back rail be-

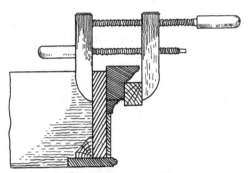

1. Section through a Cornice.

tween the ends, and square up as with carcase, and when dry mitre round the moulding, one end of which is glued first, then the front, and the return end rail last.

Cornice Frames are almost identical with plinths ; the back rail is lapped dovetailed flush at back, equalling in width the side rail plus thickness of frieze moulding ; the diagram, f. 1 above, is a section through one end ; the frame is through dovetailed at front corners, and the frieze is formed by glueing a

2. Use of Margin Gauge.

facing upon the framework, thus also forming a rebate to receive cornice mouldings. It will be noticed that the cornice mouldings project above the framework, this is to allow for dustboard, which is screwed in position and levelled off flush with moulding. After the framework is dovetailed, glued, trued, and toothed up, the facings are mitred and well warmed, then hand-screwed in position. When dry level off at bottom and finish to true width with shoulder or iron rebate plane ; then mitre round frieze moulding and glue blocks about 6 in. apart as indicated

in section, f. 1 ; mitre and glue smaller part of cornice into position, following with the large piece, hand-screwing as shown. Cornice frames made of solid hardwood require a margin gauge to glue moulding in correct position ; one or two of these gauges are placed at intervals along the frame, f. 2, thus causing a perfectly equal frieze, facilitating speedy execution of the work.

On cheap work cornice mouldings are "pitched" and fixed round the carcase with blocks, &c., on to a frame as above. In a like manner a plinth piece is "planted" round the ends and front of a chest of drawers and so becomes a fixed part of the carcase. The loose plinth and cornice frame represent the best and most convenient forms of construction.

DOOR MAKING.

Example of Wardrobe Door—Setting out—Shaping Rail—Fitting Together—Mitreing
Moulding—Glueing up –-Testing : Five-Panelled Door — Setting out—Glueing
Centre Frame—Fitting Cross Rails, &c.—Glueing up : Barred Doors—Methods of
Forming Bars—Mitreing Mouldings---Jointing Stars—Use of Templates : Framed
and Rebated Door with Curved Corners—Setting out—Shaping Rails--Rebating—
Long and Short Shoulders—Glueing up : Routering—Circular Rings for Corners—
Curved Mitres in Mouldings—Flush Doors—Laminating—Cross Clamping—Mitre
Clamping—Slipping Edges—Veneering.

Preparing a Wardrobe Door.—The five illustrations below show various
types of doors.   Their construction embraces the principles applied to all kinds
of doors which are straight in plan and section.   Fig. 1 represents a wardrobe
door with a glass panel.   After preparing the stuff, hand-screw the stiles together,
and set out divisions for mortises on inside edges ; then fix the rails and square

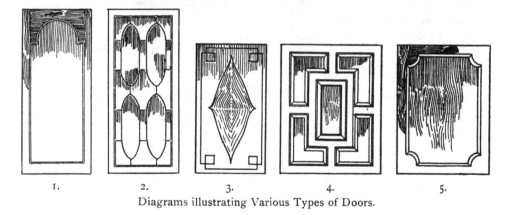

1.   2.   3.   4.   5.

Diagrams illustrating Various Types of Doors.

shoulder lines across, returning them on both sides of each piece ; gauge lines for
the rebate, which, in this case, is equal to width of moulding ; gauge mortise
and tenon lines ; cut and saw ditto, and prepare a template from the drawing
to mark the shaped top rail, cut with bow saw, and finish with files and glass-
paper ; work mouldings and rebates as described on p. 70.   Then place the pieces
on bench, and mark the stiles and rails as f. 1 opposite, fix one stile in stops
as shown, and fit the head rail, testing across the shoulder with a try square ; if
the shoulder requires shortening on one side, proceed as shown in f. 2 opposite,
until it lines exactly with the surface of stile ; repeat with bottom rail, and if
both are fitted truly, they will be out of winding one with the other.   Cut the
mitres as shown in f. 1, p. 70, and again test ; if true, with shoulders well up, or
"tight," place two bearers upon the bench, out of winding with each other ;
glue mortises with a pine stick and tenons with a brush ; then knock together
and cramp up on the bearers.   If the door is well fitted the cramps may be
removed directly after the door is squared up ; it is then allowed to dry, preferably in a hanging position.   Stuck mouldings when used as above are usually
polished before " mitreing."

Five-Panelled Door, f. 4 opposite.—The stiles, rails, cross rails, and centre frame stuff are all marked for mortises, tenons, and length; then gauge on the rebate, mortise and tenon line, and cut all mortises and tenons. Rebate the inside of centre frame, and mitre together as shown in f. 3 below, finally glueing up after the addition of hand-screwing blocks, somewhat similar to those used in plinth frame, the mitres to be tongued up before glueing together. When quite dry the rebating is completed on all the pieces, and the short rails fitted into centre first, following on with the others, each being tested separ-

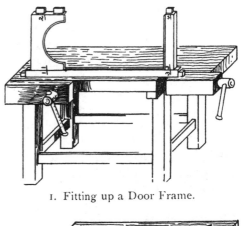

1. Fitting up a Door Frame.

2. Use of Shoulder Plane.

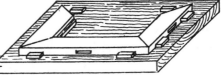

3. Fitting up the Centre Part.

ately for truth; the centre panel is fitted in the centre part, so that the cramps do not strain the framing and cause mitres to spring.

Barred Doors, f. 2 opposite, are executed by two distinct methods. The first consists of fitting a board inside the rebate after the door is glued together, and setting out the moulding lines upon the front, f. 4 alongside. Then the mouldings are mitred to the given lines and shapes, glueing the mitres only. The door is then laid face downwards on the bench, and "slats" or "bars" are fitted into the grooves at the back of the moulding, stub mortised into rails and stiles. Corners are afterwards strengthened by glueing a piece of thin calico or silk about 2 in. long where the bars meet, this is concealed by the glass "beads" when the door is complete. Second method—The frame is set out inside the rebate with slips and a striking knife, the slips equalling the distance from the frame corner to inside of bars; a second mark, $\frac{1}{8}$ in. distant from the first, is made for width of the stub mortise, and repeated for a succeeding bar; the bars or slats are then fixed in position, halving them if possible, or dovetailing the angles. Vee the diagonals, glue and fit the mouldings on face side, cutting mitres with

4. Procedure in Barred Doors.

template, f. 1 below.   All mouldings in both cases must be polished before mitreing.

Panelled Door with Hollow Corners, f. 5, p. 78.—In this case, it is assumed that the frame is rebated on in the inside of face, with a moulding glued round which projects about ⅜ in. to receive the panel (see f. 2 below). This is perhaps the best construction for doors of this kind, because if the moulding is 'stuck" on the stiles and rails, carving is required to finish the corners, but when separate mouldings are mitred round, the hollow corners are obtained by having a "circle" or ring turned, and cut into four parts for the corners.   It will be necessary to have long and short shoulders on the rails of this frame.   These are obtained by setting out the mortise lines on the edges of stiles, and shoulder line *a*, *b*, f. 2, at each end of rails.   The long shoulder *a* is returned on the front of rail, and *b* upon the back ; then proceed to cut mortises and tenons, fit and glue frame together, after shaping and rebating the stiles and rails ; when dry, the door is bevelled off, and, in order that the projection of moulding above the surface be uniform throughout, it will be necessary to router the rebate from the face side.   Prepare a router, f. 3, by screwing two pieces of wood together, and insert a ¾-in. plough iron ; set the iron, allowing it to project just the required depth of rebate, and scratch or scrape the superfluous wood away ; if the fitting of the door has been care-fully done, only a few shavings need be re-moved.   Glass-paper the face of door and glue mouldings in rebates, the mitres being curved to obtain a clean intersection.

1. A Moulding Template.

2. Rebated Frame with Moulding.

Flush Doors.—The construction of f. 3, p. 78, may be either by " laminating," " cross clamp-ing," or " mitre clamping."   It is not usual in flush veneered doors to frame the groundwork together, owing to the shrinkage of panels, and consequent splitting of veneer.   When a groundwork is laminated or clamped, shrinkage does not split the material.   For a laminated door glue either three or five thicknesses of wood together, called " three " and " five ply,"

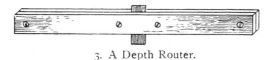

3. A Depth Router.

each layer in a cross direction, *i.e.*, in the case of " five ply," three layers are placed with the grain running in the direction of length of door, and two across, placed alternately, and well glued to-gether in veneering press ; when dry the door is planed up, and the edges slipped, and veneered on both sides.   For clamped doors use well-seasoned timber, and either " cross clamp " or " mitre clamp " the ends, the latter method making the best job ; then veneer both sides as for laminating.

Flush doors were largely used by Chippendale, Hepplewhite, and Sheraton, as this method gave the widest possible surface for decoration as well as the opportunity of making the most of good figure in veneer.

DRAWER WORK.

First Method of Drawer Making—Preparing the Stuff—Fitting the Front and Back—Cutting the Dovetails—**An Alternate Method**—Glueing up—Testing for Squareness—Slipping a Drawer—Working the Slip—Fitting the Bottom—Slot-screwing same—Necessity for Munting in Large Drawers—Fixing the Munting—" Bead and Flush " Slipping.

Before dealing with this subject, a few remarks are necessary regarding the construction of the carcase or framing respectively. The whole depth of a drawer must accurately fit the opening, and it should gradually tighten as it is withdrawn. To effect this the carcase is made slightly larger at the back, both in length and width. In the case of a nest of drawers, or a pedestal, the carcase is made wider, and the runners slightly thinner at the back. The drawer itself is also left slightly full at the back. Wax or similar substances need not be rubbed upon a well-fitted drawer.

First Method.—Proceed by first planing all the drawer stuff to thickness, scraping and glass-papering the inside surfaces. Shoot all bottom edges, and then mark the pieces as f. 1, left-hand side and back also. Plane the sides to width until they slide into the carcase, then withdraw, and pin them together and shoot to length. Now carefully fit the drawer front until it enters the opening about $\frac{1}{8}$ in., as previously mentioned. The back is left slightly longer, and is marked as follows :—Place it on the bench, then withdraw the front and lay it upon the back,

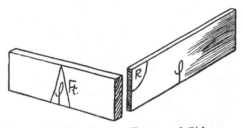

1. Marking Drawer Front and Sides.

with the inside faces together and the bottom edges level. Draw a sharp marking awl along each end, saw off the waste, and plane the sides upon a shooting board, just leaving the mark on the stuff. Gauge the thickness of

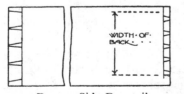

2. Drawer Side Dovetails.

sides on the front and back, then on the lap on the end grain of front, and thickness of back in the sides. Set a marking gauge to $\frac{5}{8}$ in., and gauge line for bottom edge of back in sides. The front is then grooved with a No. 1 plough iron $\frac{3}{16}$ in. deep, and $\frac{5}{8}$ in. from the edge. To cut the dovetails, space out and mark with a dovetail template, put both together in vice, and cut the dovetails at both ends, see f. 2, then proceed as explained in dovetailing.

An Alternate Method is to fit the front only into the carcase or framing entering about $\frac{1}{8}$ in., and marking the back as before. Both sides are pinned together, and the bottom edges shot true, and then squared to length. To complete the drawer, proceed as described in preceding method.   When glueing together, in each case carefully glue the dovetails on one side, and lay flat on bench, glue sockets in drawer front and back, and place in position, pressing down with the hands, then glue the other side, place dovetails in the sockets, and tap each

1. Drawer Slips.

joint with a hammer until quite close. **To test for square-ness,** use a 12-in. try square, placed against the front, and press the corners of the drawer until the sides coincide with the steel blade.   Or the diagonals of drawer may be measured, and the drawer adjusted until both lengths from corner to corner are quite equal in length.   The drawer is now ready for **slipping,** viz., pieces of wood, shaped to the sections shown in f. 1, A, which are glued into the sides to receive the bottom.

These pieces increase the running edges of the bottom, and greatly strengthen the drawer where it is mostly worn. **To work the slips,** shoot the edge of a $\frac{5}{16}$-in. piece of wood, and lay on the bench, fixing with holdfast, and allowing the edge to project slightly over the front of bench, plough the groove with a No. 1 iron, $\frac{1}{8}$ in. deep, set $\frac{5}{16}$ in. from edge, and then round with a smoothing plane and glass-paper, gauge entire width of slip and cut off with tenon saw.   The edge of the stuff is then shot again, and the process repeated.   Saw one end of the slip square in a mitre cut, and notch it to fit the back, as in f. 2.   Where a number of drawers are made, they are placed side by side on the bench, and the slips glued in position, securing two at once with small hand-screws or clips.   Drawers exceeding 2 ft. in length should have a centre munting about 2 in. wide dove-

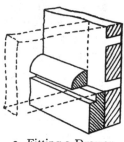

2. Fitting a Drawer Slip.

tailed into the front, rebated and screwed at the back (see f. 3); this should be glued and screwed exactly in centre of drawer, the dovetailed portion being filled in and levelled off to the edge.

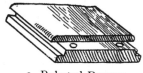

3. Rebated Drawer Munting.

Fitting the Bottom.—Shoot the front edge and square one end, then mark and shoot to length. Work a $\frac{3}{4}$-in. bevel on three sides, testing with a " mullet."   After preparing for slot-screwing, drive bottoms home, and glue two small blocks underneath, which prevents the drawer bottom shrinking out of the groove ; care must be taken not to overturn the slotted screws, for shrinkage may occur, and the bottom is likely to split.   Fig. 1, B, illustrates a " **bead and flush slip,**" suitable for small drawers.   The bottom in this case is rebated into the grooves, shouldered underneath at the front edge, and on the top for the end edges.   A mistake frequently made in this method is to rebate on one side only, causing an unsightly joint on the inside at the front.

A flush bottom to a drawer adds to the flat surface room, and in this respect is a distinct advantage over the method shown in f. 2.

CURVED WORK.

Building up Curved Rims—Preparation of Templates—Cutting the Segments—Fitting same—Band-sawing to Finished Shape—**Curved Drawer Fronts**—Cutting from Solid Stuff—Glueing up—Wide Carcase Ends—"Flushing off" Curved Fronts—**Upright and Landscape Curved Panels**—Bevel Jointed—Curved Planes—Circular Carcases—Glueing up—Planing to Shape—**An Alternate Method** for thin Panels—Ogee Shapes—Drying—Building up the Core—Toothing and Veneering—Use of Steam Box—**Curved Framed Doors**—Dovetailing the Rails—Dowelling same—Glueing up and Testing—Levelling off—**Building up Galleries and Slats**—Preparing the Template—Veneering the Curve—Alternate Method with Core—Rounding the Edge—**Building up Slats,** Cores, and Templates.

So many different methods are employed in the production of curved work that only fundamental principles can be treated in this section. A number of examples illustrating these principles are given, and a thorough understanding of these will assist in working out problems of single and double curvature. The latter kind is so involved with practical geometry that examples are given in the chapter which deals with that subject.

Kidney, oval, or circular table rims are usually built up with segments, or laminated, *i.e.*, in layers. The work must first be set out on a board, showing the thickness of rim, projection of top, and fixing or connection of legs to the frame. If this board is shaped to the top line, a template is thus formed, from the edge of which all lines indicating projections or thicknesses will be parallel. Supposing the rim to be 2½ in. wide, four layers are required to build the shape, the bottom layer is divided into four or more parts, according to the shape and size of rim, and the joints of the second layer of segments fall exactly between those of the previous

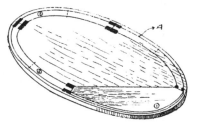

1. Preparing Curved Templates.

layer, thus overlapping each piece, so that each alternate layer has similar segments.

2. Segmental Building up.

To Prepare the Segments, mark out on board the joints of one layer in full lines, the next in dotted pencil lines. Roughly shape a piece of ¼-in. whitewood to outside line, and pin to board (see f. 1 above), mark the joint lines, and measure the distance of rim line from the edge, f. 1, A. Set a tee gauge to this size, and gauge the whitewood template. Another tee gauge is now set to inside line of rim, and gauged as before. This process is continued until all the templates are marked. Then number each to correspond with board (see diagram). Spokeshave and file the templates to true shape, and mark out required number on ¾-in. stuff. In some cases these segments are cut $\frac{1}{8}$ in. outside the lines, and the rim band-sawn after glueing is completed. Band-sawing may be dispensed with by proceeding as follows :—After the segments are marked out and sawn, work to

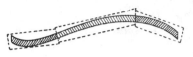

1. Building up Panels.

true shape with circular plane or spokeshaves. Fit the bottom layer on board, and pin it in position, glueing the butt joints only. Next fit and glue each segment in the succeeding layer (see f. 2, p. 83) until completed, levelling off when dry, and repeating the same process for each other layer. Remove the rim from board, withdraw the pins, and plane or spokeshave the outside of rim until it fits the board, then tee gauge to thickness, and remove the superfluous wood.

Curved Drawer Fronts are cut from the solid if wood of sufficient thickness is available. Should a 9-in. front be required, two pieces are glued together, and then band-sawn to shape. Some-

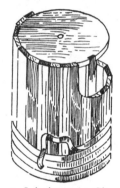

times **very wide shaped ends** are wanted in carcase work. The best plan then is to cut the shapes from best 9-in. stuff, and glue them together, levelling off when dry. The waste pieces are also glued up and used as cauls when veneering. It is advisable when several curved drawers are fitted into a carcase to finish the shape correctly by temporarily stopping the drawers so that they project slightly beyond the rails, and then levelling them down. This is called "flushing off." The stops are then removed and set back, allowing the fronts to form a small square.

Upright and Landscape Curved Panels.—Upright panels are made to any shape by bevel jointing flat pieces of wood, and glueing them together, then

2. Jointing up a Circular Carcase.

they are planed to shape with concave and convex-shaped planes (see diagram, f. 1 above).

Circular Carcases are also built up in this way. A skeleton frame is fitted to the shape shown in f. 2, and each piece or "segment" dry-jointed

3. Bending and Veneering
a Curved Panel.

until the carcase is completed. Then glue all the joints together and bind round tightly with very wet webbing, remove the skeleton frame, and thoroughly heat the whole over a shaving blaze ; this has the effect of softening the glue and drying the webbing, which contracts and forces the glue out of the joints. About twelve hours are allowed for drying, and then the true shape is set out at each end, and planed down to the lines with shaped planes.

An Alternate Method for curved panels where a number of similarly shaped ones are required, consists of bending straight-grained mahogany and veneering both sides at once between shaped cauls. This is the most economical method, but it is practically restricted to stuff not exceeding

$\frac{7}{18}$ in. thick. For quick curves or ogee forms the "core" or "ground" work is made up with thin wood, two or three thicknesses bending easily to any desired shape. As an example illustrating the first method we will take the panel shown in f. 3 opposite. Prepare pine cauls to fit both faces, plane up, tooth, size, and glue the core, pin veneer in position, thoroughly heat the cauls, and put the whole together with paper between and hand-screw down. If possible, leave it in the cauls for two or three days, so that it can thoroughly set, and when the panel is removed it should be screwed to curved bearers or clamps about 1 in. thick, which prevents casting whilst finally drying. In cases where the curve is ogee shape (see f. 1 opposite) or too quick to permit this method, substitute two thicknesses of thin stuff for the core, and proceed as described above. The landscape panel shown in f. 1 alongside would be executed by preparing cauls to fit both sides, and in steaming two pieces of bare $\frac{1}{4}$-in. stuff, the whole being hand-screwed between heated cauls until quite dry; six or eight reheatings and screwing up are necessary, and then the core only is glued up. When dry, level down any small kinks, and tooth both surfaces, and veneer on both sides with the same cauls.

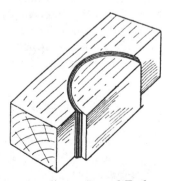

1. Laminating an "Ogee" Shaped Panel.

Description of Steam Box.—This may be improvised by procuring a large flat tin or zinc tray about $1\frac{1}{2}$ in. deep, with a cupboard or box fitting exactly over the tray, and having a door at one end; bearers are fixed inside so that the stuff rests edge downwards. This steam box is placed on a stove or other heating accommodation, causing it to fill with steam, which renders the wood pliable.

2. Plan of Violin Case.

Application of Bending to Curved Ends.—There are many instances where bending as described is used, viz., in semi-circular ends of cases, chests, and caskets. The example illustrated is a violin case with curved end, plan shown in f. 2. Prepare cauls for the wide end, fitting both sides of shape, about 6 in. wide; cut lengths of clean, straight-grained pine $\frac{1}{8}$ in. thick, tooth both sides, and lay in steam box until rendered pliable, then screw between the cauls, f. 3, and allow to remain for two hours; then reheat the cauls occasionally, hand-screwing together as before, thus absorbing and drying out the moisture caused by steaming. When quite dry, well glue the inside surfaces, and hand-screw again between the heated cauls, and allow them to remain screwed up as long as possible. The small end is proceeded with in the same way, and straight lengths are tongued between them to complete the box, to which are then glued a curved top and bottom, and the whole is then levelled off and veneered.

3. Bending a Curved End.

Building up Galleries.—Various curved galleries are used on table tops, and are constructed as follows :—Prepare a template of suitable thickness to the inside of gallery, gauge off strips of knife-cut veneer, and cross veneer one length, which will be the inner or first layer. When dry, clean off. Pin down one end to the edge of template, and carefully stretch the veneer all round the shape, making a "butt joint," and also pinning down. If veneer pins are used, they are allowed to project slightly, so that the veneer can be pressed over them, and pins withdrawn without damaging the veneer ; the second layer is glued about a foot at a time, moistened on opposite side, and laid down with a hammer ; continue with strips of veneer until the thickness is obtained, as section shown in f. 1, A, alongside. Then allow to dry, level off and tooth ; finally cross veneering with figured veneer. Shoot the edge, cross veneer, and slightly round the same when cleaning off.

1. Sections of Table or Tray Rims.

An Alternate and Cheaper Method is to first pin a veneer down, and then glue pieces of cross-grained soft wood down to form a core, which is levelled down and veneered as before (see f. 1, B).

Rounded Edges.—If a rounded edge is wanted, glue thin cross-cut wood to rim, level off flush with both faces, and round with file and glass-paper.

Waved Edges, f. 2, are set out and worked to shape with spokeshave, and then veneered.

Circular and Elliptic Shaped Slats for barred doors are also built up by this method, and practically any shapes other than those mentioned are formed by glueing veneers between cauls, as illustrated in f. 3, p. 85, but 1-in. stuff only is used, which is cramped or hand-screwed together.

2. Rim Edge—Waved.

Curved Doors.—The construction of curved framing, panelling, and doors is made rather difficult owing to the cross grain tending to weaken the joints. To obviate this difficulty, tenoning is almost entirely discarded in shaped frames, except where the curve is very slight and the stuff will allow an almost straight-grained tenon ; lapped dovetails and dowelling is therefore employed, the use of which is governed by the work in hand.

3. Various Panel Mouldings.

Wide Rails in framing are built up like curved rims, or cut from solid stuff. The former method is preferable, and is stronger in rails of much curvature, short grained solid rails reducing the strength. Stuck mouldings are not advisable in work of this description, and rebated framing with a "planted" or "bolection" moulding is most effective. These mouldings (see f. 3), unless flat and small in section and curvature, must be worked from the solid, but where circumstances permit of steaming and bending, the wood should be bent and regulated before the mouldings are worked. Veneering is necessary in most of the framing, owing to the unsightliness of the end grain when polished. This is accomplished by levelling off the work after cramping together dry, when veneering the separate pieces, and glueing the whole together. As this necessitates removing the cramping blocks, and re-glueing them, the frames are generally glued together, levelled off, and veneered (see chapter on "Veneering"). To gauge the rebate to correct depth, fix a piece of steel or plough iron into a "router" projecting the required distance and router away the extra wood. The example shown represents the curved end of a parting screen, 4 ft. 6 in. high. Sectional plan shown in f. 1, *b*, alongside. The three curved rails would carry through in each case, dowelled into the stile and outside munting, marked *c*, the short muntings being dowelled between the rails. Cut a template of the curve, and make up the rails, then prepare a curved template made from the waste stuff, and fix a piece of hard wood, set to the short shoulder line upon it (see f. 2). Mark points on the face, representing

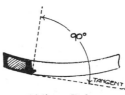

1. Elevation and Sectional Plan of a Parting Screen.

both long and short shoulders, and return them on the edges with this template or bevel, gauge, and cut, then shoot in mitre block with shoulder plane. Mark

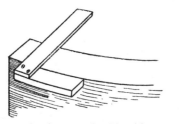

2. Setting out the Shoulder.

position of dowels on all pieces, and bore with dowel bit, gauge and work rebates for mouldings, put together dry, and level off, then take apart, glue together, and veneer, &c.

Rebating after Glueing. — If the double shoulder is of such proportion as to render dowelling difficult, set out with butted shoulders, cramp the frame together, and level off, then take apart and work the rebate, finishing as before.

Curved Doors.—Although the methods described above are applied to curved framing and doors generally, there are certain instances where dovetailing is employed to advantage. This is especially the case in doors with simple stuck mouldings on stiles and rails, as section in f. 3. Set out the shoulder lines as described for "framing," and mark the dovetails, cut these and also the shoulders, then set a dovetail in position upon the planed end grain of a stile, and mark with an awl, then cut with dovetail saw, and chop out the sockets. Extreme care must be taken when fitting, or a winding door will result. To test for squareness, measure diagonally with a thin slip of wood, and look across the stile lines to

3. Oblique Rebate on Curved Door.

judge if the door is free from winding, regulating the joints if necessary. It will be seen from the section that the shoulder is not set out square with the tangent of curve ; this would prevent the entry of panel.

CHAPTER VI.

TABLES AND FRAMED-UP WORK.

Extension Tables—Telescope—Tray Frame, and Dovetail Slide Dining Tables—Circular and Leaf Extension Tables—Elizabethan, Drawing, and French Extension Tables—Gate Leg and Framed Gate Tables—Flap Tables; Revolving Tray, Pouch, and Flap Work Tables—Envelope, Pivoted Top, and Flap Card and Chess Tables—Billiard Tables, with Working Details—Circular and Elliptical Tables—Adjustable Bed Table—Chippendale Pie Crust and Tea Tables—Hall and Pier Tables—Nested Tea Tables—Washstands—Toilet Tables—Kidney Dressing Table—Pedestal, Elliptical, French, William and Mary, and Chippendale Writing Tables—Curio and Occasional Tables—Cylinder Fall Writing Table and Secretaire—Shaving Stands—Writing Bureau on Stand—Welsh Dressers—with details and drawings to scale.

INTRODUCTION.

THE development of the table from the earliest types would be an interesting subject to consider if space would allow, for what is now the paper-hangers' "trestle and board" was once a highly prized and richly decorated form. Probably no article of domestic use has been subject to so many changes in shape and make, and the following chapter contains some fifty odd applications of the name. The term "table part" is also applied to the upper or drawer section of a pedestal sideboard.

EXTENSION TABLES.

Various methods used for extending tables are illustrated and described in this chapter. The most used is undoubtedly the "telescope" method acted by means of keyed sliders working telescope fashion in each other. The principles and workshop practice involved in tables on the slider principle are general, and much of the description of the example illustrated on Plate XV. applies also to the dovetail slide and tray frame. Reference to the plan shows the single sliders or "lopers" screwed to undersides of tops and connected to the framing; iron pins are fixed to those underneath (see sectional detail), and they stop against plates screwed to the outside sliders. Dining table clips fixed in the grooved edges of sliders form an effective stop for the double sliders, and also bind the pieces together (see also sectional view). When making the sliding part of table, well-seasoned, straight-grained wood should be selected, preferably teak or mahogany, the former wood combining good standing powers with a naturally oily surface.

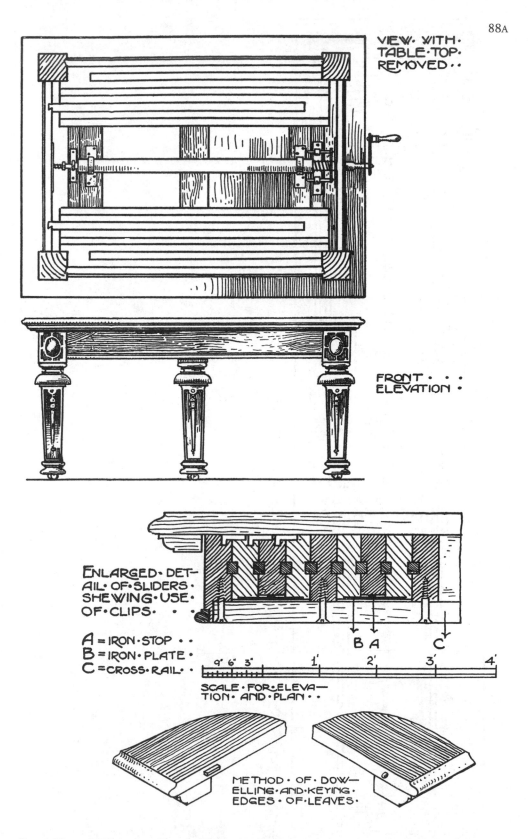

VIEW·WITH·
TABLE·TOP·
REMOVED··

FRONT···
ELEVATION·

ENLARGED·DET-
AIL·OF·SLIDERS·
SHEWING·USE·
OF·CLIPS··

A = IRON·STOP··
B = IRON·PLATE·
C = CROSS·RAIL·

B A   C

9' 6' 3'   1'   2'   3'   4'

SCALE·FOR·ELEVA—
TION·AND·PLAN··

METHOD·OF·DOW—
ELLING·AND·KEYING·
EDGES·OF·LEAVES·

PLATE XVA. A TELESCOPE DINING TABLE (CONTINUED OVERLEAF).

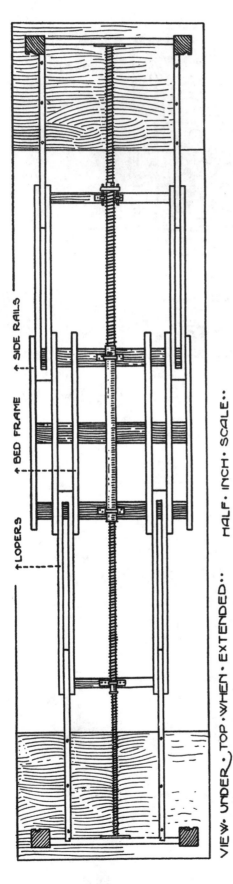

↑ SIDE RAILS

↑ BED FRAME

↑ LOPERS

VIEW · UNDER · TOP · WHEN · EXTENDED · ·   HALF · INCH · SCALE · ·

PLATE XVB. A TELESCOPE DINING
TABLE (CONTINUATION).

A template must also be prepared to length of sliders, and the top edge curved about ⅜ in. from end to end. All the sliders are then planed to correspond with the template, and when the table is complete, the curvature of bed will counteract the sagging of centre part. All grooves for clips, and also the tongues, must be worked from the curved edge. Plans show the method of fitting the outside rails into the knee part of legs, so that when the frame is closed up, there will not be open shoulders. Centre legs, mortised into the centre rail of bed, though not absolutely necessary in tables under 10 ft. in length, are certainly advisable. Patent extending dining table screws, manufactured by Messrs Fitter, of Birmingham, are used for closing or opening the table. Diagrams opposite illustrate the use of a double-action screw, which operates from one end only. It is, however, generally advantageous to use a screw operating from both ends, or, on large tables, two separate screws can be fixed. The type illustrated always keeps the centre leg in the middle of the table, when opened to any position. The plan shows the fixing of single sliders to framing, and sliders screwed to tops, the end rails being pocket screwed to top. The extra leaves are usually from 15 to 18 in. wide, and the sketches show methods of dowelling and keying; the former method being the best, is effected as follows :—Upon completion of bed framing, all the leaves and both tops should be cramped up, one upon the other, when the positions of the dowels (about 16 in. apart) are then squared across all the edges, and the stuff separated, centre lines for boring are gauged from the top faces and the dowels glued into one edge of each leaf; the dowels are best made of ebony or rosewood, and are rounded off with a dowel rounder (see Chapter V.). When finishing the tops, all the leaves are inserted and the screw tightened up, previous to carefully levelling down with plane, scraper, and glass-paper. The fixed rails in bed plane are dovetailed up the side rails and screwed, the smaller rails are necessary to carry the double-action screw. Gauge pieces at ends of double sliders are to keep them the proper distance apart, and are glued between and screwed through; the length of these pieces is from 1½ to 4 in. The overlap of sliders illustrated in plan is about 11 in., and this amount can be increased up to 18 in. with advantage.

A BILLIARD TABLE (see Plate XVI.).

The increasing production of billiard tables, and the reconstruction of earlier types to suit modern decorative requirements, has rendered this an important branch of work, chiefly done by cabinetmakers. There has, however, been a remarkable paucity of information regarding this branch, due probably to the very limited number of firms in the business. Although the standard sizes vary slightly with various firms, the construction of the framework and fixing of wooden cush are alike, the efficiency of the table, however, depending largely upon the rubber cush. These specialties are protected by patents, and used exclusively by their respective patentees. The bed frame illustrated has 6-in. square knees, and the rails are stub-tenoned into them at the corners, and bolted (see cross section and also front sectional view facing this page). The bolt heads are sunk, and a turned button or stud is glued into the holes. The bolts in end

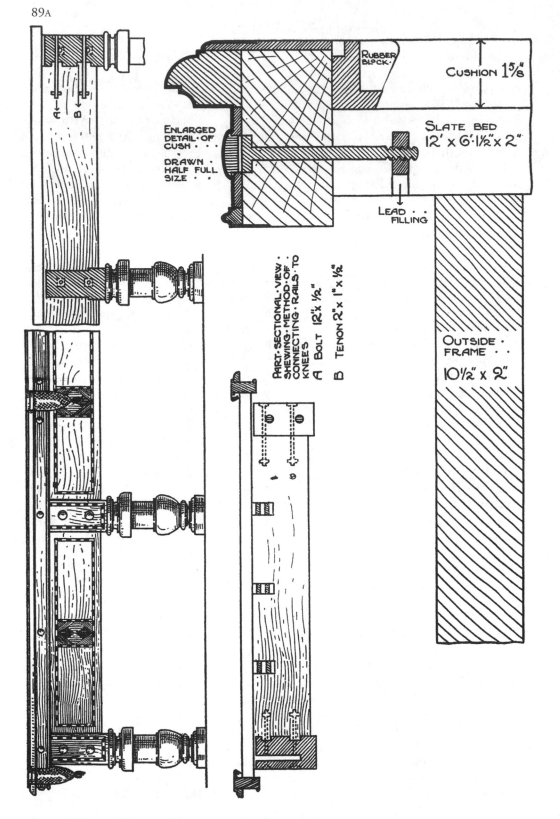

ENLARGED
DETAIL·OF·
CUSH·.·.·
·
DRAWN·
HALF·FULL·
SIZE·.·.

RUBBER
BLOCK·

CUSHION 1⅝"

SLATE·BED
12'·x·6'·1½"·x·2"

LEAD
FILLING

PART·SECTIONAL·VIEW·
SHEWING·METHOD·OF·
CONNECTING·RAILS·TO
KNEES

A BOLT 12"x ½"

B TENON 2" x 1" x ½"

OUTSIDE·
FRAME·.·.
10½"·x·2"

A
B

PLATE XVIA.   A BILLIARD TABLE, WITH DETAILS OF CONSTRUCTION.

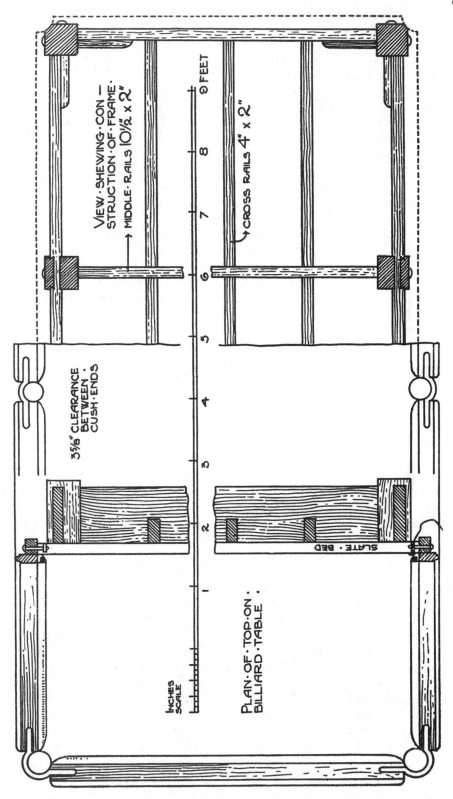

VIEW · SHEWING · CON—
STRUCTION · OF · FRAME ·
MIDDLE · RAILS 10½" × 2"

CROSS RAILS 4" × 2"

3⅝" CLEARANCE ·
BETWEEN ·
CUSH · ENDS

9 FEET

INCHES
SCALE

SLATE · BED ·

PLAN · OF · TOP · ON ·
BILLIARD · TABLE ·

PLATE XVIB. A BILLIARD TABLE, WITH DETAILS OF CONSTRUCTION.

rails are fixed lower than the front, in order to clear the front bolts when fixing up (see sectional elevation). The cross rails are of 4 by 2 in. stuff, and are also double stub-tenoned and bolted. Hard woods are used for this framing, well seasoned and bone dry. Legs are fixed to the framework by dowelling, or with a strong screwed pin into the knee parts, similar to a piano leg. The width of front rails is determined by the design, but should not be less than 9 in. The slate bed, indicated by dotted line in plan, is 12 by 6½ by 2 in. Cut away for the pockets as shown. Fillets are fixed underneath the slate at the edge to which is affixed the tablecloth. The wooden cush is built up and fixed to slate as shown in enlarged detail, and can be made wider to suit any special design ; the projection of same above slate must, however, always be 1⅝ in. Ends of cush are bevelled at the pockets, carrying the same line as rubber. Brass pocket holders are used, and screwed down in cheap tables, but invisible fixings are general in good work ; effected by bolts attached to underside of holder lug. These bolts are bored through the cush, and secured with nuts underneath. The pocket holders are also made to tenon into the cush ends, this presenting a neater appearance. 3⅝ in. clearance must be ensured through the entrance to pocket on the completed table, but the true shape of rubber cush at the pocket cannot be accurately shown in a scale drawing. It is rather flatter in form than the detail illustrated. This work forms a separate and distinct business in billiard table making. The brackets shown at ends of rails are frequently used so that the stub tenons can be made in the centre of knee parts.

A TRAY FRAME TABLE (see page opposite).

These tables are much simpler in construction than the telescope arrangement, and can be made to extend to almost any length, according to the number of trays introduced into the framing. The simplest form, and the one most commonly made, consists of one tray working inside the outer rails with dovetail key tongues. The example illustrated has two trays, and its construction will be understood from the isometric sketches. A centre leg is also introduced (as with the telescope extension) which supports the centre part when open. A minimum overlap of the trays is illustrated, and the rigidity of the table is materially increased when this amount is added to, thus permitting the use of longer tongues. To ensure an easy adjustment of the tongues the rails connecting sliders are dovetailed up and screwed without glueing them. The sectional view through table shows the inside tray made narrower, this is to permit of dovetailing the crossed rails to the middle sliders. The method of lining up dining table tops and leaves is also illustrated, ⅞-in. stuff is used for the top, and the under moulding or lining is glued to it ; these pieces are cut about 3 in. wide, with the grain in same direction as the leaves and tops. The direction of grain in lining up pieces must not be across the tops, or, where shrinkage occurs, splits will inevitably result. The method of dowelling or keying up the leaves is illustrated and described in connection with the telescope dining table facing p. 89.

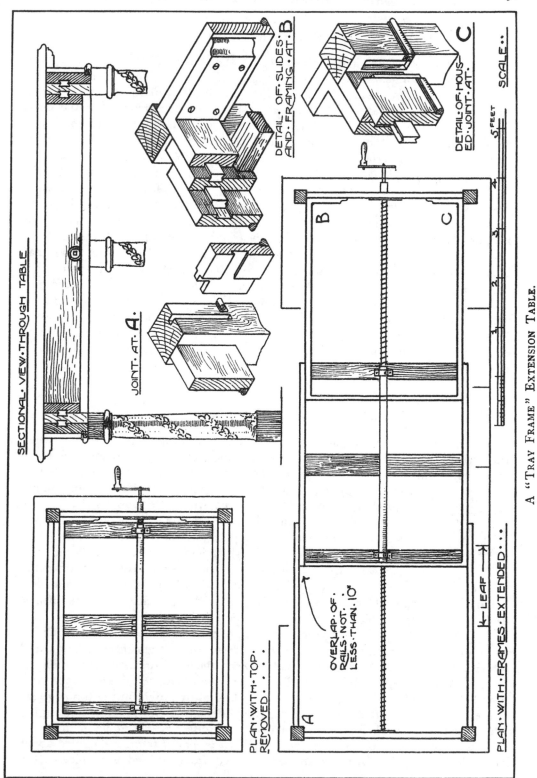

SECTIONAL·VIEW·THROUGH TABLE

DETAIL·OF·SLIDES· AND·FRAMING·AT·B

DETAIL·OF·HOUS-ED·JOINT·AT·

C

JOINT·AT· A.

B

C

5 FEET SCALE··

4

3

2

1

PLAN·WITH·TOP· REMOVED··

A

OVERLAP·OF· RAILS·NOT· LESS·THAN·10"

LEAF

PLAN·WITH·FRAMES·EXTENDED··

A "Tray Frame" Extension Table.

A DOVETAIL SLIDE TABLE (see page opposite).

The method of extension illustrated in the drawings of this type is both strong and economical. Plans show methods of arranging the sliders, the inner and outer pairs mortised and tenoned to the legs. Enlarged sectional view shows the width of sliders. The inside is again made narrower for the cross rails to dovetail into the middle pair. The general principle of extension is very similar to the tray frame, and by the addition of extra pairs of sliders and a centre cross rail to receive a leg, the table can be made to extend to a much greater length. It is a general practice with dining tables to fix castors on the legs ; these are of various patterns, ranging from an ordinary plate castor screwed underneath the leg to special castors with patent bearings, the use of the latter being desirable upon very heavy tables. Small wheels or friction rollers prevent loose or worn bearings which affect the stability of the work. Plan shows position of screw, but it should be understood that before setting out extension tables of any kind, the screw, or full particulars regarding it, must be obtained. These are made in a variety of sizes and actions to suit the requirements of dining table makers. Square moulded or "thurmed" legs are largely used in these tables, and the working processes involved in them are described elsewhere. Turned and carved legs are features of Elizabethan, Jacobean, and eighteenth century designs applied to modern dining table work.

LEAF EXTENSION TABLES (see p. 94).

The drawings on p. 94 illustrate tables with drop leaves, which, when raised, are supported by sliders working under the top, providing a fairly spacious surface if required for dining purposes. The one illustrated is circular in plan, but the shape may be varied to an infinite number of forms. Points requiring attention in this job are the under-railing and slides. View under top shows a bracket screwed underneath the top, acting as a guide for the sliders (see projected view). These sliders are also cut into the rails, and work against each other. They are made of straight-grained stuff clamped at each end, and levelled off flush with the rails. Section of under-railing is shown in sketch above, and this is halved together with mitred beads, and connected to the legs by mortise and tenon joints.

The other views illustrate the further application of the above construction to an ordinary extension table. This table separates in the centre of frame, and when extended, the leaves are inserted between the fixed tops, and rest upon the slides. A centre leg is advisable and necessary as an extra support when the table is fully extended. All sliders should be made slightly round on the top edge (as is the case with all extending tables on the slider principle) to allow for sagging when the leaves are in position, and heavy weights are placed upon the table. This is accomplished by planing each slide to a prepared template, curved about $\frac{3}{16}$ in. in its length. Grooves are also worked from this edge to receive the

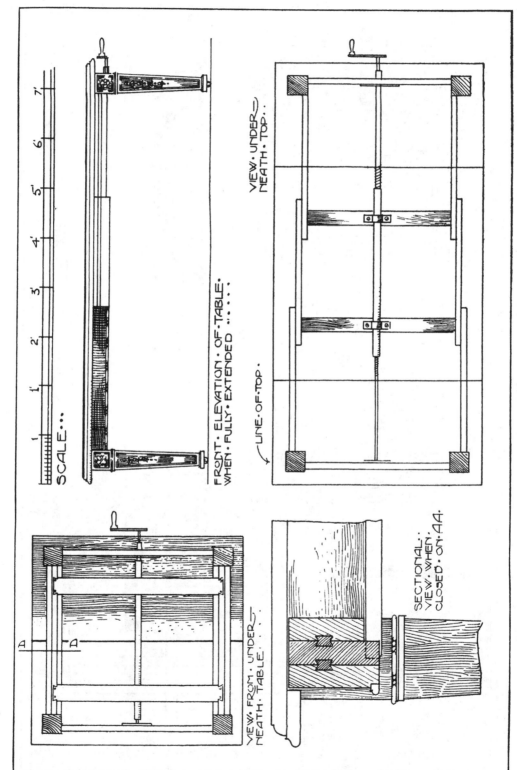

SCALE...

FRONT · ELEVATION · OF · TABLE ·
WHEN · FULLY · EXTENDED · · · · · ·

VIEW · UNDER—
NEATH · TOP · ·

LINE · OF · TOP ·

VIEW · FROM · UNDER—
NEATH · TABLE · · · · ·

SECTIONAL ·
VIEW · WHEN ·
CLOSED · ON · AA ·

A "Dovetail Slide" Extension Table.

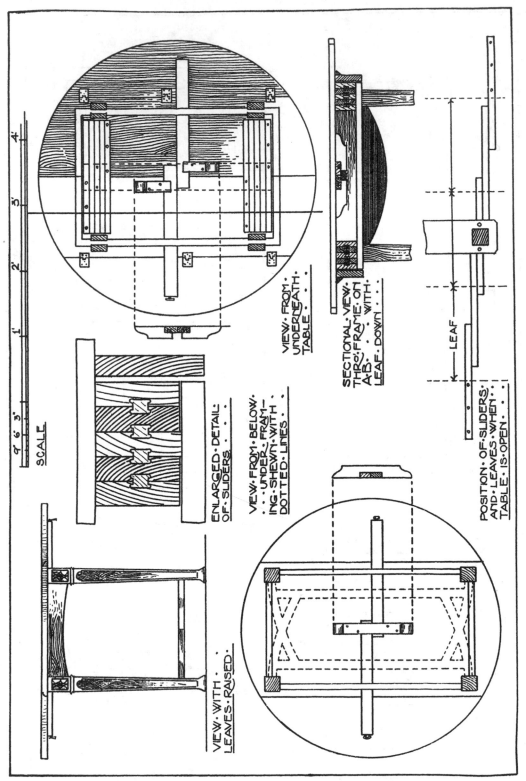

VIEW·FROM·UNDERNEATH·TABLE·

SECTIONAL·VIEW·THRO·FRAME·ON·A·B· ·WITH·LEAF·DOWN·

SCALE

ENLARGED·DETAIL·OF·SLIDERS·

VIEW·FROM·BELOW· ·UNDER·FRAMING·SHEWN·WITH·DOTTED·LINES·

LEAF

POSITION·OF·SLIDERS·AND·LEAVES·WHEN·TABLE·IS·OPEN·

VIEW·WITH·LEAVES·RAISED·

Leaf Extension Tables.

key, see sectional detail. If these sliders are well fitted, the fully extended table is curved slightly from end to end, which is sufficient in some cases to raise the centre leg a short distance from the floor. Owing to the separation of the tops at the centre of table, the supports for the top are fixed to each front, and each piece is grooved to take a short tenon or tongue mortised into the brackets, thus keeping them in position when acting with the table open. This one is not opened with dining table screws, owing to the leaves preventing their use. The sliders are stopped with the tongues.

A WELSH DRESSER (see p. 96).

This sheet of drawings represents a typical form of Welsh dresser, embodying several characteristics of this style, such as the turning, shaping, and the panelled door and drawer fronts. The stand or bottom part is made in one piece, by tenoning the bottom between the legs, trenched or housed into the ends, and rebated and screwed into the centre partition. Fig. 1 illustrates the construction under the top. This stand contains four drawers with the fronts rebated and panelled out with moulding, as shown. The cupboard doors are similarly treated. To construct the top part, housed dovetailing is used to connect the shelves with ends and partitions, whilst the carcase top is

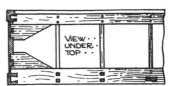

1. View showing Bracketed Carcase Rails.

lapped dovetailed into the ends. Partitions are pinned into the carcase top and wedged. The three sets of panels in some cases are formed on one long drawer front. A modern treatment for a similar dresser is shown on p. 97.

A GATE LEGGED TABLE (see p. 98).

The drawings on p. 98 show two examples of gate legged tables. They are made with numerous variations, which, however, are based on these types. The first example is an adaptation of an old Jacobean table made in oak, con-

2.

taining a drawer (see plan), which also shows the movement of the gates, which are formed by tenoning a top and bottom rail between the two inside legs (see elevation). The right hand leg fits between the table rail and the lower stretcher, with a $\frac{1}{4}$-in. iron pin bored through rails into this leg. The left inside leg is halved into the frame, and also the stretcher, as shown. A smaller kind, used for tea tables, made from 2 ft. 1 in. to 2 ft. 4 in. high, has a ridge or moulded edge round the top, called a "pie crust top" (see f. 2). In either case the leaves are connected to the fixed top with rule joints. When screwed together the complete top is temporarily clamped on the underside, which keeps it firm when moulding, shaping, or turning.

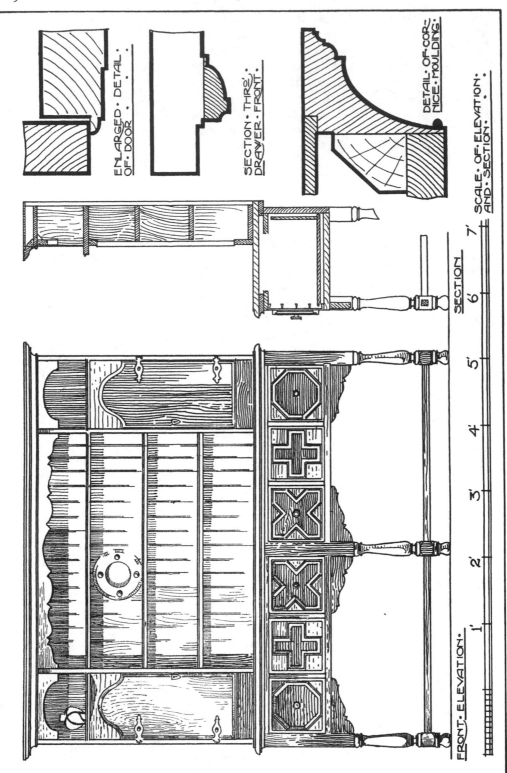

ENLARGED · DETAIL · OF · DOOR ·

SECTION · THRO' · DRAWER · FRONT ·

DETAIL · OF · COR-NICE · MOULDING ·

SECTION

SCALE · OF · ELEVATION · AND · SECTION · . · .

FRONT · ELEVATION ·

1' 2' 3' 4' 5' 6' 7'

A WELSH DRESSER, WITH JACOBEAN TABLE PART.

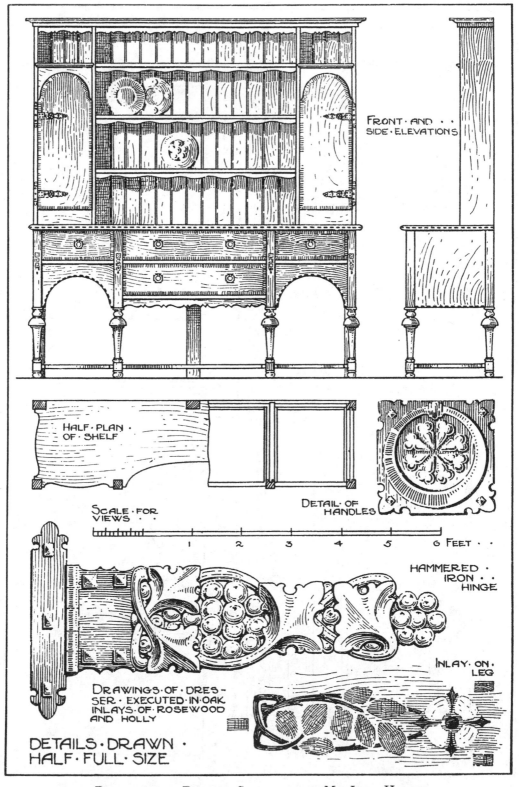

FRONT · AND · ·
SIDE · ELEVATIONS

HALF · PLAN ·
OF · SHELF

DETAIL · OF ·
HANDLES

SCALE · FOR
VIEWS · ·

1   2   3   4   5   6 FEET · ·

HAMMERED · ·
IRON · ·
HINGE

INLAY · ON ·
LEG

DRAWINGS · OF · DRES-
SER · EXECUTED · IN · OAK
INLAYS · OF · ROSEWOOD
AND · HOLLY

DETAILS · DRAWN ·
HALF · FULL · SIZE

DESIGN FOR A DRESSER SIDEBOARD BY MR JOHN HOOPER

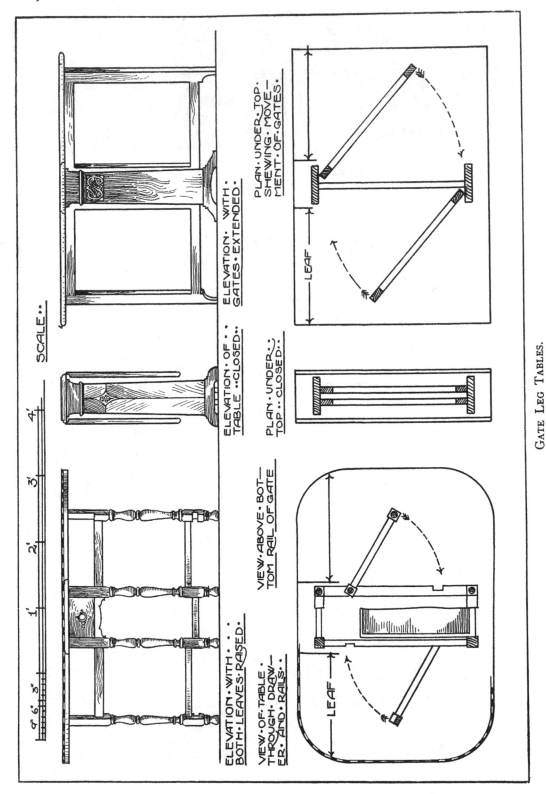

SCALE

9" 6" 3"   1'   2'   3'   4'

ELEVATION · WITH ·
BOTH · LEAVES · RAISED ·

VIEW · OF · TABLE ·
THROUGH · DRAW—
ER · AND · RAILS ·

ELEVATION · OF ·
TABLE · CLOSED ·

ELEVATION · WITH ·
GATES · EXTENDED ·

VIEW · ABOVE · BOT—
TOM · RAIL · OF · GATE

PLAN · UNDER ·
TOP · CLOSED ·

PLAN · UNDER · TOP ·
SHEWING · MOVE—
MENT · OF · GATES ·

LEAF

LEAF

GATE LEG TABLES.

A FRAME GATE TABLE (opposite).

This table, illustrated opposite, is much simpler in construction than the other, though not so decorative. The plans show two frames acting as gates, hinged to each end, and stopped when open by two blocks glued on the underside of leaves. Alternate treatment of ends, veneered and inlaid, are shown in the elevation, and with strapwork carving recessed about ⅛ in. from the face side. The centre frame is dowelled between the ends, whilst the frieze moulding is housed into the outside surfaces and returned on the edges. Owing to the end grain not affording much strength for pocket screwing, the centre top should be well dowelled into the framing.

A DRAW TABLE (see p. 100).

This method of increasing the top surface of a table by means of sliders is probably the earliest known, the first examples belonging to the Elizabethan period. The framing is first put together, with under-railing as shown, a wide centre rail is then screwed to the framing, and tops are prepared as shown in the elevation; the stuff is selected from well-seasoned boards, and to ensure permanent flatness, mitre clamps are mortised and tenoned to each end; in the case of an especially large centre top, it is advisable to make a four-panelled flush framed top. When setting out this table, make the combined thickness of top

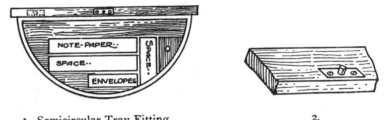

1. Semicircular Tray Fitting.   2.

and bearer when closed equal to the width of bearer under centre rail. If the rail is now cut away to receive the bearer, the centre top may be lifted slightly and the leaves pushed home. The method of connecting bearer to tops, and arrangement of sliders, is shown in plan. One pair of sliders has a rail dovetailed into their ends, thus keeping them quite parallel, and guides are fixed to rails for the outer pair. As previously mentioned, the centre top has to be slightly raised when closing the table. This is effected by tenoning wooden forks or prongs into the top, passing through the centre rail; these act as keys, ensuring the top remaining in position. Then card table centres are screwed to the top, and are loosely bolted underneath the rail. Examples of an Elizabethan and also a Dutch "Draw" table are shown on p. 101. They were measured and drawn from the actual work.

A REVOLVING TRAY WORK TABLE (p. 102).

This table, made of Italian walnut inlaid with snakewood, can be also used as a side and occasional table; semicircular trays are attached to panelled

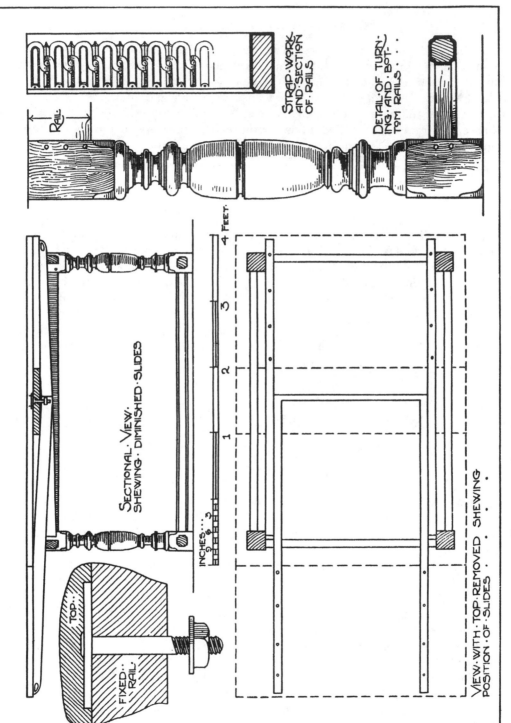

STRAP·WORK·AND·SECTION·OF·RAILS.

DETAIL·OF·TURN·ING·AND·BOTTOM·RAILS...

RAIL.

SECTIONAL·VIEW. SHEWING·DIMINISHED·SLIDES

TOP...

FIXED... RAIL.

4 FEET.

INCHES...

VIEW·WITH·TOP·REMOVED·SHEWING POSITION·OF·SLIDES.·.

"DIMINISHED SLIDE" "DRAW" TABLE OF ELIZABETHAN TYPE.

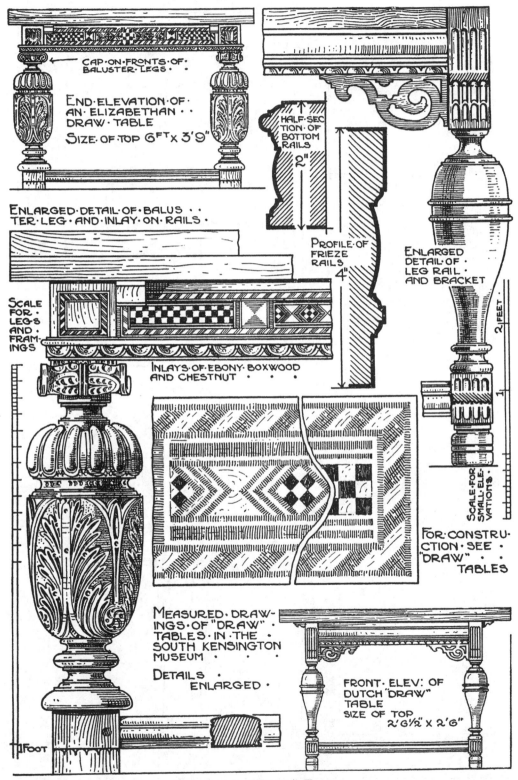

CAP·ON·FRONTS·OF·
BALUSTER·LEGS·

END·ELEVATION·OF·
AN·ELIZABETHAN··
DRAW·TABLE
SIZE·OF·TOP·6ᶠᵀ x 3'9"

ENLARGED·DETAIL·OF·BALUS··
TER·LEG·AND·INLAY·ON·RAILS·

HALF·SEC
TION·OF·
BOTTOM
RAILS
2"

PROFILE·OF·
FRIEZE
RAILS 4"

ENLARGED
DETAIL·OF·
LEG·RAIL·
AND BRACKET

SCALE
FOR·
LEGS·
AND
FRAM-
INGS

INLAYS·OF·EBONY·BOXWOOD
AND CHESTNUT·

2·FEET

1

SCALE·FOR·SMALL·ELE-
VATIONS·

FOR·CONSTRU-
CTION·SEE·
"DRAW"
TABLES

MEASURED·DRAW-
INGS·OF·"DRAW"·
TABLES·IN·THE·
SOUTH·KENSINGTON
MUSEUM·

DETAILS·
ENLARGED·

FRONT·ELEV: OF·
DUTCH "DRAW"
TABLE
SIZE OF TOP
2'6½" X 2'6"

FOOT

DETAILS OF "DRAW" TABLES.

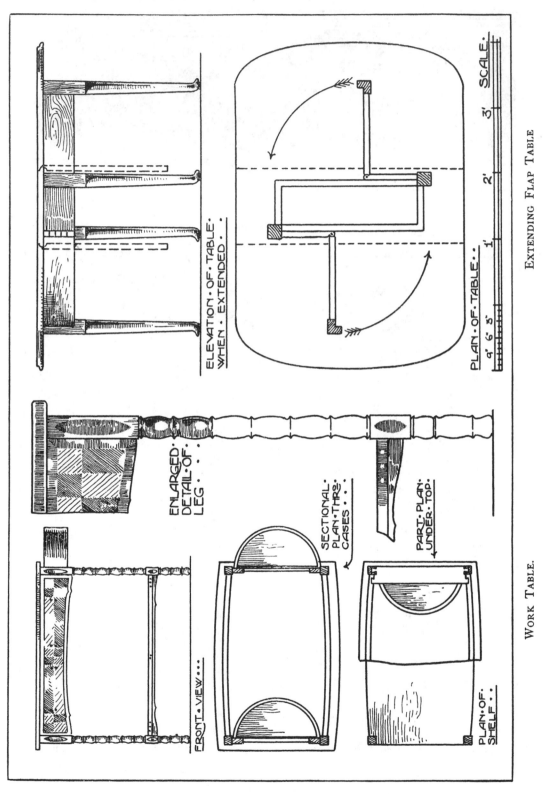

ELEVATION·OF·TABLE·
WHEN·EXTENDED·

PLAN·OF·TABLE··

SCALE·

9' 6" 3"   1'   2'   3'

Extending Flap Table

ENLARGED·
DETAIL·OF·
LEG···

SECTIONAL·
PLAN·THRO·
CASES···

PART·PLAN·
UNDER·TOP·

FRONT·VIEW···

PLAN·OF·
SHELF··

Work Table.

fronts, which revolve upon pivots let into the rails. Although the space in the trays is rather limited, it is of sufficient size for the storage of fancy work requisites. An alternate treatment of trays, fitted for stationery, &c., is shown in f. 1, p. 99. The turned legs are adaptations of "ring and ball" turning so largely used during the latter part of the seventeenth century. Both the veneered and constructive parts are straightforward, and do not require a lengthy explanation. It will be seen from the plan that the trays are attached to the framed fronts, and the pivoting is accomplished as illustrated in sketches. The pivots are fixed to the inside surfaces of rails (see f. 2, p. 99), with hole plates sunk into frames. They are placed in position when glueing up, and the top secures them, the semicircular boxes being screwed in afterwards. The diagram shows the frame projecting slightly beyond the ends of box, facilitating clearance ; a bullet catch fixed under bottom rail (position indicated in diagram) proves an effective stop.

An Extending Flap Table (Height 2 ft. 4 in. to 2 ft. 6 in.) (opposite).

This is an extending table, worked upon the gate leg principle. The movement consists of a boxed frame, two opposite corners of which are through dovetailed together, with the other corners tenoned into the legs. Two legs on fly rails, working upon knuckle joints (see plan), open to angles of 90 degs., and when closed, shut over the dovetailed angles. Elevation shows the depth of box, and also length of knee part on leg, which, when housed (see sketch), leaves a supporting ledge. Both fly rails are stopped under the leaves by boring dowels into the flaps, and allowing them to project about $\frac{1}{4}$ in. The rigidity of the table depends entirely upon accurately fitted knuckle joints. When working the top, both rule joints should be worked and hinged together, clamps are then temporarily screwed on the underside to keep the tops straight whilst shaping, moulding, and cleaning up. This type of table is also made circular, elliptic, and oblong in plan.

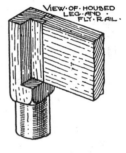
VIEW·OF·HOUSED LEG·AND·FLY·RAIL·

Work Tables (p. 104).

The tables illustrated on p. 104 are the most typical forms in this kind of furniture, and judged from a utilitarian standpoint, the box or well pattern is distinctly the best. A drawer is provided at the bottom, and, by slightly alter-ing the curved opening under folding tops, a sliding tray for small articles can be introduced. This kind also lends itself more readily to decorative treatment, having the additional advantage of being made entirely of wood, and thus not de-manding periodical renewing of silk linings. The example shown was executed at the Shoreditch Technical Institute, and was made of rosewood, with inlays of pear and purple wood. The various views show constructive details, the main features of which are the sides, formed by tenoning the rails into legs, grooving all pieces to receive the panels. The bottom also is grooved or "housed" into the

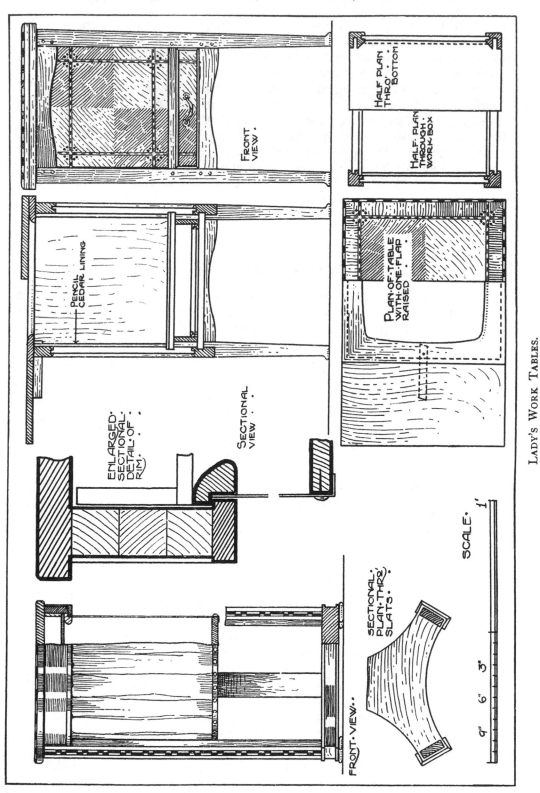

FRONT VIEW.

HALF PLAN THRO' BOTTOM.

HALF PLAN THROUGH WORK-BOX.

PENCIL CEDAR LINING

PLAN OF TABLE WITH ONE FLAP RAISED.

ENLARGED SECTIONAL DETAIL OF RIM.

SECTIONAL VIEW.

FRONT VIEW.

SECTIONAL PLAN THRO SLATS.

SCALE.

9"   6"   3"   1'

LADY'S WORK TABLES.

ends tenoned at front and back. This bottom is faced up with pencil cedar, and the interior is lined with the same material, the legs being cut away to complete the corners. Drawers in these tables can be made to withdraw from either side, and when this is desired, the bottom should be framed up with a $\frac{1}{4}$-in. panel and slotted to receive a piece screwed to drawer bottoms, utilised as a stop for the drawer. It will be observed that the top consists of two hinged flaps supported by pivoted brackets, thus necessitating the use of an underframe or top. The brackets are cut and fitted into the rails, and an iron pin is bored through each bracket into the top rail, and also into the underframe; when this frame is dowelled down to the carcase, it supports the brackets when open, and also receives the hinged flaps for which link joint hinges are used. These give a level surface when the flaps are open (see chapter on "Brasswork" for description of this hinge).

A POUCH WORK TABLE (opposite).

The diagrams show various views and details of the above type, which are chiefly made in decorated Sheraton, Adams, and Empire style. The stand, into which the lower ends of uprights are tenoned, should be cut from a solid piece of stuff if a moulded edge is required, but "laminating" is best for veneered

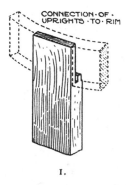

CONNECTION·OF·UPRIGHTS·TO·RIM

1.

PLAN OF TRAY

2.

work. The rim is built up on the "segment" principle (see enlarged detail), with a frieze moulding glued on the bottom edge between the legs, and allowed to project about $\frac{1}{4}$ in. in the inside to receive the pouch; when the rim is built up, it is levelled and veneered, then set out to receive the uprights, stub tenoned and housed into the rim as shown in f. 1. The enlarged detail shows the method of attaching the silk to form the pouch, and this inner rim should be turned up from a "laminated" piece of stuff. To ensure the solid bottom passing through opening of top, make diameter of bottom $\frac{3}{8}$ in. less than opening. A fitted tray is shown in f. 2 and rests upon the rim. This is made by glueing several thicknesses of veneers round a circular template. The edge is afterwards veneered to conceal the joints. Care must be taken when glueing on the bottom not to alter the shape, and it is advisable to glue this on with the template inside the rim.

WASHSTANDS.

The washstand shown on p. 106 is probably the most popular type made; its construction is simple, and when properly put together, should be a very serviceable, strong, and rigid job. The pieces forming the ends run across, and are either tenoned or dowelled into the legs. The back runs right through, either dowelled between the back legs, or framed together,

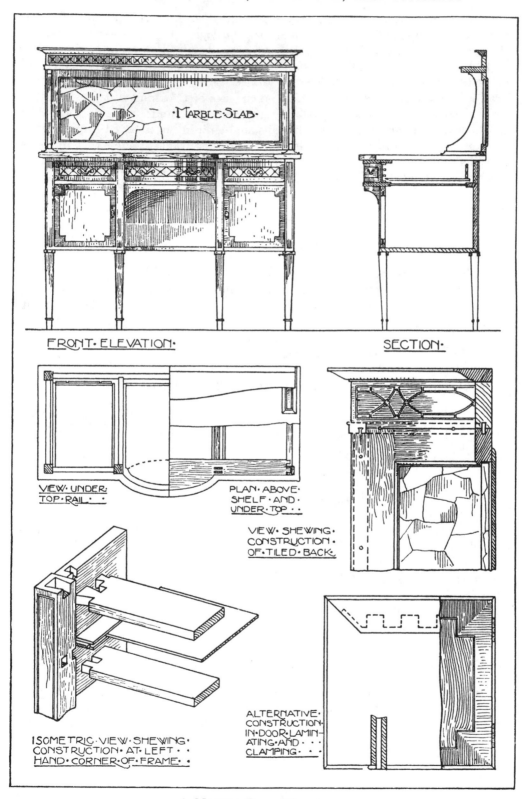

·MARBLE·SLAB·

FRONT·ELEVATION·

SECTION·

VIEW·UNDER·
TOP·RAIL·

PLAN·ABOVE·
SHELF·AND·
UNDER·TOP·

VIEW·SHEWING·
CONSTRUCTION·
OF·TILED·BACK·

ISOMETRIC·VIEW·SHEWING·
CONSTRUCTION·AT·LEFT·
HAND·CORNER·OF·FRAME·

ALTERNATIVE·
CONSTRUCTION·
IN·DOOR·LAMIN-
ATING·AND·
CLAMPING·

A MARBLE BACK WASHSTAND.

when it is screwed into rebates formed on the inside of the legs. The fixing for the top rail is shown in plan, dovetailed and tenoned, whilst the drawer rails are tenoned into the legs. Cupboard bottoms are likewise tenoned into front and back legs, with the intervening portion screwed into rebates worked on the inside bottom edges of ends and divisions, form- ing a flush or level surface under- neath. The centre bottom is stub tenoned into legs, and screwed into rebates on partitions, as with cupboard bottoms. An isometric sketch is shown on p. 106 illustrat- ing the construction of one corner with the drawer runner "housed" or "trenched" into the ends, with a small stub tenon fitting into a groove worked on inside edges of drawer rails. Corresponding grooves are also worked on the runners to receive the dust-boards. The span rail under drawer is cut from the solid, and veneered in order to cover the end grain— (which would appear darker in colour when polished), and also to obtain a

A = LOOSE BUSH
B = CURTAIN·ROD

1. A Thimble Fitting.

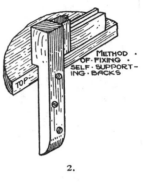

METHOD · OF · FIXING · SELF · SUPPORT-ING · BACKS

2.

richer effect by using figured veneer. Two methods are shown of making the doors: the first is "mortise and tenon mitred" clamping, which costs more than the second method, i.e., laminating. The cocked bead in both cases is glued into rebates worked on the edges, and secured while drying, with clips, hand-screws, or tape bound firmly round the door, and left until quite dry. The drawer fronts should be executed as follows :—First veneer the centre part of each drawer front, and when dry, cut margin with gauge or scratch stock, then remove veneer, and glue. Set out the pattern with pencil lines, and cut with dovetail saw to required depth, glue lines into grooves. Trim level with edge of veneer, mitre margin line round, glue in position, and then lay the cross banding with a hammer. It will be noticed from the sketch that the cocked beads on

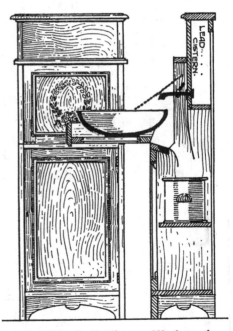

3. Detail of a Folding-up Washstand.

door are equal to the thickness of hinges, which ensures a neat appear- ance. The top part is composed of a moulded frame with the frieze tongued to the top rail, the shelf when fixed concealing the joint. When fixing the shelf notch back at each end as shown, and screw from behind. Side brackets

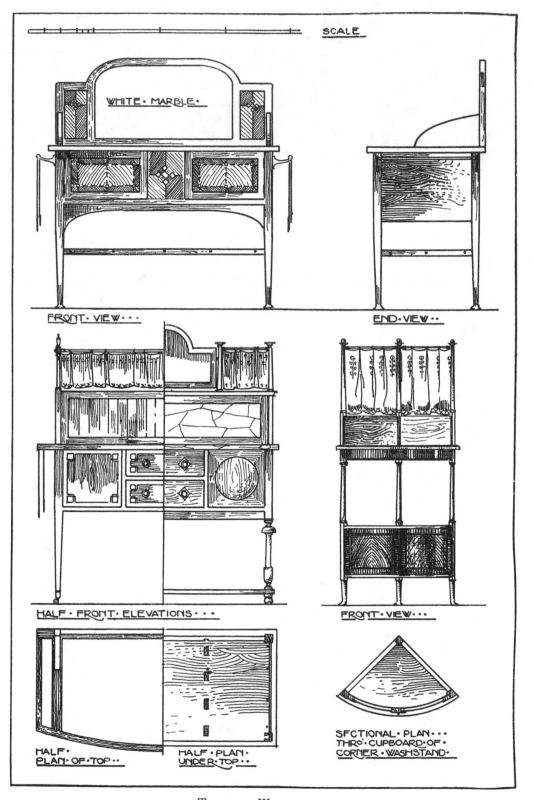

SCALE

WHITE · MARBLE ·

FRONT · VIEW · · ·

END · VIEW · ·

HALF · FRONT · ELEVATIONS · · ·

FRONT · VIEW · · ·

HALF ·
PLAN · OF · TOP · ·

HALF · PLAN ·
UNDER · TOP · ·

SECTIONAL · PLAN · · ·
THRO · CUPBOARD · OF ·
CORNER · WASHSTAND ·

TYPES OF WASHSTANDS.

are secret screwed to shelf, and also screwed from the back. A moulded base is mortised and mitred together, forming a frame, which is dowelled or screwed to the brackets and back. Holes are drilled through the marble top, and the top part may then be firmly screwed into position from under the marble. To ensure the marble top finding its correct place when fitting the job up, blocks are fixed to the underside with plaster and glue, touching the corners of framing, so that it will only drop into one position. Locks are sometimes fitted to the drawers, but bullet or French catches are sufficient for the cupboard doors. For construction of curved drawer refer to chapter on "Curved Work." The frieze is inlaid with box lines in a pattern, executing the curved grooves for lines with flat gouges, or scratching with a file end round the templates prepared to the various curves.

The drawings shown on opposite page illustrate several types, with varied arrangement in the upper part, both in design and application of material. The first example—in Italian walnut inlaid with rose and grey-wood, with a three-panelled back, the centre panel of marble—provides a not unpleasant effect contrasting with the side panels, and differing from the usual treatment of washstand backs, viz., porcelain tiles, secured with brass screws. Marble brackets and tops are also shown in the drawings. The construction of this stand introduces no features needing special mention. Doors are framed up with panels veneered as shown. A half front elevation is given, showing a different arrangement in bottom part with tiled top part, and a curtain attached to a brass rod. The pillars are of turned wood, and the rod is secured by thimble fittings illustrated in f. 1, p. 107. Backs of this character without side bracket supports, should have the stiles extra long at the bottom, forming horns that can be attached to the stand (see diagram, f. 2, p. 107). This constructive principle is further illustrated in the dressing-table with self-supporting top part on p. 111. A half elevation is also shown of a washstand in oak, with curtains above and also a glass frame. The corner stand illustrated is based upon a Sheraton example. A cupboard is made by tenoning the rails between the square part of legs, the bottom being rebated into rails and tenoned into front legs. A shelf is pocket screwed through the side rails, and curved doors fitted at the front. Fig. 3, p. 107, illustrates a fold-up washstand used where space is limited, such as in yacht and ship cabins and offices (see also folding washstands in chapter on "Office Work").

A KIDNEY DRESSING TABLE (p. 111).

Kidney-shaped dressing tables are generally made in the Louis XV. style, of oak and walnut, carved and gilt, or enamelled white. Triple glasses being a special feature of these types, the best arrangement for fixing them is to mortise the uprights through the glass rim, and cut the wide rim away about $\frac{3}{8}$ in. deep to receive the uprights, which are then screwed into the rim The exact proportion of the housing and mortise has to be carefully considered, otherwise the glass rim will be weakened. The plan shows the best way of putting this together with dowelled joints; the shaping is done after the segments are glued together. The rim should be cut roughly to shape, which permits the cutting of notches to receive cramps during glueing. When commencing to make a kidney-shaped table, a template should first be made corresponding with the line of top. The lines inside this shape, such as table rim, glass rim, moulding on top, &c., will all be parallel to the edge of the template, and when their projection has been ascertained, they may be gauged upon the template with a tee gauge. To construct the rim, prepare separate templates about 1⅛ in. wide. Four will be required for the bottom layer, lettered A, B, C, D, in diagram below, with E, F, G, H, for alternate layers. Mark out segments from templates, spokeshave to true shape, then lay in position and fit one layer on to board. This is temporarily secured by glueing at intervals with a piece of stiff paper under the joints. The second layer is then fitted and glued down, each

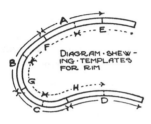

segment overlapping the joints of the previous layer, brickwork fashion, until the required height is obtained. When dry, the whole rim is levelled off, sized and veneered. The legs are then fitted into rim as shown in plan, and the stretchers tenoned into legs, halved at the centre to receive the upholstered footrest. When these are properly fitted together dry, take apart and cut away the rim to receive a drawer. Then dovetail pieces into rim for the drawer to work in (see plan), with a top and bottom rail set back for the drawer front. Prepare the drawer front from a piece of solid stuff, and put the drawer together. To obtain the sunk panel, rout away the centre part with a scratch stock, or the job may be done on a spindle machine, leaving a ½-in. margin, and finished in the corners with a chisel. Another method is to rebate the front, and mitre a slip in the rebate formed, projecting above the surface of the drawer. Compo or carved moulding is then fixed into the angles. The diagram shows the section to which the footboard is made, with a rebate for upholstery. This is screwed through the stretcher from underneath, and is finally fixed when fitting the work up. A ⅞-in. moulded top is shown with a rebated rim holding a plate glass in position. Silk is inserted between the top and the glass, which is all secured by screwing the rim down from underneath the top. For other types of dressing tables see p. 112.

A CYLINDER WRITING TABLE (see p. 113).

This rather intricate piece of cabinetwork includes a fall, circular in section, operating a sliding table part. Details of bar E are given in the chapter on "Mechanical Actions." The fall and slides are attached to an iron trammel or bar that is slotted and works along a centre. When the slider is drawn forward, the fall is opened, and closed when pushed home. A method of locking which secures the fall, slider, and drawer simultaneously, is shown in f. 1, p. 114. A is a spring bolt let into the partition B, when the bottom drawer lock bolt is out; it raises the spring bolt into the slider, and when the drawer lock bolt is down, A springs back into position indicated, thus freeing the slider. The slotted bar is connected to both cylinder and slider, and also to iron plates sunk into the ends. Both ends are prepared to form grooves for the cylinder to run

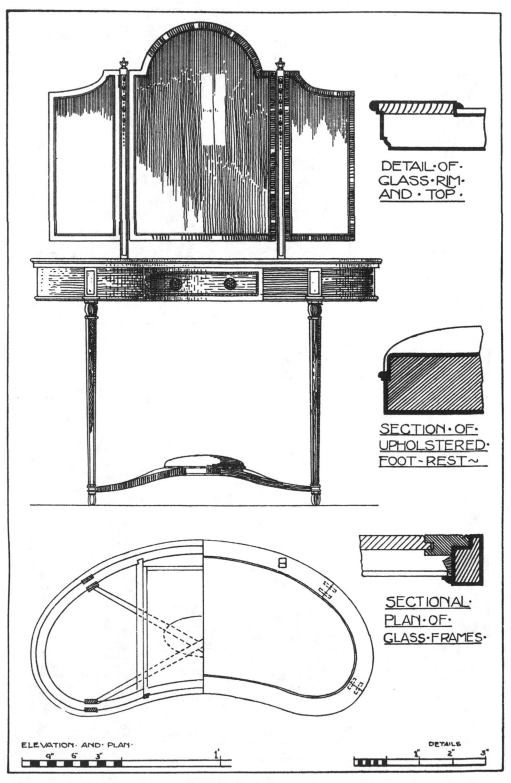

DETAIL·OF·
GLASS·RIM·
AND·TOP·

SECTION·OF·
UPHOLSTERED·
FOOT·REST~

SECTIONAL·
PLAN·OF·
GLASS·FRAMES·

ELEVATION· AND· PLAN·

9"   6"   3"   1'

DETAILS

1"   2"   3"

A KIDNEY DRESSING TABLE.

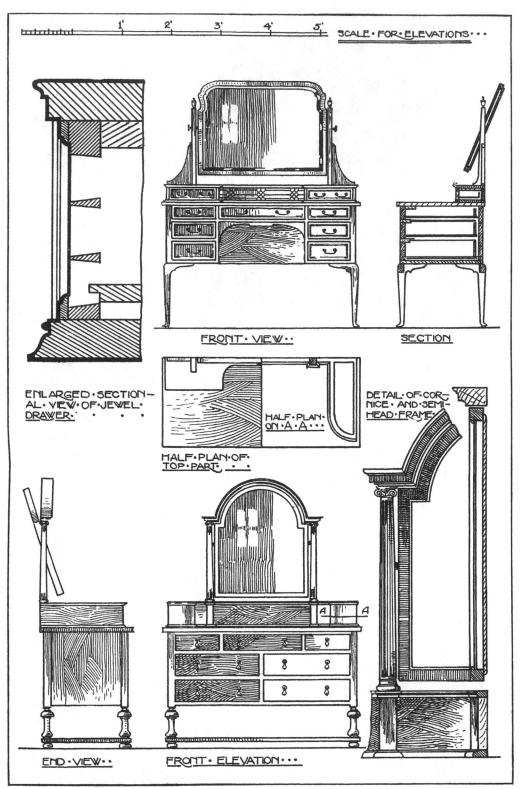

SCALE·FOR·ELEVATIONS···

FRONT·VIEW··   SECTION

ENLARGED·SECTION-
AL·VIEW·OF·JEWEL·
DRAWER·

HALF·PLAN·
ON·A·A···

DETAIL·OF·COR-
NICE·AND·SEMI-
HEAD·FRAME·

HALF·PLAN·OF·
TOP·PART·

END·VIEW··   FRONT·ELEVATION···

TYPES OF DRESSING TABLES.

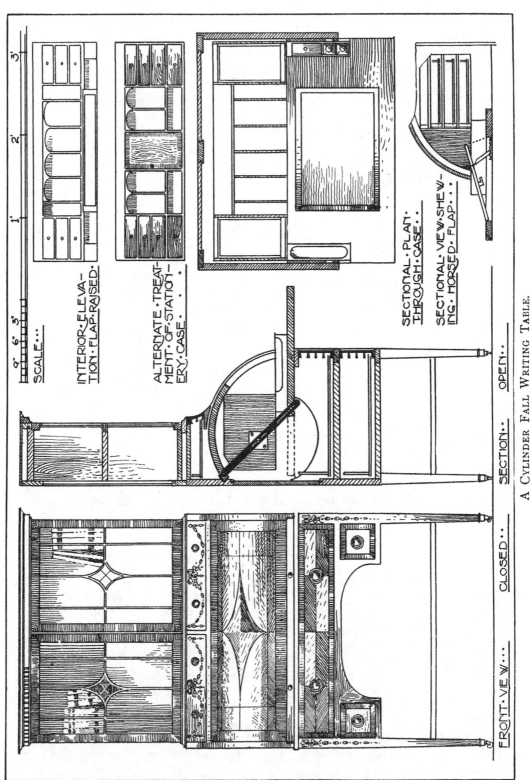

SCALE···

INTERIOR·ELEVA-
TION·FLAP·RAISED·

ALTERNATE·TREAT-
MENT·OF·STATION-
ERY·CASE·

SECTIONAL·PLAN·
THROUGH·CASE··

SECTIONAL·VIEW·SHEW-
ING·MORSED·FLAP·····

FRONT·VIEW···· CLOSED·· SECTION·· OPEN··

A CYLINDER FALL WRITING TABLE.

8

in by attaching curved brass slips near the edge, or by glueing pieces of work at the edge, outside the cylinder. Then a three-sided piece is attached to the insides, thus making a groove for the cylinder to run in. An alternate method is to work grooves with a stock and cutter attached to a centre, also rebating the end for slider (see front view). When constructing the cylinder, it may either be framed together or "coopered," *i.e.*, several strips of straight grained stuff are jointed to give the required curve, but for use with a slotted bar, the former method is preferable, owing to its better standing qualities,

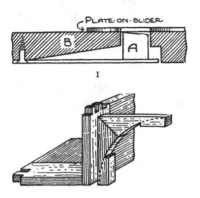

I

2. View showing Method of Fixing the Kneehole Brackets.

no shrinkage or warpage taking place. Interior fittings are illustrated. These are made quite separate from the main carcase, and screwed on to carcase ends, with packing pieces as described in Chapter XII. A stationery case is also illustrated in elevation and plan. It is used when the slider contains a horsed rack writing flap, the construction of which will be understood from the end sectional view shown, the pen and ink boxes running underneath the stationery case. The complete job is formed of three parts—(1) Bottom table or stand ; (2) Cylinder carcase with drawers above ; (3) Bookcase top part. Both ends of the cylinder part are "laminated," with a dove-tail housed horizontal division rail, and lapped dovetailed carcase top. Rebates are worked on the ends at back, so that when the carcase is dowelled to the table frame the whole back may be screwed in as shown in sectional view. The bookcase is secured by screwing through the carcase bottom. To construct the curved kneehole, a full partition is used between the long and short drawers, tenoned into legs and housed into ends, while the angles outside small drawers are clamped and rebated together, tenoned into legs, and grooved into partition. Brackets are mitred and tongued together, glued in the corners, and the front flushed off and veneered (see f. 2).

A WRITING TABLE (see opposite).

The example on p. 115, manufactured by Messrs J. S. Henry, Ltd., shows an unusual treatment of the writing part. A folding top is made, which, when opened, releases a falling front, and discloses a fitted stationery case. The front is supported by quadrant stays, similar to those used on bookcase "secretaires," and is lined for writing purposes. The construction of work such as this, where large legs are introduced, is generally to make the carcase separate from the stand. Pins are turned into the legs, see enlarged detail of leg on p. 116, and bored and glued into the carcase above. The underframing and feet are dealt with in connection with a cabinet of the same period, illustrated on p. 165. This constructive principle, viz., separate carcase, is again rendered necessary when considering the centre cupboard, and it permits the carcase bottom to be carried through in one length, rendering the fixing of pilasters at each side of door a com-

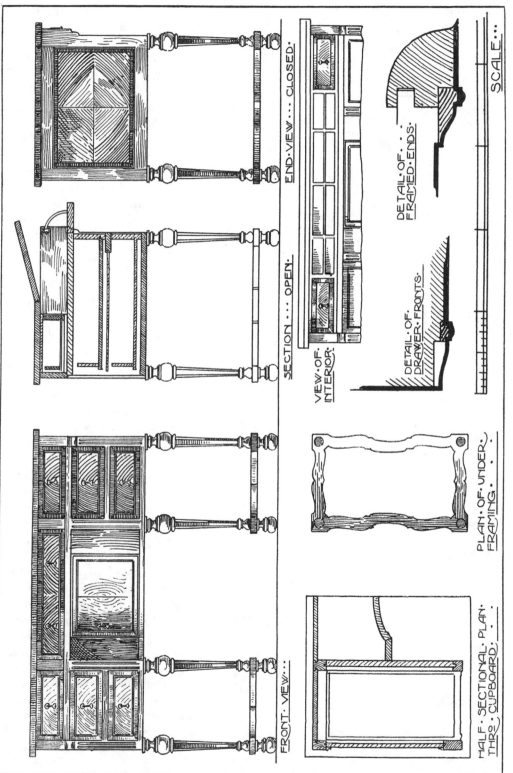

END·VIEW···CLOSED·

SECTION···OPEN·

FRONT·VIEW····

VIEW·OF· INTERIOR·

DETAIL·OF··· FRAMED·ENDS·

DETAIL·OF· DRAWER·FRONTS·

SCALE···

PLAN·OF·UNDER· FRAMING·····

HALF·SECTIONAL·PLAN· THRO·CUPBOARD····

A Writing Table, with "William and Mary" Details.

paratively easy matter.   The sectional view shows the shape of the falling front, acting between the bracketed pilasters ; false fronts are made by veneering the face, and glueing on a thin continuation of the inside pilasters.   The stationery case is of a simple arrangement, fitting into the recess formed by fixed top.

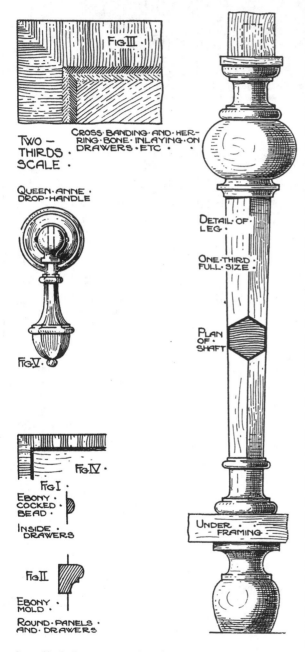

TWO —
THIRDS ·
SCALE ·

CROSS·BANDING·AND·HER-
RING·BONE·INLAYING·ON·
DRAWERS·ETC · ·

FIG III ·

QUEEN·ANNE·
DROP·HANDLE

FIG V ·

DETAIL·OF·
LEG ·

ONE·THIRD·
FULL·SIZE ·

PLAN
OF ·
SHAFT

UNDER · ·
· FRAMING ·

FIG IV ·

FIG I ·
EBONY ·
COCKED ·
BEAD ·

INSIDE ·
DRAWERS

FIG II
EBONY ·
MOLD ·

ROUND·PANELS ·
AND·DRAWERS

Alternate treatments of stationery cases are given with various other cabinets in Chapter VII., and these could be adapted to this piece of work. Fig. I. shows the edges of the stationery case, faced up with ebony beads ; f. II., the ebony moulding round drawer-end frames and cupboard doors ; f. III., the veneered treatment of top, back, and ends ; f. IV., inlay on inside drawers ; and f. V., detail of a characteristic Queen Anne "drop handle or pendant," taken from an old cabinet, and much used in this period of woodwork.

The drawings on p. 117 are of a writing table belonging to the late Louis XV. period, also called " Transitional," that is, the period between the Louis XV. and Louis XVI. styles proper. Details of the Louis XV. style are found in the general proportion and outline, ormolu mounts, "bombé," *i.e.* curved-shaped, ends and outline of plan ; the Louis XVI. feeling being quite distinct in the diaper tambour front and inlaying upon the drawer. When putting this piece of work together, it will be found advantageous to have the legs cut to shape first, by preparing a template to the outline in front elevation, and then setting the shapes out on adjoining sides of square stuff.   Both ends are then prepared, shaped inside as shown in plan, squared up, and dowelled between the legs, setting them back the required distance from the squared knee part to allow for final curvature of legs.   The back,

FRONT · VIEW

SECTIONAL · VIEW

SECTIONAL · VIEW ·
THRO' DRAWERS ·

LEATHER · LINING · ·

SECTIONAL · PLAN ·
THRO · TAMBOUR · ·

SECTIONAL · PLAN ·
AND · VIEW · UNDER ·
TOP · · · ·

SCALE ·

9" 6" 3" 1' 2'

A FRENCH WRITING TABLE, WITH TAMBOUR FRONT.

bottom, and partitions are then tenoned into the legs, setting the pieces back as before, and grooving into ends as shown in sectional view. Legs are then shaped to diagram, f. 1, from which it will be seen that the section of the leg varies in shape as well as size.   No hard and fast rule can be laid down for this kind of shaping, for the correct proportion and feeling necessary are only acquired by long experience in this work, but, in the case of carved or intricate shaped legs, a pine or whitewood leg is generally prepared, which serves as a model, and is moulded until the shaping is de-finitely settled.   When shaped, one end is then inserted between the legs, and cramped to-gether dry, with the top edge marked out to shape, as shown in plan.   The ends curved in plan are recessed into a panel, veneered and finished, with the addition of small mouldings mitred round the angles.   This can be effected by building up the end with three thickness 4-in. stuff glued together and band-sawn, recessing away the panel portion with routers and planes, and then veneering.   This is a more economical method than that usually adopted in French furniture, viz., cutting a groundwork from built-up stuff, veneering the centre part, and then mitreing round facings to form the panel borders.   This is rather a lengthy process, as all the pieces have to be carefully fitted over the curved ends.   When veneering such work, curved in plan, the cuttings from band saw are utilised as "cauls," with a thin piece of cardboard between, or a sand bag is employed, described in chapter on "Veneering."   Mounts for this work are prepared by making a pattern in boxwood or plain satin-wood carved to the required design, then forwarded to the metal worker for reproduction in metal.   "Water gilding" is the finishing process for mounts of this period, and used in conjunction with fine "chasing" on the mounts, has a very rich effect.   Notable examples of such work are to be seen in the Wallace Collection, and also the Jones Collection at the Victoria and Albert Museum, including the work of such famous artists in metal as Caffieri, Oeben, Martin Carlin, and Gouthiere.

On p. 119 a fine example of a Chippendale double-fronted pedestal table is shown.   The heads to the doors are exceptional, and novel in treatment.   The plan shows the arrangement in pedestals, giving similar cupboard and drawer accommodation at each side.   Drawers are introduced at each end, and with but slight structural altera-tion of the frieze frame, drawers could be introduced above the kneehole space.

1. View showing Shaping of Leg.

DETAIL·COR-NER·OF·FRIEZE FRAME

2.

B

CARCASE TOP·

SECTIONAL· VIEW·THRO' FRIEZE· AND·DOOR·

3.

SECTIONAL PLAN CORNER OF·PLINTH·

4.

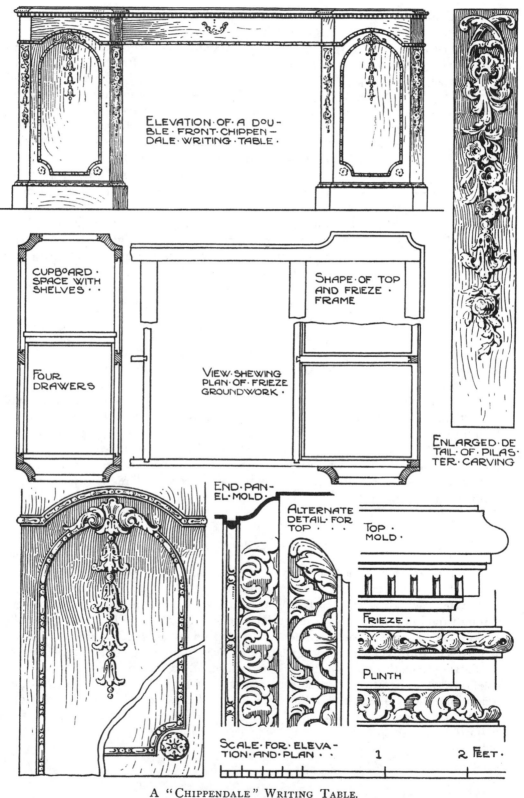

ELEVATION·OF·A·DOU-
BLE·FRONT·CHIPPEN-
DALE·WRITING·TABLE·

ENLARGED·DE-
TAIL·OF·PILAS-
TER·CARVING

CUPBOARD·
SPACE·WITH
SHELVES·· ·

FOUR
DRAWERS

VIEW·SHEWING
PLAN·OF·FRIEZE
GROUNDWORK·

SHAPE·OF·TOP
AND·FRIEZE·
FRAME

END·PAN-
EL·MOLD·

ALTERNATE
DETAIL·FOR
TOP·· ·

TOP·
MOLD·

FRIEZE·

PLINTH

SCALE·FOR·ELEVA-
TION·AND·PLAN·· ·   1   2 FEET·

A "CHIPPENDALE" WRITING TABLE.

The sectional plan shows the method of framing up the ends, essential in such a heavy piece of work.   The construction of the doors is also shown in this view, and it must here be observed that the corresponding shape on the frieze frame is effected by making both together in one length, which, after being veneered, is cut through; the top piece is then glued on to a framed-up frieze ground-work, see plan showing construction of frieze.   A top lining and also a frieze frame are next constructed, and the frieze groundwork is screwed between them. These frames are mortised and tenoned together, with mouldings mitred round the edges, the hollow corners inserted as shown in f. 2, p. 118. Sectional view through frieze and door is illustrated in f. 3, and it will be seen from this

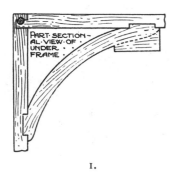

view that the door projects above the pedestal carcase top, and that the frieze is cut away to receive the frieze moulding; a block is glued to the inside of frieze, see B in diagram, which closes or fills in the cavity formed by cutting away the frieze.   Characteristic Chippendale details are also shown on same page; the carvings are cut to outline, and glued to doors and pilasters before carving up. Fig. 4, p. 118, shows the construction of

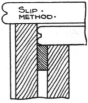

2. Detail of Nested Tables.

I.

one corner on plinth frame, with rails tongued into the corner pieces, which have been worked to section in one long length.   Cross rails of stout material, such as 4-in. by 2-in. pine, are dovetailed between the side rails of plinths, and act as strengthening braces, and also provide the necessary fixing for castors.   The "pateræ" at bottom corners of the doors are turned to section designed to suit the carved detail, and they should be shouldered with a projecting part about ¼ in. thick and bored and glued into the groundwork.   An alternate treatment to the carved corners is to introduce fluting and "reeding," frequently used in Chippendale's examples.

A HALL TABLE (see opposite).

A simple table of the above type in Austrian and brown oak, executed at Shoreditch Technical Institute, is illustrated on p. 121.   The table part construction is dealt with elsewhere in this chapter, as is also the method of pinning feet through the lower framing.   The turning is based upon the "William and Mary" period.   A pediment back is shown, the top edge moulded, a frequent constructive feature of cabinetwork, which is executed by glueing the curved part on to the groundwork, and the side pieces, of full width, on to the top edge. Fig. 1 above illustrates the constructive detail of lower framing, in which stub tenon joints with bevelled shoulders are used.   The shaping of outside portion should be executed as indicated, and thus provide a necessary hold for cramps when glueing up.

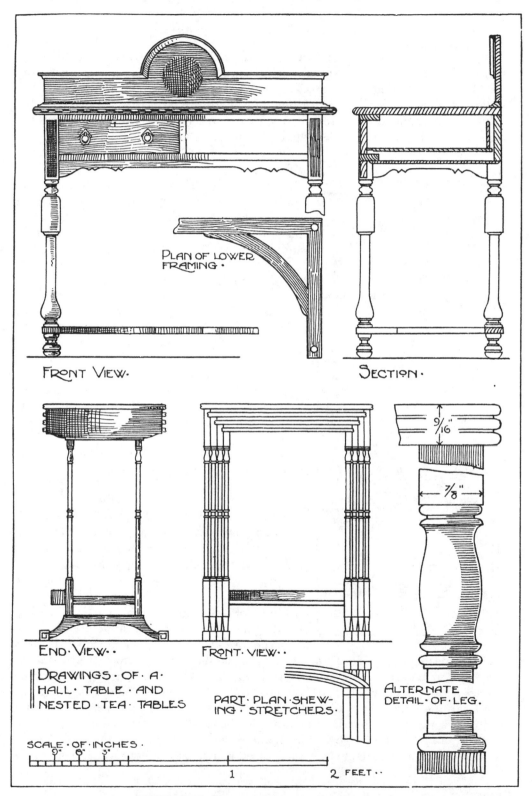

FRONT VIEW.

PLAN OF LOWER FRAMING.

SECTION.

END·VIEW·

FRONT·VIEW··

DRAWINGS·OF·A· HALL·TABLE·AND· NESTED·TEA·TABLES

PART·PLAN·SHEW-ING·STRETCHERS·

ALTERNATE DETAIL·OF·LEG.

9/16"

7/8"

SCALE·OF·INCHES·

9"   6"   3"

1   2 FEET··

A HALL TABLE, AND NESTED TEA TABLES.

NESTED TABLES (see p. 121).

These tables are called "Nested" because of their arrangement, viz., forming a nest or fitting into each other. There are two ways of making them, the method shown being most effective. It will be seen in front view that the largest table has a smaller one fitting into a groove in the side rails, and this principle is extended to the remaining two, or more if necessary. Plan shows the connecting rails, curved in order to fit each other, and built up for requisite strength. The smallest table has a shelf in addition to the rail, which adds to the general effect when all are in position, and also strengthens the smaller frame. The alternate construction is to form grooves by screwing slips on to the inside of rails, see f. 2, p. 120, but work executed in this manner is unsightly and cumbersome.

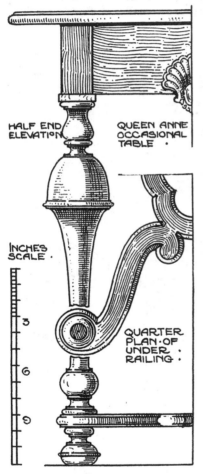

HALF END ELEVATION

QUEEN ANNE OCCASIONAL TABLE .

INCHES SCALE .

3
6
9

QUARTER PLAN OF UNDER RAILING .

AN EXTENSION TABLE (see p. 123).

This system of extension is of French origin. "Draw" frames act under the top (see plan), and afford support to the semicircular side "leaves." A rule joint connection is used. And the underframing is constructed by tongued mitres at the corners, the remainder "halved" together, stopped dovetail joints being used for connecting the straight lengths to end rails.

CURIO TABLES (see p. 124).

An original table, manufactured by Messrs J. S. Henry & Co., of Old Street, London, is illustrated, in which a maximum amount of show space is obtained. End elevation shows the glazed framing dowelled between the legs, a false bottom is grooved across the ends and back before glueing up, and forms a filling or soffit to the projecting front part, rebated into the front rails and screwed from underneath. The smaller type shown is rectangular in shape, and does not demand a detailed explanation. Curio tables shaped in plan, are also frequently made, the top made in segments, with curved frames fitting between the legs. When an elliptic or "kidney" shape is employed, a special hinge must be made. This is fixed at the centre, and is made of extra width; owing to the curved rail and top, not more than one can be used, and it is for this reason that the hinge flaps are made longer than the ordinary type. Special locks are also to be obtained for such work, which is very light in construction.

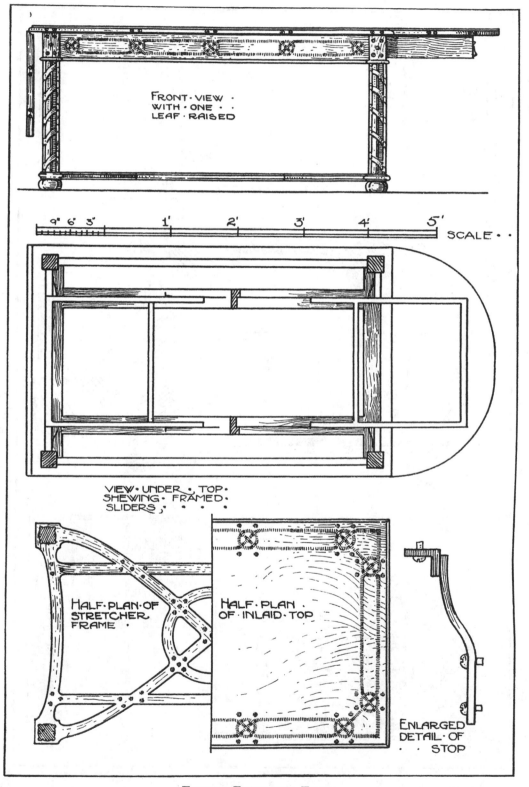

FRONT · VIEW ·
WITH · ONE · ·
LEAF · RAISED

SCALE · ·

VIEW · UNDER · TOP ·
SHEWING · FRAMED ·
SLIDERS ; · · ·

HALF · PLAN · OF
STRETCHER
FRAME ·

HALF · PLAN ·
OF · INLAID · TOP

ENLARGED
DETAIL · OF
· · STOP

FRENCH EXTENSION TABLE.

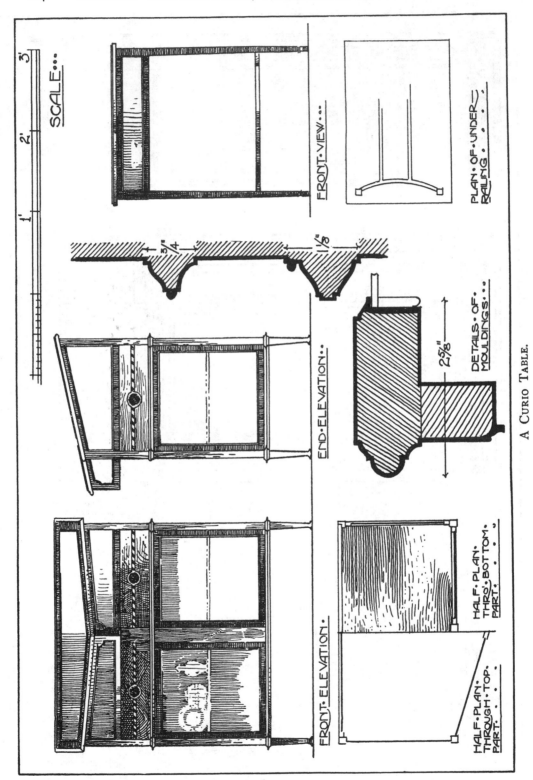

A CURIO TABLE.

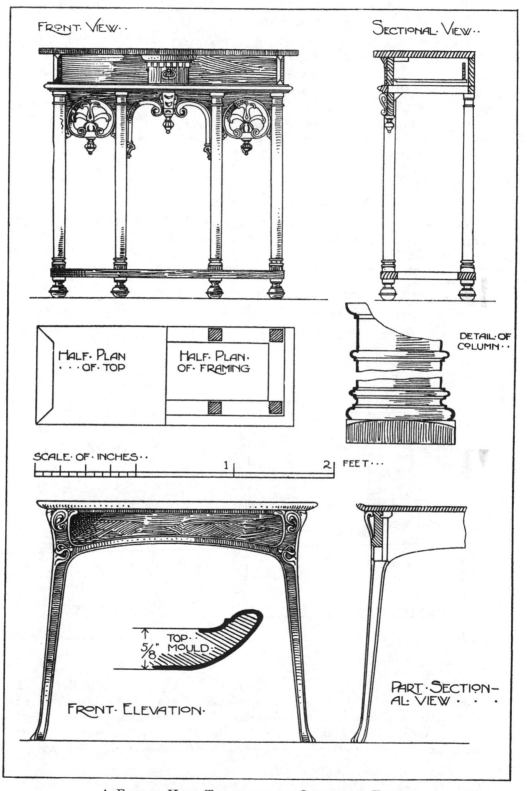

FRONT. VIEW..

SECTIONAL. VIEW..

HALF. PLAN
· · · OF · TOP

HALF. PLAN·
OF · FRAMING

DETAIL· OF
COLUMN · ·

SCALE· OF· INCHES..   1   2   FEET · · ·

TOP·
MOULD·

5/8"

FRONT· ELEVATION.

PART · SECTION-
AL· VIEW · · · ·

A FRENCH HALL TABLE, AND AN OCCASIONAL TABLE.

A HALL TABLE (see p. 125).

This is a fine example of French sixteenth century work now in the Victoria and Albert Museum, displaying excellent proportion and characteristic decoration in the fretted and carved under or " span " rails. The sectional view shows construction with a tablet attached to the drawer front. The under-railing is simple, rectangular as shown in plan, and the top is mitre-clamped. A small " console " or bracket is attached to the centre span rail under frieze, with a turned " pendant " or " drop " pinned in from underneath. The original is executed in walnut.

AN OCCASIONAL TABLE (see p. 125).

The measured drawings shown were made from the actual example in Bethnal Green Museum. It forms a part of an exhibit which is representative

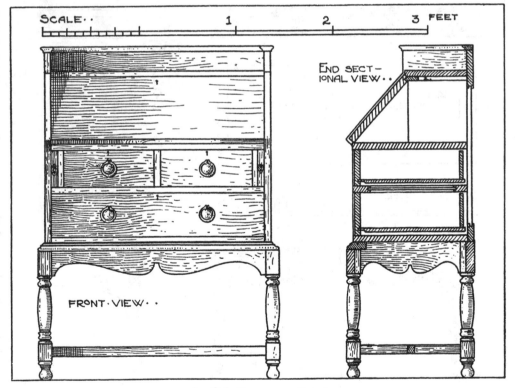

An Oak Bureau on Stand.

of the Continental New Art style, purchased by Sir George Donaldson, who presented it to the nation. The exhibit generally displays excellent technique in execution, both in wood and metal work, and there are some fine examples of inlaying. On the other hand, many of the designs are quite unsuitable for the materials employed, and require bent wood in executing them, which, however carefully it may be done in furniture, always has a natural tendency to spring back. The example given is in good proportion, and except for the carved knee parts is an effective piece, with good moulded legs and top. The construction is effected by cutting the legs to profile, and framing up with moulded rails. The carving is then executed, and continued or "run off" on to the rail mouldings.

AN OAK BUREAU (see opposite).

The example shown, upon a stand with turned legs, illustrates the necessary arrangement and construction of this class of work. The stand is

1.

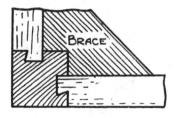

2. Holly Stationery Case.

dovetailed together with the angles braced as shown in f. 1, and a moulding mitred round front and ends. The carcase ends need special mention here, as they are common, with but slight variations, to all bureaux. It will be seen from the sectional view, that the front line of end does not carry through, but is curved round the edge of fall. This is necessary to conceal the end grain of the fall, a small part of which would otherwise project beyond the carcase ends. Many old bureaux have this small part glued on, but this is not always satisfactory, and to ensure the

necessary strength the ends should be cut from the solid. Fig. 2 illustrates a stationery case suitable for the interior. Other examples are shown as they occur in various pieces of work in other parts of the book. A general rule in fitting stationery cases is to make the carcase slightly smaller at the back, and about $\frac{3}{8}$ in. shorter than the space between ends. A bead is then glued at each end of case to fill the intervening spaces. A detailed description of the supporting "sliders" or "lopers" is given in the next chapter, in connection with an oak bureau bookcase.

A CHIPPENDALE SILVER TABLE (see p. 128).

3. View showing Column glued inside the Angle.

This type of table is, as the name implies, intended for the display of silver or curios. The illustration has been measured and drawn from an original example. The height to table top is 28 in., and the width is 21 in. A turned column (see f. 3) is fixed inside the fretwork angles; diagonal stretchers assist to keep the table rigid. The constructive features of this table do not require any special comment, and the arrangement of leg and rim or gallery will be apparent

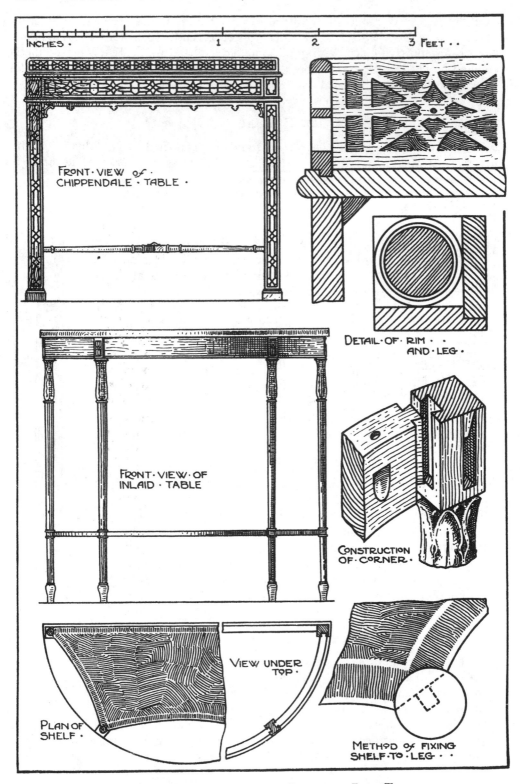

INCHES ·   1   2   3 FEET · ·

FRONT · VIEW of ·
CHIPPENDALE · TABLE ·

DETAIL · OF · RIM · ·
AND · LEG ·

FRONT · VIEW · OF
INLAID · TABLE

CONSTRUCTION
OF · CORNER ·

VIEW UNDER
TOP ·

PLAN OF
SHELF ·

METHOD of FIXING
SHELF · TO · LEG · ·

CHIPPENDALE SILVER TABLE; SHERATON PIER TABLE.

from the enlarged details. When preparing the fretwork, four pieces can be cut together by glueing paper between each piece, and separating after the frets have been polished. The angles should be glued together, and the turned column glued in position before the rail mortises are cut; barefaced tenons are used as the rails are very thin.

A SHERATON PIER TABLE (see opposite).

Pier tables were so called because of their original use in supporting a wall or pier glass, but changing fashion has displaced "pier" glasses, and "side" table is now the more appropriate and accepted term. The tops of these tables veneered with " curl " veneer, have a very rich effect, and it should be noted that the carved laurel and pateræ on knee part of leg were practically the only exceptions to Sheraton's use of inlay for decoration. The top should be prepared first, and rim, shelf, and leg lines set out upon it; templates can, then be made for rim and shelf; both front rails are forked into the rim. This is glued up in segments and veneered. The diagram shows construction at back corner, rim dovetailed into leg, and straight rail tenoned with diminished haunch; pocket screwing is shown for fixing the top, but one and a half screws sunk into the rim have a very neat appearance.

CONSOLE TABLES.

This form of table was made by all the great designers in the late eighteenth century period, although Chippendale appears to have been the most prolific producer. Its use was practically identical to a "pier table," viz., supporting a wall glass, clock, and urn candelabra or vases. The name originated from the form of bracket called a "console," which was used in supporting the top, although this term appears somewhat perverted when regarding some of Chippendale's carved extravagancies. The console table of the Adams period is very severe in outline, the legs consisting of a modified " console " shape, with carving of classic origin. Marble tops were also introduced in these tables, and it is probably for this reason that Adam's tables of this type are referred to as commode tables.

CARD TABLES (see p. 130).

A French pattern of card table, based upon a Louis XV. design, is shown on p. 130; the plan shows the side rails attached to front legs, and back rail dovetailed into side rails in box form. Fly legs and rails are used in these tables, with a finger joint connection (see enlarged detail). The back legs are fixed to the fly rails, and the centre piece between fly rails is screwed to the framing. To open the table the back legs are drawn out, and the top folded over. Curved rails, such as are illustrated, require careful treatment in executing them. They are usually cut from solid stuff, with a corner glued in, as shown

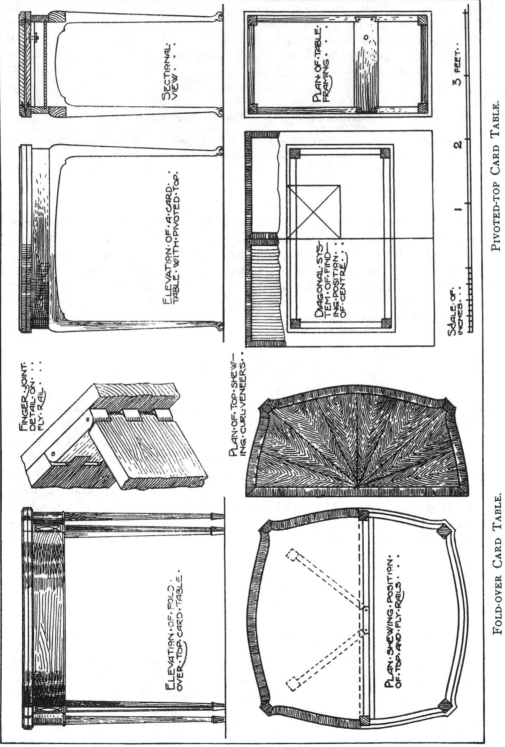

SECTIONAL VIEW.

PLAN OF TABLE FRAMING.

ELEVATION OF A CARD TABLE WITH PIVOTED TOP.

DIAGONAL SYSTEM OF FINDING POSITION OF CENTRE.

SCALE OF INCHES.

3 FEET.

PIVOTED-TOP CARD TABLE.

FINGER JOINT DETAIL ON FLY RAIL.

PLAN OF TOP SHEWING CURL VENEERS.

ELEVATION OF FOLD OVER TOP CARD TABLE.

PLAN SHEWING POSITION OF TOP AND FLY RAILS.

FOLD-OVER CARD TABLE.

in f. 1, in order to prevent the short grain breaking away which would almost certainly occur if this provision was not made. The diagram also shows the method of connection, being slip dovetailed into the knees. Although dowelling is sometimes employed, it is not recommended. This method of extension can also be applied to semicircular card tables, both types used when closed up as pier or side tables, and placed against the wall. The plan of top closed shows an effective veneered treatment. The centre part is of curl veneers, which are feathered up as shown, radiating to a centre, with border cross-banded. An alternate treatment suitable for a Sheraton table top is indicated on this page, f. 2.

A Pivoted Top Table (see opposite).

This type of card table, from the simplicity of its construction and action, easily ranks first. The plan shows the framing and line of top, open and closed. There are various systems for determining the true position of pivot, the one illustrated being the simplest. Plan of framing must be set out full size, then

VIEW· SHEW-
ING·CONNEC-
TION·OF·RAIL
TO·LEG·

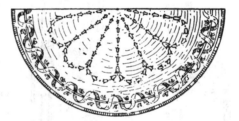

1. 2. Decorative Treatment of a Semicircular Top.

draw a centre line, divide this centre line into two equal parts, and erect a square upon one half as shown, then draw the diagonals, the intersection of which is the true position for centre of pivot. A cross rail is also necessary with this type, the pivot pin passing through is secured with nut as shown in sectional view. A receptacle for cards, &c., is provided by grooving a bottom board into the frame, with a filling-in rail tongued to one side of cross rail. The "cabriole" frame is executed by tenoning rails into knee parts of legs. Curved rails between legs are also glued to rails, and stub tenoned into legs. Cabriole legs are cut to square section first, then rounded with spokeshaves and files before glass-papering. "Claw and ball" feet are illustrated, the origin of which can be distinctly traced to the Chinese, probably suggested by animal anatomy. They should be carved up before the final finishing of leg is proceeded with. The shaded part in plan indicates a narrow lipping of cross-banded veneer with cloth centre part. Lippings are sometimes placed on the outside edges only, so that only one piece of cloth is required. This, however, generally proves unsatis-factory at the joint.

CARD TABLES (see next page).

The first illustrations represent an uncommon method of extension in card tables, first introduced by Chippendale. The leg is composed of two pieces forming an angle, rebated together, and completed by the addition of a foot. These legs were frequently " pierced " or " fretted," also " recessed," as shown in example on this page. The plans indicate the extension principle, open and closed, with hinged connections ; a groove is worked on the inside of rails, so that when the table is open, the board or tray, shown in plan shaded, can be drawn along, thus preventing the rails from closing up, and ensuring a rigid frame. The tops are hinged together, and should be framed up, with a lipping inside to receive the card table cloth. Various hinges and their uses on folding tops are illustrated in the chapter on " Brasswork."

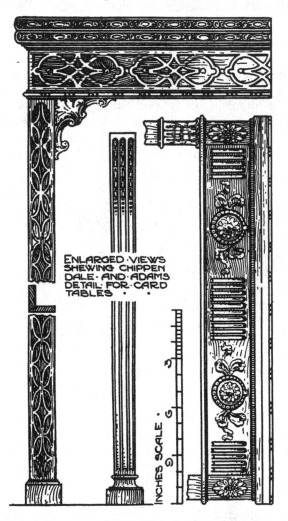

ENLARGED VIEWS SHEWING CHIPPENDALE AND ADAMS DETAIL FOR CARD TABLES

INCHES SCALE

AN ENVELOPE CARD TABLE
(see opposite).

This is a most compact and useful type, and is so termed because of the resemblance of folding flaps to an envelope. The plan under top shows the framing, and also a centre cross rail to receive the card table centre ; a drawer is also introduced into the framing. Part plan shows the flaps closed, the construction of which must prevent the possibility of warping, best effected by framing up each flap with tongued joints. When the top is rotated slightly, a spring made of flexible oak (as shown in diagram) comes into action, the button pressing against the rail, causing the dowel to push up one flap. This is then raised, and the top rotated to its full extent, when the spring returns to its original position, see dotted line in plan. A stop block is also shown, which prevents the top rotating more than the required amount. A view indicates the top open, the flaps resting on the framework ; brackets are glued into the corners, and then lined with baize. An alternate decorative treatment in the Adam style is shown on this page.

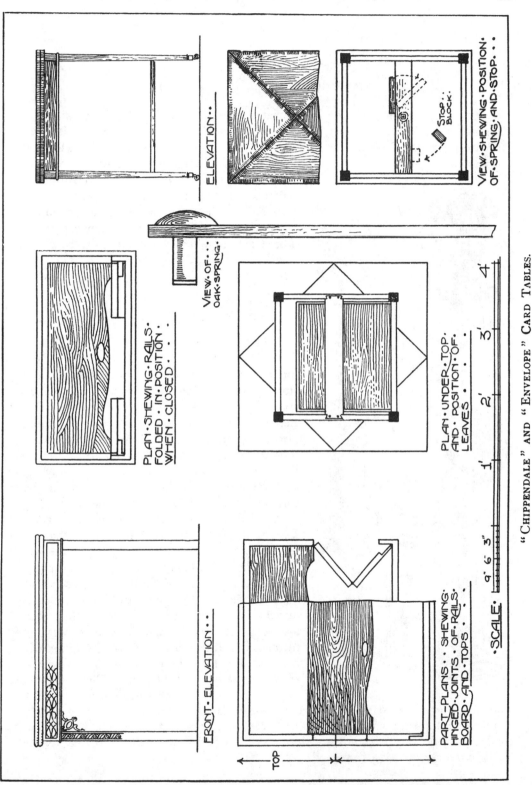

ELEVATION

VIEW·SHEWING·POSITION·
OF·SPRING·AND·STOP·

STOP·
BLOCK

VIEW·OF·
OAK·SPRING·

PLAN·SHEWING·RAILS·
FOLDED·IN·POSITION·
WHEN·CLOSED·

PLAN·UNDER·TOP·
AND·POSITION·OF·
LEAVES·

FRONT·ELEVATION·

PART—PLANS·SHEWING·
HINGED·JOINTS·OF·RAILS·
BOARD·AND·TOPS·

TOP

SCALE·

9″ 6″ 3″   1′ 2′ 3′ 4′

"CHIPPENDALE" AND "ENVELOPE" CARD TABLES.

SHAVING STANDS (see next page).

Shaving stands are made in a variety of forms, of which the three examples illustrated are the best.   The height of these stands to the table part is fixed definitely, viz., 3 ft. 6 in. for the swing glass type, but where an extension movement in pillar form is used, this rule is not binding.   The elevations have the ends dowelled into legs, with the top and bottom tenoned into the legs, and housed into ends.   Brackets are then dowelled on with a $\frac{3}{8}$-in. rod, fitting loosely between them. These act as a towel bar, with shelves above them as shown.

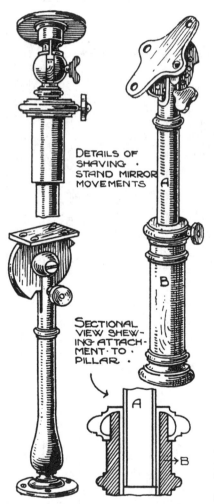

DETAILS OF
SHAVING ·
STAND MIRROR
MOVEMENTS

SECTIONAL
VIEW SHEW-
ING ATTACH-
MENT · TO ·
PILLAR .

A

B

A

B

A PILLAR SHAVING STAND.

This form of construction is applied to several kinds of tables, of which we may mention two and three tier tea tables, cake stands, and circular dumb waiters.   The constructive principles involved are simple, viz., the insertion of circular shelves between turned portions of the pillar.   This principle is further illustrated in the connection of top pillar to the standard, and elaborated according to requirements ; a collar or flange should be turned underneath the shelves, thus permitting of a light appearance on the circular rims. Various movements are attached to shaving stands in order to permit of tilting or turning the mirror.   These are illustrated on this page, and an enlarged detail shows sectional views of the column, to which the movement is attached.   The silvered mirrors illustrated are without bevels, and where these are introduced, the mirrors must be carefully blocked in the rebate so that the margin shows equally at the front.   The quickest method is to cut small wedge-shaped blocks, and these are placed in the space between glass and frame, secured by lightly glueing and fixing with a panel pin.   Rebates should be lampblacked, or an unsightly reflection will show on the glass.   In addition to blacking the rebate the glass edge is also darkened.

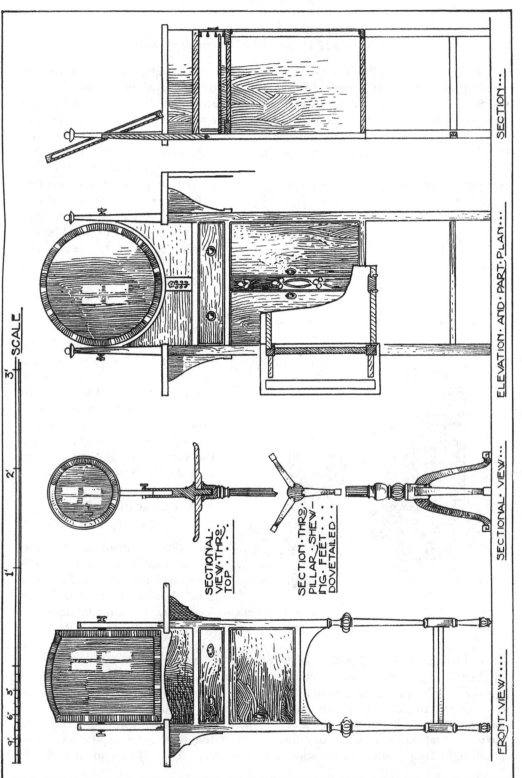

SCALE

9' 6" 3"   1'   2'   3'

FRONT·VIEW····   SECTIONAL·VIEW····   ELEVATION·AND·PART·PLAN····   SECTION····

SECTIONAL·
VIEW·THRO'
TOP·····

SECTION·THRO·
PILLAR·SHEW–
ING·FEET····
DOVETAILED···

TYPES OF SHAVING STANDS.

AN ELLIPTICAL TABLE (see opposite).

A Louis XVI. elliptical table is shown on next page, and the method of building up the rim is described in the chapter on "Workshop Practice." This rim is veneered and inlaid with brass lines, or recessed as in f. 1, forming panels veneered with amboyna or thuya wood, with a brass-cased moulding mitred round the angles, see diagram. The top should be flush and framed up. The legs are turned and inlaid with brass flutes, see f. 2, and the circular mounts under knee

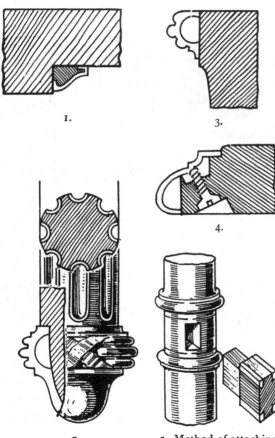

I.

3.

4.

2.

5. Method of attaching Stretchers to Legs.

part of legs fit as shown in f. 3, placed in position and screwed before shoes are put on. When the top is prepared and rebated to section shown it should be forwarded to the metalworker, who makes the rim as indicated in f. 4. Small metal blocks are inserted at intervals underneath, brazed to the rim, and "tapped" to receive set screws. The rim is then fixed by screwing from underneath through pockets cut under top. Brass shoes, shown in f. 2, are a feature of work in this period embracing many variations. With the example shown, the leg is turned away to receive the shoe, which is then screwed into the leg from underneath.

A CIRCULAR TABLE
(see opposite).

This drawing-room table, made of satinwood, is very similar in construction to the above kind, but there is no necessity for the framed top, "laminating," or even a well-seasoned solid top, veneered both sides, stands well, secured to the rim by "pocket screwing" or buttoning (see "Joints and their Application"). Fig. 5 shows a detail of the stretcher and leg mortised and tenoned together. The inlaid lines round leg are bent round an iron bar, to obtain the requisite curvature, and the stretchers are screwed to the circular shell, or they may be made as diagonal rails, halved at the centre. When inlaying the turned portion under knee, a template must be prepared to fit the leg between the mouldings, and shaped to coincide with the inlay line. The end of a file is

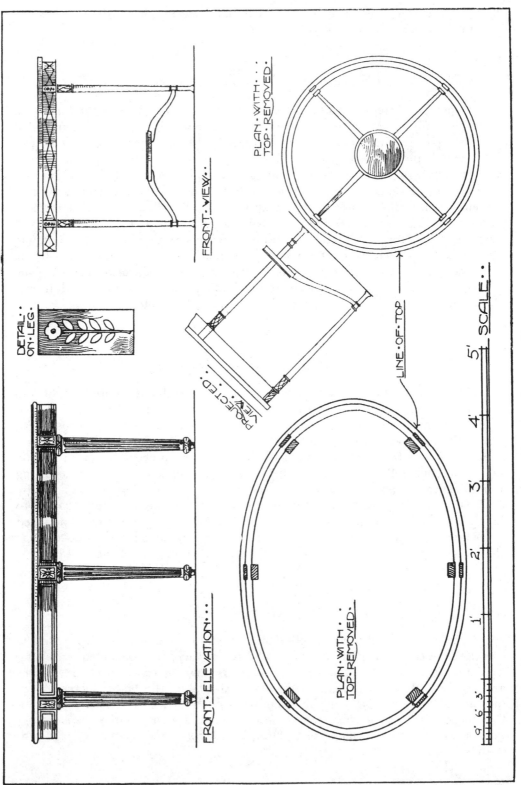

FRONT · VIEW ·

PLAN · WITH · · · TOP · REMOVED ·

DETAIL · ON · LEG ·

PROJECTED · VIEW ·

LINE · OF · TOP

FRONT · ELEVATION · · ·

PLAN · WITH · · TOP · REMOVED ·

SCALE · ·

9' 6' 3'   1'   2'   3'   4'   5'

ELLIPTICAL AND CIRCULAR TABLES.

used as a cutter, worked against the template edge until the desired depth is obtained to receive the line.

A CHESS TABLE (see opposite).

Chess or draught tables, of which the measured drawing shown is an example, only differ from an ordinary occasional table in the arrangement of the top. The illustration shows a reversible top, which, when not in use, is reversed and forms an occasional table. Sectional view shows the centre top working upon brass pins fixed on each edge, sliding in brass-lined grooves. Constructional detail of top rails shows the necessary mortise and tenon and dovetail joints, the centre part cut away to render the box enclosure more accessible. These rails are lined with baize when fitting up the work, to prevent scratching the top. A sketch illustrates the construction of bottom framing, the divisions are clamped at front and back, mortised and tenoned as shown, and the panels are bareface tongued into the rails—see also section. The materials used in this table are Italian walnut and rosewood, and it was designed and made at the Shoreditch Technical Institute.

A BED TABLE (see opposite).

The drawing shows a type of invalid table adjustable to desired height, and with tilting top. Sectional views show the box pillar tenoned into a T-shaped stand, with an inside pillar notched as shown in small sketch. This also illustrates the method of fixing the top plate B. The height is adjusted by raising the pillar, when the plate automatically descends, and prevents further insertion of the notched pillar. A partial side view shows detail of quadrant, revolving round centre C, bolted as shown in section. When the top is tilted to any desired angle, it is securely fixed by tightening the butterfly nut attached to bolt. The pierced brass bracket under top is to ensure rigidity, and is attached to quadrant, and also to a T-shaped brass plate fixed on underside of top; this bracket distributes the weight of top on to the pillar and stand.

A PILLAR "PIE CRUST" TABLE (see opposite).

Details of a Chippendale pillar table are also given on next page. The claw feet are dovetailed into the pillar, and the curved top is executed by cutting to shape, then moulding the rim and clearing away the centre part with planes and router. When a deep-centred lathe is available, the better method is to turn away the centre part, finishing the moulding with scratch stock and cutter. Oval tops of a similar character can also be worked upon a lathe, necessitating the use of a special fitting, viz., a chuck, based upon the "trammel" or "two-centred" principle.

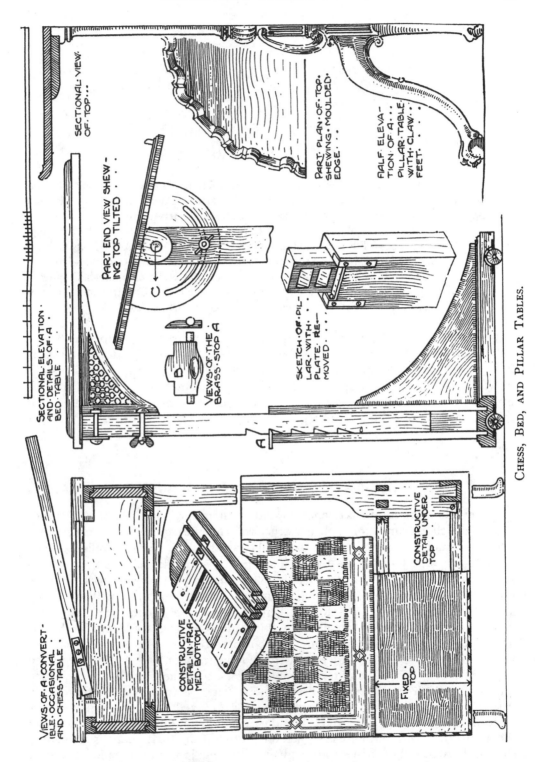

SECTIONAL VIEW OF TOP · · ·

PART · PLAN · OF · TOP · SHEWING · MOULDED · EDGE · · ·

HALF · ELEVA-TION · OF · A · · · PILLAR · TABLE · WITH · CLAW · FEET · · · ·

PART END VIEW SHEW-ING TOP TILTED · · ·

SECTIONAL · ELEVATION · AND · DETAILS · OF · A · BED · TABLE

VIEWS · OF · THE · BRASS · STOP · A

SKETCH · OF · PIL-LAR · WITH · PLATE · RE-MOVED · · ·

VIEWS · OF · A · CONVERT-IBLE · OCCASIONAL · AND · CHESS · TABLE

CONSTRUCTIVE · DETAIL · IN · FRA-MED · BOTTOM

CONSTRUCTIVE · DETAIL · UNDER · TOP ·

FIXED · TOP

CHESS, BED, AND PILLAR TABLES.

CHAPTER VII.

CARCASE WORK.

Chest of Drawers, General Proportions and Construction—Bookcases, Dwarf, Glazed Doors, and Cupboard Carcase—Inlaid and Barred Door Cases—Oak Bureau Bookcase—Sideboards—Pedestal, Leg, and Carcase—Curved and Straight Fronts—Adam and Georgian Types—Dresser Sideboard—Wardrobes—Gent.'s Hanging, and Wing Carcases—Elliptical Pedestal Writing Table—Queen Anne Flap Cabinet—Satinwood China Cabinet—Secretaire Writing Cabinet and Bookcase—Dressing Chest—Music Cabinet—Scale Drawing and Sheet of Details of Flemish Cabinet—Tall-boy Chest—Dutch China Cabinet—Full Details of Construction, Interior Fittings, Cases, Trays, Cellarets, Shelf Supports, Glass Backs, &c.

THE term "carcase" is generally applied to the "case" or "cupboard" part between the plinth and cornice. There may be a top and a bottom carcase, as in a bookcase, or a "middle" and right and left "wing," as in a wardrobe, all of which have been built up from the old chest. Sometimes a carcase may be fitted to a framed-up stand with legs, or may hang on the wall, but the title of this chapter applies the term in a general way to enclosed furniture.

A CHEST OF DRAWERS (see next page).

The illustration on next page shows the general proportions and dimensions of this article of furniture, with constructive principles general in carcase work. The ends can be framed up or used solid as shown. Division rails between drawers are stub tenoned or housed into the ends (see also chapter on "Joints and their Application"). Carcase rails at top should be 3 in. wide, with brackets glued at each end for dovetailing, thus economising material without losing strength. These rails are set back behind the drawer fronts (see section); a useful detail when a top rail under a thick moulded top would appear heavy. This detail is repeated at bottom. The bottom stand is a constantly recurring feature in carcase work, and is constructed by through dovetailing a ground frame of $\frac{7}{8}$-in. stuff. A length of moulding worked to the section shown is then mitred round three sides of the frame, and is cut to elevation when thoroughly dry. Sectional view shows the dust-boards grooved into the rails, with a corresponding rail at the back, forming a complete dust-board frame under the drawers. This is the better method, although the dust-board is frequently slid in between the runners after glueing up the job, and completed by the addition of a panelled back, or as described in "Workshop Practice and Construction." Refer also to that chapter for processes connected with manufacture of carcases and drawer-making. The drawers in this example are made and flushed off and faced up before mitreing and glueing the mouldings. A raised tablet at centre is introduced, projecting $\frac{1}{8}$ in. above the ground-work facings.

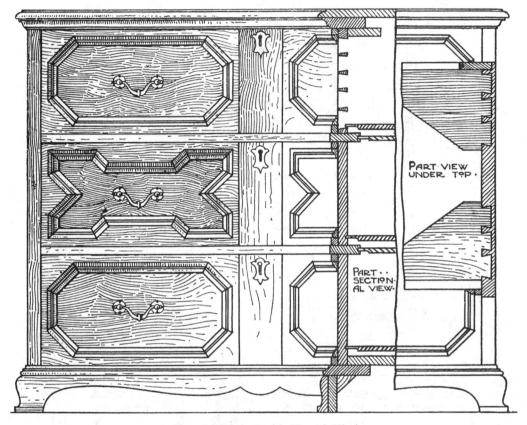

A Chest of Drawers with Shaped Plinths.

BOOKCASES (see next page).

The example on next page is a typical bookcase regarding general proportions, although the arrangement of doors, &c., occasionally vary, such as, for instance, open glazed or barred doors in the bottom part, and a narrow frieze in place of the drawer. The depth of book space, *i.e.*, the distance between inside of door and back, should never be less than 10 in., and this distance is frequently increased to suit special requirements. There are four methods employed to support the adjustable shelves, one of which is illustrated on p. 143. Holes are bored $\frac{3}{8}$ in. deep at intervals of $1\frac{1}{2}$ in. inside both

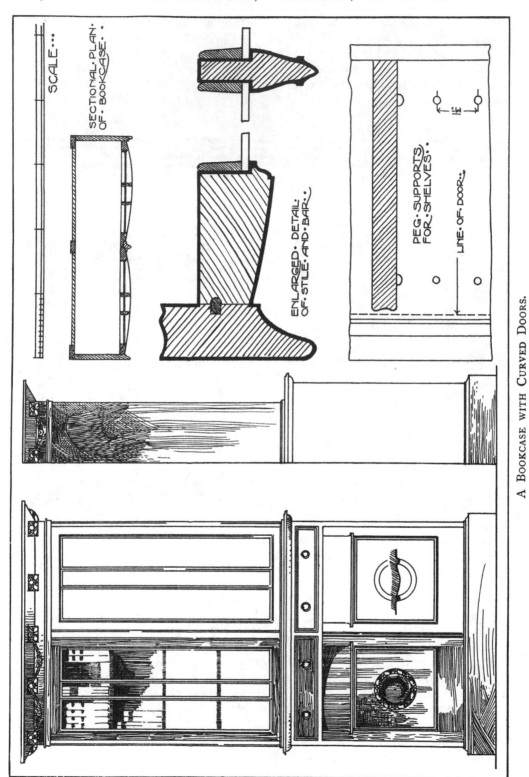

SCALE···

SECTIONAL·PLAN· OF·BOOKCASE·.

ENLARGED·DETAIL· OF·STILE·AND·BAR·.

PEG·SUPPORTS· FOR·SHELVES··

LINE·OF·DOOR··

A Bookcase with Curved Doors.

ends, and turned wooden studs (see f. I.) are inserted to support the shelves. To ensure accurate spacing for these holes, set out the distances upon a slip of wood, gauge a centre line, and bore holes with a $\frac{3}{8}$-in. dowel bit (see f. II.). Glue a stop at each end, so that the slip may be placed on the carcase end and secured with a small hand-screw, then bore through the holes. A stop is fixed to the dowel bit, so that all are bored equal depth. To prevent the shelves slipping forward, they can be hand-screwed together, and bored with a bit, and when separated semicircular cavities are left which drop over the head of stud (see f. III.). Another method of supporting shelves is with brass studs (see f. IV.) ; $\frac{3}{16}$-in. holes are made in the ends as before, and the underside of shelf is bored to fit the circular head with a centre bit ; when the shelf is in position, the underside is quite flush. A third method, used only in conjunction with a pilastered carcase, is to fix saw-tooth racks on to the ends, and insert small cleats or fillets to receive the shelves where required (see f. V.). Tonk's patent fitting for

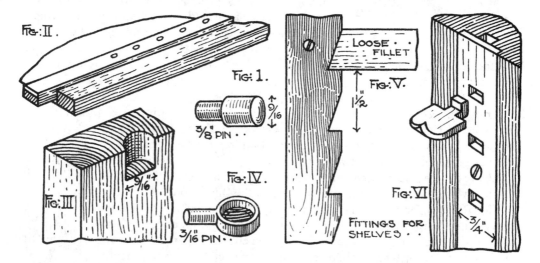

adjustable shelves consists of strips of $\frac{1}{8}$-in. iron with rectangular holes cut at intervals to receive a small spiked clip. The ends are grooved to receive these irons with a special plane, and the irons are inserted and screwed down flush (see f. VI.). To insert the clip, the small projection is first placed in the hole, and the clip is then brought down square with the irons, a small spike serving to prevent the shelf moving forward when in position. The construction of top doors curved on the front only in plan, will be understood from the diagrams. A dust bead is inserted into hanging stiles, which renders the case almost dustproof.

AN INLAID BOOKCASE (see p. 145).

The design shows an effective treatment executed at the Shoreditch Technical Institute. The panels demand an executive process similar to the "diaper" patternwork of the Louis XVI. period. The chequered diamonds are prepared first by cutting strips of rosewood and satinwood veneer to required width. These are then glued down on to paper, and when dry one end is cut obliquely (see A A in f. I. below). A cutting gauge is set from this edge and a cut made on either side of the veneer: this marks three diamond shapes in one length with rosewood outside. Half the number of those prepared are required with satinwood outside, and these are proceeded with as above.   The lines surrounding the chequered diamonds are next

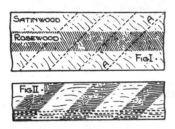

Cutting Veneers for Diapers.

dealt with; veneer is glued on paper, as indicated in f. II., the edge shot, and pieces gauged off ⅛ in. wide. Set out the panel on paper, and commence fitting up the surface from one corner, glue down a mahogany piece first, and then glue down a piece of line. Follow this up by glueing down the chequer pattern, then the line, and next the mahogany. This process is continued until the whole surface is glued on to stiff paper, which when dry is transferred to the panel groundwork and veneered with cauls in the usual way. After the

surface has been cleaned off with the toothing plane, the small ebony diamonds are cut in with a chisel. It is advantageous to use stiff brown paper for this process, damped and stretched on to a clamped board, described in the chapter on "Drawing," &c. The inlaid cornice frieze also introduces processes not dealt with elsewhere. "Curl" mahogany and rosewood are the materials used, and the lancet-shaped pieces are cut by pinning six or eight thicknesses of veneer between two thin pieces of hard wood, taking care that the centre line of each curl is directly under the centre line of the lancet which has previously been drawn on the thin wood. Then cut with a fine bow or fret, and finish carefully to shape with files. Carefully glue the pieces of veneer on to paper, butting each edge against a straightedge to ensure accuracy, and then cut the pointed pieces in a similar fashion, testing them carefully between the other veneers before separating them. These pieces are then glued down, and when dry are ready for veneering. The inlaid mouldings are executed by veneering the edge surfaces, and inlaying the corner lines, cutting in the squares with a chisel. Diamond and square shapes

FIG. III.

are frequently introduced into barred doors, and these are executed in a manner similar to the small six-sided panels in this example. Prepare a piece of ⅞-in. whitewood to the inside line of slab, and cut the ⅛-in. slab round this piece, mitreing the corners. Temporarily pin the pieces to template, and complete the joint by making dovetail saw cuts at the angles, into which veneers are glued, forming a dovetail key (see f. III.). The straight bars are then V-jointed, and strengthened with strips of linen glued in the angles.

The satinwood diamonds should be toned down in the polishing to prevent too sharp a contrast with the rosewood and the mahogany should be kept to its natural colour.

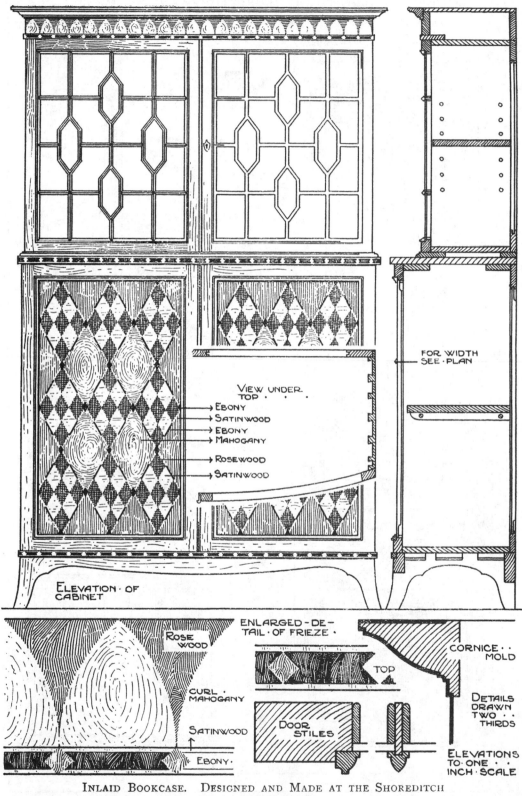

VIEW UNDER TOP

→ EBONY
→ SATINWOOD
→ EBONY
→ MAHOGANY
→ ROSEWOOD
→ SATINWOOD

FOR WIDTH SEE·PLAN

ELEVATION·OF CABINET

ROSE WOOD

CURL· MAHOGANY

SATINWOOD

EBONY·

ENLARGED·DE- TAIL·OF·FRIEZE·

TOP

DOOR STILES

CORNICE·· MOLD

DETAILS DRAWN TWO·· THIRDS

ELEVATIONS TO·ONE· INCH·SCALE

INLAID BOOKCASE. DESIGNED AND MADE AT THE SHOREDITCH TECHNICAL INSTITUTE.

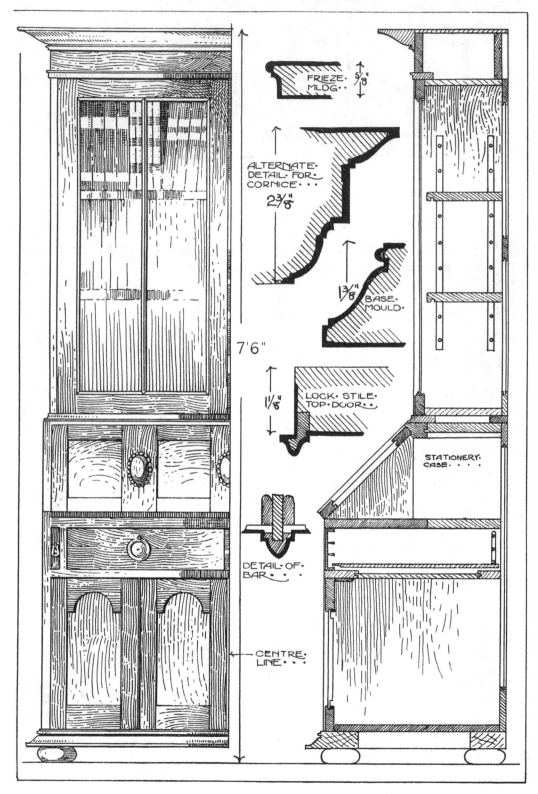

FRIEZE·
MLDG.··

5/8"

ALTERNATE·
DETAIL·FOR·
CORNICE···

2 3/8"

1 3/8"

BASE·
MOULD·

7'6"

LOCK·STILE·
TOP·DOOR···

1 1/8"

STATIONERY·
CASE···

DETAIL·OF·
BAR···

CENTRE·
LINE···

AN OAK BUREAU BOOKCASE (see opposite).

Good general proportions are represented in this example, which was manufactured by Messrs J. S. Henry & Co. The height of bureau fall varies from 29 to 30 in. from ground line when horizontal, the same as for writing tables. The bureau carcase is made quite separate from the bookcase, with slides or lopers to support the fall; these draw out about 13 in., and are stopped by boring $\frac{3}{8}$-in. holes 16 in. from the front edge to receive a short dowel inserted when the loper is run in through the drawer opening; this dowel stops against the edge of the division when the loper is drawn forward, and prevents it being entirely withdrawn. A slip of billiard table cloth is glued to the top edges of lopers, commencing $\frac{1}{2}$ in. from front edge, to prevent marking the face of fall when horizontal. The sectional view shows a $\frac{1}{4}$-in. groove worked underneath the shelves, this is to receive bookcase leathers, which are held in position by glueing a wedge-shaped slip in the groove behind the leather strip. An alternate method of supporting the shelves is shown. Grooves are formed in the ends and an L-shaped stud is inserted (see sketch), which leaves the lug projecting to support the shelves. Shelves in bottom carcases are in most cases supported by either of the methods previously described, or fillets may be used, screwed to the carcase ends.

Lug Shelf Support.

A DWARF BOOKCASE (see next page).

A part plan of the plinth frame belonging to this piece indicates the construction; the mitres being tongued and blocked, beads are inserted between the wing and centre carcases, which facilitate fitting up and allow the door to clear the end. The construction of the carcase corner is also shown glued up and rebated right through, and filling pieces are glued in to fit the column, then levelled previous to veneering the end and also the front edge. Quarter columns are worked by planing up four squares of stuff and glueing them together with paper between the joints; after the turning and reeding are completed, the joints are forced apart with a knife, toothed to remove paper and glue, and each piece is fitted into the angles provided for them. The decoration of this frieze consists of a pattern recessed $\frac{1}{8}$ in. from face side called "recessing," but this decoration is frequently accomplished by glueing fretted patterns into the groundwork, although not so satisfactory. To glue the frets, prepare a board and lightly cover with thin glue, place the fret upon a heated caul, and transfer the toothed surface when warm to the glued board, well press all parts down, when sufficient glue will adhere to the surface; then lift off and place in position and

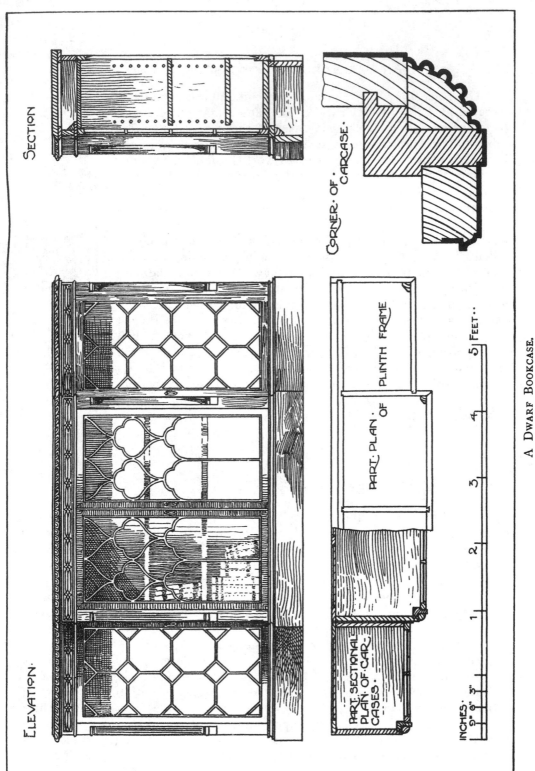

SECTION.

CORNER · OF · CARCASE ·

ELEVATION.

PART · PLAN · OF PLINTH FRAME

PART · SECTIONAL · PLAN · OF · CAR- · CASES ·

INCHES · 9" 6" 3"   1   2   3   4   5 FEET··

A DWARF BOOKCASE.

screw tightly down with a flat piece of wood and hand-screws. If the glueing has been carefully done, there will only be sufficient glue upon the fret to secure it, without any spare glue oozing out when hand-screwed. To construct a wing carcase door, prepare eight L-shaped bars dovetailed together from $\frac{3}{16}$-in. stuff, and three square forms also dovetailed together; mortise the L-shapes into the frame first, and then V cut straight lengths across the door between the points; now place a straightedge across the rails to mark the position of vertical slats on the cross pieces, these are halved together where they cross, and glued up; when dry, lay the three squares into bars and carefully mark position with a knife, then cut through and finish the V joints with a chisel. The squares should then fit exactly in position. Glue together, and strengthen all joints by glueing a strip of thin linen into all the angles. This method of procedure ensures accurate fitting, and the short length will follow through in straight lines. Building up curved slats is described in "curved work" section of the chapter on "Workshop Practice and Construction."

A GEORGIAN SIDEBOARD (next page).

The front elevation on p. 150 is drawn with a part finished, the other portion a sectional view, showing how the various parts are made and fitted together. It is reproduced by permission of Messrs J. S. Henry & Co. The bottom carcases are used for cellaret and cupboards, but if required a large carcase could be constructed having the same appearance, blocked and screwed into position on frieze and stand. The "claw and ball" feet are then tenoned into the base. False ends are necessary if a cellaret drawer is required in the pedestal, in order to allow free passage of the drawer past the edge of door. In making the frieze frame, the groundwork is set back to allow of the moulding being mitred round. This moulding is worked to within about 5 in. of each mitre, the high part left is for carved corners. The sideboard top part is framed together, and dowelled as shown in the separate sections. Both hoods above the columns are mitred and tongued at the corners, and a block is glued in for turning the fluted coves. These hoods are fixed over the back as shown in sectional view in B B. A curved shelf is dovetailed between, and mouldings are glued round the hoods mitreing into the moulded edge of shelf at the inside front corners. A turned ring or circle forms the convex mirror frame, which is scribed over the back framing, and is also cut away to form a rebate. The circle is glued and screwed, the carving pieces and key piece at head being scribed into position before they are carved. Pins are turned at both ends of pillars, and glued into the hoods and bases. Various cellaret fittings are described in connection with an Adam sideboard in this chapter, either of which could be substituted for the more ordinary lead-lined drawer illustrated in the sectional view, but this is most satisfactory, and accommodates more bottles than either of the methods previously described. The left-hand pedestal is usually fitted with a shelf only, but two or three shallow trays at the top, fitted for small articles of plate or cutlery, and cupboard space underneath them, is an excellent arrangement.

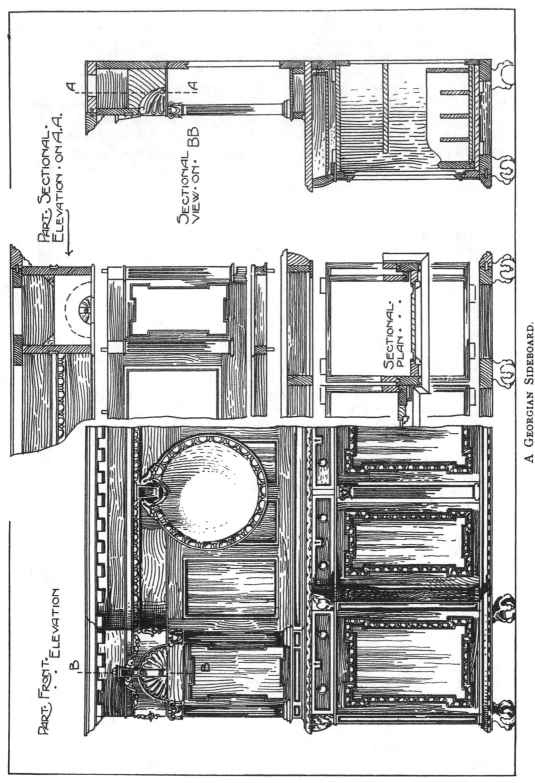

PART. SECTIONAL.
ELEVATION · ON A.A.

A

A

SECTIONAL.
VIEW · ON · BB

SECTIONAL.
PLAN · · ·

PART. FRONT. · · ELEVATION

B

B

A GEORGIAN SIDEBOARD.

A SIDEBOARD (see next page).

Much simpler work is illustrated in these drawings, the whole of the bottom part being in one piece. The view with top removed shows dovetailing of top drawer rail into the divisions, which runs right through and acts as a division between the centre cupboards; the ends are tongued into the legs, and the curved frieze rails over doors are slip dovetailed down into legs. The method of putting this piece of furniture together is as follows :—Tenon the divisions into bottom, tongue and dowel the divisions into the front legs, slip dovetail the bottom drawer rail in position and dovetail down the top rail. Both ends of carcase bottom are tenoned into the legs as shown in sectional view through bottom. The curved portion of base moulding is worked upon the solid, and all returns to breaks are mitred round, glued into rebate in ends, and set back at the front, housing where they cross the ends. Trays are fitted into the left-hand cupboard space, and the other is fitted with a cellaret drawer, lead lined, having divisions ; both cupboards, enclosed by circular doors, are fitted with a centre shelf. The sectional view shows construction of top part, the frieze rail being veneered to show the grain carrying right through.

AN ADAM SIDEBOARD (p. 153).

This type of sideboard is made in the Adam, Hepplewhite, and Sheraton styles; proportions and outline are similar, the decoration varying according to style. Both pedestals are made separate from the centre table part, and connected by screwing. The construction of pedestals and the arrangement of cellaret drawers are almost identical in the different styles, the original types containing plate racks and a spirit lamp for warming them, but these are not introduced in modern work. A "Tambour" front is frequently used to enclose the space under the long drawer, then used as a cupboard, and the square drawers are fitted with sliding trays for cutlery (see sketch). The cellaret drawer, inside the pedestal, is oblong in plan, divided up for bottles and lead lined. This is an excellent arrangement, as it economises space,

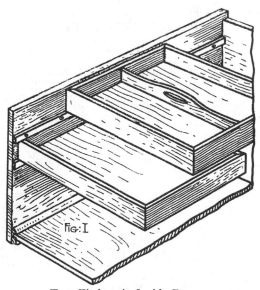

Tray Fittings in Inside Drawer.

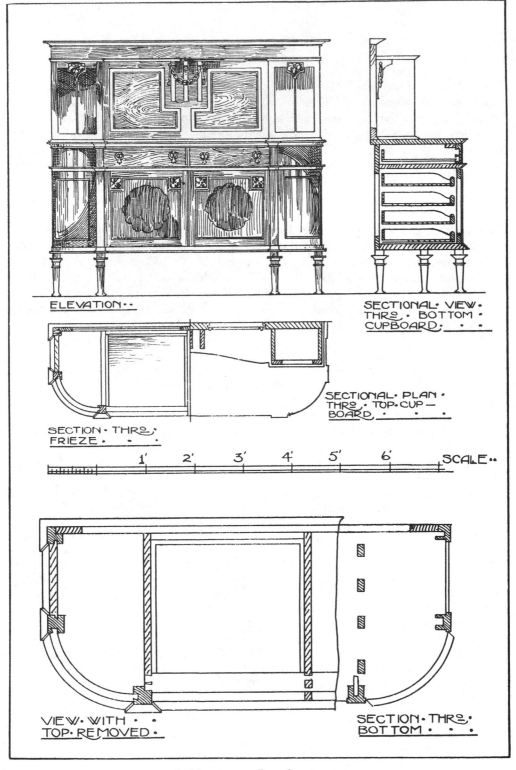

ELEVATION · ·

SECTIONAL · VIEW ·
THRO · BOTTOM ·
CUPBOARD · · ·

SECTIONAL · PLAN ·
THRO · TOP · CUP —
BOARD · · · ·

SECTION · THRO ·
FRIEZE · · · ·

1'   2'   3'   4'   5'   6'   SCALE · ·

VIEW · WITH · · ·
TOP · REMOVED ·

SECTION · THRO ·
BOTTOM · · ·

A MAHOGANY LEG SIDEBOARD.

PLATE XVII.   MAHOGANY SIDEBOARD. DESIGNED AND MADE AT THE L. C. C.
                   SHOREDITCH TECHNICAL INSTITUTE.

PLATE XVIII.   PAINTED SIDEBOARD BY MR. AMBROSE HEAL (HEAL & SON LTD.).

PLATE XVIII.   SIDEBOARD, PAINTED (DESIGNED BY P. A. WELLS (OETZMANN & CO.).)

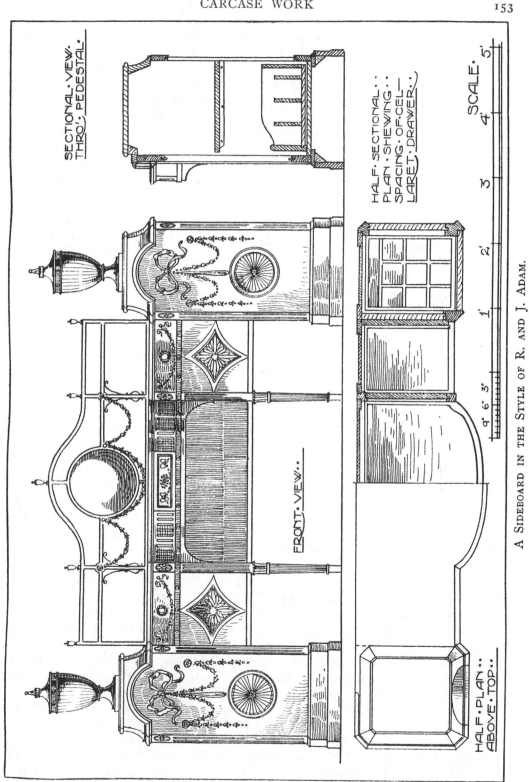

SECTIONAL·VIEW·
THRO'·PEDESTAL·

HALF·SECTIONAL·
PLAN·SHEWING·
SPACING·OF·CEL—
LARET·DRAWER·

SCALE·

9' 6' 3' 1 2' 3 4' 5'

FRONT·VIEW··

HALF·PLAN··
ABOVE·TOP··

A Sideboard in the Style of R. and J. Adam.

but the alternate fittings shown in f. II. and III. below and fixed to pivoted doors are also a feature of these sideboards. The sectional plan shows connection between centre part and pedestal, with false end dovetailed into carcase bottom and rails, and set back behind the pedestal pilaster with the drawer front overlapping. The half plan above top shows the joint line of tops, dowelled up dry, with the moulding worked on sides and front and run off at the back. Shaped tops of pedestals are executed as follows : — Rails are dovetailed into pilasters from back to

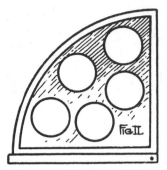

"Quadrant" Cellaret Fitting.

Semicircular Cellaret.

front, with a rail stub tenoned between them at the back ; these form a groundwork into which moulded pieces 3 in. wide are mitred round to coincide with the centre top. The built-up moulded hood is then glued in position, and the curved piece mitred, scribed, and glued. The part under this curved moulding is then cut away, and levelled off flush to receive the door. Doors are made from solid stuff, and clamped as shown in section, or laminated. The carving is cut to outline first, glued to the door, and finished in position.

WARDROBES.

There are many types of wardrobes, consisting of one, two, and three carcases, which are termed "Hanging," "Gentlemen's," and "Winged" wardrobes, according to their form and interior arrangement. The example shown on p. 155 is a "break-front winged wardrobe," and consists of a centre carcase containing four drawers and five sliding trays enclosed by doors. Both wing carcases are in this case fitted with a bottom drawer, intended to receive hats, &c., or an enclosure may be substituted, fitted with a hinged lid. Rails are screwed to the carcases about 9 to 12 in. from the top, to which the brass hanging pegs are screwed, these peg rails also supporting a shelf; but where the height of a wardrobe is insufficient for both drawer and shelf, the peg rail is fixed close to the carcase top, and additional swivel hooks are also screwed underneath the top. Half plan of plinth frame shows its construction, with moulding mitred round ; both cross rails and the back are made wider to allow for this extra thickness, whilst the cornice frame is mitred at the front corners, with lap dovetailed back rail ; a moulded top is screwed to this cornice frame, and brackets are dowelled into position. Arrangement of carcases will be understood from the diagram, the division between the drawers and trays being carried through full width. Trays are supported by two methods ; the neatest consists of grooving the tray side, and screwing hardwood slips against the ends ; the second method is to screw bearers of $\frac{3}{4}$-in. stuff to the ends and run the

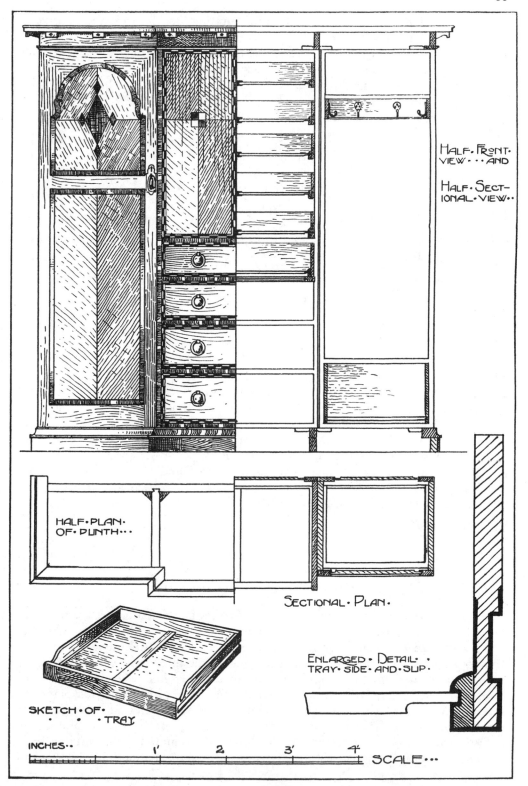

HALF·FRONT·
VIEW···AND

HALF·SECT-
IONAL·VIEW··

HALF·PLAN·
OF·PLINTH···

SECTIONAL·PLAN.

ENLARGED·DETAIL·
TRAY·SIDE·AND·SUP.

SKETCH·OF·
·   ·   ·TRAY

INCHES··   1'   2   3'   4'   SCALE···

AN INLAID WARDROBE.

trays between them.   It is expeditious in putting up the carcases to glue a
strip of $\frac{3}{16}$-in. stuff with beaded edge against the centre carcase ends; this
simplifies fitting the carcases together, and also prevents the edge of the door
rubbing against the end.   To fit the carcases up, set the plinth true upon a
level floor, place carcases in position, hand-screwing together where necessary,
testing and measuring pro-
jections, &c., then screw the
ends together, and also screw
down to the plinth; the cornice frame is also set in position, and screwed through the
carcase tops.   Now prepare
two dozen $\frac{3}{4}$-in. whitewood

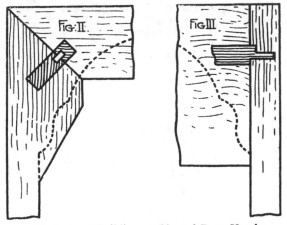

Methods of Building up Shaped Door Heads.

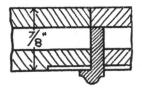

1. A Rebated Astragal
Joint.

blocks about 3 in. square, and glue and screw them to the carcases only in the
angles of plinth and cornice.   It will be necessary to unscrew the dust-board
from the cornice to effect this.   These blocks are shown in the front sectional
view, and ensure the carcases finding their correct position when fitting up again.
Both small doors are glued up in three thicknesses, the centre piece crosswise,
with an astragal moulding, as in f. 1 above.   Figs. II. and III. show different ways
of constructing the curved door heads, i.e., "mitred and tongued" and "tenoning" rail into stiles.   In both cases the shaping is done after glueing up,
then rebated, and the corners rounded.

A WINGED WARDROBE (next page).

This type of wardrobe is built up of five parts, named plinth, cornice, surbase, hanging carcase, tray carcase, and cornice, as illustrated in the key diagram.
False ends are fitted into the tray carcases, which allows the trays to slide past
the door edges when opened.   This is a general rule in carcases when both doors
are fitted inside the ends, and is, of course, not required when the doors are
hung over the ends. $\frac{3}{4}$-in. stuff is used for the false ends, with slips placed at
intervals in the space formed to prevent casting, and screwed through both
pieces from inside.   Heavy glazed doors are usually centre pivoted, and a stay
is fixed to the door and carcase at the top to prevent the door swinging back
too far.   The diagram shows the front top rail of surbase about 4 in. wide, and

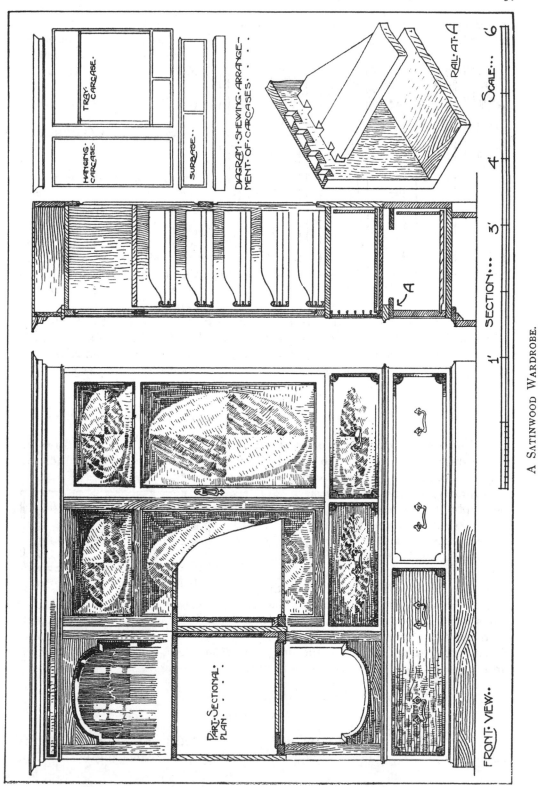

TRAY·CARCASE·

HANGING·CARCASE·

SURBASE·

DIAGRAM·SHEWING·ARRANGE-MENT·OF·CARCASES·

RAIL·AT·A

SCALE... 6'

SECTION... 3'

4'

A

1'

FRONT·VIEW··

PART·SECTIONAL·PLAN·

A SATINWOOD WARDROBE.

made up to give extra width for dovetails. Figs. I., II., and III. below show methods of making glass backs for large wardrobe doors. This example is reproduced by permission of Messrs J. S. Henry & Co.

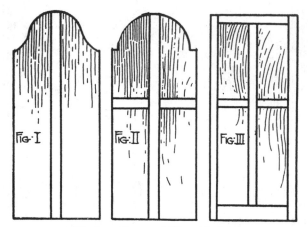

Various Types of Glass Backs.

A HANGING WARDROBE
(see opposite).

This is shown in front and sectional elevation. The large carcase is lap dovetailed together, with a framed-up back screwed in, and then wide pilasters are glued into the front. Reeded columns are fitted over the corners of carcase and surbase, whilst all moulding lines follow round the column lines. Refer also to chapter on "Practical Geometry." The best construction for the door with an elliptical glass panel is to mitre the frame together with tongued joints, then cut and rebate the ellipse, and glue a small moulding round on the outside edges as shown.

A GENTLEMEN'S WARDROBE (see opposite).

This consists of a chest of drawers, surmounted by a tray cupboard. In cases where the outline is similar to the diagram, and drawers are substituted for the tray cupboard, a "Tall-boy" chest is formed —accurately speaking, two chests of drawers, one upon the other—with plinth or stand, and a cornice. False ends are necessary in this tray carcase, and as blocking the carcases for position is impracticable in the ordinary way, fillets are prepared, cut through as in f. IV. alongside, a plan of bottom part. Both small pieces are glued down, and the darkened

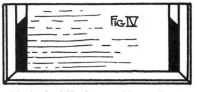

Method of Keying an Upper Part.

parts are fixed to top carcase. To mark for position, touch each bearer with glue, set top part in position, and, when dry, turn the carcase over and screw down each bearer. To make the shaped feet, cut them out of 5-in. solid stuff, and tenon in the pieces to complete the foot.

A WARDROBE.

The wardrobe illustrated on p. 160 was exhibited at the Arts and Crafts Exhibition in 1906. It was designed and made in Cuba mahogany by Mr E. J.

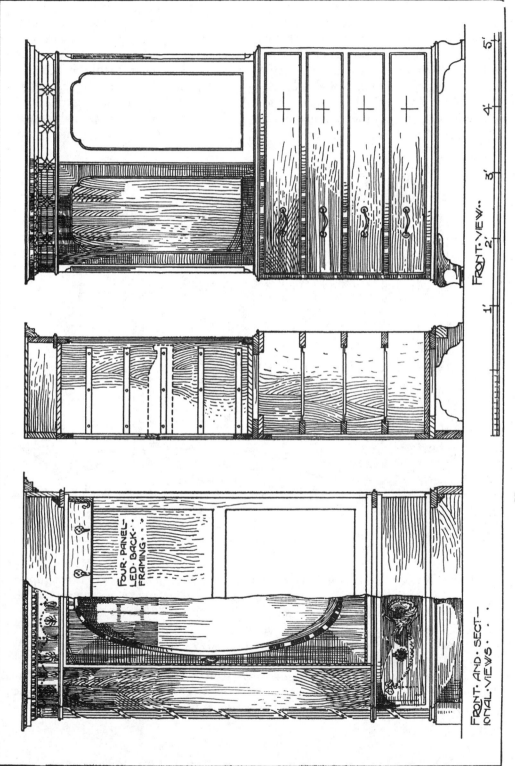

FOUR·PANEL-
LED·BACK-
FRAMING·.·.

FRONT·AND·SECT—
IONAL·VIEWS·.·.

FRONT·VIEW·..   1'   2'   3'   4'   5'

HANGING AND GENTLEMEN'S WARDROBES.

Minihane, and is well suited for a large bedroom or landing. As a piece of carcase work its construction is quite simple, consisting of three carcases, a plinth, and cornice. The centre part, with two doors, is fitted with trays and drawers, and the two wings provide good hanging cupboards, and a bonnet box. The design, which resembles the older type of "armoire" more than the modern wardrobe, is notable for its fine proportions, and in the simple but effective treatment of the doors, which are flush panelled and veneered with small figured stuff. The play of light on the diagonal markings in the pattern was a marked feature in the design. This effect is often lost sight of in the choice of veneers and figure,

A Mahogany Wardrobe by Mr E. J. Minihane

especially in satinwood stuff, which, when polished, presents a surface upon which some extraordinary changes in light and shade effects are visible, according to its position in the room. This kind of work must be carefully planned, and the figure matched as near as possible in regular lines, or a distorted pattern will result, which will always be made more prominent by the polish and light. The raised mouldings on the doors were grooved in, and the moulding on each side was "run out," so as to form the flat diamond-shaped stops which give a distinctly decorative treatment to the constructive detail of the doors. The "run outs" are easily worked on the spindle machine.

An Elliptical Writing Table (see next page).

This piece of furniture is introduced here in order to illustrate principles relating to carcase work which is shaped in plan. The application of these principles is constantly occurring in work of this kind—for example, in kidney-shaped and circular carcases—and it should be set out upon a 1-in. board in preference to paper, so that the templates can then be taken direct from the board. The method of making templates from a board is fully described in Chapter V., and in work of this character it is most important.

Commencing with the plinth, the necessary templates are obtained for the segments, and also the plinth mouldings. Then proceed to obtain the templates for frieze and drawer fronts; the top is marked direct from the board. When making the plinth frame, glue all the segments up, clean off the inside and brace them as shown in diagram. Next level the outside and veneer same (for description see chapter on "Veneering"), and then add the pilaster bases and the plinth moulding. The cross braces serve to strengthen the plinth frame, and also act as bearers for the carcases. The construction of the large carcase is shown in sectional plan, and the outside is built up or "coopered" with pieces of dry material about $1\frac{1}{4}$ in. thick, and 5 in. wide. These are bevelled and tongued together, planing to the true shape on the template after glueing up. Both inside ends are then constructed, framed together, glued between the pilasters, and finished off with curved pieces and door.

The drawer rails are now tenoned, the top rails dovetailed, and the carcase bottom fixed; this bottom runs right through the job, pinned at the divisions and pilasters, dovetailed where possible, and rebated and screwed. Fix runners on the ends, and prepare the dust-boards; the whole carcase is then ready to glue up. A diagram also illustrates the construction of frieze frame, with top rail set back behind the drawer fronts; this does not demand further explanation regarding construction; a moulding is glued under frieze, also in segments. Wherever possible, such furniture as this should be made in parts for convenience both in making and transit, but this is not always practicable in shaped work. In this case the frieze is definitely dowelled and fixed to the main carcase, the plinth being blocked and temporarily screwed. Another principle in connection with carcases containing drawers is to flush off the fronts after the drawers are fitted. To effect this, temporarily stop the drawers with their fronts projecting slightly beyond the rails, and level down. Take out the drawers, tooth, veneer, and clean up, and insert the drawers again, stopping them the required distance from edge of rails. This method is quickest in the end, and it ensures all the "squares" being equal, and with good effect. Details are shown of the top; this is framed together, moulded on the edge, and a lipping of cross-banded mahogany about $1\frac{1}{4}$ in. wide surrounds the leather lining; the moulding details and alternate treatment for pilasters are drawn two-thirds full size.

A writing table top of this size is best made in one solid piece, with a narrow cross-banding of satinwood round the leather lining. Two or more

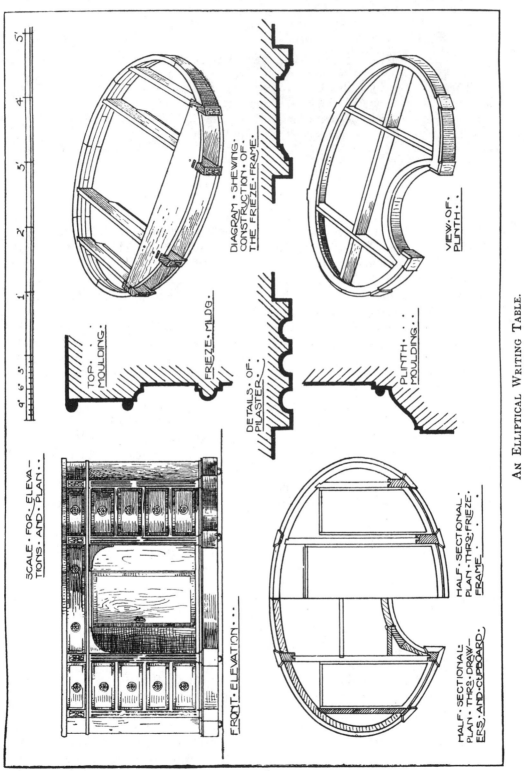

DIAGRAM · SHEWING · CONSTRUCTION · OF · THE · FRIEZE · FRAME ·

VIEW · OF · PLINTH · ·

TOP · MOULDING ·

FRIEZE · MLDG ·

DETAILS · OF · PILASTER · ·

PLINTH · MOULDING · ·

SCALE · FOR · ELEVA — TIONS · AND · PLAN · ·

FRONT · ELEVATION · · ·

HALF · SECTIONAL · PLAN · THRO · DRAW — ERS · AND · CUPBOARD ·

HALF · SECTIONAL · PLAN · THRO · FRIEZE · FRAME · ·

An Elliptical Writing Table.

skins are used butted together across the top with a simple edging or border. When shrinkage occurs in panelled tops, it creates unsightly cracks or breaks in the leather.

A QUEEN ANNE CABINET (see p. 164).

This cabinet is made up of a carcase and surbase only. In the majority of cases where a curved cornice is introduced, it will be found advantageous to carry the framing and ends right through, and make a dust-board rebate by using the cornice moulding, which is glued round the framing and ends, and allowed to project about ½ in. above them. The surbase is made first, and is tongued and dovetailed together with the ogee moulding mitred round. This is followed by preparing the top and bottom members as indicated in sectional view, and glueing them round also. Two cross rails and also the back rail are made wider, notched out to receive the moulding, when the surbase is tried up; the framing and ends are set out upon the top side, and made with wide top rails reaching to ½ in. below top line of job. Enlarged scale view of carcase bottom shows the method of connection to the framing, with a panelled back screwed into rebates. The bottom moulding in this carcase is rebated and glued into position, as shown in section. To prepare the cornice moulding, templates must be cut to shape for marking out the stuff; the front piece follows the outline of the carving, and the moulding is stopped a few inches each side of the centre piece. This requires extra thickness, obtained by glueing on a piece of stuff to the moulding before it is cut. It will also be necessary to slip dovetail a rail curved in outline between the pilasters in order to carry the moulding; also two rails between front and back for extra strength; the moulding is then mitred all round. Mention has been made of the dust-board; ½-in. stuff is used, finished to bare thickness. The large curve can be bent into the rebate, and secured with glue and screws. The side pieces are bevel jointed, and worked to true shape before glueing in. The end grain of these dust-boards must be at the front. In addition to glass shelves, which would require light metal bar supports, the back and sides are sometimes lined with silvered plate glass, fitting close against the back and ends, and fixed by rebated mouldings screwed round the outside of each sheet. This sectional view shows an alternate treatment for a silk-lined cabinet with a wooden shelf supported by brass studs.

A "WILLIAM AND MARY" CHINA CABINET (see p. 165).

(Manufactured by Messrs J. S. Henry & Co.)

The top part of this cabinet is constructed very similarly to the previous example, i.e., Queen Anne cabinet, with framed ends running right through,

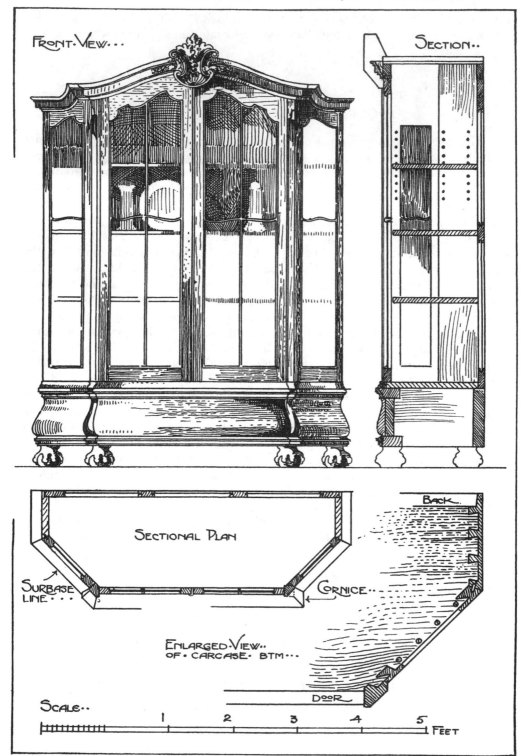

FRONT·VIEW···

SECTION··

SECTIONAL PLAN

BACK.

SURBASE
LINE···

CORNICE···

ENLARGED·VIEW··
OF·CARCASE·BTM···

DOOR

SCALE··

1   2   3   4   5   FEET

A QUEEN ANNE CHINA CABINET.

PLATE XIX.

164A

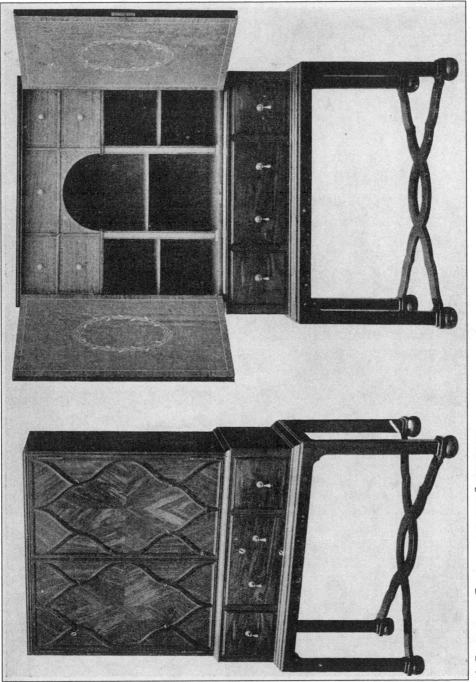

A CABINET IN COROMANDEL AND SATINWOOD.
DESIGNED AT THE L. C. C. CENTRAL SCHOOL OF ARTS & CRAFTS, AND MADE BY J. H. BRANDT.

PLATE XX.

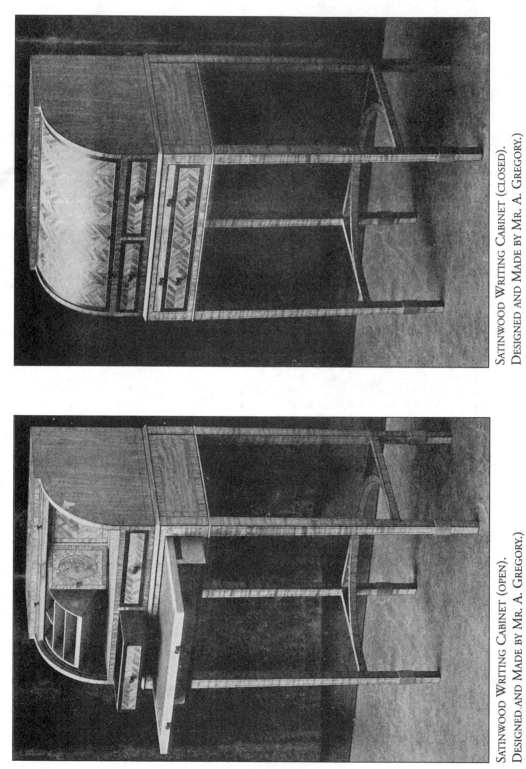

SATINWOOD WRITING CABINET (CLOSED).
DESIGNED AND MADE BY MR. A. GREGORY.)

SATINWOOD WRITING CABINET (OPEN).
DESIGNED AND MADE BY MR. A. GREGORY.)

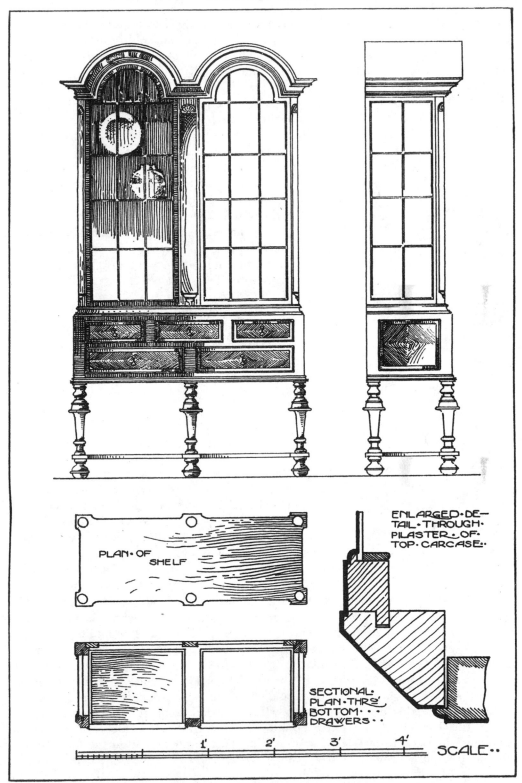

PLAN·OF·
SHELF

ENLARGED·DE—
TAIL·THROUGH·
PILASTER·OF·
TOP·CARCASE·

SECTIONAL·
PLAN·THRO'·
BOTTOM···
DRAWERS··

1'   2'   3'   4'   SCALE··

A "WILLIAM AND MARY" CHINA CABINET.

and a front rail dovetailed in between to receive the cornice moulding, and a pilaster stub tenoned into the rail.   An additional straining rail is also dovetailed between the semi-head to the back rail.   The bottom part of this cabinet has six legs, with either a shelf or a curved underframing above the feet; detail of moulding for this part is shown below.   This shelf or framing is fixed to the shafts by turning ¾-in. pins on to the feet, with corresponding holes in shelf and legs.   Place the shelf in position, well glue the pins, and cramp together.   The carcase is constructed by framing up the ends, setting the panel back, and mitreing a moulding round; the back is either framed up and

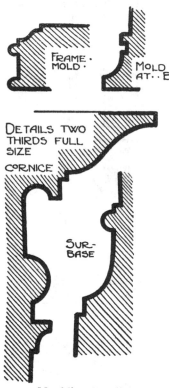

Moulding Details.

rebated in, or a solid piece dowelled between the legs.   The correct and best method of making the legs is to cut them from 4-in. stuff, and reduce the knee parts after turning, but, as this is an expensive procedure, a more economical plan is usually followed.   This consists of turning pins on the legs, and dowelling them into the posts on carcase.   In either case the centre legs are twin tenoned into surbase.   Rebated and moulded drawer fronts look exceedingly well (see detail on section), and effectively conceal any shrinkage in the drawer front.

A SATINWOOD CHINA CABINET

(see opposite).

China cabinets are made in an infinite number of forms, and the types reproduced on the opposite and following pages are such as introduce sound constructional features and characteristic details of the styles they represent.   The cabinet on p. 167 is made up of three carcases, the centre one curved in plan like a flat ogee.   It is not necessary to make separate cornices for this light form of carcase.   The ends run through, and pieces are dovetailed between the ends to form the frieze, which is veneered and inlaid.   The columns also carry through to the frieze moulding.   This is of kingwood cut over the corners as with the columns, with the small remaining piece of column glued on to the frieze.   A cornice is built up as shown in diagram, f. 1, p. 168.   The inlaid portion, circular in plan, is also cut over, the straight lengths of moulding glued down, and the cornice completed by the addition of a full top with moulded edge, screwed down from inside the carcases.   To mitre round the base moulding, all columns are grooved ⅛ in. deep to receive these mouldings, which are turned in the form of a ring, with straight lengths between them.   The diagram on the same page shows

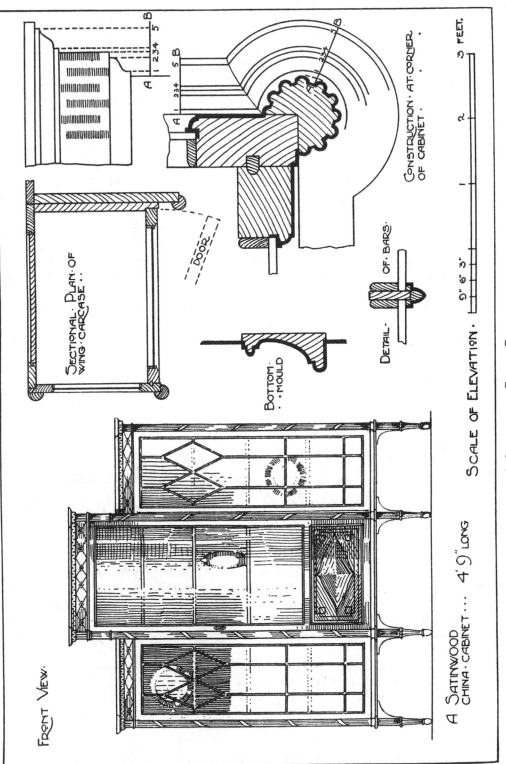

CONSTRUCTION AT CORNER OF CABINET.

SECTIONAL PLAN OF WING CARCASE.

DOOR

BOTTOM MOULD.

DETAIL OF BARS.

FRONT VIEW.

A SATINWOOD CHINA CABINET .... 4' 9" LONG

SCALE OF ELEVATION. 0" 6" 3" 1 2 3 FEET.

A SATINWOOD CHINA CABINET.

how to obtain the true mitre, when both are worked to the same section, and is further explained in chapter on " Practical Geometry." The shelves and interior parts of china cabinets are usually lined with silk or velvet, the shelves having a lipping or margin of polished wood about $\frac{1}{2}$ in. wide. This is formed by gauging round the edges, and recessing the wood about $\frac{1}{16}$ in. deep (see f. 2 below). When the material is glued down, the edge is concealed by this

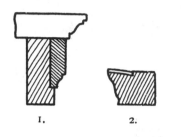

1.   2.

lipping, and a level surface is obtained upon the top side. Glass shelves are also largely used, $\frac{3}{8}$ in. thick, of plate glass, with slightly rounded edges, and are supported by screwing eyes into the cabinet angles, or as shown in accompanying details, f. 3 and 4. Although reeded and carved columns are used in this example, inlaid or marquetried columns are frequently met with in these cabinets, and demand very careful treatment when laying the veneer. It will be quite obvious to the reader that when several pieces are cut into a veneer to form a design, it will easily break upon attempting to bend it. The marquetry is therefore backed up with a piece of linen or silk, firmly glued on, and which, when slightly moistened, allows of bending round the column without splitting. Well glue the toothed column and wait until quite chilled, then pin down one edge of the veneer,

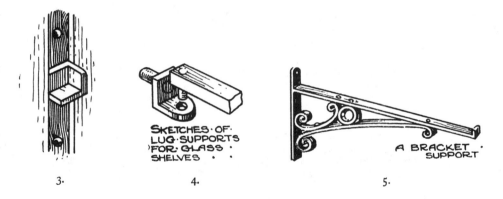

SKETCHES · OF · LUG · SUPPORTS 'FOR: GLASS · SHELVES · ·

A BRACKET · SUPPORT

3.   4.   5.

and carefully bend into position, binding tightly with wet webbing, until the whole is bound up. Thoroughly heat over a shaving blaze, which melts the glue, and at the same time dries the webbing, which contracts and expels the glue. The bottom space in the centre carcase may have either a fitted drawer or cupboard with an enclosing door—each would be equally effective—flush veneered and inlaid.

Fig. 5 shows a bracket support used when a fixing can be obtained at one side only, as frequently occurs with glass-lined cabinets.

A QUEEN ANNE WRITING CABINET.

On p. 170 are drawings and details of a fine type of writing cabinet. Its design is associated with the early Queen Anne period, and although it is not, as a rule, made up now, it contains many good features in its construction. Some of the old examples are veneered with the cross sections of walnut and lignum vitæ, the broad writing flap offering a suitable position for this type of work and decoration. The curved frieze was sometimes used as a drawer, especially in chests of drawers, and in some instances the top carcase was raised on legs. Italian walnut is the most suitable wood for a cabinet of this character, the striped figure being used to produce the "herring-bone" pattern on the drawer fronts. The ends of the carcase and the front edges of the drawer bearers were sometimes faced with cross-grained slips and rounded off, an expensive though very effective detail. The spacious inside carcase gives ample scope for nests of drawers, pigeon holes, and small lockers, and no one could wish for a more convenient and roomy cabinet. It is also known as a "Secretaire."

The section shows the falling front supported by rule joint stays. The inside of the fall would be lined for writing purposes, and sometimes it would include another small flap which could be raised to any slope.

The sectional view also shows the rebated joint of the carcase bottom

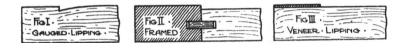

Methods of forming Lippings.

and corresponding rebate on the fall. During the eighteenth century Sheraton produced many examples of this kind, ornamented with characteristic details and veneering, and further improved the mechanical action of the fall. This was effected by introducing pilasters at each side, and allowing the interior to overlap the same on the inside; a cavity was thus formed between the stationery case and the carcase ends, in which a club iron movement operated. This is fully explained in the chapter on "Mechanical Actions," and has the advantage of providing a support almost entirely invisible from the front. The constructive features of this cabinet do not require special comment, the drawings conveying all necessary information apart from actual workshop practice.

Varieties of Linings.—This section of work, properly speaking, belongs to "Table Lining," an industry confined to covering flat surfaces of tables with leather or substitutes for same, and lining cabinetwork with velvet or other material of a like character. A few words regarding this branch, however, are very necessary when the lining of falls is being dealt with. "Lippings" are first necessary to receive the leather, f. I., II., and III. showing methods of forming them; the first example being only used in cabinet shelves, and effected by gauging a

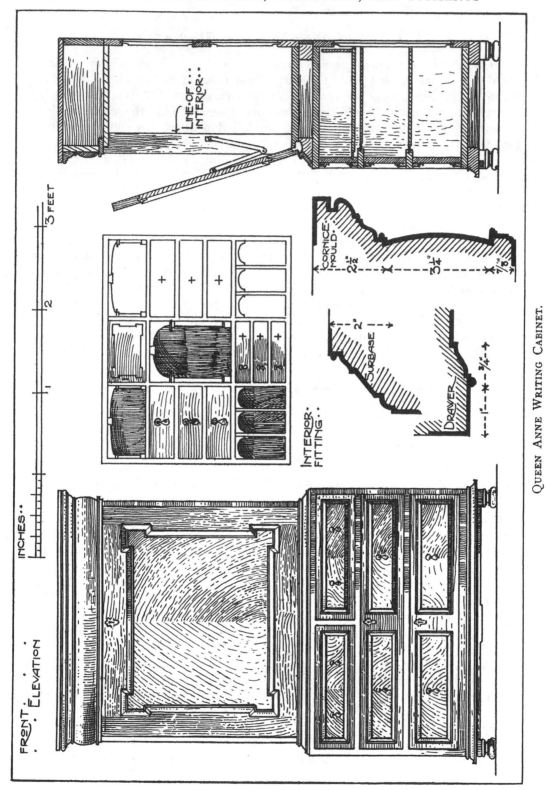

QUEEN ANNE WRITING CABINET.

line from the edge, cutting down to depth with a chisel. The best lining is "Morocco," a fine kind of leather, prepared from goat-skin, tanned with "sumach," and so called because it was first prepared by the Moors; "Roan" is an imitation of the above, made from sheep-skin; and "Skiver" is a more inferior imitation, prepared from split sheep-skin, and dyed to a large number of colours. Linings are fixed with a special preparation of paste to a toothed groundwork, and finished flush with lipping. With large surfaces the skins are butt jointed when laying. Various fancy borders complete the work, and these are executed with a heated branding tool, consisting of a wheel with a pattern upon the edge. This presses down the material, leaving a repeat pattern, in some cases gilt. The neatest finish is, however, without the gilding, and is termed "blind" bordering.

A SECRETAIRE BOOKCASE (see next page).

Secretaire bookcases were quite a feature of eighteenth century work, and many fine examples were made by Chippendale. The top parts were enclosed by barred doors, or flush, as shown in the illustration, p. 172. The writing drawer is drawn forward, and the front released by pressing

1. View showing Position of
Thumb Catch.

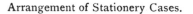
2.

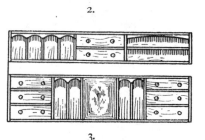

3.
Arrangement of Stationery Cases.

thumb catches fixed to both the sides (see f. 1 above); one edge of front is rebated, and also the bottom, see enlarged detail. Dolphin hinges are fixed as illustrated, and quadrant stays prevent the drawer front falling lower than a horizontal line. Dolphin hinges are described in detail in the chapter on "Brass-work." The bottom of the drawer, $\frac{7}{8}$ in. thick, is either cut from solid stuff and tongued into the sides, or it can be framed together—see also enlarged end view of drawer. It is prevented from withdrawing beyond the distance required by fixing two pieces of springy oak underneath, which fit flush into the bottom when inserting the drawer, and stop against the drawer when withdrawing. The upper doors are mitred, clamped, and veneered, with carving glued on after polishing, bottom doors framed and rebated. Fig. 2 shows the arrangement of stationery case, and f. 3 an alternate detail, with height increased to $8\frac{1}{2}$ in.

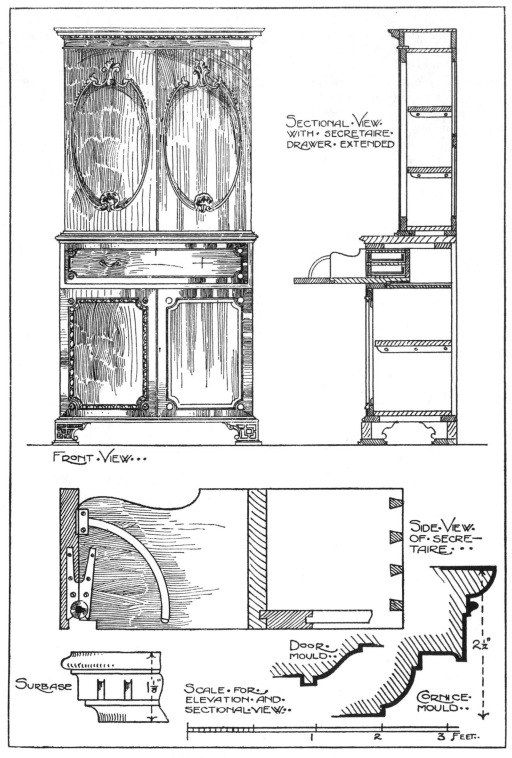

SECTIONAL·VIEW·
WITH·SECRETAIRE·
DRAWER·EXTENDED

FRONT·VIEW···

SIDE·VIEW·
OF·SECRE-
TAIRE···

DOOR·
MOULD··

SURBASE

SCALE·FOR·
ELEVATION·AND·
SECTIONAL·VIEW··

CORNICE-
MOULD··

3 FEET.

A SECRETAIRE BOOKCASE.

JARDINIERES.

This type of furniture, see f. 1, was generally used for ferns, &c., standing in front of large wall mirrors, but modern ideas of decoration have almost displaced them. The shape is shown in plan, the interior being divided into two parts, and lined with lead or zinc. Bevelled jointing is used for the curved ends,

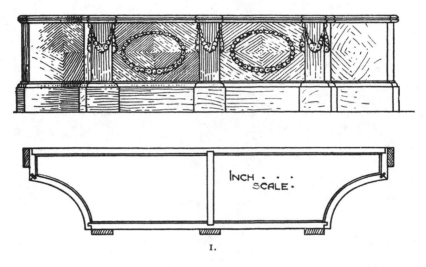

I.

the curved plinth rail being cut from solid stuff, veneered and moulded. The cap moulding is framed up, the interior linings having a flange or collar lapping over the inside edge. Smaller types of jardinieres are common, and are used for fern pots on tables and stands.

A DRESSING CHEST (see next page).

The drawings on p. 174 show, in the bottom part, a suitable treatment when the chest stands alone, with a small separate toilet mirror placed upon it. The upper part illustrates a construction frequently employed in dressing-chest top parts, viz., in the circular mirror, drawers, and shelf. The methods adopted in executing such work are of a general character, and apply to many other examples of

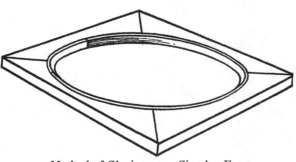

2. Method of Glueing up a Circular Frame.

this kind. A diagram shows the construction of the carcase, and a full drawer

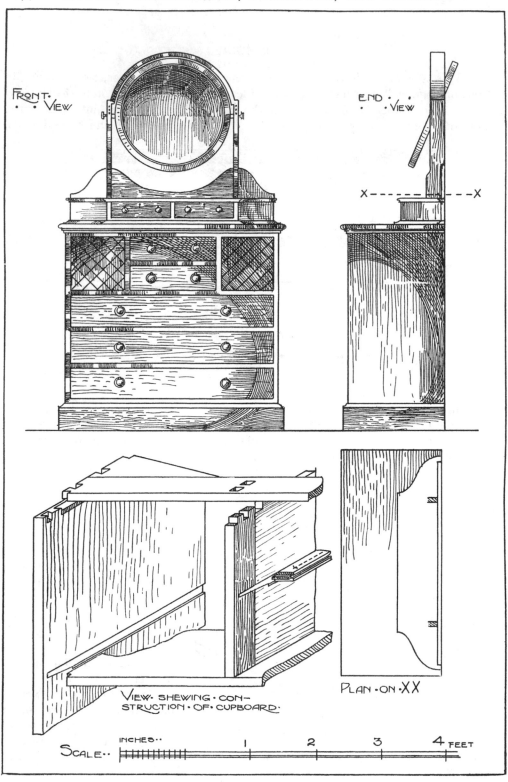

FRONT. VIEW

END. VIEW

VIEW. SHEWING. CON-
STRUCTION. OF. CUPBOARD.

PLAN. ON. XX

SCALE.. INCHES.. 1 2 3 4 FEET

A DRESSING CHEST.

division is introduced to serve also as cupboard bottoms, these being dovetail housed into the division and end ; the drawer runner is also shown, and the method of connecting it to the rail. A circular glass frame with cross-banded front is made by preparing a framing of whitewood (see f. 2, p. 173), the inside cut to the mirror size. This acts as a mould for building up the glass frame. Three strips of thin pine are prepared with toothed faces. One piece is sprung into the opening and forced against the wood. The butt joint should be cut slightly long to allow the strip to press against the shape. This process is repeated with the other strips, which should be warmed and glued before they are sprung into

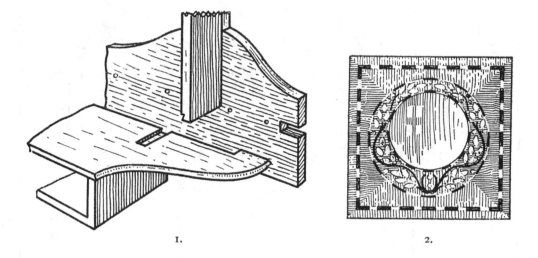

1. 2.

position. If carefully done, cripples in the stuff will not occur, and the joint can be rubbed down with the hand. Upon completion of glueing and drying, the frame is withdrawn and veneered, or faced up and moulded according to the design. The connection of the standards is illustrated in f. 1. The small carcase is made as shown, and the standards are slip dovetailed into the shaped shelf. The back is also shown, but this would be screwed in position after the standards were fixed. This shaped back is notched at both ends, and the shelf fits into the back rail, thus allowing the moulding to run through to the back line. Segmental building up is used for the shaped head, or it may be cut from solid stuff, and dovetailed into the standards. Fig. 2 shows an alternate treatment, veneered and inlaid, for the cupboard doors.

MUSIC CABINETS.

The arrangements for holding music in furniture are very diverse, ranging from a fitted seat to a substantial cabinet, with tray-lined upper part. The dwarf music cabinet shown on p. 176 has four drawers fitted in the lower part,

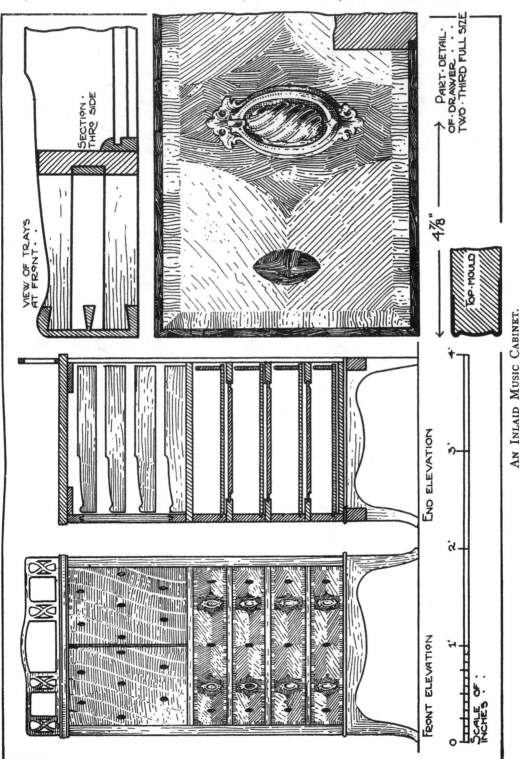

SECTION.
THRO' SIDE

VIEW OF TRAYS
AT FRONT.

PART·DETAIL·
OF·DRAWER.·.
TWO·THIRD·FULL·SIZE

4⅞"

TOP·MOULD

END ELEVATION

FRONT ELEVATION

4'   3'   2'   1'   0

SCALE OF
INCHES.

AN INLAID MUSIC CABINET.

providing storage capacity for bound volumes and portfolios, and a cupboard
fitted with sliding trays intended for sheet music.   Music cabinets of this
type are essentially a product of the twentieth century, many of them
embracing mechanical features in falling fronts to racks, &c.   The decorative
treatment of the example shown is in Italian walnut with inlays of snakewood.
The cupboard doors are mitre clamped and veneered, and the lines are
inlaid to the curved design
shown by cutting a template of
¼-in. hardwood.   This is temporarily fixed in position, and
grooves are cut with scratch
stock and cutter as indicated
in f. 1 alongside.   The process
of building up the veneered
patterns on drawer fronts is
described in Chapter IX.   A
curved stand is illustrated, built
up with square shoulders and
veneered.   The tray detail is
similar to that described in connection with a tray wardrobe in
this chapter, with slips fixed to
false ends (see also enlarged
detail).   A front elevation of a
music cabinet with falling front
is shown in f. 2.

1. Use of Scratch Stock against Curved Template.

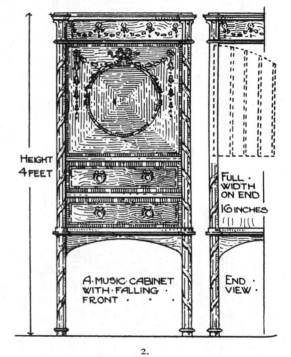

2.

A FLEMISH CABINET
(see pp. 178, 179).

The measured drawings of
this cabinet and the enlarged
details are taken from an example in the Victoria and Albert
Museum.   The part sectional
view illustrates the construction
of this piece, as it would be made at the present day, differing slightly from the
original.   Fine proportions and details are a feature in this cabinet, notably the
pilasters and the spacing of doors and panels.   The split turning and strapwork
on pilasters are of ebony, as are also the large ball feet.   An enlarged detail
shows the method of framing up the door, rebated to receive the splayed part,
which is mitred round and fits into the rebated frame.   Reference to the front
elevation also shows the method of fixing the feet.   Blocks are cut to fit inside
the corner of the plinth, and the feet are pinned into them.

12

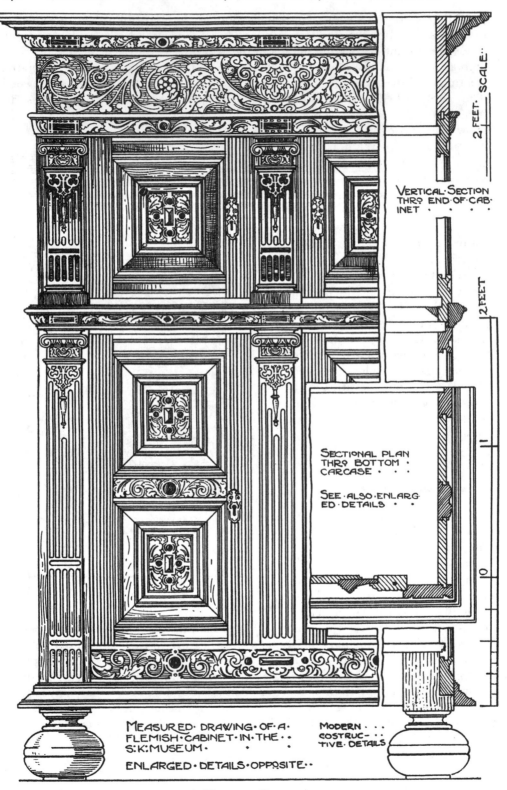

2 FEET · SCALE ··

VERTICAL·SECTION
THRO END·OF·CAB·
INET · · ·

2 FEET

SECTIONAL PLAN
THRO BOTTOM ·
CARCASE · · ·

SEE · ALSO · ENLARG·
ED · DETAILS · ·

MEASURED · DRAWING·OF·A·
FLEMISH · CABINET · IN·THE · ·
S:K:MUSEUM ·   ·
ENLARGED · DETAILS · OPPOSITE · ·

MODERN · · ·
COSTRUC· · ·
TIVE · DETAILS

A FLEMISH CABINET.

FRIEZE · MOLD · ·

CORNICE · · MOLD ·

EBONY INLAY

EBONY

SURBASE MOLD · ·

SCALE = TWO-THIRDS

ENLARGED · DE-TAILS · OF · FLEM-ISH · CABINET · ·

DETAIL · OF · PILAS-TER · CAP · STRAP-WORK · AND · BASE

DETAIL · OF CENTRE RAIL · ON · DOORS ·

DETAIL OF SPLIT TURNING ON · · PILASTERS · · ·

HALF · VIEW · OF · DOOR · PANELS ·

PILASTER · BASE ·

DETAIL · OF · · DOOR STILES

DETAILS OF FLEMISH CABINET.

A TALL-BOY CABINET.

This is a development of the "tall-boy" chest of drawers, in which a stand is substituted for the lower chest. The stand is quite characteristic of modern Queen Anne work, other examples of which are given elsewhere in the book.

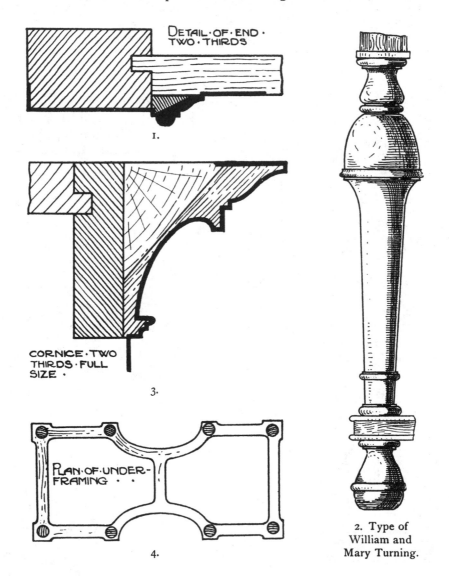

DETAIL·OF·END· TWO·THIRDS

I.

CORNICE·TWO THIRDS·FULL SIZE·

3.

PLAN·OF·UNDER- FRAMING · ·

4.

2. Type of William and Mary Turning.

The ends are put together first, and framed up as shown in detail, f. I, the divisions and bottoms are then connected, and the apron piece or curved rail in front is fitted over the bottom, as shown in sketch ; it is secured by dowelling, and stub

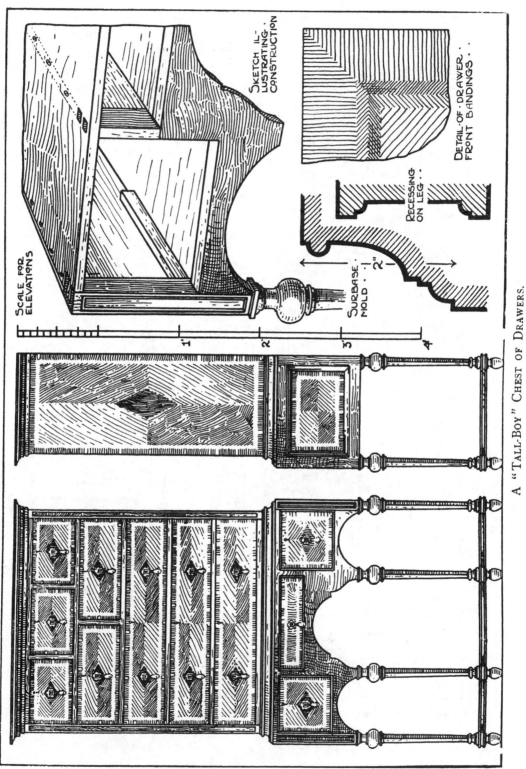

SKETCH IL-
LUSTRATING
CONSTRUCTION

DETAIL OF DRAWER
FRONT BANDINGS

RECESSING
ON LEG

SCALE FOR
ELEVATIONS

SURBASE
MOLD 2"

1' 2' 3' 4'

A "TALL-BOY" CHEST OF DRAWERS.

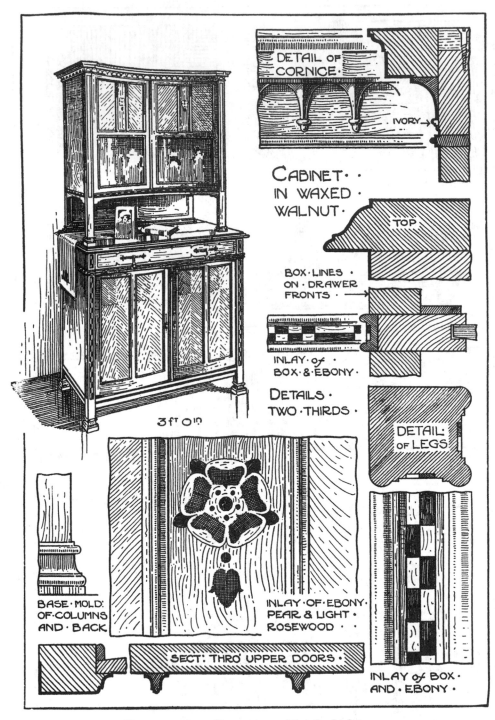

DETAIL OF CORNICE.

IVORY →

CABINET · · IN · WAXED · WALNUT ·

TOP

BOX · LINES · ON · DRAWER · FRONTS · →

INLAY · of · BOX · & · EBONY ·

DETAILS · TWO · THIRDS ·

DETAIL: OF LEGS

3 FT 0 IN

BASE · MOLD: OF · COLUMNS AND · BACK

INLAY · OF · EBONY, PEAR · & · LIGHT · ROSEWOOD ·

SECT: THRO' UPPER DOORS ·

INLAY of BOX · AND · EBONY ·

DESIGN FOR A CABINET BY MR A. J. JESSOP.
(Reproduced by permission of the Editor of the "Cabinet Maker.")

tenoned into the legs. The centre legs are made separately, and turned pins about $\frac{3}{4}$ in. diameter fit into the apron piece. Details of the leg for this cabinet are shown on p. 116 in connection with a writing table of the same period. The enlarged detail of turning, f. 2, on p. 180, is of the William and Mary type, executed in oak. When either kind of leg is used, the underframing is made separately, and the feet have turned pins fitting through the frame into the leg above. Fig. 3 is a sectional view of the cornice moulding with cross-grained facings, a special feature of Queen Anne work. The end panel mouldings and the surbase in this job are also cross-grained. Fig. 4 is a plan of the underframing.

The illustration on this page shows a simple arrangement for a bureau flap, by which the supporting slider is withdrawn or pushed home as the flap is opened or closed. It can be applied to any bureau flap which is supported by the usual

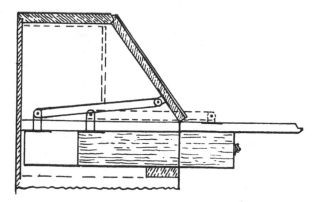

Simple Arrangement for a Bureau Flap.

slider, as seen in the designs on pp. 126 and 146. The movement is made of thin plate brass 1 in. in width. Both ends are riveted to a short piece of the same material, and in such a way that the centres work true and easy. These pieces are again fixed into a flat plate which is prepared for screwing into the slider and flap as shown. To obtain the length of the bar, pull out the slider to the required distance, in this case about one-third of its whole length, take half that distance from the bottom edge of the flap to the centre of the bar, and then from that point to the back end of the slider is the length of the brass bar, allowing for the plate. When this movement is used the solid shelf is not carried right through, or it is cut short at both ends to make a passage for the flange to work. The pigeon-hole case is made short and the filling-in piece cut to allow for the bar. For other movements see chapter on "Brasswork."

CHAPTER VIII.

BEDSTEADS AND MISCELLANEOUS FURNITURE.

Designs, Working Details, and Full size Diagrams of French, Four-Poster, and Ordinary Wood Bedsteads—Clock Cases—Grandfather, Section of Carcase, Details of Mouldings, Hinges, &c.—Balloon and Hanging Clock Cases, and how to make them—Chippendale Commode with Curved Front and Ends—Adjustable Pole and Wing Fire Screens—Folding Draught Screen—Swing Toilet Glass with Drawers—Wall Mirror—Hanging and China Cabinets—Combination Hall Stand and Seat—Revolving Bookcase—Dinner Waggon—Grand Piano—Corner Cabinet—Rising Dumb Waiter—Hall Seat—Pedestal.

APART from the special furniture for dining, drawing, and bed rooms, there are many articles such as clock cases, screens, &c., which are used in all. These are described in detail in the following pages, and it would be possible to enlarge on furniture for kitchens, bathrooms, and nurseries, which would, however, only mean a repetition of constructive principles given in such chapters as those on Table and Carcase Work.

A FRENCH BEDSTEAD (see opposite).

This type of bedstead has been almost superseded by the English pattern, in which the wooden rails are dispensed with, and iron bars with key blocks on posts substituted, but a general description of wooden bedsteads would be incomplete without an example of this kind. The sectional detail of foot on p. 185 shows the posts faced up and fluted; the foot end is built up in three thicknesses and cross veneered on both sides. This construction is usual with large panels in French furniture, and is rendered very necessary when dealing with large flat surfaces. The end is housed into the posts, and the carved mouldings are glued on after polishing. The head is framed up with the wide bottom rail, carving, and paterae as at foot. Both capping mouldings may be worked in the solid, and fitted to the shapes, or they may be

Connection of Rails at Ends.

worked to a template and glued on to the face sides, veneering the top edge after levelling off. Box spring mattresses are generally used with those

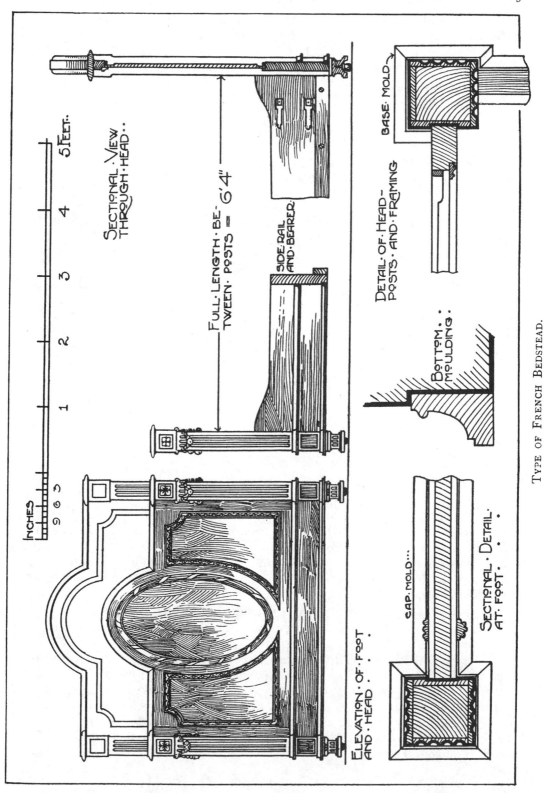

SECTIONAL·VIEW·THROUGH·HEAD··

FULL·LENGTH·BE-TWEEN·POSTS = 6'4"

SIDE·RAIL·AND·BEARER·

INCHES

9 6 3

1 2 3 4 5 FEET·

ELEVATION·OF·FOOT·AND·HEAD··

BASE·MOLD

DETAIL·OF·HEAD-POSTS·AND·FRAMING

BOTTOM··MOULDING··

CAP·MOLD···

SECTIONAL·DETAIL·AT·FOOT·

TYPE OF FRENCH BEDSTEAD.

bedsteads, and fillets are screwed to the inside of rails for supporting them. The rails are stub tenoned and bolted to the ends, see diagram on previous page, and also the view of a French bedstead bolt in f. 1 below.   The nut should be cut into the posts, and the spaces filled in with pieces of wood.

BEDSTEADS (see opposite).

These bedsteads do not require any detailed description of the construction, and are only given as types.   The attachment of side rails, however, must be noted; they are similar to an iron bedstead, with side rails and key blocks screwed to the posts, see f. 2.   Chain mattresses are frequently used in conjunction with iron or wood side rails.   Fillets should be fixed to the mattress frame underneath, close to side rails, thus preventing the frame from moving about; wooden slats are

I.

2. Detail of Key Block.

also occasionally used notched into rails, and are made of some serviceable wood about 3 in. wide and $\frac{3}{4}$ in. thick.

FOUR-POSTER BEDSTEAD (see p. 188).

The bedstead on p. 188 is of this type, and was manufactured by Messrs Heal & Son, of Tottenham Court Road.   It consists of a framed-up head, with turned posts at the foot supporting a canopy or tester.   These beds were most frequently made during the Elizabethan and Jacobean period, and the bed itself was usually a "truckle" or "trundle" type, quite separate from the posts and canopy; and could be drawn out when required.   A later development of this type of furniture is the French pattern, with construction similar to that illustrated on p. 185.   The head and foot frames are attached by rails, with a canopy projected from the head.   Chippendale and Sheraton both produced very ornate specimens of four-poster bedsteads, in which the use of drapery was a prevailing feature, drawn up into folded swags at the sides when not in use.   The framing and posts of these latter types were connected with rails—a decided improvement on the earlier examples—and canopies were panelled and made in the form of a cornice, fitting on to the head framing with holes bored at the bottom to receive turned pins on the pillars.   Fine examples of bed pillars are shown in the

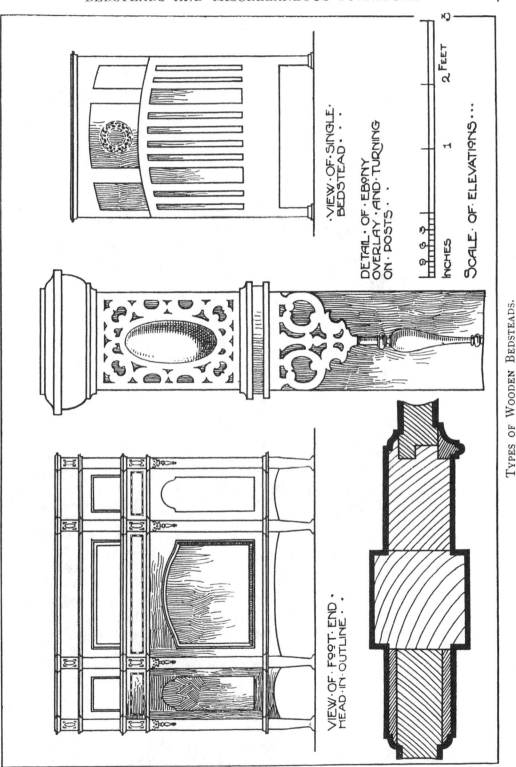

·VIEW·OF·SINGLE· BEDSTEAD·

DETAIL·OF·EBONY OVERLAY·AND·TURNING ON·POSTS·

SCALE·OF·ELEVATIONS···

INCHES 2 FEET 3

VIEW·OF·FOOT·END· HEAD·IN·OUTLINE·

TYPES OF WOODEN BEDSTEADS.

original books of Chippendale and Sheraton, and well repay careful study. The Elizabethan types are well represented in the Victoria and Albert and Bethnal Green Museums. The very ornate character of these early four-poster beds is accounted for by the social customs of the period, when the bed-chamber was frequently used as a reception-room.

A Modern "Four-Poster."
(*By Heal & Son.*)

CLOCK CASES.

A "hanging" or wall clock is shown on next page. It was executed at Shoreditch Technical Institute, and consists of a carcase formed by slip dovetailing the bottom between the sides, and the top is lap dovetailed. The front is veneered and inlaid with corner edgings of cross-cut kingwood on the sides and bottom. The plan shows the method of fixing the front, tongued into the sides and bottom, and the back is rebated and screwed. A door in this case is not required for access to the movement; if this is necessary the back is removed by unscrewing it. The movement is fixed to the end by a bracket attached to the back plate, screwed to the ends or riveted through. Before setting out or designing clock cases, the movement should be obtained and the case made accordingly.

A BALLOON CLOCK CASE.

The "balloon" clock case, also shown on next page, is simple in construction, but the veneering may prove troublesome unless properly handled. A sectional view shows the construction, viz., a block of beech or mahogany is cut to outline,

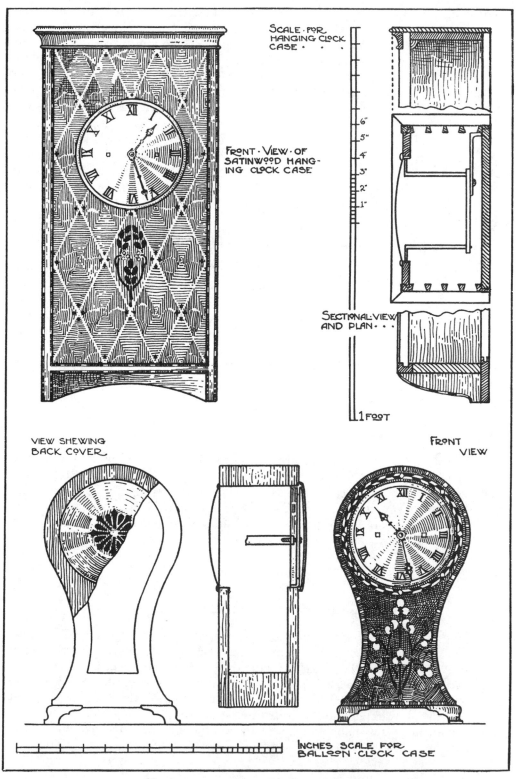

SCALE·FOR
HANGING·CLOCK
CASE···

FRONT·VIEW·OF
SATINWOOD·HANG-
ING·CLOCK·CASE

6"
5"
4"
3"
2"
1"

SECTIONAL·VIEW
AND·PLAN···

1 FOOT

VIEW·SHEWING
BACK·COVER

FRONT
VIEW

INCHES·SCALE·FOR
BALLOON·CLOCK·CASE

HANGING AND BALLOON CLOCK CASES.

with allowance inside for a short swing pendulum, the back and front are glued upon this shape and levelled off. Well tooth and size the case, and prepare pine cauls to fit the shape (see f. 1), also prepare three stiff pieces of cardboard to cramp under the cauls. Well glue the groundwork and allow to chill.

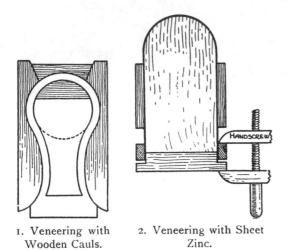

1. Veneering with   2. Veneering with Sheet
   Wooden Cauls.   Zinc.

Thoroughly heat the small caul and cardboard, and place the veneer in position at top, also a block inside case (see diagram), hand-screw caul to the shape, and carefully bend the veneer down each side, then place the side cardboards and cauls in position, and well cramp together across the case ; a strong block placed inside will prevent the joints breaking under pressure. The hand-screws should be fixed at the top first, and the veneer will then lay down without buckling. The usual movement is shown in this case. The bezel is attached to the movement and forms a rebate in front, which fits into a circular hole, and a cover is fixed at the back. Brass straps from the bezel are secured and tightened by set screws in the back rim as shown in section.

BRACKET CLOCKS.

This is a term applied to nearly all small clocks, and originated in the late eighteenth century because of their position, *i.e.*, standing on a wall bracket. The semi-head is a typical shape (see f. 2), the veneering of which is accomplished by screwing a piece of stiff zinc firmly to two blocks ; another block is also screwed temporarily to the bottom. The pressure is obtained by cramping as shown, and hand-screwing right across the flat sides.

GRANDFATHER CLOCK CASES.

The measured drawings and detail of a clock case, reproduced by permission of C. Vickers, Esq., represent the characteristic detail and proportion of the transitory period between William and Mary and Queen Anne. The influence of the latter period is clearly indicated in the semi-headed door and curved part of hood, as well as the bulbous shaped terminals of Dutch origin at the top. This example also illustrates the application of fancy hinges, shown in detail, and their position on the door ; the centre is brought forward and causes the door moulding to clear the groundwork immediately it is opened. This con-

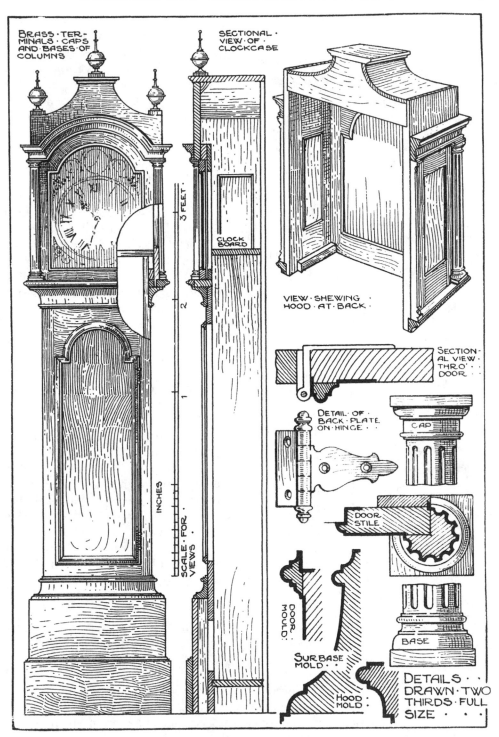

A GRANDFATHER CLOCK CASE.

structive principle is also shown in the Queen Anne cabinet in Chapter VII. A perspective view of the hood shows the method of connecting it to the shaft,

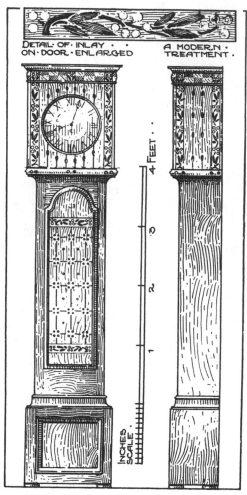

DETAIL·OF·INLAY· · ON·DOOR·ENLARGED

A MODERN TREATMENT.

4 FEET · ·

INCHES SCALE ·

A Modern Grandfather Clock Case.

the sides of which are as indicated in sectional front elevation, with a fillet fixed, and so forming a groove for the hood fillet to run in. The side panels are in this case of glass, but pierced brass panels are frequently used in eighteenth century work. The construction of end panels is determined by design, with a wide rail connecting them at top, the curved portion of hood being bent round and strengthened from inside. A back is fixed to the shaft portion of case, filling in the opening of hood when in position. Moulding details, characteristic of this period in woodwork, are shown, and the fixing of same is illustrated in sectional view; this also shows the construction of the shaft, with stiles running through to ground, and the surbase mitred round bearers or cross bars screwed to ground frame, and completed by the addition of the surbase moulding. Details of brass caps and bases of pillars are illustrated on p. 191, and also the plan of the column and door. An alternate decorative treatment suitable for modern work is indicated on this page, in which simplicity of outline is the keynote, the decoration being obtained by the judicious arrangement of contrasting figures in veneer, and the application of inlay.

A CHIPPENDALE COMMODE (see opposite).

The drawings show a Chippendale commode, shaped in plan with "bombé" front and carved legs, and "tern" feet. This piece, like many of Chippendale's productions, is distinctly Louis XV. in character, from which period many of his shapes and ornament details were taken—the "Rococo" detail being perhaps the most conspicuous instance. Many points, involved in the production

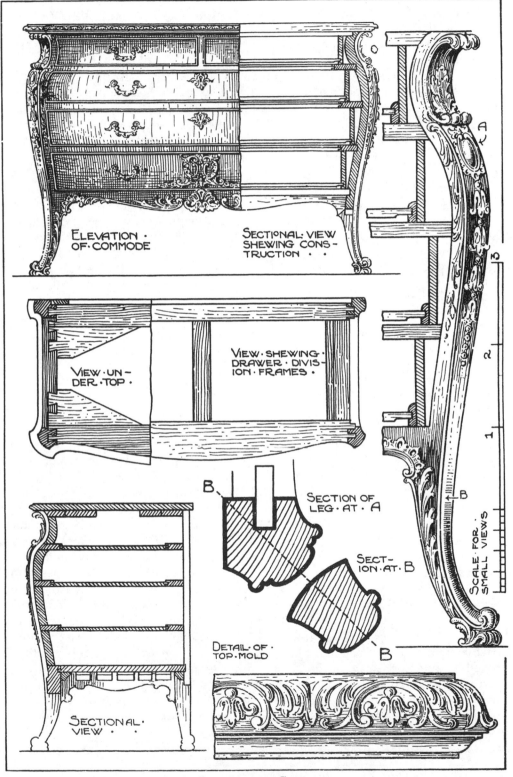

ELEVATION · OF · COMMODE

SECTIONAL · VIEW SHEWING CONS- TRUCTION · ·

VIEW · UN- DER · TOP ·

VIEW · SHEWING · DRAWER · DIVIS- ION · FRAMES ·

SECTION OF LEG · AT · A

SECT- ION · AT · B

DETAIL · OF · TOP · MOLD

SCALE · FOR · SMALL VIEWS

SECTIONAL · VIEW · ·

A CHIPPENDALE COMMODE.

of commodes, in this and also the French periods, are embodied in this example. The elevation, section, and plan illustrate the main characteristics, and when work of this character, shaped only in plan, is to be produced, it is customary, in addition to a working drawing conveying main details to the workman, to supply a carved pinewood model of one corner, carved up until the proper proportion and curves are decided, glueing on extra stuff where necessary, or, as an alternative, modelling clay is used upon a wooden groundwork. The best construction is then determined from the model, and templates can be prepared for legs and other shapes from the model. With "bombé" front work it is necessary to make a complete commode in soft wood, which is then modelled or carved up to the design. The advantage of such procedure is obvious, when considering that any alteration to the actual commode in an advanced stage would necessitate almost reconstructing the whole piece.

Wing of Draught Screen.

When cutting the legs, a template must be prepared to an outline on the diagonal line B B (see enlarged detail on p. 193). The legs are marked out to this template, and cut to shape—it will be necessary to square two sides of the front legs above the line of carcase bottom—and when this is accomplished, rails, bottom, and end are prepared. These latter are shaped in section only, and are best cut from 6 or 9 in. stuff, and glued up to the required width ; one end must be scribed to the inside of leg and dowelled up, completing the end by dowelling into the straight back legs. It is certainly advisable in work of this kind to glue up both ends before fitting in the front part, grooving the ends for division frames and bottoms before doing so. The drawer rails must be marked from the model. For this reason the fronts are simply driven in hand tight on the model, thus permitting proper templates to be made from rails. These are cut square to the line of greatest projection, and mortised and tenoned into the legs, completing each drawer rail or division by framing up as shown in sectional plan.

Drawer fronts are best cut from solid stuff to the approximate front shapes, and then fitted into the spaces, and stopped by temporarily glueing blocks behind them. The "bombé" shape can then be worked with planes and "floats," leaving the carved part, and when completed the fronts are withdrawn and gauged to thickness (see sectional view). If necessary the fronts are veneered with sand bags, and the carving shapes are glued on. The drawers can then be put together, as illustrated in the enlarged detail. Sides are set in from each end of drawer front, and slip dovetailed into the fronts. Pieces are then glued to the legs between the division frames and behind the drawer fronts, inserting guides in line with inside edges. It should be noted that with this method of construction it is necessary to make the end rails of drawer divisions of greater width in order to provide the extra material for drawer sides to run upon.

PLATE XXI.   SATINWOOD WARDROBE. BY THE BATH CABINETMAKING CO.

PLATE XXII. MAHOGANY CHINA CABINET.
DESIGNED BY MR. GEORGE JACK, AND MADE BY MESSRS. MORRIS & CO, OXFORD STREET.

FOLDING SCREENS.

The simplest and commonest type of screen is the threefold kind, consisting of framed-up wings with silk or wood panels. Knuckle joint screen hinges are used for connecting the wings, the fixing of which is described in chapter on "Brasswork." The sketch on p. 194 illustrates one wing suitable for a draught screen. A heavier type used in hotels, clubs, &c., has a moulded joint between the wings which renders it quite draught-proof. Special hinges are necessary for this screen, which are also described in the chapter on "Brasswork," and the joint itself is dealt with in "Joints and their Application."

FIRE SCREENS (see p. 196).

The Sheraton fire screen illustrated consists of a flush frame, rebated for glass and tapestry. Standards are tenoned into feet, and these are connected by the curved rail under panel; a rail is also fixed at the top in the back side, not shown in plan. It is readily adjusted to any height, and for this reason the standards are grooved, the frame fitting inside them. Screw movements are illustrated for supporting the frame, but springs fixed at either side of the top rail pressing against

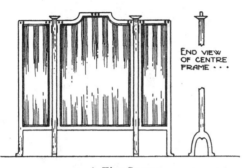

END VIEW OF CENTRE FRAME · · ·

1. A Fire Screen.

2. Pole Screen Fitting.

the back are more satisfactory, on the same principle of those illustrated in f. 2. A winged fire screen is illustrated in f. 1, the outside wings are hinged to the centre frame, and the outside stiles of these frames are carried through in the form of a leg.

POLE SCREENS (see p. 196).

A Louis XVI. example is illustrated, drawn in elevation and plan, and f. 2 on this page shows a steel spring attachment. The panel is adjusted by simply pushing upwards or downwards. These pole screens were fashionable in the eighteenth century, and Chippendale, Hepplewhite, and Sheraton designed them in their own styles. The design of the one shown is similar to Sheraton work, as he adapted the Louis XVI. details. Various methods were used for the construction of the base, the commonest of which were the triangular block with curved sides, and the claw feet; but the method shown in the design tends to lessen the length of the pole and gives it a better proportion. They were usually made of satin or rosewood, and the shape of the screen frame varied from circular, shield, and oval, to square or rectangular.

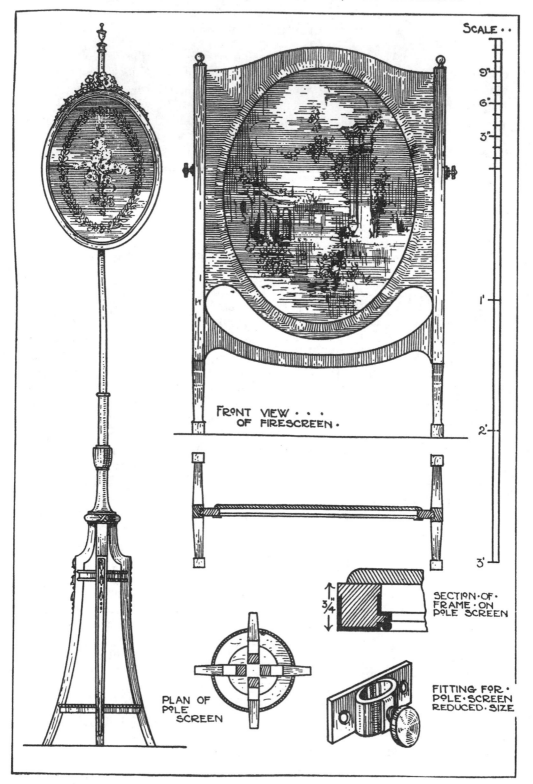

SCALE ..

9"

6"

3"

FRONT VIEW . . .
    OF FIRESCREEN.

1'

2'

3'

3/4"

SECTION · OF ·
FRAME · ON ·
POLE SCREEN

PLAN OF
POLE
    SCREEN

FITTING · FOR ·
POLE · SCREEN
REDUCED · SIZE

POLE AND FIRE SCREENS,

A CORNER CABINET (see p. 198).

As mentioned previously in connection with the drawing of a hanging cabinet, these examples adequately illustrate the constructional features of corner cabinets. A drawer is introduced in this example, although it is not recommended where there is not sufficient running surface. The drawer is similar in shape to the plan, and as the sides are of necessity very short, two muntings are fixed underneath the drawer (see f. 1) with centred dovetailed grooves. Runners are also fixed to the drawer rail and back, with a dovetailed key piece fixed upon it and sliding in the dovetailed groove. These act as guides when working the drawer. The construction of the top carcase is

1. View showing Underneath Side of Drawer.   2. Clamp on Top.

illustrated, showing the dovetailed joints of carcase top. A solid top with carved edges is used to form a cornice. Fig. 2 illustrates the method of clamping this piece to avoid the end grain for carving upon. To fix the bottom in lower carcase, groove about $\frac{1}{4}$ in. deep into back frames and pilasters, tenoning at front. When the carcase is glued together screw the bottom through back frames and well block the angles underneath. Both bottom doors are flush veneered with mouldings mitred round. Clamped ends prevent the doors casting, and they are also veneered on both sides. The detail of moulding is shown and also the meeting joint.

A DINNER WAGGON (see p. 199).

Dinner waggons are intended to carry extra dishes and dining-room accessories not immediately required on the table, and as such should contain good shelf, cupboard, and drawer space. This is amply provided for in the type illustrated, which is far superior to the "shelf and column" variety. Revolving castors should be fixed on the feet, for easy transit about the room. The lining under the top should be framed up and slot screwed to the top. A sketch indicates the connection of drawer rail with side, with the mitred moulding above the pillar. The doors should be of three-ply oak, and the panelling obtained by glueing $\frac{1}{2}$-in. strips of oak on the surface, the outside margin being mitred round the edge of door. This serves a double purpose, i.e., in concealing the three-ply joints, and showing the required margin for panelling. When the pieces have been fitted and glued to the groundwork, it is levelled off and cleaned up before mitreing and glueing the mouldings (see detail of door mould). The drawer fronts are rebated to receive the moulding, see sectional view of drawer front on the line A A.

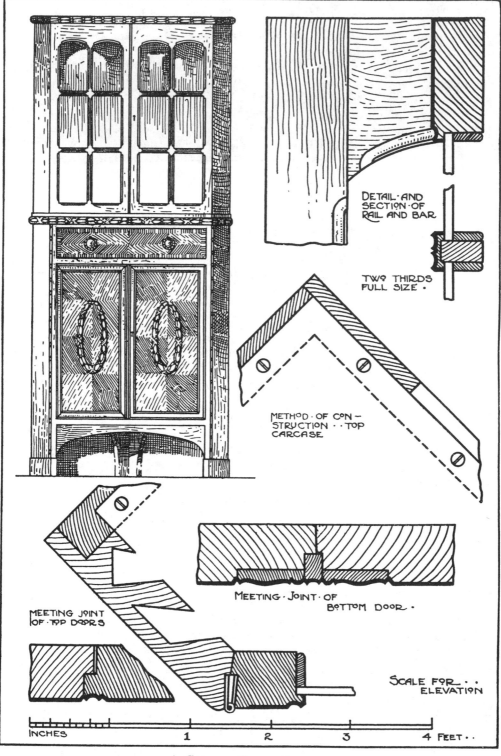

DETAIL·AND
SECTION·OF
RAIL AND BAR

TWO THIRDS
FULL SIZE·

METHOD·OF·CON-
STRUCTION··TOP
CARCASE

MEETING·JOINT·OF
BOTTOM·DOOR·

MEETING JOINT
OF·TOP·DOORS

SCALE FOR··
ELEVATION

INCHES   1   2   3   4 FEET··

A CORNER CHINA CABINET.

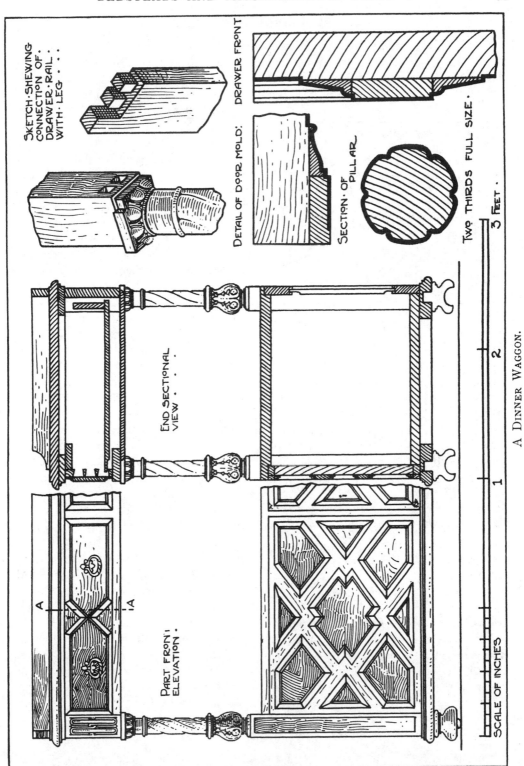

SKETCH·SHEWING·CONNECTION·OF·DRAWER·RAIL·WITH·LEG·

DRAWER FRONT

DETAIL OF DOOR MOLD·

SECTION·OF·PILLAR

TWO THIRDS FULL SIZE·

END SECTIONAL VIEW·

PART FRONT ELEVATION·

A DINNER WAGGON.

FEET·

SCALE OF INCHES

REVOLVING BOOKCASES.

There are three different methods of construction used in these bookcases, the best type being illustrated on next page. The sectional view shows detail of centre post, in this case of pine faced up with walnut; it also shows the shelves grooved into the post. This is further illustrated in the plan, in which is seen the construction of the framed shelves. These are secured on the outside by the pilasters, screwed to the shelves, or, as in the majority of cases, screwed laths instead of the solid piece. A patent revolving action is illustrated, much easier to manipulate than the other details described below. The plan also shows the shape of base board, with socket plate screwed in position. The second constructive detail is given on this page. A post is boxed up of $\frac{7}{8}$-in. stuff, and both ends are filled in with a block. The revolving process is effected by means of a turned pillar, bored through the pillar bottom, with a 1-in. pin turned at top, forming a shoulder as shown, which receives the whole weight of bookcase. A base is made of $1\frac{3}{4}$-in. stuff X, to which the centre pillar is mortised, and bolted as shown, and is further strengthened by the addition of four brackets. A third construction consists of building up the bookcase with a faced-up centre post, and fixing a short pillar to the X piece. The bottom of bookcase rests upon four flush plate castors, sunk into the base, and revolves upon them, but this is the least satisfactory method for this kind of bookcase. The system of jointing shelves as illustrated is undoubtedly the best, but four shelves are frequently used to form one tier, and the joints are concealed by the book stops, the position of which is shown in the diagram on this page. The solid side supports illustrated on next page are an unusual but effective treatment, executed in Italian walnut, with inlays of rosewood, snakewood, and ebony, and herring-bone inlays of Italian walnut. Spots are introduced in lines with the shelves, concealing the screw fixings.

Views of a Revolving Bookcase.

HALL-STANDS (see p. 203).

Although hall-stands are generally simple in character, seldom exceeding the bare accommodation for wearing apparel, sticks, and umbrellas, they

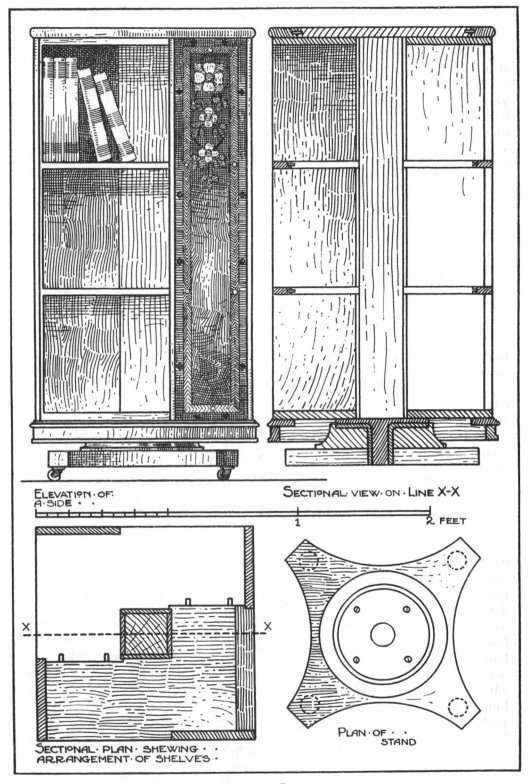

ELEVATION·OF·
A·SIDE · ·

SECTIONAL· VIEW·ON· LINE X-X

1 2 FEET

SECTIONAL· PLAN· SHEWING · ·
ARRANGEMENT· OF SHELVES ·

PLAN· OF · ·
STAND

A REVOLVING BOOKCASE.

are made more imposing and useful when the hall is of sufficient size to receive a large piece of furniture.   The example illustrated has the added advantage of providing for ordinary requirements, and also a seat with receptacle for indispensable accessories.   The hanging capacity could very well be increased by adding another panel to the back—thus increasing the space between enclosures—and also by inserting cross rails between the side frames, and adding pegs as required to serve for hats.   The features of this stand are a panelled back with pilasters and consoles supporting the cornice.   The whole of the front part is framed together and mortised to the back framing.   Fig. 1 is a sketch showing the construction of the back.   It will be noticed that the shoulder line falls behind the pilaster, thus avoiding an unsightly line across the top rail.   The arrangement of tenons and tongue will also be seen from this

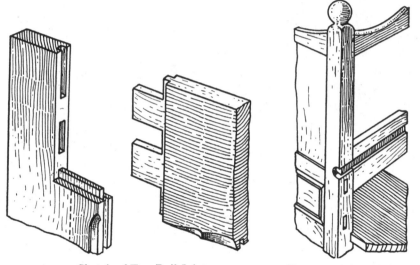

1. Sketch of Top Rail Joint
with Stile.

2. Sketch showing Construction
of Enclosures.

diagram.   The bottom part of back is panelled with a flush surface at the front, not shown.   Fig. 2 is a sketch showing the inside return of enclosures.   A space is left underneath the rail for withdrawal of pan into the centre part.   The outside returns of enclosures are panelled similar to front, and the bottom is grooved in position, as shown in section.   All stiles are allowed to run right through to floor line, and a skirting is mitred round after the whole job is together.   The sectional view also shows the arrangement of cornice.   Brackets are fixed at intervals, and the moulding between the consoles is made wider to overhang the brackets.   Wooden pegs are tenoned through the back frame, and secured by wedging from behind; they should be cut square to profile, and worked to an octagonal shape.   A sketch is also shown of the pan section with rolled edge.   This forms a supporting flange or collar, necessary in some stands. The arrangement of the seat will be understood from the diagram.   A three-sided frame is made, housed between the enclosures, with a clamped top hinged to the back rail.   The bevelling at panel heads in the back is obtained

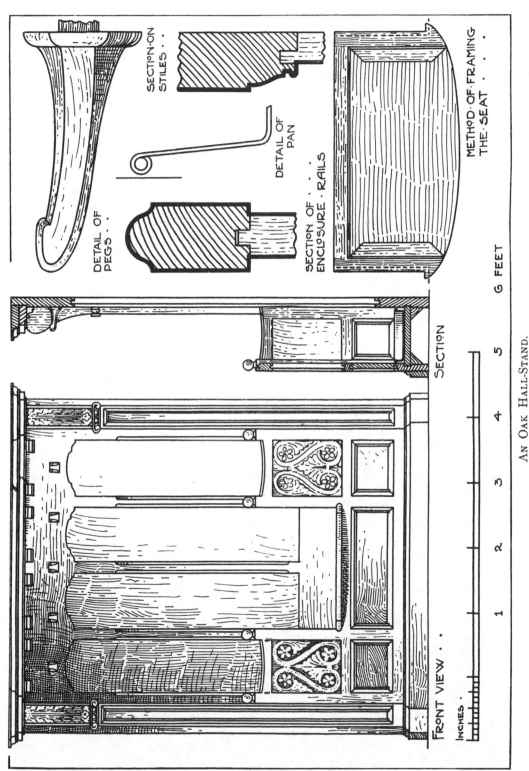

DETAIL OF PEGS · ·

SECTION-ON STILES · ·

DETAIL OF PAN

SECTION OF · · · · ENCLOSURE · RAILS

METHOD · OF · FRAMING THE · SEAT · ·

SECTION

FRONT VIEW · ·

INCHES ·

1 2 3 4 5 6 FEET

An Oak Hall-Stand.

by setting back the panel from the face, and spokeshaving the square edge of rail to the required shape.

A HANGING CABINET (see opposite).

The hanging cabinet illustrated here with veneered doors is also referred to as a medicine chest, as distinct from the other example with moulded and glazed doors, used for the display of china. A separate carcase with surmounting cornice is frequently met with, but appears hardly necessary in such small work. The construction employed in the first example is to carry the outside ends right through to the dust-board. The inside ends are attached to the carcase top by pinning, and the rest of joints, carcase top to sides, and bottoms to ends, are housed and dovetailed. The frieze rail is grooved into the ends, and veneered when glued up. Enlarged detail of cornice mouldings is given, the decoration composed of alternate East and West Indian satinwood dentils. The carcase back should be framed up, and the shaped piece at bottom tongued to the panelled frame, thus avoiding unsightly shoulder lines.

A HANGING CHINA CABINET (see opposite).

This example, together with the above and the corner cabinet also dealt with in this chapter, practically embodies all the points likely to be met with in this class of work. The plan shows the back frames rebated and screwed together, and tongued into the pilasters. The carcase top and bottom are rebated, dovetailed, and screwed into the frames and pilasters. The top is moulded with indentations carved at intervals, the bead run out as shown. The door frame is dovetailed together, and the moulding on edge of bars is also run out. To work the wave bars, they must be shaped to plan before cutting the elevation curves and matching the moulding.

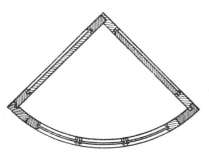

Sectional Plan of Corner Cupboard.

A PEDESTAL (see opposite).

The drawing of a Chippendale pedestal is given to illustrate general proportions and method of preparation for carvings. Sheraton, Hepplewhite, and Adam also produced these pedestals, and the differences consist rather in the decoration than in the proportion and construction. The actual groundwork is very similar in all cases. The shaft is mitred and tongued together, and well blocked inside ; the base is built up and veneered, and a subsidiary top is dowelled to the shaft. The carvings are roughly cut to profile, rebated and scribed to the groundwork. These are glued in position, and screwed where possible from the inside, and finally carved to drawing. The sectional view shows the building up of the curved top.

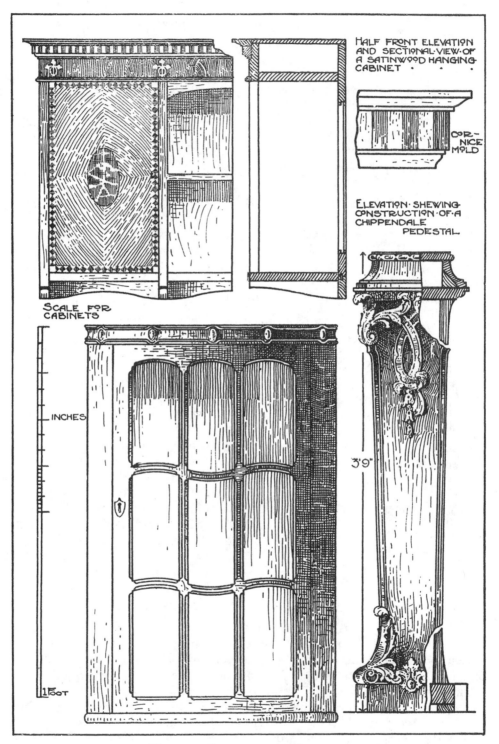

HALF FRONT ELEVATION
AND SECTIONAL VIEW OF
A SATINWOOD HANGING
CABINET

COR-
NICE
MOLD

ELEVATION SHEWING
CONSTRUCTION OF A
CHIPPENDALE
PEDESTAL

SCALE FOR
CABINETS

INCHES

1 FOOT

3'9"

Hanging Cabinets and Pedestal.

A TOILET GLASS (see opposite).

This pattern toilet glass with drawers below is both serviceable and decorative, and the bottom part is put together as shown in sketches. Secret lapped dovetailing is used for the top, and a rebate is thus formed to receive the moulding at the ends ; this is also continued along the front edge.

The inside vertical divisions should be housed and slip dovetailed into the top and bottom, with similar joints in the horizontal divisions (see sketch on next page). Bevelled dovetailing in top drawers is also illustrated with cocked beads round edges. The glass frame is mortised and tenoned together and veneered with Italian walnut on the face side, a $\frac{1}{4}$-in. edging of purplewood is glued round the frame, firmly bound with tape until dry. If any difficulty is experienced in bending the edging, a heated iron bar will expedite matters. The wood is moistened on the outside and bent round the bar until the desired curve is obtained (see f. 2). To make the feet a length of moulding is worked to section shown, and cut off in lengths. These are mitred and tongued together, the curves cut and the feet screwed to the carcase.

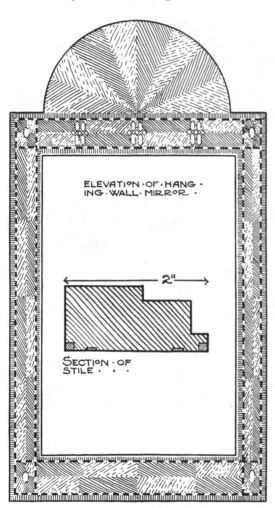

ELEVATION · OF · HANG · ING · WALL · MIRROR ·

2"

SECTION · OF STILE · · ·

1. Inlaid Hanging Wall Mirror.

A HANGING WALL MIRROR (see above).

The frame in f. 1 is the modern successor to the carved girandoles and candelabra mirrors of the late eighteenth century. Rosewood is the material used, with a groundwork of mahogany, and the inlay of satinwood. After setting out the pattern full size on paper, the veneers are cut and fitted, then pinned to groundwork and the joints secured with strips of paper. When the veneer is laid the grooves are scratched for inlay and the lines inserted.

2. Bending Lines round Heated Bar.

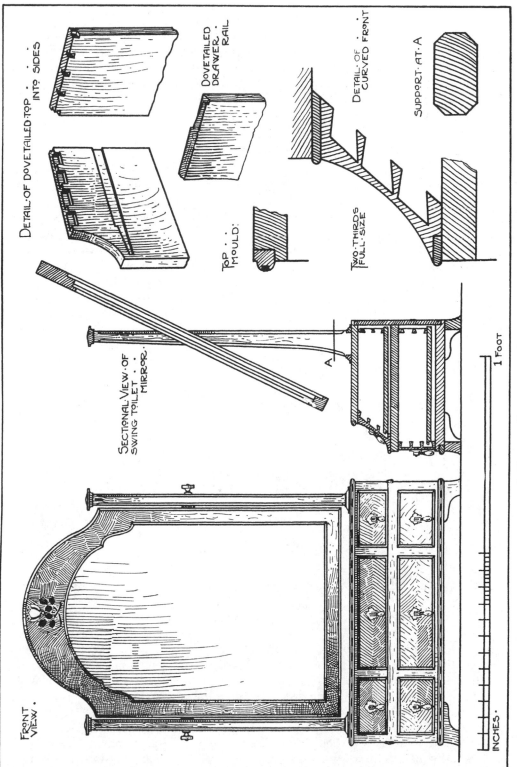

DETAIL·OF·DOVETAILED·TOP·INTO·SIDES

DOVETAILED DRAWER·RAIL

DETAIL·OF·CURVED·FRONT

SUPPORT·AT·A

TOP·MOULD·

TWO·THIRDS FULL·SIZE

SECTIONAL·VIEW·OF SWING·TOILET·MIRROR·

A

FRONT VIEW·

1 FOOT

·INCHES·

A TOILET GLASS WITH DRAWERS

A HALL SEAT (see opposite).

This simple hall seat in oak with carved strapwork frieze (executed at Shoreditch Technical Institute) illustrates the general proportions and sizes of this class of furniture. The back frame is moulded and housed into the posts, tenoning the top and bottom rails, with the cap moulding dowelled to framing. The seat is tenoned at the front and well blocked underneath, with span rail stub tenoned into legs and screwed to seat.

A DUMB WAITER.

This article of furniture, curiously but appropriately named, is intended for use as an additional receptacle for dishes. It is also made in circular form of two tiers to stand in the centre of a dining-table, revolving as required. Dumb waiter movements for the circular type can be obtained to fit a turned pillar with plate or flange screwed to the top. The drawings below illustrate the rising and falling pattern, the sectional view showing the waiter with top raised. A reference to the other sectional view shows a roller fixed in the post, and the sliders connected with webbing. When not in use, the springs fixed to outside slides are pressed in, allowing the top part to descend, at the same time effecting a rising action in the shelf, this fitting under the top. To counterbalance the difference in weight between the shelf and top, sheet lead should be fixed to the underside of shelf. A sectional plan of pillar is also shown, with the outside slide grooved, which is to receive a corresponding projection left on the shelf, an additional preventive against running untrue. The pillar is boxed up as indicated in plan, mortised into the stand at bottom, and further strengthened by the addition of curved brackets, a centre rail connecting the two pieces at the bottom. Horizontal supports for shelves are in bracket shape attached as shown to the sliders, the top bracket is also

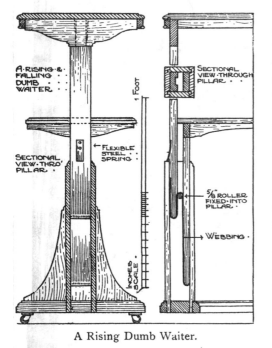

A Rising Dumb Waiter.

fixed to the lining up of top. A centre rail is introduced between the inside sliders under the shelf, acting as a gauge or binding between both slides. Various materials were used in dumb waiters to connect the slides at bottom, such as cord and catgut, working upon a double roller, but the fixing of these materials is unsatisfactory, and webbing fixed as shown in sectional view is strong and permits of proper fixing, as well as providing a much increased running surface. An ovolo moulding is worked round three sides of the pillar at top, the outside edges left square with a brass plate inserted to provide a seating for the spring.

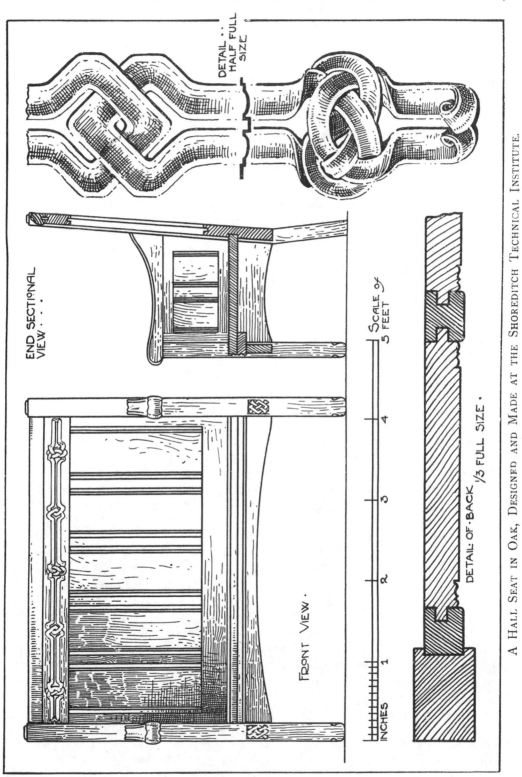

DETAIL·. HALF FULL SIZE

END SECTIONAL VIEW·. . .

FRONT VIEW.

SCALE of 5 FEET

INCHES 1 2 3 4

DETAIL·OF·BACK ⅓ FULL SIZE·

A Hall Seat in Oak, Designed and Made at the Shoreditch Technical Institute.

CHAPTER IX.

VENEERS AND VENEERING—MARQUETRY AND INLAYING.

Veneering, Decorative and Constructional—Veneers, Saw-Cut, Knife-Cut, Hand-Cut—
Burrs—Curls—Feathers, &c.—Preparation—Laying—Finishing on Flat and Curved
Surfaces—Treatment of Old Work—Marquetry—Buhl Work—Inlaying, Wood,
Metal, Pearl, Ivory—Stringing—Banding—Parquetry—Intarsia.

VENEERING is an old and decorative art. In the British Museum some
examples of Egyptian work may be seen which are thousands of years old.
From that day to this it has influenced the construction and design of household furniture. In ancient Rome the choicest and costliest pieces of work were
the tables veneered with rare woods. In Italy cabinets were veneered with
tortoiseshell, ivory, and ebony, and inlaid with pearl and precious stones. In
the Dutch and French work of a later period it reached an exalted place in
furniture decoration, and in our own eighteenth century the masterpieces of
Sheraton and Hepplewhite which are so much coveted to-day are a witness to
the utility and decorative advantages to be found in veneering. To the ordinary
householder the word "veneer" means to cover up cheap and shoddy work, or
to make a whitewood cabinet look like a mahogany one. Hence the mistaken
idea that all veneering is bad work. That such work is done must be admitted,
and this makes it more difficult to convince the public that veneered work, when
it is well and rightly done, and shows that it is veneer, is the best and most
effective work for the following reasons :—1. It is the only way to use the rare
woods such as "curls" in satinwood and mahogany, "burrs" in walnut or
amboyna, and cross-grained but pretty wood which would only twist if used in
the solid. 2. The extra layer of veneer tends to strengthen and preserve the
wood upon which it is laid. This is best illustrated in the Queen Anne work,
most of which is walnut veneered on oak, or yellow deal, which must have
perished but for the veneer. 3. That veneering gives the only opportunity
for flat decoration in furniture, by using the grain of the wood for designs in
panels and on wide surfaces. 4. The process needs more care and thought in
the selection of wood, its preparation, application, and finish, than ordinary
"solid" work requires. These explanations are necessary because of the mis-
understandings as to the right use of veneer, and the suspicions which naturally
arise from them.

Veneers are cut in two grades or thicknesses, which are known as "saw-
cut" and "knife-cut." The first named are the thickest, and vary in thickness
from $\frac{1}{32}$ to $\frac{1}{16}$ in. They are cut from the log with a large circular saw, and

PLATE XXIII. CABINET WITH DUTCH MARQUETRY -- LATE SEVENTEENTH CENTURY.

PLATE I. CHINA CABINET IN COROMANDEL, PALM, AND SATINWOOD.
DESIGNED AND MADE BY MR. W. WILLINGALE.

usually produce twelve or fourteen sheets to the inch. "Knife-cut" veneers are much thinner, and with the new machines it is possible to get from fifty to a hundred in the inch, the very thin ones being used as picture mounts. These are cut with rotary and flat knives. In the former the log is well steamed and fixed between two stocks (like a leg in a lathe), and directly under a knife its whole length. The log is then forced round, and on to the knife, which drops the required thickness at each revolution. By this process it is possible to get veneers almost any width, and by cutting spirally the grain is accentuated and enlarged as in the figured maples used for ships' cabins. The flat knife acts somewhat like a plane. The log is fixed on a rising table, and the blade works backwards and forwards, and takes a sheet off horizontally, the knife being parallel with the grain. Before the introduction of machinery veneers were cut by hand, and were usually $\frac{1}{8}$ in. thick, which would allow of them being planed.

Burrs are the excrescences, or warts, which grow on the outside of the tree trunk, and although a deformation (see chapter on "Timber"), they produce beautiful wood, and are very valuable. The best known are amboyna, Italian walnut, yew, elm, cherry, and ash. Burrs are sold in "parcels," and in single "leaves," both knife and saw cut. It is often possible to get good figure from the "butt" ends of a log; these too are treated and used like the "burrs."

"Curls" and **"Feathers"** are produced by the separation of the heart at the junction of a branch with the main trunk, and consequently are limited in length from 9 in. to 4 ft. They are usually confined to mahogany and satinwood, and good ones always fetch high prices.

The different "figures" or "mottles" in mahogany are known as "fiddle back," found chiefly on the outside edges of Honduras wood, running across the grain, and named from the similar figure in maple on the backs of violins. "Rain mottle," very like fiddle back, but with much longer mottlings. "Plum mottle," from dark elliptical marks in the wood at frequent intervals resembling the shape of a small plum. "Roe" is the name given to the showy dark flakes, which, when broken, give such a fine effect of light and shade. They run with the grain in a zigzag line, and though a similar figure is associated with East Indian satinwood the "roe" on mahogany is usually wider. "Stopped" or "broken" mottles are also found on the outside wood, and consist of flame-like marks and irregular figures of varying and spreading forms. West Indian satinwood is either "mottled" or "flowered" against the "roe" of East Indian. These names would apply to figures in all woods more or less, and they are found singly or together. "Stripe" is applied to good Italian walnut. "Streaky" to plain rosewood. "Blistered" to walnut and maple cut spirally to enlarge the figure. "Silver grain," "clash," or "felt," to the figure in oak, and "lacy," to the rays in plane, but names vary in different yards and localities.

Preparation.—For all general purposes the best hard wood to veneer upon, called the "ground," is plain Honduras mahogany, principally because it warps and shrinks less than most woods. In soft timbers the best is American yellow pine, which also warps less and contains less resin than other pines. Whatever wood is used, it should be clean, dry, and as uniform in texture and straight in grain as possible. A very hard wood like ebony, rosewood, yew, or satinwood, should not be veneered on a soft wood like pine or basswood, as the ground is likely to absorb more than its share of the glue. Where light-coloured veneers are used, as oak, holly, maple, or satinwood, the glue should be whitened with flake white or bleached with oxalic acid. If this is not done there is a danger of the dark glue being forced into the veneer and showing through when cleaned off, thus spoiling the whole surface. In all veneering there is a danger from what is known as the "pull" or shrinkage in drying, which causes warping. The following methods are adopted to prevent this, and as they are all good, they should only be used where they apply best to the circumstances and the nature of the work to be done :—(1) Veneer on the heart side of the wood. If reference is made to the chapter on "Timber" (Shrinkage and Warpage), it will be seen that a board warps away from the heart, so that the "pull" of the veneer is somewhat balanced by this natural force. (2) When wide surfaces are to be covered, it is a good thing to cut the boards up the centre, and reverse the edges before rejointing, when the forces of contraction are fairly equalised. (3) A method adopted in France is that of cross-veneering, especially for panels which have a finished pattern on the face. Plane the panel perfectly flat, size both sides, and with "knife-cut" veneer it at right angles to the grain of the wood. This makes a "three-ply" or "lamination," and is generally successful, if the panel is kept flat when drying. (4) By mitre clamps, as in bureau flaps (see chapter on "Construction"); and (5) if the wood is dry and well chosen, sized on the face to prevent undue absorption of moisture, damped on the back, and kept flat when drying and until dry, it should keep flat. The reason for damping the back is to equalise the pull or swelling of the fibres caused by sizing the face, and this effect of moisture and evaporation, or drying, is one of the most important things to watch and understand in veneered work. It is a good thing to shrink veneers between hot cauls, so tending to lessen the "pull."

To prepare the wood, plane perfectly flat and true, and when dry fill in and level all holes. If the hole is a large one a similar piece of wood should be let in, diamond shaped, but a small hole can be filled in with plaster of Paris, or glue and sawdust. The surface should then be "toothed" with a "toothing plane," a small plane with single, upright blade, which is milled or grooved on the face, so that the edge has sawlike points (see sketch). In sharpening this plane, the "burr" must not be rubbed down as in a cutting blade. The toothing should be done both up and down and across the board, and all over it. The surface should then be sized with a little thin glue, and when dry it may be necessary to slightly tooth it again as the sizing may have caused some irregularities to rise on the face. The veneer too may need toothing to remove any rough surfaces left by the saw. A careful workman will examine both wood and veneer before laying. To cut thin veneers a sharp chisel and a straightedge are the best tools to use, but in the thicker or saw-cut sheets it is better to use a saw, either dovetail or tenon, or a veneer saw shown in f. 1, next page. When veneers are dry they buckle and split easily, and need very careful handling and cutting.

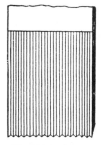

Toothing Iron.

Laying.—Two methods are used: one with a "hammer" for knife-cut veneers, and the other with "cauls" under pressure for the thicker or "saw-cut" sheets. The hammer is usually home-made, of beech or ash, with a blade of $\frac{1}{16}$-in. steel let into the head, and pinned through as shown in f. 2 below. The edge of the blade should be rounded to prevent cutting. Other tools for hammer veneering are a hot flat iron and a "swab" or sponge. When everything is quite ready—glue, clean, hot, and fairly thin—cover the ground quickly with a large brush, and see that it is free from any little specks of grit; then carefully lay the veneer on, flatting it with the hand, damp it with hot water, and pass the flat iron over rapidly without much pressure. Hold the hammer in the right hand, with the left pressing on the head, and starting in the centre work it backwards and forwards with a zigzag motion (f. 2) towards the outside edges, going over the whole surface quickly, and repeating the strokes from the centre until the air and surplus glue are forced out. To test the laying, tap the veneer with the fingers or hammer handle; a hollow sound will

1. Veneer Saw.   2. Showing Use of Veneering Hammer.

soon show any blisters or air spaces and if these occur, damp again and use the hot iron sparingly; or lumps may appear where the glue has clogged, which the hot iron and hammer should disperse. Wipe off, and stand on one side to dry where the air can get round both sides, and hand-screw a clamp across to keep flat whilst drying. Blisters are sometimes found when the veneer is dry, and to get them down properly it will be necessary to prick or slit them to let the air out, then warm them with the iron and flatten with hammer.

Saw-cut veneers cannot be laid with a hammer except in narrow strips such as cross-bandings. It is necessary to use wood or metal "cauls" under pressure either from hand-screws or veneer press. Wooden cauls are best made of mahogany or pine and out of 1-in. stuff. In hand shops they are usually kept for this purpose, either flat or curved, and they need only be quite flat and hot when used. Metal cauls are usually of zinc plate, thin in curved work such as piano falls, and $\frac{3}{16}$ in. thick for flat surfaces. To lay a panel with hand-screwed cauls, get everything ready, caul quite hot, hand-screw set about right, thick pieces of stuff for clamps, and odd paper and veneer pins handy. Cover the ground with glue and let it set slightly, a precaution necessary to prevent the veneer sliding and swelling too quickly, and doubly secure it by tapping pins into the edges or where the holes may not be seen afterwards, and do not turn the pins over unless on waste places; cover the veneer with a layer of paper, and on the top of the paper a piece of green baize, and then lay the hot caul

1. Veneer Clamp.

on round side downwards to ensure the glue being driven from the centre; in no case should cauls be laid on with hollow side down. Lay the clamping pieces across and hand-screw down, fixing the centre ones first and the ends last. Clamps are only necessary for wide panels, as hand-screws can be used all round a small one. Clamps should be slightly round on the inside edge to ensure the centre of the panel being pressed first. Fig. 1 above shows a regular clamp with iron screws at each end. In large shops a veneer press is used where the clamps are part of a stand and the

2. A Small Veneer Press.

pressure is much greater; whilst in many cases the press is combined with a hot table, either gas or steam, where the cauls are heated and the veneer laid in a very expeditious and effective manner. Two views of a small press are shown in f. 2. When paper is not used, metal cauls should be rubbed with soap to prevent sticking, and in large flat surfaces it is a good thing to have a layer of thick flannel or baize between the paper and the caul, as it helps to press into any little irregularities which the hard caul could not touch.

In curved work it is always advisable to use a caul, even when laying knife-cut veneer, and when the curve is too difficult to

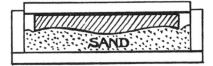

3. Sand-box for Curved Work.

test the fit of the wooden caul, sand-bags are used. These are easily made with strong calico, and should allow for at least an inch of sand at all points. They can be heated on the stove or hot plate, and it must be remembered that they retain the heat longer than the wood or metal cauls. Sand-bags, however, can only be used for hollow or serpentine surfaces. They should be laid in a box made for the purpose, f. 3, previous page, and the veneered face gently fitted down to the sand before final pressure is put on, and the sand must not be too hot. The most practical thing to do in curved work, such as hollow, round, or ogee fronts, is to keep the waste outside piece from the sawmill (or reverse shape), and use it as a caul, or failing this, build up a bit of pine and have one cut. In large surfaces like cylinder "falls," the most effective method is by building up a "saddle" or double caul out of pine, as shown in f. 1 below, with a thin ¼-in. board which should easily warp to the curve, as a hot caul. This

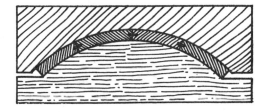

method takes a little longer in preparing the "saddle," but it is the best in the long run, as it ensures direct pressure all over the fall, or a sandbox can be used. The other method is to screw at least four ribs inside the fall, one at each end, and prepare similar ribs to fit the top. Warp a thin board for hot caul as near to the curve as possible, and the ribs can

1. A Saddle for Curved Work.

then be hand-screwed down one over the other—the more ribs the more likely a good job.

Circular Pedestals are usually veneered with knife-cut, and a slightly curved hammer. This is not a difficult process if the veneer is flat, but the joint must overlap and be left for a time until the pedestal has partially dried, so as to reduce the shrinkage at the joint, which may be cut with chisel and straightedge and laid with a warm iron and hammer. The same method applies to a column, and if further pressure is needed as in laying saw-cut, bind it round with wide tape or webbing, which, if slightly damped, will draw taut and act as a caul. In work of this kind the outside of the veneer should be covered with canvas to prevent fracture.

Coves are usually made of thin stuff, and if veneered the board will warp nearly to the shape required, or it can be steamed to the curve and fixed to a saddle and then veneered.

Flatting is often necessary when veneers are inclined to buckle, and is essential when using burrs, brown or pollard oak, or in fact any veneer which is "bumpy" and likely to be troublesome in laying. The best method is to damp the veneer and press it between hot cauls until dry,

2. Pattern in Veneer.

except in rosewood and satinwood, which are both oily woods and need not be damped. As a further precaution against "pulling," some men prefer to flatten and shrink all veneers between hot cauls before laying, and the less water used in all cases the better.

End Grain Veneering is not a very safe process, but is sometimes necessary. The wood should be sized three or four times to close up the pores.

Setting out and "**Fixing**" patterns in veneer is a job requiring skill and care. Suppose a flat design such as f. 2 above has to be prepared for veneering.

Set it out carefully on a board, prepare template of one corner of the inside and outside shapes, and mark them out on the veneer where the grain is most suitable; cut them out roughly with saw or chisel, then finish the curve, of inside pieces first, with marquetry saw and file, shoot the joints, lay it on board and fix it with three veneer pins driven partly home; fit up other pieces to it, taking care that centre joints are in line; then fit up outside pieces in a similar way, being careful that the grain is in the right direction.   When complete, glue

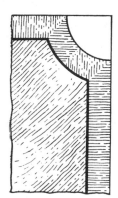

1. Curved Corner in Bandings.

slips of paper over all the joints, tapping them down with a brush to escape the pin heads; when dry draw out pins, and the panel should be ready to lay.   If a line has to be taken round the diamond shape, it should be laid up to the curve, slightly glued at joint and held in place by pins driven outside at intervals, and then gently bent over towards the inside; when set, the pins are removed and the outside pieces fitted up to the line.   The above process has to be changed for light-coloured veneers, as satinwood, in which the pin holes would show badly.   To escape this the pieces are laid on paper with just a little glue near the edges to fix them, the paper, strong cartridge, being stretched on the board by damping it and glueing the edges.   The paper slips over the joints are not necessary in this case, as the top side of the veneer is laid on to the paper.   Where pins are at all likely to injure the veneer this paper method should be used, but it is a safe one for all; and where veneer is very brittle and the grain short in the design, it is safer to back it with paper before cutting out shapes, and if a fret saw is used, back it also with a piece of $\frac{1}{16}$-in. stuff.   For curved shapes the pattern is developed (see Chapter X.) on the flat and fixed as above, but a thin layer of glue should be put between the veneer and paper to prevent the former splitting when laid on.

Cross-Banding can be laid with the hammer; a slight damping will swell the outside fibres, and prevent the ends cocking up through the same action by the glue on the inside.   Thin slips of paper should be laid over all the joints to prevent the air getting in, and to hold the band up to the joint when drying.   The cross-band round a panel end or drawer front can be laid at one time if done in this way.   Fig. 1 above shows a curved corner for a panel, and how to match the mitres.

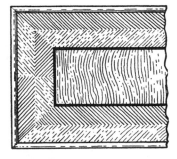

2. Herring-Bone Veneering.

Herring-Bone patterns are usually applied to Queen Anne Italian walnut work, on drawer fronts, ends, and frames.   It should be done with good striped wood, or it fails in its purpose.   Fig. 2 shows a part of a drawer front with herring-bone banding.   The strips are carefully cut obliquely across the sheet with straightedge and chisel, or on the edge of a board with a cutting gauge, shot with an iron plane, and laid with the " hammer," or the pane end of an ordinary hammer, the inside strip first, all round, and the outside one laid up to it, care being taken that the grain matches; or the pattern can be built up on paper and laid altogether, centre and bands as well. Joints are made in the middle and the grain reversed. Paper should be laid over all joints as previously explained. Cocked beads are usual on such drawer fronts.

Cleaning Off and Finishing.—It is most important that no veneered work of any kind should be cleaned off until quite dry, or it will tear up or blister in the cleaning. If there is any paper to remove it can be toothed off with the fine toother, or a little warm water and a sponge, but the less water used the better; the rest of the work must be done with the scraper, and very carefully too, or it may easily work through. In a panel where the grain goes in different directions, the scraping should be done with it, as well as the papering to follow; and where there is other work to do to the job, as in a table, the final clean off should be left to the last. The veneered portions which are left loose for a time should be watched in case of casting or warping, which may occur in the best executed work owing to changes of atmosphere or the natural working of the wood. To prevent this, keep the work hand-screwed down between clamps, and out of draught, heat, or damp.

Old work requires special treatment, and it would be absurd to lay down any fixed rules for it. But there are a few instances in which some general hints may be useful, and as such these are given. As a rule veneer on old work is fairly thick and can be toothed or even planed. Where there is a blister it is a sign that the glue has perished, and it may be possible to cut a slit and insert fresh glue, and then

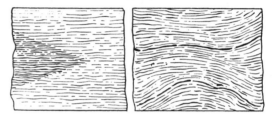

Joints in Veneers.

press down with a hot caul. But if this is on a top it will leave a bad mark where the slit was cut, or holes, if the veneer had been pricked. In this case it would be better to find a new or old piece of stuff, if possible, as near to the grain and colour as could be, and cut it in diamond shape, as in sketch above. If the grain is wavy the joint should be made to fit it, especially in burrs or pollard woods, in which irregular shapes should be let in, but in all cases square pieces or butt joints look very bad. The same hints apply to a bruise or fracture, either in the veneer or solid wood. It sometimes happens that an old top has to be completely stripped off, and this may be done by damping and a hot flat iron rubbed over the surface a few times. If the veneer has to be preserved it can be raised carefully by inserting a thin-bladed knife underneath, a palette knife being well suited for the job. The pieces of veneer should be carefully laid on a board in preparation for the restoring process, which would be similar to fitting up a panel, but the old glue would have to be removed by repeated work with sponge and toothing iron, and the veneer well flatted before any restoring could be done.

Stringing and Banding.—Strings are thin lengths, ranging from "hair lines," which are not much thicker than drawing paper, up to ⅛ in. square. They are prepared and sold in 3-ft. lengths, at a few pence per dozen, according to size, and are stocked in black, white, box, and purple, but any kind can be cut to order. The bandings are sold in similar lengths up to 1 in. in width. They vary in design, of which a few are shown in

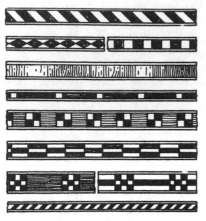

1. Types of Bandings.

f. 1 alongside. It has already been explained how to lay lines or strings, in a veneered pattern, and this applies to any shape, straight, circular, or elliptic, but where lines have to be inlaid into a plain or solid panel, other methods are used. Where special shapes such as "ovals" or ogee corners and curved lines are to be inlaid, it is done with a template, and the groove to take the line is routed out against the edge of template by the tang end of a file, or a bradawl, the end of which has been filed square to take the required line. In circles or lines which are parts of such, a small block of $\frac{1}{2}$-in. stuff can be glued on to the panel, with paper underneath for easy removal, and a hole bored in it to take an ordinary dowel. A strip of $\frac{1}{2}$-in. stuff about 1 in. wide can be used for the arm, and bored about 2 in. from the end to drop over the dowel in the block. At the other end the piece of steel for routing can be driven through at required distance, and with one hand on the dowel end, and the right hand guiding the steel, the groove is easily worked. Fig. 2 on this page shows the arrangement which is easily adapted to such work. For all straight work, where there is an edge to work from, a "scratch stock" is used, f. 3 below. This is a little

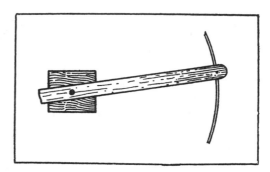

2. Router for Curved Lines.

home-made tool which is useful in many ways, as in scratching flutes and mouldings. Its make has already been described in Chapter III., and it can

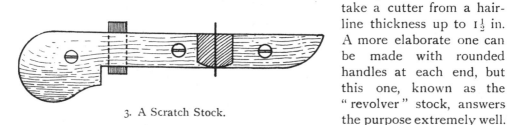

3. A Scratch Stock.

take a cutter from a hair-line thickness up to $1\frac{1}{2}$ in. A more elaborate one can be made with rounded handles at each end, but this one, known as the "revolver" stock, answers the purpose extremely well. Fig. 1, next page, shows one with a movable fence and butterfly screw. When the routing is done the lines are touched with thin glue, and pressed into the groove by the end of an ordinary hammer. The same tool is used for routing in the wider bands. The edge of the cutter is best kept square like a scraper, and in using the stock, somewhat like a gauge, only with both hands, the worker must be careful to keep it tight up to the edge, and hold it firmly to prevent wobbling.

For cross routing a "double cutter" should be used. This is made by leaving a small "knife" on each edge of the blade, and if used first it prevents the edge from being frayed. Lines and bands should not be cleaned off until quite dry, or they will sink below the surface as the glue beneath them sets and contracts.

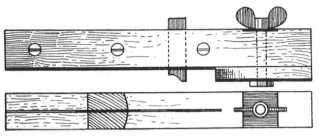

1. Scratch Stock with Movable Fence.

Square lines are used for edges round table tops, &c., and are simply laid in a rebate on the corner. Special devices are resorted to for holding them

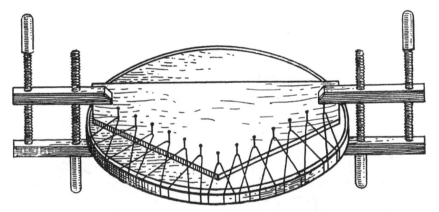

2. Method of Lacing an Edge to a Table Top.

whilst drying. If on the edge of a door frame, they can be bound round with tape, but for the edge of an oval, or any shaped table, the following method is practised, f. 2 above. Drive some screws into a piece of stuff about 2 in. apart

3. Building up Bandings.

and $\frac{1}{2}$ in. out of the wood, and on the underside of the top drive other screws about 2 in. from the edge and also 2 in. apart. Hand-screw the piece of stuff down to the top about 4 in. from the edge, and with plenty of tape the edge line can be bound on from screw to screw,

and laced up effectually whilst drying. Lines can be steamed and bent to almost any curve by gradually bending them on a piece of hot gas pipe, keeping them well damped in the process. This applies chiefly to the thicker and square edges rather than to the thin lines which will, as a rule, bend quite easily round a circle. Sometimes, in repairing, a few feet of banding has to be made up by the cabinetmaker. Fig. 3, p. 219, shows how to build it up. A few strips of cross-grained ebony and satinwood are carefully jointed and glued up alternately, and if a line is wanted on each side the faces can be prepared when dry and veneered with a caul, the grain going in the same direction as the ground.

1. Box for Inlaying Lines in a Tapered Leg.

When dry the bands can be cut off the edge, and are ready to inlay. Or if a plain cross band is wanted, cut a piece the required thickness off the end of a 2-in. board, and lay the veneer on the end grain faces. An endless variety of bands can be obtained in this way in any woods, thickness, or width. The old

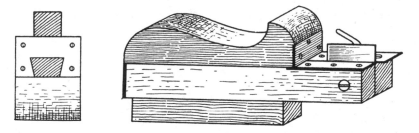

2. A Line Gauge.

Tunbridge work, so much used on workboxes and desks, was built up in a similar way. Fig. 1 above shows a box for inlaying lines in tapered column. Made out of 1-in. stuff, it can be fitted with a screw as shown. A screw through the other end should suffice to fix the column, and the line is routed from the outside edge of box.

String Gauge (f. 2).—This is a very useful home-made tool for gauging strings, especially when they have to be cut by hand. The top curved part moves freely in a dovetail groove, and is stopped by the adjustable plate shown in f. 3, which also gives a view showing a thin brass lever, which keeps the string down whilst being pulled through. The knife is fixed with a screw in a saw kerf, and has a bevel on the edge like a chisel. To use the gauge, fix it in bench screw by the block shown underneath, adjust the plate to the required thickness of string, lay string in and drop the lever, push the top of gauge towards the

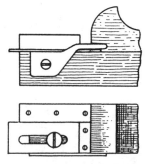

3. Parts of Line Gauge.

knife with left hand, and pull string with the right. It may take two or more pulls through the gauge before the string is cut to desired thickness. The thin plate on the end of the stock is necessary to keep the sliding top from moving out. The diagram is about half size.

Marquetry was developed in France during the eighteenth century, and chiefly through the reign of Louis XVI. The word means to "mark," to "impress," to "cut into," and the process, which was made possible by the introduction of veneers, is as follows :—A tracing of the design is glued on to the sheet of veneer which is to form the ground, and other veneers to form the design are glued on the back with paper between them. They are then cut on what is known as a "donkey" (see below), which is a stool with a frame fixed at the end, on which the saw runs horizontally, and to which is also attached an upright clamp, something like a harness maker's, worked by a treadle. The cutter sits astride the stool, holds the veneers in the clamp, and moves them about with his left hand, whilst he works the saw with the right. The saw frame can be adjusted so as to cut on the slope and ensure a good fit. Marquetry cutters are generally men who do nothing else, thus becoming highly skilful in the work, and as a rule they make their own saws, which are extremely fine, out of clock spring steel. When the cutting is done, the design is laid out on a board, and the pieces shaded where required. This shading, which is really scorching, is done by dipping the veneer into hot sand, and when completed the whole design is glued down on to paper, and handed over to the cabinetmaker to lay. If any engraving is required, it is done when the marquetry is cleaned off. Veneers are now stained all colours, so that it is possible to obtain very naturalistic effects in a flower design. The Marie Antoinette toilet bureau in the Jones Collection at South Kensington,

Using a Marquetry Cutter's "Donkey."

shown on Plate XXVIII., is decorated with this process. The Dutch were also famous marquetry cutters, and the fine Stuart cabinet, Plate XX., is a noted example, together with the clock case, Plate XXI., both probably made in England. The fans, shells, &c., which were a common feature on second-rate furniture a few years ago, and are still used, are cut and shaded in the manner described above. For further reference to marquetry work see chapter on "Styles."

Buhl Work.—This was invented by André Boulle, a noted Frenchman who became famous as a cabinetmaker in the reign of Louis XV. (see chapter on "Styles"), and "buhl," as it is spelt in England, was named after him. It is really the inlaying of metal into tortoiseshell firstly, and when this became scarce, into wood or composition which passed as tortoiseshell. He used brass and silver chiefly, which was afterwards engraved. The cutting was similar to marquetry, and Plate XXIV., p. 222, shows a wardrobe in the Jones Collection by Boulle.

The work was continued by an artist named Berain, and the later work was so arranged to save material that the ground furnished another design, a device known as "boule" and "counter boule." This inlaying in metal has never found much favour in England, but metal was used by some of the eighteenth-century designers, amongst them Sheraton. When brass lines or bands have to be inlaid Salisbury glue should be used, or the glue should be mixed with plaster of Paris. Files and emery cloth are used to clean off metal inlay, finishing with a little oil and pumice powder.

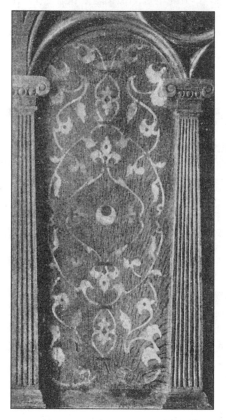

Inlaid Holly and Bog Oak Panelling from Sizergh Castle in the Room at the Victoria and Albert Museum.

Inlaying differs from marquetry from the fact of its being applied to solid work into which pieces are inlaid. It was largely used on furniture in the Jacobean period, and the illustration on this page shows a panel of holly in oak from the Inlaid Room of Sizergh Castle, Westmorland, date about 1600, now in the Victoria and Albert Museum. In inlaying proper the pieces are cut out, laid on, and marked round, and then holes cut to receive them. The edges of the pieces for inlaying should be slightly bevelled to make sure of a good joint, and the bottom of the hole pricked to make keys for the glue. Chess squares are sometimes inlaid into a solid piece, or "overlaid," a term used when the layer is thicker than veneer, with the squares which have been glued up in nine strips, and cross cut again, and then laid on the ground in the usual way, with a caul, the odd strip allowing for the alternate square at each cut.

Mother-of-Pearl is used largely in veneering and inlaying on such things as clock cases, mirror frames, caskets, and small cabinets. It can be bought prepared for use from 10s. to 15s. per lb. in pieces from 1 to 2 in. broad in irregular shapes and about a thin $\frac{1}{16}$ in. thick. The qualities are "snail," which is the ordinary shell; "Japanese," wavy and varying in colour, and "blue," or "green," or "pink," which are the most expensive, and obtained in smaller pieces. Pearl can be cut with a very fine saw, or filed to any shape, but where the shape is thin or delicate, it should be backed up on stiff veneer with paper between, before the cutting is done. When inlaying, the underside of the pearl should be roughened with a file, and the ground pricked to give a better hold for the glue. Owing to its brittle nature it will not bear much pressure, and the weight of a flat iron or iron plane should be sufficient. When a caul and hand-screw are used there is a danger of breaking the pearl without knowing it, as its underside is often hollow. A little plaster of Paris should be mixed with

PLATE XXIV. 222A

BUHL WARDROBE FROM THE JONES COLLECTION,
VICTORIA AND ALBERT MUSEUM.

DUTCH MARQUETRY
CLOCK.

PLATE XXV.

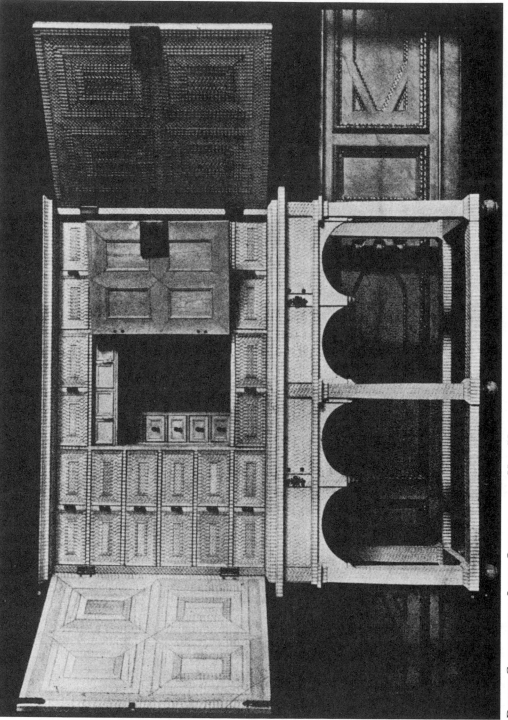

DUTCH CABINET WITH IVORY OVERLAY, FROM HAM HOUSE.

the glue, which should be used quite hot.   The face side is usually polished, so that if carefully inlaid it should need but little cleaning off.   Where this is necessary use a scraper, or a fine file, then rub down with flour paper, and finish with pumice powder and rottenstone.   To prevent the pearl powder penetrating the wood, first give it a rubber of light polish, which can be easily removed at the final clear off.   It is often necessary to cut a line design into the surface of pearl, which resists the engraver's tool, and this is done by covering the surface with a thin coat of beeswax brushed on warm.   The design is then scratched through the wax down to the pearl, and nitric acid poured into the scratchings.   In the course of an hour the acid will have burnt away the pearl, and after a good washing in water the wax can be cleaned off, and the mastic run in the lines to complete the design.

Ivory is another rare material used for inlaying.   It is obtained in fairly large pieces, 12 to 14 in. long, and 4 to 5 in. wide, and a good veneer thickness or in lines and solid squares.   It can be cut in a similar way to pearl, and inlaid with a caul.   The underside should be toothed, and the ground pricked as in pearl.   For cleaning off, scrape or file and finish with fine paper and pumice powder, the polishing being done with a buff rubber and whiting. Ivory can be made flexible by soaking it in pure phosphoric acid until it has ceased to be opaque.   It must then be washed in cold water, and dried with a clean, soft rag, and if it again becomes too hard to bend, a soaking in hot water will produce flexibility again.   The cheap substitutes for ivory are ivorine, bone, and celluloid.

Tortoiseshell is a rarer material than pearl or ivory.   It can be cut and inlaid in a similar way to pearl, and cleaned off by scraping and papering, and is polished with dry whiting or rottenstone.   A composition to imitate tortoise-shell, with red-coloured background, was introduced into the later buhl work, but it was far from being successful.

Parquetry is the geometric veneered work found on Louis XV. and XVI. work (see table on p. 117), composed largely of diapers of the same wood.   It is well adapted for small things, such as clock cases or caskets, and is built up on paper as explained in the satinwood veneering, and laid with a caul.

Intarsia is a name given to the early inlaying originating in Italy in the fourteenth century, when realistic perspective effects were obtained with veneers which were laid on piece by piece.   It may be called "pictorial" inlaying, and much of it has been recently done in the "New Art" Continental Work, illustrated in the examples in Bethnal Green Museum, although it has not affected the cabinet trade generally.   Its success depends upon the selection of the grain and colours of the wood, and in recent years the Gold Medal in the National Competition has been granted for work of this character.   Some remarkable and beautiful effects are obtained when combined with good colour and design.

Overlay Work.—This is a type of veneering done with stuff which was thick enough to mould, or the term would be applied to any material which was laid over another.   The famous examples are those of the Italian and Dutch periods when ebony and ivory were lavishly used.   "Facing up" is a workshop term applied to it when thin solid stuff is used as against the thinner veneer.   The cabinet on Plate XXV. is a fine example of seventeenth-century Dutch overlay work in ivory. It is reproduced by permission of the Earl of Dysart, and is in that nobleman's fine collection at Ham House. The "waved" surface and mouldings are a special feature of Dutch work in the seventeenth century, found on frames, chests, and cabinets, but ivory is the exception owing to its cost and rarity. The "waves" vary in design and give a pleasing effect of light and shade. They were made by a hand machine, which causes the waves to be slightly irregular in shape. A full description of the machine may be found in a French book, by A. J. Roubo, dated 1769, to be seen in the library at South Kensington. These mouldings are still made in various sizes and "waves," but stained sycamore is used in place of ebony. They cost about 3d. per foot and upwards from $\frac{1}{2}$ in. to 1 in., and, as a rule, can be obtained at any of the good veneer merchants, who also supply pearl, tortoiseshell, strings, bands, and other materials for inlay, overlay, marquetry, and veneering.

Oyster Shell Veneering.—This name is given to the type of veneering found on old Dutch cabinets. The veneers have been cut transversely from branches of lignum vitæ, or laburnum wood, so that the markings of the rings give an oyster shell appearance, hence the name. The joints between the pieces are usually square, and the pattern is built up by the methods already described, viz., pinning to the ground and glueing paper over the joints, or glueing each piece to paper. Cleaning off requires great care, and a circular motion to the rubber. The inside of the doors on the cabinet (Plate XXIII.) are good examples of oyster shell work. For other illustrations of pattern building in veneer, see pages 104, 130, 145, 155, 160, 175, 176, 181, 189, 190, 192, 205, 206.

CHAPTER X.

FOREMEN'S WORK—PRACTICAL SETTING OUT AND APPLIED GEOMETRY.

Foremen's Duties, Definition of—Working Drawings—Description of Rods—Purpose of Working Drawings and Rods—Method of Preparing same—Elevation, Section, &c.—Specimen Rods—Preparing Curve Templates, and Application of—Moulding Sections for Machine—Turning and Fretwork Details—Cutting Lists—Necessity for Method of Preparation and Checking—Duplicate Lists—Allowances for Cutting —Taking Measurements and Templates—Development of Room—Measuring Angles, &c.—Taking Details of Existing Work—Strapwork, Posts, &c.—Squeezing Wax for Carvings, Recipe for—Method of Using—Casting in Plaster—Flat Relief Work— Supervision in Workshop—Requisitions—Time-sheets, &c.—**Specimen Requisition—Equipment of Drawing Office**—Draughtsmen's Table—Sizes of same— Accommodation—Storage of Rods—Marking Rods—Roll Paper—Wall Roller for same—Instruments—**Estimating**, Methods of—Specifications—Special Clauses— Specimen Estimate in Detail—**Applied Geometry**—Reduction and Enlargement of Mouldings—Proportionate Reduction—Drawing Entasis of Column—Spacing of Flutes and Fillets—Reduction and Enlargement of Mouldings—Alternate Method— Intersection of Bracket Mouldings—Intersection of Raking and Curved Mouldings —Necessity for Curved Mitre—Joining in a Straight Mitre Line—Intersection of Raking Mouldings on Pediments and Overdoors—**Gothic Arches**—Method of Drawing same—Names and Terms applied to ditto—Combinations—**Geometry of Gothic Detail**—Foliation, &c.—Trefoiling—Cusping—Quatrefoiling, &c.— Chippendale Cluster Columns—**Development of Curved Surfaces**—Method of Measuring Curved Lines—Development of Pillar or Vase-Shape for Marquetry— Necessity for Development—Method of Developing Splayed Veneers—Octagonal Pillar Shape—**Development of Marquetried Knife Case**—Veneering same— Method of Developing—Allowance for Curvature and Bending—True Shape of Flutes—Preparing Zinc Templates—Veneering with Sand-bags—**Hopper Development**—Application to a Wine Cooler—Obtaining Bevels—Making the Carcase— Dovetailing and Keying same — Working the Mouldings and Rebates — Other Methods—**Elliptical Doors**—Method of Projection and Development—Preparing the Stuff—Obtaining Segments and Bevels—Necessary Templates—Marking out the Material—Fitting together—Glueing up—**Circular Dome**—Drawing the Ribs— Rebate Line in Crown—Construction of Bed Frame—Sections of the Mouldings— Mitre Intersection—Securing the Panels.

SETTING OUT, AND FOREMEN'S WORK.

THE duties of foremen differ according to the size of a firm and the class of work done, but foremen's work in its broadest sense is very comprehensive, and embraces the practice of the various branches of setting out, estimating, supervision, and organisation. In large firms where there are several shops, each controlled by a foreman, the duties are more limited in character, and consist chiefly of issuing the job orders, drawings, and cutting lists, and in generally supervising the production of the work. All setting out, full sizing, estimating, &c., is then conducted by draughtsmen in the drawing office of the works. Under these circumstances, individual foremen's work will naturally vary, but in shops of a comparatively small size, the foreman will estimate, set out, keep time-sheets, prepare orders for fittings and generally supervise the work in its progress, from the perspective sketch or design to the actual completion of the job.

Working Drawings are really full-size representations on paper of the object required to be made, and consist usually of the elevation, plan, and section arranged in such positions as to occupy the smallest space consistent with the workman's ability to read them. In nearly every instance these working drawings are made full size; scale drawings tend to confuse the workman in transferring to full measurements; and again, a slight error may creep into the scale drawing which would be considerably magnified when made up full size. A rod is a thin board upon which is set out the plans and sections of certain repetition work, panelling for example, which does not demand fully drawn elevations. These rods are usually made of $\frac{1}{2}$-in. pine planed smooth on both sides with the edges shot perfectly straight.

Purpose of Working Drawings and Rods.—They convey to the workman all the necessary information concerning the work in hand, and they should indicate clearly all the measurements, true curves for shaping, details of turning, fretting, carving, inlaying, &c., and also the construction. Many points have to be considered in setting out the drawings and rods. Economical and effective construction, properly proportioned moulding sections; a sympathetic interpretation of the designer's suggestions as expressed in the scale drawing; facility in separating if necessary for transport, and suitability of the work to a specified purpose. A half front elevation is usually sufficient on the working drawing, and a "section" showing the arrangement of the various pieces, portions for dovetailing, &c., is superimposed on the first view. This section is really a view of the interior parts where the job is divided by a vertical cutting plane, an outline of blue pencil serving to distinguish this view from the elevation. Where the work is shaped in plan, such as a serpentine front sideboard, a "sectional plan" also is required, which is again superimposed on the drawing and outlined with red pencil. A comprehensive study of the illustrations in the chapter on "Carcase and Table Work" will indicate to the reader suitable positions for determining the sections and elevations.

Preparation of Rods.—Specimen rods are shown illustrating the setting out of a library bookcase and panelling respectively, f. 1 and 2 alongside. The bookcase is set out as follows :—Mark thin lines indicating the total height of job and the heights from floor line of the plinth, table top, frieze, cornice, &c. ; use a thumb gauge off one edge to pencil perpendiculars between these divisions for the line of doors, frieze, back, &c., draw in the moulding sections, detail of drawer dovetails, section of door rails, width of back framing, &c. The whole section of the job cannot be shown on an 11-in. board, so wave lines are drawn right through the section and the true over-all width is marked on the rod. Complete the setting out by lining in with an H.B. pencil. Sectional plans are shown in a separate rod, f. 2, as described above, showing position of ends, divisions, and doors, and also showing constructive detail such as the dust-proof beads and details of shutting stiles, rebated ends for back, &c., that do not occur in the section. Fig. 3 is a specimen rod of panelling, showing sectional view of plan and side elevation.

Preparing Curved Templates. — Upon completion of the drawings or rods, the templates necessary for marking shapes on the wood are next prepared. These apply to shaped brackets, curved rails, mouldings, and segmental templates requisite for building up curved ends or drawer fronts. Quarter-inch whitewood is used, and the shapes

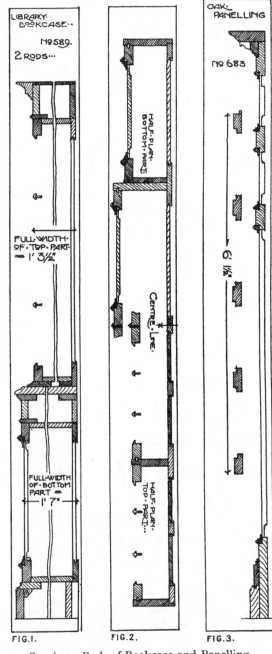

Specimen Rods of Bookcase and Panelling.

are transferred to this by placing the thin wood under the drawing and in pricking points at intervals along the curve ; these points on the template stuff are then joined up with pencil lines and the template cut to shape.

Moulding Sections are then prepared for use in the machine shop. The true outlines are marked upon tracing paper, with the required run in length of each section marked also, see f. I. alongside.

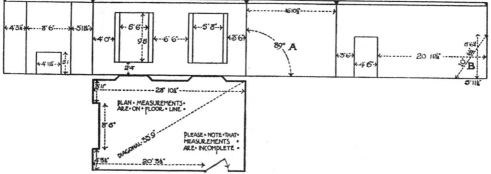

OAK· BOOKCASE·   N.º 589·

CORNICE·
IO'RUN'···

BAR·MOLD
40' RUN'···

BEADS·116 FT.

BED·MOLD
9'6"RUN'··

FRIEZE·MOLD
9'6"RUN'··

12 STILES·AND
RAILS· TO· THIS··

TABLE· TOP.

LINING·UP·
2·TO·THIS··

PLINTH·MOLD
2 TO THIS··

PANEL·MOLD·
26 FEET·RUN··

I. View showing Arrangement of Sections on Tracing Paper.

Turning or Fretwork Details are also traced off ready for the machinist's use. Such systematic procedure is always advisable, and is conducive to economical production and smooth progress through the various shops.

Cutting Lists are lists of material giving particulars of each piece required for making the job. They are prepared as in the specimen opposite, and bound in book form with perforated edges to tear away easily. Thin paper is interleaved and carbon paper is inserted when making the entries, which makes a duplicate list for office reference. About fifty items are entered upon one sheet, and each piece is numbered on the working drawing to correspond with the numbers contained in the first column. Allowances for cutting are usually $\frac{1}{2}$ in. extra in length, and $\frac{3}{16}$ in. for width. See also chapter on " Workshop Practice."

Taking Measurements and Templates. — When work of a special

2. View showing Development of Room with Measurements and Angles.

character is to be executed, involving specific measurements, such as fireplaces, fitted corners, window seats, panelling, &c., preparatory sizes must be obtained before the work is set out. A scale development of the room is prepared (see f. 2 above), with actual measurements figured in. All angles and corners should

CUTTING LIST.

No. 837. SHEET A.

JOB—*Satinwood Wardrobe.* ORDER NO.—*B326.*

CUSTOMER—*H. J. Smith, Esq.* DATE—*Jan.* 3, 1909.

No.	For	Length.		Width.	Thickness.	No. of.	Wood.	Remarks.
1	**Large Carcase**.	Ft.	In.	In.	Inches.			
2	Carcase ends - -	4	$10\frac{3}{4}$	$20\frac{1}{2}$	$\frac{7}{8}$	2	Hond. Mahog.	
3	,, top - -	4	0	19	$\frac{5}{8}$	1	,, ,,	Faced with
4	,, btm. - -	4	0	$20\frac{1}{2}$	$\frac{5}{8}$	1	,, ,,	satinwood.
5	,, division -	3	$11\frac{1}{2}$	$20\frac{1}{2}$	$\frac{7}{8}$	1	,, ,,	
6	Upright ,, -	0	$9\frac{1}{4}$	18	$\frac{7}{8}$	1	,, ,,	Clamped front.
7	False ends - -	3	11	18	$\frac{7}{8}$	2	,, ,,	
8	,, end facings -	3	11	2	$\frac{7}{8}$	2	,, ,,	
9	Shelf - - -	3	$10\frac{3}{4}$	$18\frac{1}{2}$	$\frac{7}{8}$	1	,, ,,	
10	**Large Carcase Back.**							
11	Stiles - - -	4	$10\frac{3}{4}$	$4\frac{3}{4}$	$\frac{5}{8}$	2	,, ,,	All wood to
12	Top rail - -	3	$9\frac{1}{2}$	$3\frac{1}{4}$	$\frac{5}{8}$	1	,, ,,	be well seasoned,
13	Btm. ,, - -	3	$9\frac{1}{2}$	$12\frac{1}{2}$	$\frac{5}{8}$	1	,, ,,	free from knots,
14	Cross ,, - -	3	$9\frac{1}{2}$	3	$\frac{5}{8}$	1	,, ,,	and suitable for
15	Munting - -	3	10	3	$\frac{5}{8}$	1	,, ,,	veneering upon.
16	Panels - - -	1	$10\frac{1}{2}$	$19\frac{1}{2}$	$\frac{1}{2}$	4	,, ,,	
17	**Doors.**							
18	Hanging stiles - -	3	1	$2\frac{1}{8}$	$1\frac{1}{8}$	2	Cuba Mahog.	
19	Shutting ,, -	3	1	$2\frac{3}{8}$	,,	2	,, ,,	
20	Top and btm. rails -	1	$9\frac{1}{2}$	$2\frac{1}{8}$	,,	4	,, ,,	
21	Cross rails - -	1	$9\frac{1}{2}$	$1\frac{7}{8}$	,,	2	,, ,,	
22	Top panel - -	1	$7\frac{3}{4}$	$11\frac{1}{2}$	$\frac{5}{8}$	2	,, ,,	
23	Btm. ,, - -	2	8	$19\frac{3}{4}$	$\frac{5}{8}$	2	,, ,,	

Remainder of fifty items filled in as above on Sheet A. Next fifty items on Sheet B.

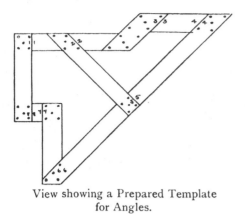

View showing a Prepared Template
for Angles.

be carefully measured, and the angles subtended by wall lines and floor lines indicated in the development by degrees or figured triangles, see A and B.   Rough templates are prepared, in some cases, made of ½-in. pine, and scribed to the wall or floor lines (see sketch).   These are screwed together whilst in actual position, and are marked as shown at the joints.   If the work is to be executed at any great distance from the drawing office, the pieces may be unscrewed and packed in a bundle.   They may then be readily screwed together again in the drawing office, and the work set out upon them.

REQUISITION FOR BRASSWORK.

JOB—*Satinwood Wardrobe.*   ORDER No.—*B*326.
CUSTOMER—*H. J. Smith, Esq.*   DATE—*Jan.* 3, 1909.

Please supply—

	Approximate Cost as per Estimate.		
	£	s.	d.
Two brass wardrobe locks and catches with drop handles, ⅝ inch to pin, two-lever, one each right and left hand	0	7	0
Four 2½-inch brass till locks, two-lever, ⅝ inch to pin	0	3	8
One pair brass centre hinges, 3 inches long	0	0	8
Three pairs 2½-inch brass butts	0	1	1½
One pair 6-inch wardrobe-door stay	0	1	8
Four pairs brass swivel coat hooks	0	3	0
Six pairs brass hat and coat hooks	0	2	6
One pair brass flush bolt, 6 inches long	0	1	3
„ „ „, 3 inches long	0	0	7
Six pairs drop drawer handles	0	9	0
All the above fittings, with screws for same, to be silvered and oxidised	1	5	0

(*Signed*)....................................
Foreman.

Taking Details.—Existing carving or recessing, when required to be duplicated, should be cast in plaster and forwarded as specimens.   Squeezing wax recipe, as follows, viz. :—Suet, 1 part ; bees' wax, 2 parts, or wax, 5 parts ; olive oil, 1 part, or wax, 4 parts ; common turpentine, 1 part.   The ingredients only need melting together and allowed to cool.   If stiffening is required add a little flour.   The wax is then fit for use and should be well pressed into the interstices of the work, and then carefully removed.   A counter-impression of the original will thus be formed in wax, into which plaster of Paris and water, mixed to a cream-like consistency, is poured.   Experience will soon determine the best thickness for properly running into the finer parts of the mould. When the plaster is set quite hard, the wax is drawn away, and the plaster representation of the decoration will remain.

Details of Flat Relief Work or frets can be obtained by placing thin paper over them, and in rubbing the paper with heelball. If carefully done the pattern

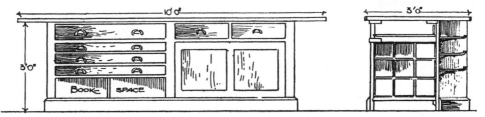

1. View of a Draughtsman's Table for Full Size Drawings.

will show in black and white masses ; these are termed "rubbings." This method is a very handy one, and the rubbings are not only accurate but permanent.

Equipment of Drawing Office.—Fig. 1. above illustrates a draughtsman's table suitable for large working drawings ; the height should be about 3 ft. A firm top made of $1\frac{1}{4}$-in. yellow pine with ebony slips on each edge, securely buttoned to the framing, is most suitable. The front is fitted with a cupboard and drawers for storage of books, instruments, &c., and trays for imperial size design sheets. Iron brackets are screwed to the back for supporting rod boards, and a space at the end is also utilised for rolled drawings. Slips of wood about 1 by $\frac{1}{4}$ in. should be glued at each end of rolled drawings to prevent

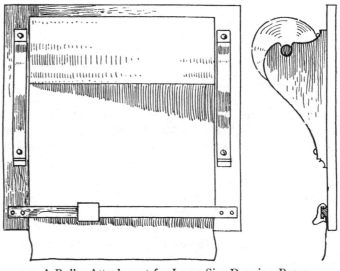

2. A Roller Attachment for Large Size Drawing Paper.

tearing during the frequent rolling they are subjected to in the workshop. Rods are labelled with the description and order number on the board or on a wooden tag attached to one end, and are stored in wooden racks after use, if required for future reference. Paper for working drawings can be obtained in rolls about 4 ft. wide, and about 1,000 yds. long. A wooden roller is inserted in the centre, and supported by strong brackets (see diagram f. 2 above); one end of the paper is placed under a lath, which has a sliding knife attached.

When paper is wanted, the required length is drawn under the lath, and separated from the roll by drawing the knife along it.

Instruments.—The following are the usual instruments required :—A 4 ft. fourfold rule, one set of cardboard scale rules, a case of drawing instruments, large wooden or celluloid set squares, a wooden bevel with adjustable top, two large wooden tee squares, one with movable head and set screw, two trammels, a beam compass with adjustable heads, tracing paper, and a straightedge.

ESTIMATING.

Estimating for cabinetwork demands a very careful attention to details. Scale drawings or perspectives and specifications are supplied to the foreman or estimating clerk, from which he prepares the prime or factory cost. Many factors affect the practice of estimating, and it is only by a broad knowledge of procedure, and a careful study of fluctuating market prices in certain timbers, fittings, discounts and rebates, that estimates can be systematically prepared. Local rates of labour, extra wages and expenses for fixing, must also be calculated. The differences of working various woods also require attention. Time limits and contract clauses, with penalties for incompletion of work within a definite time, and the consequent possibility of paying extra wages for overtime, lighting charges, &c., must also be allowed for.

Repetition Work is more economic than the first model, as it does not require extra templates, cutters, and working drawings, and is duly considered when estimating for quantities. Only the basis of estimating is dealt with here, involving methods in daily use in firms where it is carried beyond the comparative guesswork that prevails in some of the smaller shops.

Specifications always accompany architects' drawings, and must be carefully followed in estimating ; they contain all information not conveyed by the drawing, such as quality of wood, machine or hand wrought, with descriptions of special fittings, finish, &c. The first step in estimating is to ascertain the superficial area of timber in each thickness used, which is entered upon a printed form arranged as indicated on next page. The wardrobe illustrated on p. 155 is taken as a specimen job. When the timber items are complete, labour is dealt with and entered as shown. Work involving the co-operation of other departments is also entered under their respective titles. Fittings should be specified in detail, with the estimated cost attached to each, providing the requisite information as to price, &c., when ordered by the foreman or stockkeeper. Space is also allowed for extras, in which is entered additional expenditure not coming under previous heads. Glue, &c., is a constantly recurring item, and comparatively large when veneered work is dealt with. Workshop expenses include the salaries of manager and foreman, rent, taxes, light, and general upkeep. These are based upon an average for the previous twelve months, and reduced to a certain percentage of labour cost. This method of estimating in detail upon prepared forms has the additional advantage of constituting a valuable record of executed work, and is extremely useful for purposes of reference.

FACTORY ESTIMATE.

JOB—*Satinwood Wardrobe.*   ORDER No.—*B326.*
CUSTOMER—*H. J. Smith, Esq.*   CLERK—*H. J. E.*

Wood.	Thick.	Feet.	@	£ s. d.	Wood.	Thick.	Feet.	@	£ s. d.
Cuba Mahog.	1⅛"	12	1/2	0 14 0	Satinwood -	1½"	2	1/9	0 3 6
" "	⅝"	15	7d.	0 8 9	" -	¼"	3	1/2	0 3 6
Hond. "	⅞"	98	8d.	3 5 4	" -	⅜"	5	7d.	0 2 11
" "	⅝"	39	6d.	0 19 6	W. Ind. veneer	...	16	10d.	0 13 4
" "	½"	73	4½d.	1 7 4½	E. Ind. veneer	...	44	8d.	1 9 4
" "	⅜"	52	3½d.	0 15 2					
" "	¼"	9	2½d.	0 1 10½					

Labour.

Cabinetmaking	-	-	...	12 0 0	
Polishing	-	-	...	3 15 0	
Machining	-	-	...	3 5 0	

Extras.

Silver oxidising all brass-work, as per estimate Messrs .... | ... | 1 5 0

Glue, glass-paper, screws, &c. - - - - | ... | 0 10 0

Workshop expenses, 20 per cent. of labour cost | ... | 2 8 0

Fittings.

	@	£ s. d.
Bevelled and silvered plate glass - - -	...	0 12 6
Two pairs wardrobe door locks -	3/6	0 7 0
Four pairs till locks -	11d.	0 3 8
One pair centre hinges -	8d.	0 0 8
Three pairs 2½-inch brass butts - - -	4½d.	0 1 1½
One pair wardrobe door stay - - -	1/8	0 1 8
Four pairs swivel coat hooks - - -	9d.	0 3 0
Six pairs hat and coat hooks - - -	5d.	0 2 6
One pair 6-inch flush bolt	1/3	0 1 3
" 3-inch flush bolt	7d.	0 0 7
Six pairs drawer handles -	1/6	0 9 0

Carried forward -	...	28 14 11½	Brought forward -	...	28 14 11½

Total -   -   - | ... | 35 10 6½

ACTUAL COST, £ s. d. ....

REDUCTION AND ENLARGEMENT OF MOULDINGS.

The diagram f. 1. shows a method of proportionately reducing a cornice moulding. Draw the section in the rectangle *a b c d*, produce the lines *b d* and *c d*, and with *d* as centre and *d c* radius, describe semicircle *c e*, join *b* to *e* and *c* to *f*. Two right-angled triangles are now formed. Supposing the height is required to reduce to *g h*, erect this perpendicular, and from *g* draw a horizontal until it cuts the triangle in *g'*. From this point drop a perpendicular into *c d*. Draw horizontal divisions from section to *b d*, and from these intersections draw dotted lines to apex *e*, which divides the line *g'h'* in the same ratio. Dotted horizontals are now drawn from 1, 2, 3, &c., representing the divisions for height of moulding. To obtain the projections, with point *d* as centre, radius *d h'*, describe a quadrant *h' i*. Then draw *i j*, divide this line as shown and transfer to *k g*. Drop perpendiculars until they intersect the corresponding horizontals, and draw new the section of the moulding.

Fig. II.—An approximate method of drawing a column is illustrated in this figure. First draw the half plan, showing flutes and fillets, determine the height of column and draw the division lines 1, 2, 3, &c., at equal distances apart. Divide the space between 1 and 5 in plan into four parts, and number as indicated. The bottom part of the column has parallel sides, the divided parts above diminishing one space in each division. Project the numbered points on to their corresponding division lines, which, joined together, shows the required curve or outline. The method of projecting the true elevation of flutes and fillets will be understood from the drawing. The points on each semicircle are projected to the divisions, and the flute lines drawn through these points.

Fig. III. is used for both reduction and enlargement of a given moulding, A representing a cornice moulding required to be reduced one-third. Draw section A in rectangle *o c a b*, from *o* and *a* describe arcs intersecting in *d*, and draw triangle with *o a* as base, and *d* as apex. Divide *d o* into three equal parts, and from *p* draw a perpendicular from the horizontal divisions on *o a*. Draw lines radiating to apex until they intersect with *p p'*, and from these points draw horizontal projectors. Construct the triangle *o e c*, and divide one side into three equal parts, then draw the horizontal *q u*, and divide proportionately to *o c*. Draw *v p* on section B, and transfer the length *q t* to *p r*. Continue with the other spaces, from which drop perpendiculars until they intersect with horizontal projectors, and draw the outline of the section. If the moulding is required to be enlarged, fix the compasses to proposed height, and with *o* as centre cut *a b* produced in *e*. Perpendiculars raised from the intersection of this line with the horizontal division 1, 2, 3, &c., will represent the proportionately increased spaces for height line. This is transferred to another part of the paper. To obt·.in the projections describe the quadrant *a w*, with centre *o*. Measure the distance from *a* to where *o e* cuts the quadrant. Transfer this distance from *w* to *y*, and draw line *o y*. The intersection of this line with the vertical divisions accurately represents the new projections.

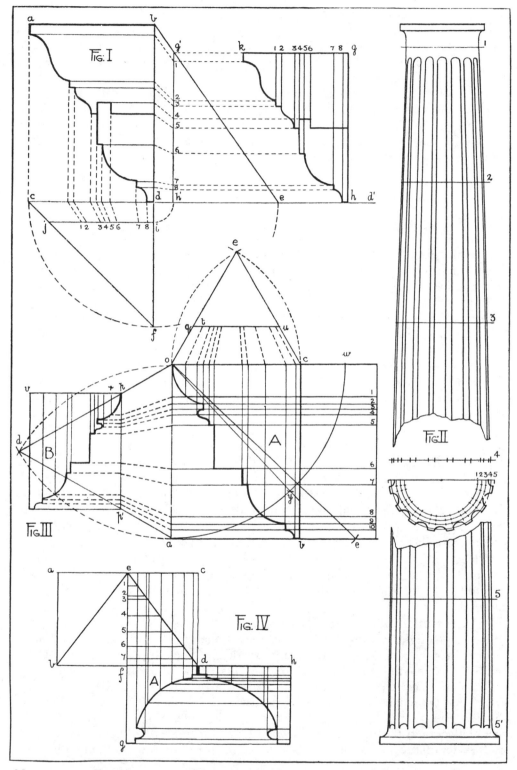

METHODS OF ENLARGING AND DIMINISHING MOULDINGS AND SETTING OUT COLUMN.

Intersection of Bracket Mouldings, f. IV. previous page.—Let *a b c d* represent the plan of a clock bracket, *b e* and *e d* the mitre lines. The projection of the front piece of moulding is greater than the sides, and therefore a section is required that will intersect accurately with the side pieces; *f g* is the height of the side moulding, and A the section. Erect perpendiculars from profile, draw horizontals 1, 2, 3, &c., and also horizontals from profile. Transfer the line *e f* and divisions to *h d*, and the true section of front piece can be drawn by joining the intersecting points between the perpendiculars and horizontals as shown. When mitreing together the mitres are marked with a bevel set to the angles of the plan, when both pieces will truly intersect.

INTERSECTION OF RAKING AND CURVED MOULDINGS.

Enlargement of Cornice Moulding.—The illustration in f. I. is a further application of the properties of a triangle in the proportionate division of lines, and applies equally well to either enlargement or reduction of a given moulding. The rectangle A B C D encloses the profile of a cornice moulding, the height of which is to be reduced to the length of line X X. Draw the profile as shown in rectangle and produce the horizontal D C to any length D C D. From the fillets or squares of the mouldings and the centre of the large ogee drop perpendiculars to C D, place compass point in C and describe quadrants from each perpendicular until they cut the line A E. The line A E is now considered as the base of a triangle, the apex situated at any convenient point on the line D D. From A and E draw the sides of the triangle to complete the figure. Draw a horizontal from X X until it cuts the triangle in F, and drop the perpendicular F G. To obtain the proportionate division of this line, draw horizontals from profile until they cut A E numbered 1, 2, 3, &c., and from their points of intersection draw lines radiating to apex, cutting F G in 1', 2', 3', &c., then draw horizontals which will represent the new heights of the moulding. To find the projections, drop perpendiculars from profile into C D, and with point C as centre describe quadrants cutting C E in *a*, *b*, *c*, &c., join these points to apex, and with G as centre, describe quadrants cutting D C. Erect perpendiculars from these points, and trace the profile through the intersection. To enlarge the moulding produce C D and also the triangle sides. Determine the height as with X X, and the new heights and projections may then be obtained in a manner similar to the former example.

Intersection of Curved Mouldings, f. II.—Where curved mouldings are mitred to straight lengths and both pieces are identical in section, curved mitres are required to ensure an accurate intersection of the various members. Draw outline of curved and straight mouldings, in this case a corner of a piece of framing, and also the section of moulding A. From the points numbered 1, 2, 3, 4, &c., erect perpendiculars. From point B draw the radius line and transfer the divided line D E to D' E'. With compass point in B, describe arcs cutting the perpendiculars, and through the intersection trace a curve; then make concave and convex templates in zinc or veneer to mark the mitre lines upon the moulding.

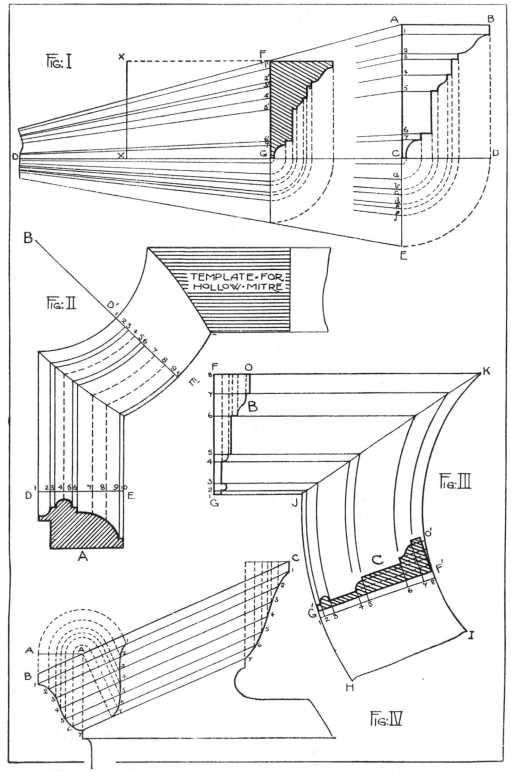

METHODS OF DIMINISHING MOULDINGS—FINDING CURVED MITRES AND
INTERSECTION OF RAKED MOULDINGS.

Intersecting in a Straight Mitre Line.—Fig. III. previous page shows this method, which is effected by altering the section of the curved piece. Make F G H I the outline of mouldings, and J K the mitre line. Draw section B on straight length, and from F G draw horizontal projectors until they cut the mitre line; from the points of intersection in this line draw arcs until they cut F' G', and erect short perpendiculars upon 1, 2, 3, &c. Transfer the height line F O to section C, and draw horizontal projection parallel to G' F' until they cut the perpendiculars. Through these points a new section or profile is traced, the members differing in width only to the original section on the straight length.

Intersection of Raking Mouldings, such as occur in overdoors and pediments, are illustrated in f. IV. Draw the line B C, and decide the section of front piece first, then draw lines parallel to B C, and from the intersections with profile 1, 2, 3, &c., draw projectors at right angles to B C, and with A as centre swing arcs on to A A and drop perpendiculars. The section of the end piece is obtained by joining up the points of intersection. The method of obtaining the profile at C will be understood without further explanation.

GOTHIC ARCHES.

Geometrical constructions of Gothic arches are shown opposite, and are named as follows:—Fig. I. Semicircular. Fig. II. Stilted Semicircular; the springing line of semicircle is raised or "stilted" above the supporting columns. Fig. III. Lancet; two sided, terminating in a sharp point, used in two, three, and five fold combinations. Fig. IV. Equilateral. Fig. V. Segmental. Fig. VI. Pointed Obtuse or Drop. Fig. VII. Pointed Segmental; the centres being below the springing line as in segmental. Fig. VIII. Three Centred. Fig. IX. Four Centred; the centres in this case are the corners of a square, but proportions vary. Fig. X. Ogee. Fig. XI. Three Centre. Fig. XII. Pointed Trefoil; constructed upon equilateral triangles. Fig. XIII. Trefoiled; constructed with squares. Fig. XIV. Equilateral Trefoliated; an arch with trefoils. The upper side of an arch is called the "extrados" and the inside "intrados" or soffit.

THE GEOMETRY OF GOTHIC DETAIL.

The subject of Gothic woodwork, traced through the many periods of Mediæval Art, is such a large one that only a few general characteristics, examples, and bases of construction can be dealt with here. Some of Chippendale's designs contained features borrowed from Gothic architecture, such as cluster columns, &c. A few of the terms used in connection with Gothic work, and illustrated in the diagrams, are as follows:—"Foliation," which was introduced as the Gothic style developed, and consisted of foliating

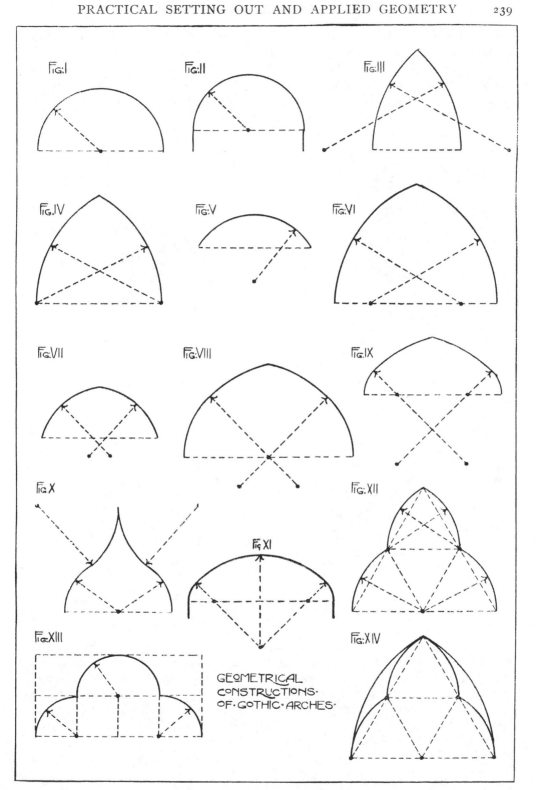

GEOMETRICAL
CONSTRUCTIONS·
OF·GOTHIC·ARCHES·

TYPES OF ARCHES.

the spaces in tracery; f. I. shows a circle "trefoiled," and this is obtained by drawing the equilateral triangle *a b c*, and in bisecting each side and drawing lines through these points to the opposite apex; from *a*, with radius *a c*, describe a circle, also from points *b* and *c*; then from centre *d* describe an enclosing circle, and the remaining lines of the figure are drawn from these four centres.   Fig. II. is also a "Trefoil" of different proportion.   The foils are described

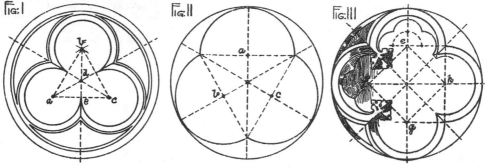

Diagrams illustrating "Trefoiled" Circles.   A "Quatrefoil" with Cusping.

from *a*, *b*, and *c*, which are the bisecting points of each side.   Fig. III. is the "Quatrefoil."   Draw a square with diagonals produced, bisect each side, and draw *e, f, g, h*; then from these points describe the foils.   The leaf shape between each foil is called a "cusp," a variation of which is "chamfer cusping," see B on f. VI. on p. 241.   Fig. III. also shows "trefoliating" in each foil, the construction with a semicircle being obvious.   Fig. IV. is the method of drawing the "foliated" circle

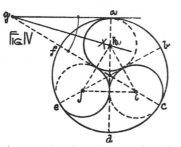

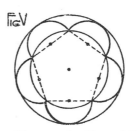

Diagram showing Constructive Lines   Diagram of a Cinquefoil.
        for "Trefoliated" Circle.

in f. VI.   Describe the large circle, and divide the circumference into six equal parts, join the points *b, e*, &c., and draw the tangent *a g* until it cuts *c f* produced; bisect the angle formed, obtaining the point *h*; then transfer the distance *a h* to *c i* and *e j*; with radius *a h* describe a circle using *h* as centre, and proceed similarly with centres *i* and *j*.   The required lines are thickened in, and each space "trefoliated."   Fig. V. is the "Cinquefoil."   Describe the pentagon in a circle, bisect each side, and draw each foil with these points as centres.

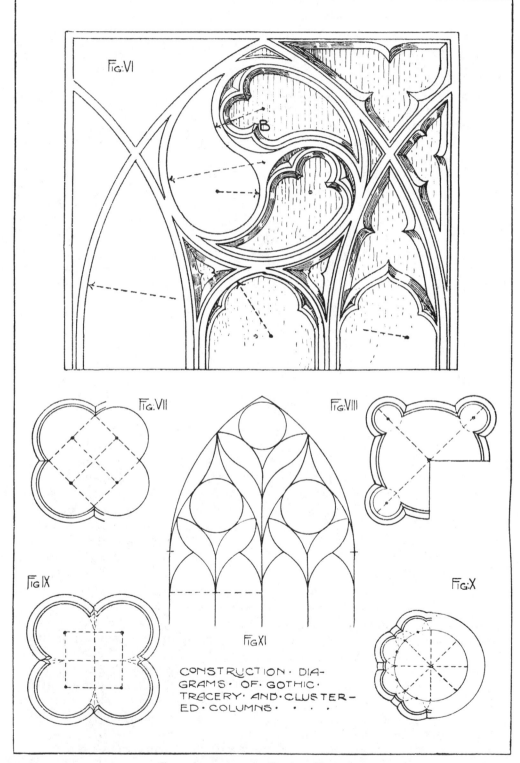

CONSTRUCTION OF GOTHIC TRACERY.

THE DEVELOPMENT OF CURVED SURFACES.

The figure shown on this page is an example which illustrates geometrical projection and development. A half plan of a vase or knife case is drawn (see diagram) first, see a_1, b_1, c_1, d_1, and also the elevation $a\,d\,b\,c$. These shapes are frequently made of solid stuff, and decorated with carving, especially in work of the Adam period, but veneering is also much employed. When veneering is necessary, the decoration must be so arranged as to permit the veneer being laid in narrow strips, as it is obviously impossible to cover it with a single sheet of veneer. Inlaid flutes of boxwood are shown in this example, with a groundwork of mahogany. To draw the elevation accurately, divide the outline of elevation with horizontal lines at intervals as 1, 2, 3, &c. Where the lines intersect with $c\,d$, drop perpendiculars into $a_1\,d_1$, and with e as centre describe arcs. Divide the arc $a_1\,d_1$ for flutes and spaces in $a\,b\,c\,d$, &c., and draw lines radiating to e. Then project points from $a\,b\,c$ on reference line 8 in plan into reference line 8 in elevation, and proceed next by projecting the points of intersection on No. 7 line in plan into No. 7 in elevation, and so on with all the reference lines. Trace curves through these points for the true elevation, and then the curved heads of flutes are drawn freehand. In considering the shape of the flutes, it must be borne in mind that although they diminish towards the bottom the sides are not perfectly straight when laid out on a flat surface, owing to the curvature of the groundwork in plan. The veneers must be bent round a curve when laid in position, and a slight swell in each side is necessary to obtain an accurate and well-fitted joint between the pieces. This allowance for bending is more apparent when working to full size measurements, than from the small illustration given.

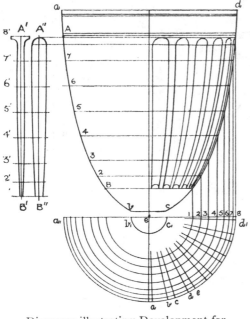

Diagrams illustrating Development for Veneers on Vase Shape.

To Obtain the True Shape of a Flute and space to which zinc templates are made, find the true length in the stretch out line of A B, and place it at the side of the diagram, see A B′ and A″ B″; transfer the divisions also, and draw short horizontal lines; number these as with reference lines corresponding with the plan and elevation. Then measure the true size of a flute on the plan reference line No. 8, and transfer to the corresponding reference line on A′ B′, then the true size of a flute on reference line No. 7, which is also transferred to reference line No. 7 on A′ B′. Continue in this way until all the true measurements are obtained and transferred, when the outline can be drawn through the resultant points, and then complete the flute by describing a semicircle at top.   The shaped pieces between the flutes are also measured and drawn in this way, both templates being prepared of tin zinc, and tested carefully in the groundwork before cutting the shapes.   Three or four pieces may be secured in the groundwork with veneer pins and strips of paper glued over the joints.   When quite dry the pins are with-

drawn, and the groundwork glued previous to veneering. Sand-bags are the most effective if firmly hand-screwed down upon the veneer.

I. System of Measuring Curved Lines.

The constructions, developments, and projections explained below involve much measurement of curves, and a simple system of measuring must be thoroughly understood before proceeding with the more complicated diagrams.   Three lines are shown in f. 1, a, b, and c above, representing a compass line, ogee, and elliptical curve respectively.   To measure the true length of a draw a straight line on tracing paper, mark a point d on this line, place this point over D and then place the sharp point of a pricker through them.   Rotate slightly until the straight line coincides with the curve at e, and place the pricker in this point and again rotate slightly ; the length of the line is transferred in this way to the straight line, and any divisions or points upon the curve as g h are also marked in their relative positions.

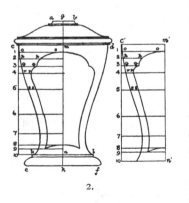

2.

The branch of practical geometry described below can be applied to finding true shapes of almost any curved work before groundworks are prepared.   It frequently happens that the true shapes or developments are required before any practical work is proceeded with, especially when marquetried decoration has to be prepared.   Fig. 2 alongside is a square pillar in vase form with curved outline, each face being panelled with a contrasting veneer.   Such shapes must be developed and drawn upon a flat surface, as the actual shape of curves are foreshortened when drawn in elevation.   Draw the outline and shaped panel a b c d e f, f. 2, with centre line g h, from c drop a perpendicular until it cuts the produced line k l. Divide the elevation with horizontals arranged as in diagram, and number the intersections with the perpendicular c k′ as 1, 2, 3, &c.   Draw the centre line at the side of diagrams and the horizontals c′ m′ upon this line, with the divisions as numbered in 1′, 2′, 3′, &c.   This is best accomplished by drawing a straight line on tracing paper, and pricking the true length upon it as described above, drawing the horizontals from 1, 2, 3, &c.   Now transfer the reference line of elevation on to the development with points of intersection marked o o upon it, and continue with reference line No. 2, marking the position of points p p.   Proceed with the succeeding lines until all the points are obtained, and draw the developed outline through them.   The veneers are cut to these shapes, and when glued to stiff paper or lined are bent over each face, and should

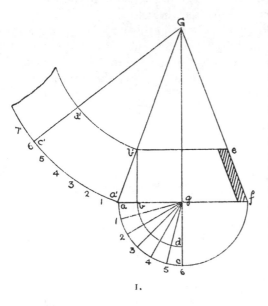

I.

accurately fit the outline.   The panel curves will likewise fit into the position indicated in elevation.

The diagram f. I shows the general method usually adopted for finding the true shape of veneer required for covering a circular conical shape.   The application of these principles to various other forms should suggest themselves to the reader, as, for example, conical or splayed niches, heads, &c.   The elevation is represented in f. I alongside, by *b' e* and *a' f*.   Produce *a' b'* and *fe* until they intersect in G the apex of a cone; divide the plan into any number of equal parts indicated by 1, 2, 3, &c., and draw lines radiating from these points to the centre *g*, then draw the perpendicular *b' b* and describe the arc *b d* with *g* as centre.   The quarter plan of the frustum of cone is now indicated by *b*, *d*, *g*, and the size of veneer must be the length of the line (*b d* × 4) for top edge, and (length of line *a c* × 4) for the bottom edge. The curve of the veneer or development is found by describing the arcs *a' c'* and *d' b'* with G as centre.   Mark the divisions 1, 2, 3, &c., on *a c* along the arc *c' a* and join these points to G, the joint line for veneer is shown by each of these, and the whole length of veneer required is (*c' a'* × 4).

Geometrical projection and development applied to an octagonal shape is illustrated in f. 2.   The outline is drawn first, and to obtain the correct representation of the intersections of adjoining faces in elevation, a plan is required, *a b c*, &c.   Draw the diagonals *bf*, *cg*, &c., and divide the elevation by drawing horizontals for reference lines numbered 1, 2, 3, 4, &c.   From reference line No. 2, drop a perpendicular cutting the diagonals *bf* and *cg* in plan, and continue also with 3, 4, and 5.   These lines are now drawn parallel to each side of the octagon, and represent sectional plans of the elevation on the

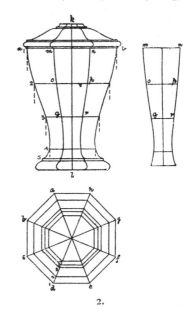

2.

cutting planes or reference lines.   Project the points marked *a b*, &c., on diagonal *d h* to the reference lines, and proceed similarly with the points on diagonal *a e*, then complete the elevation by drawing the angle lines through these points.

To Develop one Surface.—This method will be understood from the description given in the previous example ; draw the centre and reference lines, when the points for the curves are obtained by measuring the distance of *m n o p*, &c., from the centre line of elevation, and transferring to the diagram.

BEVELLED WORK DEVELOPMENT.

The term "hopper" is generally applied in cabinetmaking to work that tapers towards the bottom, instances of which occur in pedestals, wine coolers, caskets, &c. The method of obtaining the true cuts at the angles is shown in f. 2 alongside—a wine cooler. Part is shown of a four-sided example, and the further application of the principles involved are illustrated in the splayed corner diagram. A simple and straightforward way of executing this class of work is to regard the job as a series of "planes" or thin sheets of metal ; developments are thus rendered easier, and confusion, due to multiplicity of lines, should not result. The plan is shown by *a e, d h*, and *b f, c g*; project the elevation from these points after ascertaining and marking the height. In order to obtain the true shape of each piece, one end is first rebated into the horizontal plane. Use *g'* as centre and

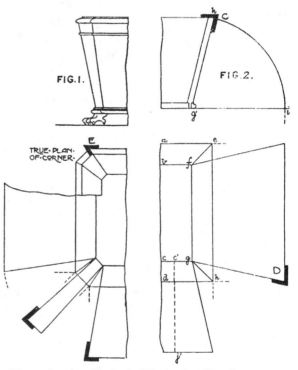

Views showing Method of Projecting Developments.

with radius *g' h* describe an arc cutting the bottom line produced in *i*. Produce the lines *a e*, and *d h*, and drop a perpendicular from *i*, joining the points as shown, which when completed represents the true shape of the ends. Make *c' j'* equal to *g' i*, and produce the line *e h*, join the points obtained which will give the true shape of front and back, and the bevels are exactly alike in both cases.

When making the carcase, prepare the stuff and plane edges to fit bevel C, mark the shape of each piece on the outside, using bevel D for this purpose ; then mark mitre lines on top and bottom edges with a set mitre, and cut and plane to the lines. The development of the splayed corner should be clear from the diagram f. 1, the cuts being obtained by setting an adjustable bevel to 67½ degs.

Bevel the edges as before to bevel C and mark the half mitres on each edge (see bevel E) and then cut and plane to the lines.   To strengthen the joints, tongueing is sometimes employed, and dovetailing is excellent if "facing up" is possible, whilst "keying" is effective for veneered work.

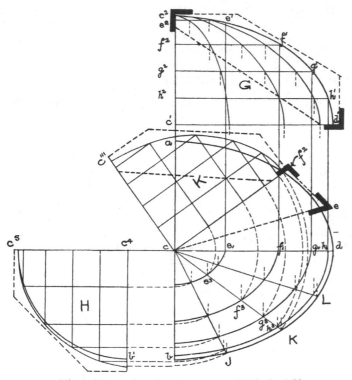

1. Views illustrating Development of Elliptical Shapes.

AN ELLIPTICAL DOME.

Many illustrations could be given of vases, domes, wine coolers, &c., of circular and elliptical shape, but the example shown adequately illustrates the method of projection and of obtaining the necessary bevels and cuts, and also the construction of these forms. Wedge-shaped segments are used in this case, but the segmental building up, as in a circular table frame, can sometimes be employed to advantage.   Dry, well-seasoned wood is of course an essential in this work, and it will be found advantageous to roughly cut the segments to shape first, and then allow them to stand about for some time until the shrinkage is quite complete before finally jointing and glueing up to shape.   Subsequent shrinkage would in most cases be almost impossible to remedy.   To obtain the segments and bevels requisite for glueing up the shape, first set out a semi-ellipse full size upon a board (see f. 1 above), with $a\,b$ the minor axis, and $c\,d$ half major axis.   Determine the number of segments in the dome, and draw to the joint lines radiating to C.   Five

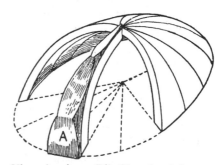

2. View showing a Rib Chamfered down to Outline.

templates are necessary to mark the segments, the first of which is obtained by drawing the line $c^1\,d^1$ at any convenient distance above the plan.   Erect the perpendicular $c^1\,c^2$ equal to the height of the dome, and describe a quarter ellipse with a trammel. The figure $c^1 c^2 d^1$ will now represent a half elevation of the dome, diagram G. The dotted line indicates the outside line of the template, and the inside line is gauged from this edge after it is cut. The segment is obtained in a like manner. The finished curved line is a true quadrant or quarter circle, see $c^5 c^4 b^1$. Three remaining templates are now required. The development of one is given in diagram K, showing the method, and its application will be obvious. To find the true shape of segment marked K in plan, proceed to rebate that part of the dome into the horizontal plane. Draw the quarter ellipse marked $e f g h$ in plan, and erect perpendiculars, cutting the elevation in $e^1 f^1 g^1 h^1$. From these intersections with the elevation $c^2 c^1 d^1$ draw horizontals to centre line, and transfer the revisions to $c'''c$ in K diagram, and then draw the projection parallel to base line cf, with c as centre radii $e^3 f^3 g^3 h^3$. Describe arcs cutting cf, and erect perpendiculars from these points until they intersect with the horizontal projectors. Trace the curve through these points of intersection, and proceed similarly with J and L. To find the plan of each piece, draw the dotted line $f e$,

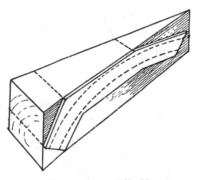

1. Marking out the Rib Shapes—
1st Stage.

equidistant from intersection of K and L, with base line of dome, the bevels indicating the joint line at the base.

Marking out the Material.—The thickness of each piece required is obtained by joining the points marked with dotted line in f. 1, G, p. 246, and drawing a line parallel to it outside the template line. Cut a wedge-shaped piece

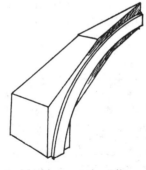

2. Marking out the Ribs—
2nd Stage.

for segment $c f e$ in plan, and plane the upper surface. The sides of this piece represent the vertical planes K and L. Place the template K on one side level with the top edge, and then mark out (see f. 1 above). Proceed likewise with template L, and join the sides together with pencil lines as shown, and then cut to shape. All the segments are thus prepared, and the templates are then cut again to the true curve lines. Carefully adjust the template on one side of a segment, and mark out (see f. 2 alongside). The other edge is also marked in this manner. Then chamfer away the corner of material down to curved lines (see f. 2, A, p. 246), and cut and plane the inside of the segment from line to line. This chamfering down to the curve is necessary to ensure the pieces being glued up accurately, and also as a guide when finishing elliptic work to shape, but it is dispensed with in a circular form ; these are usually turned both inside and outside upon a lathe. When all the segments have been cut, bevelled, and chamfered, they are fitted in position as shown in A, f. 2, p. 246. Dowelling the joints is advisable, and when the position of dowels in the joint is decided, a pin is driven in the centre of each intended dowel hole ; this is allowed to project $\frac{1}{8}$ in. above surface, and filed to a sharp point.

Then carefully set the pieces together, and press. Corresponding centres will then be marked on the other piece; after which withdraw the pins and bore the holes. Horizontal lines are drawn upon the stuff as a guide when boring, and if lines are also drawn on the plan the brace and bit can be held directly in position above them. The dowel holes will be bored in line with each other. Glueing up is then proceeded with, and a grip is obtained for hand-screws by glueing blocks at intervals. Each quarter ellipse should be glued up separately, and then fitted together. For glueing up circular segmental forms, refer to chapter on " Curved Work."

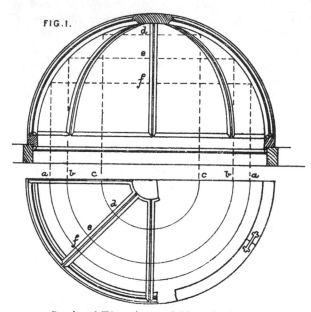

FIG.I.

Sectional Elevation and Plan of a Dome.

A CIRCULAR DOME.

Fig. 1 represents a circular dome in sectional elevation, and the view is obtained by drawing the trimmers or bearers first, and then the semicircles which indicate the thickness; and the section of the bottom frame and curved crown is also drawn in. The rebate line of the crown is obtained by striking an arc line from the bottom rebate, thus permitting the free entrance of glass or panel. To obtain the elevation of the ribs, draw part plan of dome and the semicircles a b and c. Then draw the dotted perpendiculars until they cut the inside line of rib, joining the points with dotted horizontals. Project points of ribs from f e and d on to corresponding dotted horizontals, and draw the curves for ribs through these points. This method is approximate only, but sufficiently accurate for purposes of representation. The construction of the bed frame is shown in plan, seg-

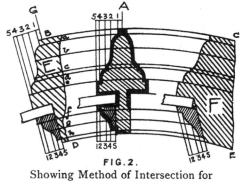

FIG.2.

Showing Method of Intersection for Mouldings on Curved Bars.

ments are butt jointed, dowelled, and secured with hand rail bolts. To obtain the sections of mouldings in the dome it will be necessary to draw a portion of the bed frame plan upon a board (see f. 2, A, B, C, D, above). Draw line A radiating to centre, and then the section of the rib upon this, and the curved lines *a, b, c, d,* &c.   The section E shows the moulding of the bed frame exactly similar to the rib section.   The large moulding of crown (see F) is again the same section, but owing to the splayed rebate of this piece, the bead moulding must be worked to the section shown.   This is obtained by drawing projectors 1, 2, 3, &c., parallel to the rebate line, and through these intersections with $f\,g$ and h trace the outline of ogee moulding.   A good mitre intersection is thus obtained, or if scribing is used in conjunction with tenoning or dowelling for connecting the ribs to the crown, the scribed joint will show a true mitre line.   This example of a dome is most suitable for a passenger lift, and is usually executed in hard wood, with framed, panelled, and fitted interior.   The wood or glass panels are best secured by screwing the bead mouldings.

CHAPTER XI.

NOTES ON THE HISTORIC STYLES OF FURNITURE, WITH EXAMPLES OF MODERN WORK.

Gothic — Renaissance — French — Elizabethan — Jacobean — Queen Anne — Eighteenth Century—Chippendale—Hepplewhite—Sheraton—Adams—Victorian—Present Day —List of Historic Houses open to Public.

It would be impossible to give anything like a full account of the development of the various styles of furniture in the course of one chapter, but as no book on cabinetwork would be complete without some reference to so important a feature in the craft, it is thought advisable to refer, however briefly, to the designers and makers of past periods.

The tendency of modern furniture design shows a direct influence of some style, and no one in the trade can afford to ignore it. Many are content to simply copy old examples, and houses are still furnished and decorated after the manner of the Queen Anne, Georgian, or Adam periods. On the other hand, it is much more desirable that the styles should be studied with a view of adapting them to modern taste and requirements, and there can be no doubt that attempts in this direction would receive public support.

Cabinetmakers, whether master or man, may at any time be called upon to restore, copy, or make furniture of any period, or based upon some style, and a knowledge of these styles should be as much a part of their "kit" as any one of their tools. A large number of books are published which illustrate the work of different periods. A short list will be found at the end of the book, and it is to them that reference should be made for fuller information.

Gothic.—Up to the end of the sixteenth century the details of woodwork and furniture followed very closely on the prevailing style of architecture, and especially so during the Gothic periods, which covered a course extending over three centuries, roughly, from the twelfth to the fifteenth. The gradual changes from Early English (thirteenth century) to Decorated (fourteenth century) on to the Perpendicular (fifteenth century) can be seen in the woodwork by the tracery on panels, the mouldings, and the developments of the arch, from the lancet as the earliest, the "decorated" or "geometric" in the fourteenth century, and finishing with the flatter or four-centre arch in the fifteenth and sixteenth centuries. Examples are given in Chapter X. These details are still applied to church furniture in chairs, seats, altar, side or "credence" tables, choir stalls, pulpits, font covers, and screens, but are not used in household articles. An old fourteenth-century cabinet is shown in the first chapter, but the pulpit and

PLATE XXVI.

250A

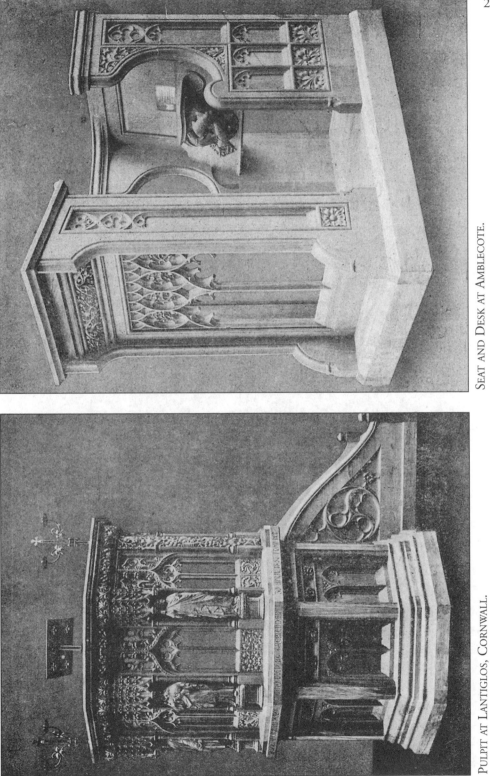

SEAT AND DESK AT AMBLECOTE.

MADE BY HARRY HEMS & SONS, EXETER.

PULPIT AT LANTIGLOS, CORNWALL.

PLATE XXVII. A LATE SEVENTEENTH CENTURY CHEST OF DRAWERS.

seat on Plate XXVI. are modern examples of Gothic work from the workshops of Harry Hems & Sons, Exeter. The pulpit, designed for the church at Lantiglos, Cornwall, is made chiefly of English oak, a timber which Mr Hems prefers to use whenever possible. The seat is in Hungarian wainscot, which, though less costly and easier in the working, does not possess the fine qualities of the English timber.

Renaissance or Classic Revival.—With the "revival of learning" there came great and sweeping changes in the domestic arts, and with them also came more luxurious living. The movement began in Italy and spread to France. The work known as "Historic French" is associated with the reigns of Francis I. from 1515 to 1547, and of Henri II. up to 1559. The furniture, made chiefly of walnut, was richly carved with classic details of a mixed order. Acanthus leaves, dentils, egg and tongue, with "cartouche" or moulded panels were some of the details applied to cabinets and other furniture, whilst most of the friezes and table frames were bulged and carved with "nulling." Curved and broken pediments and twisted columns were features of the style, which towards the end of the century became very much debased.

In England, Henry VIII. gave every encouragement to the revival, and patronised Italian artists and workmen as well as the German artist Holbein, whose name is associated with much of the work of the period. Panelling with a circle is associated with his name. Classic details were mixed with Gothic, and made up what is known as the Tudor style, beginning with Henry VII. in 1485, and ending with the more familiar "Elizabethan" in 1603. The fortified castle became less necessary, and the manor house developed. Haddon Hall and Hampton Court are well-known and fine examples of the Tudor style. The woodwork, as in the Gothic days, followed the architecture, and we find that cornices, pilasters, columns, &c., resemble as far as possible the classic orders, although in the transition stage many Gothic features were retained. The fireplace was the most important piece of work in the room, and it was in this period that the first extending or "drawinge" table appeared, shown in chapter on "Tables." Legs of tables were heavy and shaped like an acorn. "Court" or cheese "cupboards" were built up out of the chest; the linen panel, an earlier detail, was discarded for one which was split into five small panels of various design, square, circle, and diamond shaped, whilst the circular-headed panels with scalloped edges were a feature in the chimneypiece. The great halls would be furnished with long tables and stools, with heavy oak chairs for use at the head table, whilst the ponderous bedstead was the most prominent piece of furniture in the bedroom. Much of the work was inlaid, and towards the end of the reign it was largely influenced by the Flemings, and so by the accession of James I. it had become heavier and coarser in detail. (See Chapter XIV. for types of panelling.) Afterwards came the Jacobean style, followed by that sometimes described as "Stuart," lasting up to 1688, when James II. ceased to reign. The Elizabethan details and forms were continued, but were added to. Chairs, tables, settles, chests, dressers, and cabinets came into more general use, many with moulded fronts as in the illustration. The court or cheese cupboard became the principal article in household furniture. The decorative details were varied by split turning and frets laid on or cut in the solid, and acorn drops on tables and chairs, whilst the carving developed into incised and simple gouge and strap work. Towards the end of the period, and during the Cromwellian and Stuart days, the gate table was introduced, and chairs were stuffed or caned. The style and details varied according to the taste and patronage of the monarch. Charles II. favoured the French artists, and much work of French origin was brought over to add to the magnificence of the Court.

William and Mary, 1689 to 1702.—Up to the end of the seventeenth century the furniture manufactured in England had been made chiefly of oak, but with the advent of the Dutch influence walnut was used. The **S** shaped and cabriole leg with curved under stretchers, chairs with wide and curved splats in the back, bureaux, and chests of drawers on a stand or lower carcase (see illustration, Plate XXVII.), inlaid grandfathers' clocks, and card tables with " candle " or circular corners, took the place of the heavier and more severe oak work of the previous century. The Dutch style prevailed under the reign of Queen Anne, 1702 to 1714, and continued to influence the furniture of the reigns of George I. and George II. right up to the year 1750. During this period the court cupboard had developed into a dresser, a type common to Yorkshire and Wales. Most of the walnut work was veneered on yellow deal and oak with " herring-bone " patterns on the drawer fronts, and round edges to carcase ends and fronts of drawer rails, which were faced up with a solid slip with the grain at right angles. The bureaux were made in two parts, an upper carcase with two drawers, and a framed-up stand (usually with cabriole legs) with one drawer. Somewhat later a cupboard or china cabinet was added to the bureau, and " tall-boy " chests of drawers with a curved frieze were introduced. Wall mirrors are a special feature of the Queen Anne period. They were usually flat with pierced and shaped wings and pediments, whilst the moulding was often carved and gilt.

Georgian.—If all the furniture made during the reigns of the four Georges is to be termed " Georgian," it would cover a period of 115 years, from 1714 to 1829, but the time had come when the style of furniture was no longer to be known by the name of the reigning monarch, but by the designer. The term Georgian, however, can well be given to the pre-Chippendale period, which almost covered the reigns of George I. and George II., from 1714 to 1750, in which year Chippendale must have been preparing his book of designs, published four years later. " Georgian " furniture proper is a continuation of the Dutch and French styles, which were also influenced by the architecture of the period. This period included such a carver as Grinling Gibbons, who died in 1721, and architects of the Christopher Wren school, such as Kent, Gibbs, and Ware, many of whom designed furniture and woodwork. No great change took place until the middle of the eighteenth century, when the king no longer dominated the style, and the craftsman received due recognition.

Chippendale.—Thomas Chippendale was a carver by trade. He lived and worked at Worcester, and later came to London, when he started business in St Martin's Lane. In 1754 he published the first edition of his book entitled " The Gentleman's and Cabinet Maker's Director," copies of which are now very rare, and fetch a high price. A later edition was published in 1762. The book

PLATE XXVIII.

252A

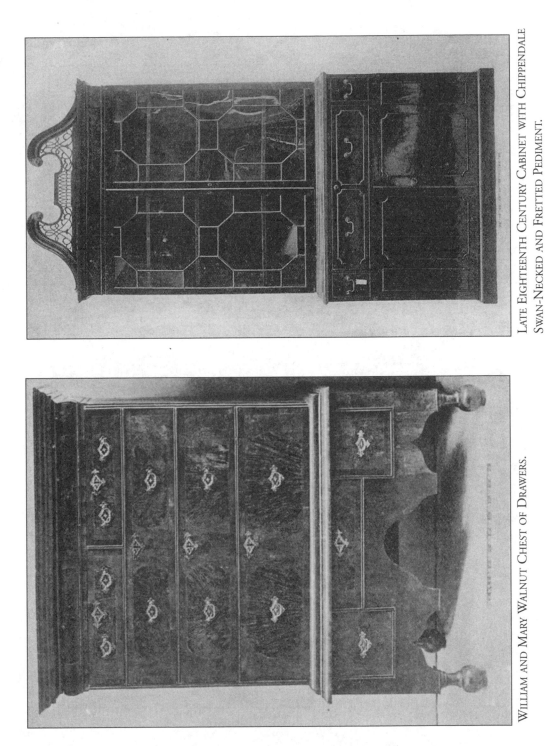

LATE EIGHTEENTH CENTURY CABINET WITH CHIPPENDALE
SWAN-NECKED AND FRETTED PEDIMENT.

WILLIAM AND MARY WALNUT CHEST OF DRAWERS.

PLATE XXIX.

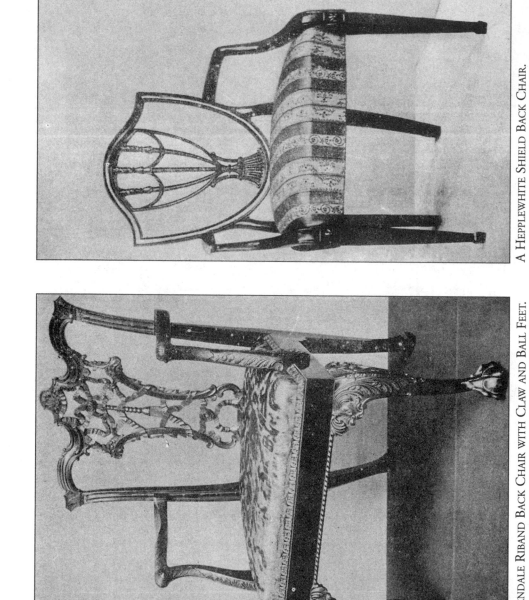

A HEPPLEWHITE SHIELD BACK CHAIR.

CHIPPENDALE RIBAND BACK CHAIR WITH CLAW AND BALL FEET.

contained designs for all kinds of furniture, from tea kettle stands to organ cases. Mahogany was just being shipped into England in large quantities, and he made it his chief material. Chippendale based his designs on Chinese, Gothic, and Louis XIV. and XV. work. The "frets" and "traceries" found in his pediments, friezes, chair legs and backs, &c., and his Pagoda cabinets, are the direct result of the Chinese influence. The Gothic was not successful, and he did not pursue it to any great extent, so that his style may be termed Chinese-French. Of all his furniture perhaps his chairs are the best known, the four noted examples being the "Lattice" (Chinese), "Ribbon," "Ladder," and "Wheatsheaf," or pierced "splat" backs. The last-named he evidently borrowed from the Queen Anne chair. In legs he used the cabriole, with club and claw and ball foot, plain or moulded square, tapered, pierced, or square, with fret laid on ; but he designed an endless variety of legs and backs ; and the same may be said of his barred doors for cabinets and bookcases. An example is seen in Plate XXVIII., a cabinet of a later period with a swan-neck and fretted pediment. Other details peculiar to Chippendale are the "Pagoda" steps on the tops of china cabinets, "pie-crust" edges on small tea tables, broken and swan-necked pediments, classic cornices, raised mouldings on flush-panelled doors, and French curves and shells of Louis XV. (known as "Rococo" details) on carved and gilt pier glasses. Most of his work was made in the solid, and he did not use inlay and but very little turning.

R. Gillow, the founder of the present firm, was in business at Lancaster in the last year of the seventeenth century. He came to London, and established the famous house in Oxford Street. The firm earned a reputation for first-class work, which they sustained throughout the nineteenth century. Though not creating a special style, their work was influenced by the eighteenth-century designers. The firm is now amalgamated with Waring & Co.

G. Hepplewhite.—The next firm of note to follow Chippendale was that of A. Hepplewhite & Co., who published "The Cabinetmaker and Upholsterer's Guide" in 1789, a book of designs which went through three editions by 1794, A. Hepplewhite being the widow who published the book and continued the business of her husband, G. Hepplewhite. These designs are more refined than Chippendale's, being based on classic details, and the later French style of Louis XVI. The "shield," "oval," and "honeysuckle" chair backs are best known. The legs are usually turned or tapered, and curved, and, as a rule, Hepplewhite's chairs are all open-backed, i.e., not stuffed over. His barred doors are curved, with a "swag" introduced, while his pediments have delicate scrolls or swags hanging from a vase as centre ornament. All through there is a delicacy of detail as compared with Chippendale's heavy work. Hepplewhite specialised in "tall-boy" chests, knife boxes and vases, toilet glasses and bedroom furniture. He used veneer, and other woods than mahogany, and some of his chairs were painted. His work is recognised by special details such as "swags" on chairs and barred doors, wheat-ears carved on chair backs, vases introduced as ornament, carved mouldings, the water-leaf—a favourite detail in carving—sideboards with hollow corners, the "husk" in borders of table tops, and in the "fluted" frieze and "reeded" legs.

Sheraton.—Not much is known of Thomas Sheraton except his work, and this has proved him to be *the* "master" cabinetmaker. He was born at Stockton-on-Tees in 1751 and served his time at the bench, after which he came to London and worked as drawing master, author, and cabinetmaker, although it is doubtful if he ever made up his designs; and he was also known as a "local" preacher. He lived in Soho, and one can imagine the struggles he had to bring out his famous book by the record of a friend who writes of his "threadbare coat," and scantily furnished room, which was "half shop and half dwelling-house." In 1791 he published his book, "The Cabinetmaker's and Upholsterer's Drawing Book." His designs, as opposed to Chippendale's flamboyant, and Hepplewhite's finicky details, were straightforward, simple, and severe. Like the last named he was influenced by classic and Louis XVI. details, but he brought them down to his material. He too designed oval and shield back chairs, but the greater number were square or with a slightly curved top rail. He introduced more turning, discarded any underframing in his chairs, and favoured stuffed all-over seats except where they were caned, as in his painted examples. He curved his barred doors, put domes to the tops of his china cabinets, and introduced a quantity of drapery both inside and outside. His sideboards were usually *round* at the corners, and he utilised the brass rail at the back very largely, as well as introducing the pedestal and leg sideboard. Sheraton was most famous for his veneered work and mechanical actions. On some of his furniture there is not a single moulding, and he was the first to use satinwood to any great extent, as well as to design a "kidney" writing table. There was no end to his ingenuity in contrivances for double and triple mirrors, rising desks and artful combinations. His "slotted bar" action is described in the chapter on "Mechanical Actions." He designed the first wardrobe, as we know it, with centre carcase and wings, and was very fond of using the "tambour" shutters for commodes and small tables. In his last days, which were the first years of the nineteenth century, he published other designs much inferior to his earlier work, due, no doubt, to the fact that he had to gain a livelihood and so pander to the bad taste of the period into which he was drawn. For types of chair backs, see Chapter XVI. on "Chair Making," &c.

R. and J. Adam.—The brothers Robert and James Adam were architects who, during the years from 1750 to 1790, designed many large houses in London, including the Adelphi and Portland Place. The furniture associated with their name was designed for the houses, which were built in classic style and decorated with delicate Roman details. Classic mouldings; dentil, egg and tongue, acanthus; vase and urn; swags, husks, scrolls, mythical figures, key borders, garlands and wreaths, honeysuckle, pateras, flutes and reeds, were all treated with particular refinement and painted or stuccoed on walls and ceilings, carved on furniture, woven into carpets, or cast on fireplaces. Much of their furniture was painted and gilt, the painting being done by such notable artists as Angelica Kauffmann, Pergolesi, and Cipriani.

There are many designers of furniture whose names are not so well known as those already given, but they deserve some mention here.

M. Lock and H. Copeland published "A New Book of Ornaments" in

PLATE XXX.

254A

A SHERATON WRITING TABLE.

A SHERATON WRITING TABLE.

254B

PLATE XXXI.

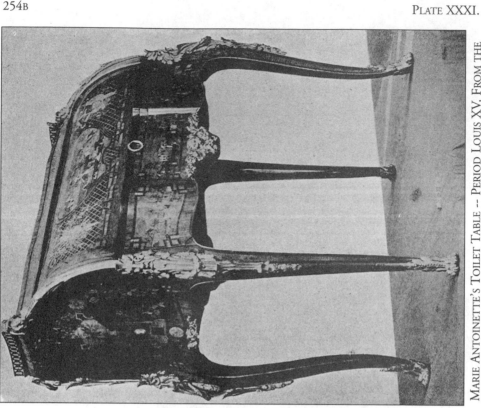

MARIE ANTOINETTE'S TOILET TABLE -- PERIOD LOUIS XV. FROM THE JONES COLLECTION.

PIER TABLE IN THE ADAM STYLE.

1752. Their original drawings can be seen in the National Library at Kensington, and consist of designs in the Rococo style.

Thomas Johnson, carver, published books in 1758-1761. His designs were largely Rococo.

Ince and Mayhew published in 1762 "The Universal System of Household Furniture," with designs in the Chippendale style, and the cluster column table.

J. Crunden, "The Joiner's and Cabinetmaker's Darling," published 1765 and 1796.

Robert Manwaring, cabinetmaker, published "The Cabinet and Chairmaker's Real Friend and Companion" in 1765, and a later edition in 1766. His designs were chiefly for chairs with interlacing and natural "rustic" backs, but his work closely resembles Chippendale's.

Thomas Shearer, cabinetmaker, published designs similar to Sheraton's in "The Cabinetmaker's London Book of Prices and Designs of Cabinet Work," issued by the London Society of Cabinetmakers in 1793.

Thomas Hope published "Household Furniture and Interior Decoration" in 1807. This was an attempt to revive Greek and Roman forms in the construction of chairs, tables, sideboards, &c. It is sometimes spoken of as the "English Empire style," and was the forerunner of the early Victorian.

French Styles.—The style named after Louis Quatorze (XIV.) covers a period of seventy-two years, from 1643 to 1715. In its early stages it followed the Renaissance details of preceding epochs, but gradually developed into the heavy curves, S and cabriole legs, and magnificence of detail which characterised the taste of the times. Most notable is the work of André Charles Boule (known in England as Buhl), who was the king's cabinetmaker. His inlaying and technical methods are described in the chapter on "Veneering and Marquetry." The reign of Louis Quinze (XV.), 1715-1774, includes the "Regency," i.e., the first eight years of the king's minority. The style soon developed into what is known as "Rococo," and is commonly spoken of as "rock and shell," and "pebble and splash" ornament. Oeben and Riesener were celebrated cabinetmakers of the period. The former designed the King's Bureau, the famous piece of cabinetwork known as "Le Bureau du Roi," now in the Louvre. It is one of the earliest known "cylinder falls," and is magnificently decorated with "ormolu" mounts.

Louis Seize (XVI.), 1774-1793.—In this reign there is a distinct return to simpler lines and details. Legs of tables and chairs were straight and tapering, and the mounts were more refined. Brass mouldings and galleries, and marble tops were favourite features, and veneering and marquetry were largely used. The diaper patterns in veneer, though commenced in Louis XV.'s reign, may be associated chiefly with Riesener in Louis XVI. work, whilst Gouthière, who also worked in the previous period, did his finest work in the same years. One special feature of this period is the "lacquer" work known as "Vernis Martin," the name of its inventor. From this may be dated the French polish of modern furniture.

Empire, 1799-1814.—This style was influenced by the Egyptian, Roman, and Greek work, chiefly the latter, and was developed during the Napoleonic period. Chairs, tables, and cabinets were designed principally to illustrate the mythologies. Caryatides, sphinxes, rams, and a mixture of animal and human figures were used to enrich them. Mounts were retained, but were simpler, and were confined to bases and caps for columns, and mouldings for panels. Brass lines and bands were frequently used in panels, and the backs of chairs, whilst metal grilles or silk took the place of the barred doors when the style made itself felt in England. "Pillar and claw" tables are a feature of this period.

Victorian.—The furniture made in the early years of this period was an unsuccessful attempt to copy the "Empire" style, without the brass mounts, and there is probably no time in the history of English furniture when taste was at such a low ebb. This is the more remarkable coming after the brilliant half of the previous century, and it was not until after the "fifties" that serious attempts were made to improve matters. Up to this time the best examples were heavy and cumbersome, such as the pedestal sideboards with low wooden or mirror backs and mouldings overweighted with carving, the smaller "chiffonier," the "pillar and claw" tables, of which the oval "Loo table" was one specially designed for the game of Loo, and which is still made, though in diminishing numbers. Chairs and "sofas" were made with ponderous curves, and covered with horsehair, whilst "what-nots" in burr walnut, and mirror frames with Tunbridge work in all colours of the rainbow, were among the smaller articles. The introduction of new woods produced some changes. Thus, mahogany wardrobes gave place to birch and bird's-eye maple, and they too had to make way for ash and American walnut. There was a period when "black and gold" cabinets were quite a rage, and rosewood was revived with marquetry, only to be discarded in its turn. A later development was in "spindle" rails and "fretwork," and with bevelled glass came a great trade in "overmantels." As early as 1835 Augustus Pugin, an architect, published his "Designs for Gothic Furniture," which did little more than draw attention to the need for reform, although many of his designs were made up. Bruce J. Talbert, who designed for Gillows, published a book in 1868 entitled "Gothic Forms applied to Furniture," and in 1876 another on Jacobean work, whilst in the same year, 1868, Mr Charles Eastlake published his "Hints on Household Taste," which ran into several editions. Mr Eastlake, who was an architect, designed work for Jackson & Graham, a firm of high repute in those days, and both his and Talbert's designs had a widespread influence in the cabinet trade. They were responsible for the return to what was called "Early English" work, chiefly in oak. Talbert designed the "Pet" sideboard, so named from the pet animals carved in the panels; and he introduced the carcase sideboard with high or low back, spindle galleries, turned supports to shelves, and reeding and fluting along door rails and drawer fronts, with incised work in the panels, all largely a revival of Jacobean detail. Eastlake worked more closely to Gothic influences, and his designs are suitable only for oak work.

William Morris, 1860-96, by his work and lectures on decorative art created a deep interest in all that went to the building, beautifying, and furnish-

PLATE XXXII.

256A

ITALIAN WALNUT INLAID CABINET.
DESIGNED BY MR. GEORGE JACK AND MADE BY MESSRS. MORRIS & CO., OXFORD STREET.

PLATE XXXIII.

A MAHOGANY WARDROBE. DESIGNED BY MR. J. H. SELLERS.

Plate XXXIV.

256c

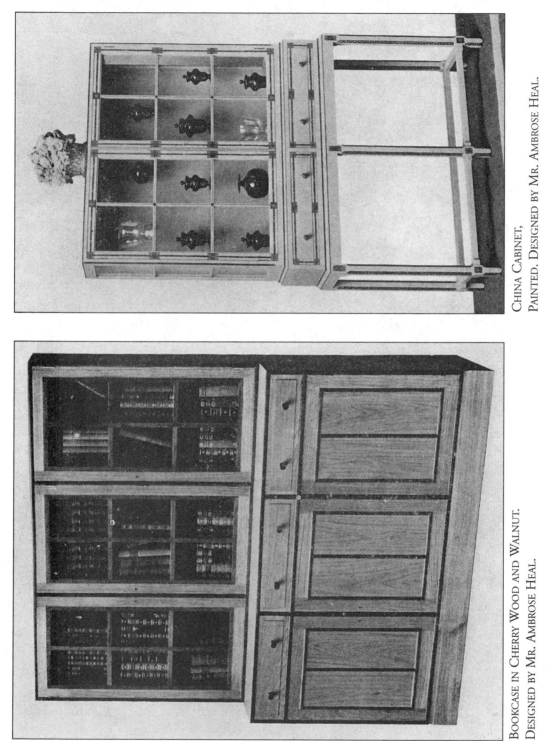

China Cabinet,
Painted. Designed by Mr. Ambrose Heal.

Bookcase in Cherry Wood and Walnut.
Designed by Mr. Ambrose Heal.

SIDEBOARD VENEERED WITH BURR ELM. BY E. W. GIMSON.

PRINT CABINET IN ITALIAN WALNUT WITH RAISED INLAY. BY E. W. GIMSON.

ing of a house. He designed furniture, textiles, and carpets, and wall-papers which have had a world-wide sale. The furniture had a tendency to Gothic forms, and much of it was painted, carved, or inlaid. But he is best known by his wonderful designs in wall-papers and textiles, which were based on natural forms entirely. In 1861 he established the firm of Morris & Co., of Oxford Street, and was largely responsible in forming the Arts and Crafts Society. The two cabinets illustrated, one as the frontispiece, are examples of the fine type of work done by this firm. They were designed by Mr George Jack, and are reproduced by permission of E. H. Marillier, Esq.

Satinwood China Cabinet. Designed by Mr R. Waterer, Jun., of Messrs Waterer & Sons, Chertsey

The "New Art" development, which took place in the last years of the nineteenth century, led rather to eccentricity in form and construction than to any well-based ideas of reform in taste. A laudable desire for simpler furniture resulted in the manufacture of goods which were neither simple nor sane, and produced a temporary return to rough and ready methods of construction, which were admirably suited to the rude necessities of bygone centuries, but insufficient for modern needs. A marked feature in the work was the revival of inlaying as a decorative medium, but this too was very largely carried to excess. In England the influence of New Art was but moderately felt as compared with France or Austria, where the ordinary lines of furniture were distorted into shapes quite unsuitable for constructional woodwork. Examples of this work may be studied in the Bethnal Green Museum. In America there has been a similar movement, known as "The Mission Style," which is more or less a revival of Gothic and Jacobean forms applied to modern work.

Modern Work and Designers.—Present-day tendencies are in the direction of sound principles in design and construction, based on past work and traditions. These traditions illustrate some of the finest efforts of English craftsmanship, which if applied to modern requirements should lead to the production of furniture equal to any of the best periods.

The photograph above shows a fine satinwood cabinet with some interesting details in design and construction. It was designed by Mr R. Waterer, jun., and made for the Countess de Morella by Messrs Waterer & Sons, of Chertsey, one of the few good and old-established firms where handwork is done, and where it is still possible for a young craftsman to get an all-round training. The cabinet was designed as a centre case with a framed-up table part on eight legs, which were cut out of the solid and are finished with what is known as the "Spanish foot," a detail found on chairs and tables of the late Stuart period. The case is made up of eight frames dowelled into posts which run up in a line with the legs. The bottom is screwed up into a rebate, and the top, which is thicknessed up, is dowelled down to the frames. The doors are hinged at both ends, and plate-glass shelves rest on metal pins in each post. Altogether it is a piece of work which called for fine skill and intelligence on the part of the maker.

Mr Ambrose Heal, of Heal & Son, Tottenham Court Road, is a well-known designer of modern furniture. The painted china cabinet (Plate XXXIV.) is a charming example, and the cherry-wood and walnut bookcase (Plate XXXIV.) shows a simple and successful combination of good lines and colour. The firm has also revived the wooden bedstead, and make up the "four poster" (p. 188), which, with spring mattress and frame, is free from any objection on the score of health and cleanliness. The "cupboard chest" in oak, chestnut, or painted deal, is an attempt to supply useful and good cottage furniture. Mr Heal also designed the special bedroom suite for the King's Sanatorium. In recent years he has been the pioneer of painted furniture. The sideboard in Plate XVIII., in silver and blue, is an example of simple and effective treatment in colour.

The designs of Mr Gordon Russell (Plates XLVII. and LIII.) show a real understanding of the beauty of English woods, and are fine examples of sound workmanship.

The wardrobe (Plate XXXIII.) and china cabinet (Plate XXXIX.) designed by Mr H. J. Sellers, of Manchester, illustrate the finely decorative results to be obtained by the right use of figure in mahogany and satinwood.

All the above-named designers are exhibiting furniture in the Palace of Arts at Wembley.

The fine satinwood wardrobe in Plate XXI. is an excellent specimen of modern work based on eighteenth-century design. It comes from the Bath Cabinet Makers Co., and the walnut sideboard in Plate XL. is from the same firm.

The oak sideboard, also in Plate XL., was designed by Mr Fred Skull, of High Wycombe. It is very pleasant in its proportions and simple outlines, and the knobs, turned in yew-wood, add a distinct interest to the design.

The Furniture Design and Cabinet Making Classes in the L.C.C. Institutes have turned out some fine pieces of craftsmanship. The Frontispiece (Plate I.), a china cabinet in coromandel, palm, and snakewood, and the cabinet in Plate XIX., come from the Central School of Arts and Crafts. The sideboard in Plate XVII. and the satinwood writing cabinet in Plate XX. are from the Shoreditch Technical Institute. The last-named piece won the Silver Medal in the City and Guild Competition, 1920.

Mr Charles Spooner is an architect who is also a furniture designer. The furniture in the room (Plate V.), and the oak dresser (Plate XLI.), are typical examples of his work on simple and traditional lines.

Mr Frank Stuart Murray, of the firm of Durand, Murray, & Seddon,

PLATE XXXVI. 258A

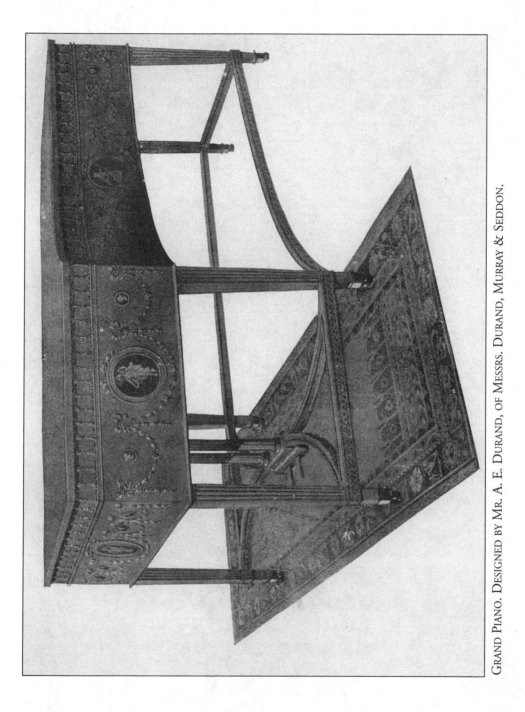

GRAND PIANO. DESIGNED BY MR. A. E. DURAND, OF MESSRS. DURAND, MURRAY & SEDDON.

AN EIGHTEENTH CENTURY GARDEN SEAT AT JESUS COLLEGE, OXFORD.
GARDEN FURNITURE BY MR. J. P. WHITE, PYCHTLE WORKS, BEDFORD.

Plate XXXVIII.

258c

A Model of the Saloon on the S.S. Mauritania. Designed by Mr. Frank Stuart Murray.

CHINA CABINET IN SATINWOOD AND MAHOGANY. DESIGNED BY MR. J. H. SELLERS.

PLATE XL.   258E

WALNUT SIDEBOARD BY THE BATH CABINETMAKERS CO.

OAK SIDEBOARD. DESIGNED BY MR. F. SKULL. SKULL & SON, HIGH WYCOMBE.

PLATE XLI.

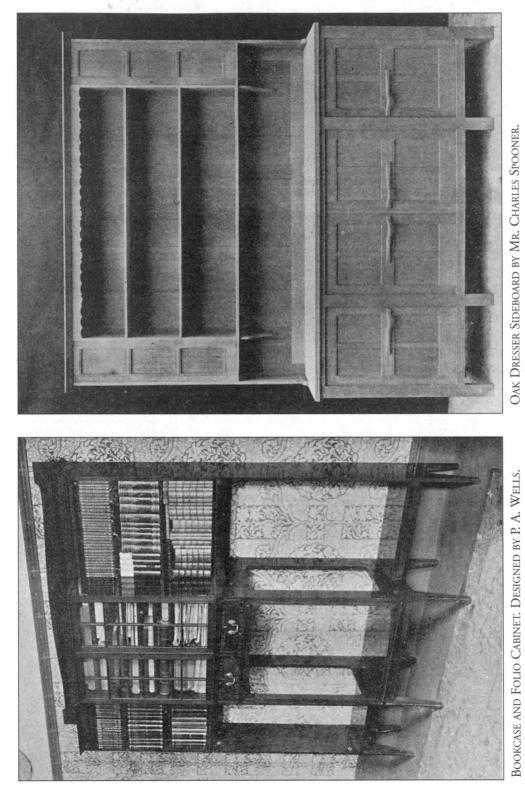

OAK DRESSER SIDEBOARD BY MR. CHARLES SPOONER.

BOOKCASE AND FOLIO CABINET. DESIGNED BY P. A. WELLS.

has for many years been recognised as one of the leading designers of furniture and decoration, and has completed many large and important commissions, the most recent being the decorations and fittings for the Cunard liner S.S. "Mauretania." A model of part of the saloon is shown in the photograph (Plate XXXVIII.) of the decoration and panelling in one bay of the smoking-room. The woodwork in the saloon is of Italian walnut, and this type of work requires a special knowledge of ship construction. Joints have to lap to allow for "camber" and expansion, and the fittings are made to templates. The grand piano (Plate XXXVI.) was designed by Mr A. E. Durand.

Good furniture for the garden is worthy of special attention. The eighteenth-century seat on Plate XXXVII. was photographed in the grounds of Jesus College, Oxford. It is made of beech, and is of the same period as the "wheel-backed" chair, the forerunner of the "Windsor" pattern. The length is 3 ft. 10 in. and depth 17 in., height of back from seat 25 in., and seat from ground 18 in. The shaping of the seat shows it to have been specially made for two. The sets of garden furniture below it are by Mr J. P. White, of Pyghtle Works, Bedford, the top one, in teak, showing a marked eighteenth-century influence, with some of the delicacy of Adam detail associated with strong construction suitable for outdoor use.

The late Mr E. W. Gimson was also a well-known designer and maker of good furniture. The Italian walnut cabinet and sideboard (Plate XXXV.) show a considerable degree of original treatment, especially in the inlay, which is thick enough to allow for a slight modelling of the leaves.

Historic Houses Open to the Public.—In concluding this chapter, attention should be drawn to the number of famous mansions containing fine collections of historic furniture, which, by the courtesy of the owners, are open to the public at stated periods. Hatfield House, on Bank Holidays: Easter, Whitsun, and August; Audley End, Saffron Walden, on Wednesdays, 2 to 4 P.M.; Claydon House, Bucks, by permission; Haddon Hall, Derbyshire, every day in the summer months; and Chatsworth and Hardwick are also open when the family is not in residence. Strangers' Hall, Norwich, contains an extremely interesting and varied collection which can be seen on payment of 6d. Hampton Court Palace is open every day but Friday; Petworth House, Sussex, famous for its Grinling Gibbons' carvings, on Tuesdays and Fridays at 11 o'clock only; Goodwood House, near Midhurst, when the family is away; and Battle Abbey, Hastings, Tuesdays only, 12 to 4 P.M. Knole House, Sevenoaks, most celebrated for its examples of Jacobean work, is open on Thursdays and Saturdays, 2 to 5 P.M., and Fridays and Bank Holidays, 10 to 5 P.M., admission 2s., reduced for parties. At Penshurst Place, also in Kent, a fine old hall with trestle and "high" tables, centre fireplace and open roof, can be seen on Mondays, Tuesdays, Thursdays, and Fridays, 2 to 6 P.M., admission 1s., by ticket obtained at the Post Office or "Leicester Arms." Ightham Mote, near Sevenoaks, is open on Fridays, 11 A.M. to 1 P.M. and 2 to 6 P.M., admission 6d. Fine collections of furniture of all periods may be seen at the Victoria and Albert and Bethnal Green Museums, and French furniture in the Wallace Collection. A very interesting collection can be seen at the Geffrye Museum in Kingsland Road, N.E., open daily.

CHAPTER XII.

CONSTRUCTIONAL AND DECORATIVE BRASSWORK, MOVE MENTS, AND FITTINGS.

Hinges, Butt, Centre, Screen, Desk, Card Table, Piano, Dolphin, Rule Joint, Wardrobe,
Quadrant, &c.—Hinge Plates—Locks, Cut and Straight Cupboard, Pedestal, Box,
Wardrobe, Link Plate, Bird's Beak, Till Drawer, Bureau, &c.—Thumb, Bale, French
and Bullet Catches—Cupboard Turns—Toilet Glass Movements and Screws—
Wardrobe, Quadrant, and Rule Joint Stays — Escutcheons — Castors — Bolts —
Cabinet Handles—Galleries—Mounts—Sideboard Rails—Movements for Music-
Stools—Library Chairs—Cylinder Fall Desks—Harlequin Tables—Shaving Mirrors
—Rising Dumb Waiters and Cellarets—Bed Tables—Locking Movements.

CABINET brasswork can be divided into two parts, viz., the purely constructive
and the decorative. It would be impossible to describe in detail all the various
types in either part, but descriptions of the most important are given, together
with their application to special kinds of furniture. Some examples not named
in this chapter will be found with the designs on pp. 134, 136, 143, 168, 171,
172, 183, 186, 191, and 195.

Hinges.—Types of hinges are shown opposite. Fig. 1 is an ordinary
" **Brass Butt**," made from 1 to 6 in. long, polished or sanded, and pressed (as in
f. 2), or solid, the latter being the best quality known as arrow butts. These
hinges are used on doors generally, and sometimes have turned knobs at each end
of the knuckle, a later addition being the " Rising Butt " for room doors. Fig. 2
is the " **Stopped Butt**," used for box lids, &c., the flange of which should stop at
right angles. Butt hinges are also made to lift off. Cross garnet and H hinges
screw on the front. Fig. 3 is the **Back Flap** with wider flanges for fall-down
flaps, and f. 5 the **Rule Joint** flap hinge with one flange longer to allow for the
hollow on the joint. A special rule joint hinge is shown on p. 267, the bend
preventing any cutting away in the joint. Fig. 4 shows the **Strap Hinge** as
used for desks and jobs which have but narrow fixing room. Fig. 6 is the patent
Reversible Hinge for screens, and f. 7 the non-reversible. Another form of strap
hinge is shown in f. 8, whilst f. 9 and 10 are the **Knuckle Joint Screen Hinges**
used on screens with a draught-proof joint. Fig. 9 is the movement top and
bottom, and f. 10 is fixed in the centre (see following pages for fixing). Fig. 11 is
the **Dolphin Hinge** for secretaire flaps (the dotted lines show alternative shape,
see p. 172), and f. 12 is the **Piano Hinge**, made in lengths from 5 in. to 4 ft. On
p. 263, f. 1 shows the **Quadrant Hinge**, very useful for flaps and lids, and only
where it is possible to cut away the stuff for the quadrant to pass. Fig. 2 the
Wardrobe Hinge, with one wide flange to screw to the carcase end for extra
strength, and f. 3, 4, 5, and 6 are types of link joint or **Card Table** hinges for

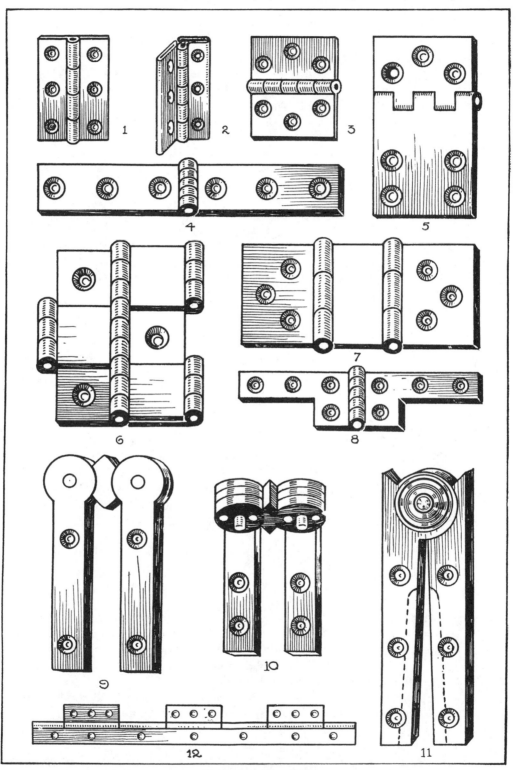

TYPES OF HINGES.

edge and top use, leaving a flush surface on either, as against a knuckle in a butt hinge. Fig. 7 the **Centre Hinge**, with hole plate for the carcase and pin plate for the door, and f. 8 is a similar hinge with a **neck**. These centre hinges are used for wardrobe and other heavy doors which are fitted with plate glass, and the diagrams on p. 266 show methods of centring and fixing. Fig. 9 shows a **Wardrobe Stay** which is cut for space. The thumb-screw would be reversed, and screwed up under the top, and the end plate is also screwed on the door. Figs. 10 and 11 are the **Ball and Socket** movements for toilet glasses, and f. 12 is the **Screw** used for similar purposes on smaller swing mirrors of the Hepplewhite type. **Dovetail Centres** are also used as a movement on common work.

Spring Catches are shown in f. 13, which is the "**Bullet**," or "**Bale**," and 14, the French catch, both suitable for pedestal and small cupboard doors when a lock is not required. "**Thumb Catches**" are used to fix upright secretaire flaps.

Locks.—These vary in size, and are usually measured on the length, and are "right" and "left hand" as needed, terms used to indicate the direction in which the bolt shoots. Fig. 15 is a "**Cut**" cupboard lock, made to cut flush into the stile, whilst f. 16 is a **Straight** cupboard lock to screw on to the stile, in which the bolt shoots either hand. Fig. 17 shows a **Pedestal** or **Linkplate** lock, used where the door shuts on to the carcase end, and the bolt shoots through the link, whilst f. 18 is another of a similar make when the lock is cut on the carcase end. The other way up it serves also as a **Desk Lock**. The links are shown, but in the lock they would not be seen. Fig. 19, the "**Bird's Beak**" lock, sunk in a mortise, and used sometimes for piano and other falls. When locked the beaks spring into holes in the plate. Fig. 20 is the **Box Lock**, with a similar action to the one used on desks, and f. 21 shows a simple fastening known as **Cupboard Turn** or **Button**. **Till Locks** have a single bolt, which shoots up into the bearer above, and are used as drawer locks. **Patent Piano Locks** have a similar action, but the bolt is notched to take two spring catches up in the plate. A specially good type of lock is the **Brahma**, with a nozzle which forms a plate for the keyhole. As a rule keyholes are protected with escutcheons to fit the hole or plates which are fixed around them. Wardrobe locks have a shooting bolt for key, and a spring catch for the handle. The main thing to remember in cutting locks on, is to carefully gauge the centre of the pin for the keyhole, which should be bored first.

Bolts are "**flush**" when the barrel is not seen and the plate is level with the face, and **open** and "**straight**," or "**necked**," when the barrel is outside. **Spring Bolts** screw on the face, and are cased to cover the spring.

Castors.—Round **Socket** for turned, and square for tapering legs, with brass or china wheels. Others have a screw with a plate and ring, whilst large ones have only an iron pin with a plate for screwing. A new patent is the Ball Castor, which moves in a cup on ball bearings.

Quadrant Stays.—Fig. 1, p. 264, shows an ordinary quadrant used for flaps and falls. They are made in various sizes, and some have a spring near the end of the plate, which has to be nipped in before the flap can be closed. Care must be taken to fix it at the same radius, or trouble will follow.

Rule Joint Stays, f. 2.—This is the more common form of support or

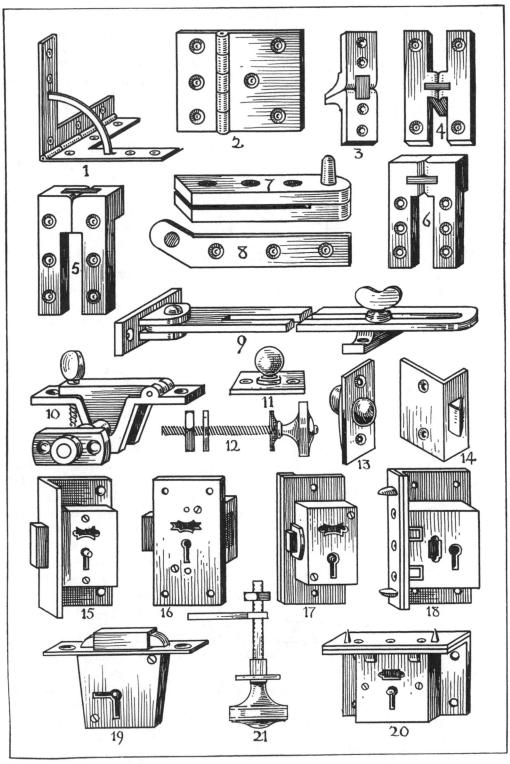

TYPES OF HINGES, GLASS MOVEMENTS, LOCKS, &C.

"stay" for a flap, and takes its name from the centre joint, which is similar to a rule. To fix it, take half the length from pin to pin and mark off from A to B and C, then fix the plate at C and draw a square line from B as shown. The centre must then be fixed exactly on the line. The diagram may be read as a fall-down flap or box lid raised, but the same method in fixing must be adopted.

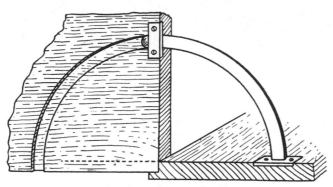

1. Quadrant Support for Flaps.

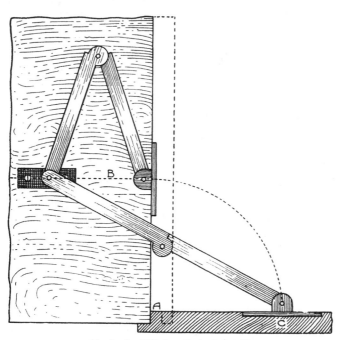

2. Method of Fixing Rule Joint Stay.

The dotted part shows the flap closed. Heavy, square flaps are supported by a long stay of thin metal, made in a similar way to a steel rule, or by a knee iron which shuts up behind a pilaster, see f. 1 opposite.

Cylinder Fall Movements. — These vary according to the job. Two simple methods are used, shown on next page. Fig. 2 opposite is an angle or quadrant iron cut out of thin $\frac{3}{16}$-in. stuff, and fixed to the radius as indicated, the centre working on a pin in a plate. Fig. 3 is the **Fan Iron,** cut out of sheet stuff, and in both cases the end of the fall is rebated to take the thickness. With the fan iron it is necessary to fix a thin false end on the inside to cover the iron. Either can be worked with or without a tongue on the end of the fall, and if there is a sliding flap it can only be pulled out after the fall is up. Fig. 4 shows a more complex but combined movement, which is known as the **Slotted Bar.** Sheraton appears to have been the first to adopt it. The bar is of $\frac{3}{16}$-in. iron, and about $1\frac{1}{4}$ in. wide. To find the centre for any given radius to the fall, draw the bar in position when both fall and slider are shut, as seen at A, and repeat the drawing when both are open, as at C. Where they cross will be the centre, and if set out again half way as at B, the length of the lower slot is obtained, whilst A gives the lower end of the upper slot and B the top end. A small plate fixes the centre pivot, and a filling-in end will be necessary to cover the bar. A tongue on the fall is preferable. The shaded portion shows the position of the stationery case, and the diagram illustrates the movement for the secretaire cabinet in the chapter on "Table Work." The lower carcase might have to be cut away to take the length of the bar, but this depends on thickness of rail, and care must be taken to make the slots work smoothly on the pivot. This movement works best when the fall is less than a quarter of a circle. American roll-top desks have no "movement," but work in a groove like a tambour. The ogee or bead slips are rebated one in the other, f. 1, next page, and are wired, hinged, or glued on to canvas. Other movements, which are nearly all patents, are screws for music-stools, centres for revolv-

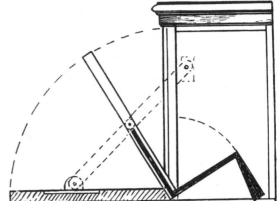

1. Method of Supporting Heavy Flaps.

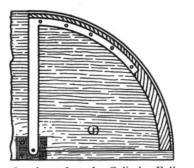

2. Quadrant Iron for Cylinder Falls.

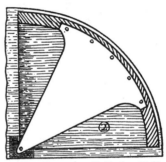

3. Fan Iron for Cylinder Falls.

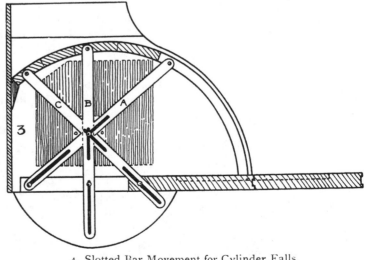

4. Slotted Bar Movement for Cylinder Falls.

ing chairs and dumb waiters, reversible joints for shaving mirrors and bed tables (see chapter on "Tables") reading flaps for chairs, automatic lockings (see chapter on "Office Work"), and harlequin table movements, as well as a number of patent devices for invalid furniture and office cases.   Extending screws for dining-tables

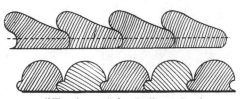

1. "Tambours" for Roll-top Desks.

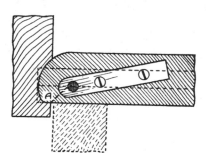

2. Fixing a Butt Hinge on Door inside Carcase End.

3. Butt Hinge fixed on to Carcase End.

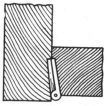

4. Method of Finding Centre and Fixing Centre Hinge.

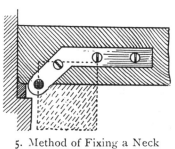

5. Method of Fixing a Neck Centre Hinge.

are described in the chapter on "Tables." On some old "diners" brass clips were used to lock the extra leaves together. An iron bracket has taken the place of the wooden one, with a finger joint, for cheap Pembroke tables. Special methods of supporting shelves are illustrated in chapter on "Carcase Work." Tiles are fixed to washstand backs with a special screw, and pivots are made for card table tops. The quality of all brasswork varies with the price; cheap locks are made with iron cases and brass facings, and iron is often faced up with very thin brass.

Setting out and Centring Hinges. —A reference to the double sheet of shutting joints will at once illustrate the different types of centres for hinges, and fixing becomes a simple matter if due thought is given to the setting out before any fixing is begun.   In ordinary butts the gauge should be set from the outside of the flange to the centre of the pin, and a line gauged on the edge to cut to.   Fig. 2 above shows the "butt" used on a door when fixed inside the carcase.   The knuckle will show full, and the whole thickness of the hinge at the knuckle is cut into the door stile, but it tapers towards the back to the thickness of the flange, whilst the opposite flange is let in flush as shown.   On cheap work the whole hinge would be cut into the door and the carcase flange screwed on the face.   The gauge mark on the carcase is the same as that on the door, plus the distance the door stands in.   Fig. 3 shows a similar hinge when the door shuts on to the carcase end and when the cutting in is equalised.   In this case the door would swing round clear of the end.   Fig. 4 is the plan of a centre hinge showing a method of finding the centre.   Divide the thickness of the stile into three as seen in the dotted lines.   From the corner of the rebate A strike a mitre line to cut the first dividing line, which gives the point, and if this point is taken along the line about an eighth of an inch it will ensure a clearance when open, as the diagram shows. The same centre will give the rounding for the back of the door. Fig. 5 opposite gives the neck centre, used when it is necessary to clear a break or moulding on the carcase or pilaster. The centre is usually on the front line of the door, but its position depends entirely on the projection to be cleared. In both cases it is safest to make a zinc template from which both top and bottom parts can be marked off. The special rule joint hinge shown in f. 1 below is much simpler than the ordinary flat one. In this the flange is bent underneath instead of being cut into the wood, thus saving the danger of an open joint when the flap is down, and allowing any variation in the depth of the square. The hinge was invented by Mr W. E. Degerdon, and a table maker will at once see its practical advantages. The setting out for both hinges is the same, and the centre must be under the square as shown, which a gauge line underneath the top will give. The centre for striking the joint

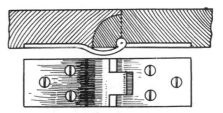

1. Patent Rule Joint Hinge.

is from the intersection of the square line and the thickness line of the hinge. It is usual to cut the small flange into the top first, and then cramp the joint up tight and mark off the opposite flange. Fig. 2 shows top and centre parts of the knuckle joint screen hinge. A the plan of the top, and B showing the double joint and pin, with C the centre in which the piece D is mortised into the stile of the screen and pinned through, the knuckle part being cross-cut to allow this to be fixed. In another make of this hinge the flange D is cut into the edge of the stile and screwed in an upright position. The patent reversible screen hinge has made the above somewhat out of date and is much simpler to fix, but no other screen hinge gives such a good draught-proof joint.

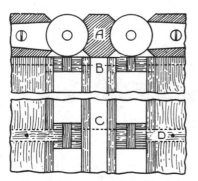

2. Top and Centre of Knuckle Joint Screen Hinge.

Decorative Metal Work.—Up to the seventeenth century most of the metal fittings on furniture were of iron. Hinges, lock plates, handles, &c., were highly decorative in character, but the seventeenth and eighteenth centuries brought other woods than oak into use, and brasswork came into general favour. Much good work is often spoiled by bad metal fittings, and handles often go a long way to make or mar a job. Handles have varied in shape with the periods of furniture, and we have Louis, Empire, Queen Anne, Chippendale, Adam, and other forms of metal work. In the nineteenth century wooden knobs were prevalent, but it has long since been the custom in the metal trades, which cater for cabinetwork, to produce fittings in "style," and it is for this reason that we give a selection of handles on the next page. Fig. 1 shows a Louis XVI. knob, full size. Fig. 2 is a plan of the top, and f. 3 the back plate with section below. The decoration is of a type much imitated by the

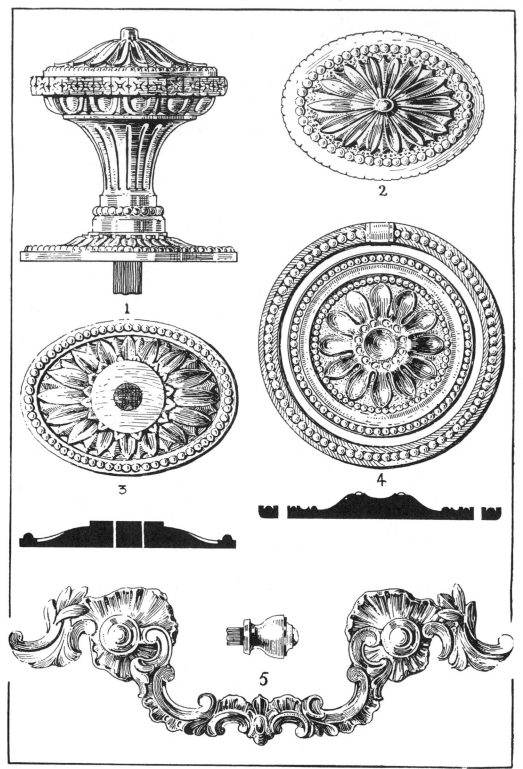

TYPES OF FRENCH HANDLES.

English furniture designers of the eighteenth century, especially Adam. The knob would be fixed by the spindle going right through and fastened with a nut. Fig. 4, p. 268, is a ring drop handle of the same period, but later, the handle itself being rectangular in section as seen by the diagram underneath. Fig. 5 is a Louis XV. type with Rococo forms, which were sometimes also copied by Chippendale. The illustrations were drawn from the actual examples kindly lent for the purpose by Messrs Shirley & Co., of Percy Street, London, as was also f. 3 in the next set on p. 270, where examples from pieces of furniture in the Museum at South Kensington are shown. Fig. 1 is a silver handle from the famous eighteenth-century satinwood toilet table, painted by Angelica Kauffmann. The back plate is slightly raised in the centre and delicately engraved with a swag. Fig. 2 is from the same cabinet on a smaller drawer. Both are extremely dainty and all that a handle should be. Fig. 3 is of modern make, but based on one of early eighteenth-century date. Fig. 4, a small keyhole plate from an old bureau, and f. 5, a cabinet door handle, evidently taken from an iron one of an earlier period. The handle in f. 6 is typical of the later eighteenth century, and is taken from an old mahogany card table. The spindles go right through the drawer front and fix with a nut on the inside. The shape of the drop and back plate vary considerably, as only single sets for each job would be made. Figs. 7, 8, and 9 are peculiar to the Queen Anne furniture, and sometimes the drop is made of solid metal, but 7 is often of thin stuff and halved. An escutcheon or keyhole plate is shown in f. 10, and f. 11 is a small brass handle from an old bureau. Needless to say that scores of patterns might be given, but those shown are typical. Iron handles are again coming into favour, and oxidised copper and white metal are also in demand. Drawer "pulls" are fixed, and are both sunk into or screwed on the face. "Flush handles" are usually sunk into the plate which is cut into a drawer front or sliding door level with the face. Both are chiefly used in office and shop furniture. Special handles are made for chair backs and butlers' trays.

Mounts are generally of brass, and vary from the richly modelled "ormolu" mounts on the French work to simple rings, caps, and bases, for clock case and other columns. "Ormolu" is an alloy of various metals, and the elaborate mounts made of it are best illustrated on the Marie Antoinette toilet table in the chapter on "Styles." The cabriole leg lent itself to such decoration, but this style of metal ornament has not found much demand in England. **Galleries** are often used on the tops of small tables and cabinets, and brass mouldings fixed round the edges of table tops, of which examples are given in the chapter on "Table Work." In eighteenth-century work brass "grilles" of thin wire or heavier metal were used in doors of cabinets and bookcases, and the shutting bead was often of brass. Sheraton, Hepplewhite, and Adam sideboards were fitted with brass rails at the back (see the Adam sideboard, p. 153), and the grandfather clock cases of the same period often mounted with a quantity of brass. Galleries, sideboard rails, beads, and mounts of various description are to be obtained ready for use, but on special jobs they have to be made. Picture and window rods, cornice poles, portiere rods, wardrobe hooks and yokes, and brass towel rails, with all furnishing fittings, come more or less into outdoor fitters' work.

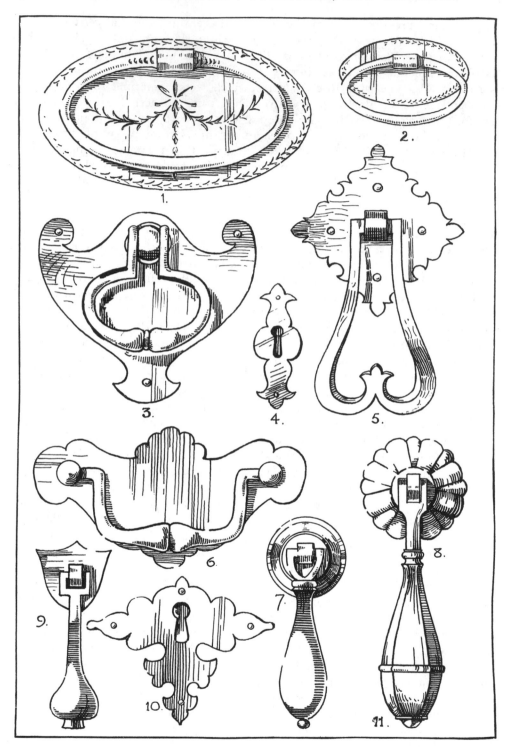

TYPES OF DROP HANDLES.

CHAPTER XIII.

MACHINE TOOLS AND MACHINING—MOULDINGS.

Machines, Hand and Power, Planing, Thicknessing, Mortising, Dovetailing, Grooving,
Moulding, Jointing, Mitreing, Boring—Saws, Circular, Band, Frame, Fret—Lathes
and Lathework—Examples of Mouldings, Classic, Gothic, French, Jacobean,
Eighteenth Century.

MACHINERY now plays an important part in the production of furniture. It
has introduced a new type of workman now known as a machinist, and another
who is a "fitter up" of the work turned out by the machine. Much has been
said both for and against machinery, but there must always remain a very large
residue of work for the skilled cabinetmaker which the machine can never do.
Hand machines are chiefly confined to small circular saws, worked with handle
or treadle; "fret" or "scroll" saws of the American type, small lathes, and
mortising machines. They are all valuable in a small shop where power is not
obtainable, but since the advent of the electric motor these hand machines
are not so much in demand. The small circular saw with a rising table and
boring attachment is one of the most useful machines in a shop, for apart from
the usual sawing it can be utilised for cutting grooves, rebates, and starting
tenons, whilst the boring attachment saves time in dowelled work.

It would take up too much valuable space to give illustrations of all the
machines used, and though a knowledge of the uses of such should come within the
cabinetmaker's experience, it must be said that they are quite secondary to
his need for skill and resource at the bench. The three examples illustrated
are made by Messrs Wilson Bros., Holbeck, Leeds, who have kindly lent
the photographs for reproduction. The band saw on Plate XLII., p. 272, is
made on the latest improvements, fitted with ball bearings which reduce
the strain and are dust-proof, both values which increase the life of a
machine. Both wheels are covered with rubber, and the table cants, and
has an extension. Such a saw is indispensable in a machine shop. On the
same Plate a "hand feed planing, jointing, and moulding machine" is shown
for high speed running. Besides planing and surfacing, this machine does
jointing, chamfering, and rebating, and sticking light mouldings such as
sash bars, &c. The "circular saw" shown on Plate XLIII., p. 273, has a
rack rising top and self-acting feed, and is fitted with an adjustable canting
fence. It is suitable for tenoning, ripping, and cross-cutting, grooving, tongueing, and moulding, with the addition of a cutter block. This firm also
supplies the patent "chain" and "hollow chisel" mortising machine. The
chain works on the principle of a dredger, and cuts a very clean mortise
with a circular finish at the base, and the "hollow chisel" is an ingenious and

simple device which cuts a straight square mortise with an upright or horizontal motion. A twist bit is encased in the chisel which has open sides to clear the core, and the action in feeding is simple and easy. "The vertical spindle" moulding machine is a great time saver, especially on curved work, but on straight intersections, such as the mould of a wardrobe door, the corners have to be finished by hand.

Among the later additions to wood-working machinery are the "dovetailing" and "sand-papering" machines. For the former Messrs Wilson have a handy apparatus which fixes to the "spindle" table. The dovetail cutter is inserted into the top of the moulding spindle, and the apparatus can be easily fixed to other makers' machines. It is specially suitable for drawer work. The sand papering is done on a divided flat table, under which a large drum revolves flush with the table top. The sections of the table are easily moved back when the paper has to be renewed on the drum. Tenoning tools are now made to fix to an ordinary hand mortiser, and the tendency is towards combination in machines, and there is one known as the "General Woodworker." It combines a band, circular, and fret saws, and mortising, boring, and moulding machines. It is of necessity a heavy machine, but such a combination economises the space considerably. Overhead fret saws are now the rule, an improvement which allows stuff of any width to be cut. Small masters usually have all machine work done out at the mill, for it is only where there is a big output that machinery on a large scale can be laid down, but electric power is so convenient now that a small motor can be fixed to a saw bench or a lathe with both economy and convenience.

Lathes are run by foot and power. A convenient size for a foot lathe would be a 4 ft. 6 in. bed, to take a table leg between the centres. Cone bearings are used on the best lathes, and "gut" bands, with a four-speed driving wheel, and cone pulley. Special "chucks" are made for "oval" and "square" turning, the latter being known as "**thurmed**." To thurm on a small lathe the stuff must be fixed on a wheel, so that only one side of it meets the chisel, but on a larger machine it is fixed to a "drum," and the larger the drum the nearer to a square the turning will be, but it is never dead square in section. Chucks are made to turn various shapes, and fancy turning, twists, &c., are done with "eccentric" chucks and cutters. Turning tools, chisels, and gouges are sold in sets of eight, up to 1 in., or singly as required.

MOULDINGS.

Mouldings are said to be "stuck" when worked on the solid; "bolection" when rebated, and laid on the angle, and are consequently above the face frame; "bedded" when laid in a groove; or "housed" and rebated when glued in a rebate with a long and short shoulder to the frame. All these types are illustrated in the chapter on "Joints and their Applications." Mouldings "project" as in a cornice above the eye, and "recede" in plinths, but are generally both on a surbase or table part. Almost any section can be worked with the "hollow and round" hand planes, or with a "scratch" (see "Workshop Practice"), and where there is an undercut or recessed "member,"

Plate XLII.

New Hand-Feed Planing, Jointing and Moulding Machine.

Improved Band Saw ith Ball Bearings.

PLATE XLIII.

CENTRAL RACK RISING TOP CIRCULAR SAW BENCH.

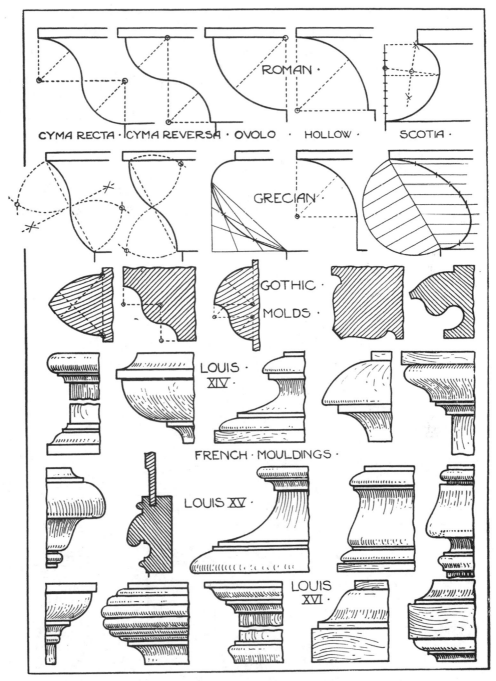

CYMA RECTA · CYMA REVERSA · OVOLO · HOLLOW · SCOTIA ·

ROMAN ·

GRECIAN ·

GOTHIC · MOLDS

LOUIS XIV ·

FRENCH · MOULDINGS ·

LOUIS XV ·

LOUIS XVI ·

TYPES OF MOULDINGS.

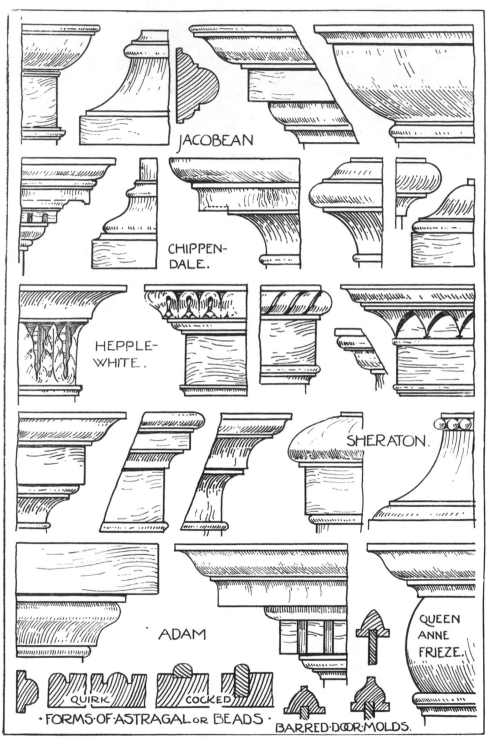

JACOBEAN

CHIPPEN-
DALE.

HEPPLE-
WHITE.

SHERATON.

ADAM

QUEEN
ANNE
FRIEZE.

QUIRK   COCKED

·FORMS·OF·ASTRAGAL·OR·BEADS·   BARRED·DOOR·MOLDS.

TYPES OF MOULDINGS.

as in the French mouldings of the Rococo period, the machine can only work the two faces or part of the recess, and the finishing must be done by hand.

Types of Mouldings are shown on pp. 273 and 274. The first two rows are the Grecian and Roman, based on circle and elliptic lines, from which all others are developed or varied. In Gothic sections the hollows are deeply recessed. Louis XIV. mouldings follow the classic details, as did the earlier designers of Francis I. and Henry II. in what is known as "Renaissance" or Historic French. Louis XV. mouldings are peculiar for their "thumb" or "nosy" projections and deep recesses, whilst those of the Louis XVI. period are more severe, and of simpler classic. On the second page, our own Elizabethan and Jacobean followed the classic models with reserve, and adapted them to the special position. Chippendale cornices, &c., are based on the classic hollows, rounds, ogees, and astragal; and Hepplewhite introduced "enrichments" as a special feature in his cornices. Sheraton was sparing with mouldings, but where he did use them, in cornices or surbase, they were plainer than those of his contemporaries. R. and J. Adam used refined and delicate details of a classic character. The curved, or "bulge," frieze of Queen Anne is peculiar to that period of English work. Types of the "astragal" or "bead" are shown with some sections of barred door mouldings. When a series of beads are worked together without a "quirk," they are called "reeds," whilst a number of rebates or steps of equal depth are known as "annulets." When the bead has a square or "step" added to it, it becomes a "torus," and all these names, with "fillet," "flute," and "facia," are derived from the classic architecture and vary in their applications. Types of mouldings suitable for all positions will be found associated with the special designs throughout the book, and it is obvious that no hard and fast line can be drawn in the design of details which lend themselves to such an infinite variety of forms.

CHAPTER XIV.

PANELLING AND FITMENTS.

Early Types of Panelling—Preparation of Walls—Plugging and Battening—Fixing
Grounds for Tapestry Hangings—Methods of fixing for Dados, Fireplaces, Skirting
Boards, Ceilings, Cornices, &c.—Fitment and Fireplace for Georgian Room, full
Details of Cornice and other Moulds — Gothic Framing, Tracery, Linen-fold
Panels — Patent Mansfield Robinson Panelling — Design for Colonial Adams
Room with Fitments—Details of Elizabethan Types of Panelling, &c.—Sheraton
Fireplace and Mantel—Georgian Fireplace and Mantel, with Complete Details—
Scale Drawing of Jacobean Room with Section of Cornice Frieze, Panel, and
Base Moulds, &c. — Photograph of Room at Versailles — Details of French
Curved Panelling.

FROM the fifteenth to the eighteenth centuries it was the custom to cover the
walls of rooms, galleries, halls, and corridors with oak panelling. In the earlier
types the panels were small (see Plate XLV.), but in the seventeenth century
the size was increased. Sometimes only two-thirds of the height of the wall
was covered, which allowed for a plaster frieze, but as a rule the panelling reached
to the ceiling, which was either of open beams or of decorative plasterwork.
Towards the end of the Georgian period, the custom declined, and wall-papers
or silk damask coverings were in vogue, a fashion which continued to the
latter part of the Victorian era. The taste and fashion about that time
reverted again to fitted rooms, due, no doubt, in some measure to the demand
for a suitable environment and background for costly objects of art, the collecting
of which had begun to assume considerable proportions. Modern fitments
are, therefore, a revival of early work, and many of them are copies of, or
based upon old examples. Probably more has been done in the direction
of panelled libraries and dining-rooms, and the movement has extended to
fitted bedrooms. To obtain a thorough knowledge of decorative interior
woodwork, the actual measuring and drawing of good examples in national
museums and mansions cannot be too strongly urged upon the student.
The necessary procedure in executing such work is described in the
following pages, and the examples shown are those which introduce the
maximum amount of constructive and decorative detail consistent with
limited space.

Taking Measurements, Templates, and necessary particulars before proceeding with the work, are described in Chapter X., and the setting out of rods and preparation of working drawings are also dealt with there. Before dealing with the general constructive details in fitments, we must first consider the preparation of walls for receiving panelling, &c. In most cases brick walls are the foundation, and when these have any suspicion of dampness about them—and always with new buildings—they should be thoroughly covered with several coats of a preparation consisting of varnish bottoms and paint. Tar also is used as a damp preventive on brick walls. In addition to this, the backs of the framing are also painted, which prevents the damp penetrating into the wood, causing it to swell and buckle. All fixings must necessarily be secret, and this can generally be effected by firmly screwing the framings before fixing the mouldings, or by slot screwing as described in Chapter IV., and further illustrated in its application to a fireplace (see f. 1). Brick walls must be well plugged at intervals to provide a secure holding for screws. The plugs are shaped as in f. 2, and the pockets are cut with a strong cold chisel, or "plugging" chisel, in the brickwork, when the plug is driven in flush with the surface. When cut as shown, the plug is forced into a screw-like position and seldom works loose. The least effective form of plug is the square taper type, which has a tend-

HALF·VIEW SHEWING· SLOT·SCREW FIXING·ON· FIREPLACE·

1.

ency to draw out of the hole when nailing or screwing. Concrete or cement facings cover some walls, and fixings are usually obtained by plugging as described above. "Grounds" are necessary when tapestry or damask panels are required.

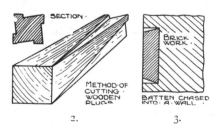

SECTION·

BRICK WORK·

METHOD·OF CUTTING· WOODEN PLUGS

BATTEN CHASED INTO·A·WALL·

2.   3.

These grounds are prepared from 3 by ⅜ in. yellow deal, and are also known as battens. The exigencies of the work sometimes demand the grounds to be fixed flush with the wall surface, and this is accomplished by cutting or "chasing" away the cement to receive the batten, which is then cemented in flush (see f. 3), and slightly bevelled in section to form a key. Before **fixing door linings**, the battens are fixed round each opening, and screwed to plugs in wall, the inside edge being bevelled to form a key for plaster (see f. next page). The architraves can then be put together, either "framed up" or "mitred and keyed" and slot screwed into position. Wide architraves necessitate the use of a wider ground, and this is obtained by "framing" the grounds and fixing as illustrated in f. below. As a further illustration of the process of plugging and battening walls see opposite page. This sketch shows grounds for tapestry above a dado, and also provides the necessary foundation for fixing the pilasters, mouldings, and cornice. The position of plugs for panelling is also indicated. Testing with plumb line and level is necessary for groundworks, the inequalities of wall line being adjusted by packing out the battens or removing superfluous wood with a plane.

Preparation of Ceilings for Panelling.—**Beam Ceilings**, composed of main beams, divided by smaller ones, do not require any special treatment. In modern work their use is restricted to casing round the girders, the modern successors in constructive building work to the old-fashioned oak or chestnut beams which supported the floors. The joists provide an excellent fixing, and the cased beams are pocket-screwed as illustrated in the section of main beam in f. 1, p. 280. The cross beams are shouldered over the rebates, and wall plates fitted as shown. Mould-ings complete the work, when scribed round all the openings.

A FRAMED
UP-SET OF
SKELETON
GROUNDS

USED FOR
WIDE ARCHI-
TRAVES · ·

Framed Ceilings consist of suitably designed framing, with carved or inlaid panels, the openings being accentuated by carved or decorated mould-ings. Numerous examples could be given of framed ceilings involving special constructive features, but space will not permit. A description only of the preparation can be attempted. The frames are made and fixed in segments fixed to the rafters, and richly carved bosses are generally introduced as a decorative feature to conceal the screw fixings. Gilt framing with silvered Venetian glass panels is an uncommon and effective treatment. Long lengths of moulding are first fixed one way of the ceiling, and then squares or rectangles are formed by scribing short lengths between them. The panels are composed of four pieces of glass, resting upon rebates of moulding. The corners are secured at the centre with a carved patera, and the scribed joints of mouldings are concealed with bosses scribed over the mouldings and screwed to the ceiling. Screws in work of this character are very frequent, and the ceiling must first be boarded with $\frac{1}{2}$-in. stuff, firmly screwed to the rafters.

Fixing Fireplaces and Panelling.—Slot screwing is essentially a fixer's joint, and much used in interior work. The process of fixing by this method is as follows :—First decide and mark the position of the job and screws for this secret fixing, and scribe the work to fit the wall properly, then plug the wall and turn screws into plugs until they project about $\frac{3}{8}$ in. from the surface. Dab the head with moist lamp black, and place the job in position, pressing it against the heads, which will leave black marks ; then bore a hole for head about $\frac{3}{8}$ in. lower than the mark, and cut the slot to receive same (see p. 277).

Replace the work, entering the heads in the prepared holes, and force it down, completing the job by additional pocket screwing where possible.

Panelling is made and fixed in segments, which are so arranged as to joint behind pilasters or mouldings. When extra long lengths are required a

GROUNDS
3" × 3/4"

View showing Arrangement of Grounds and Plugs for Panelled Room.

convenient position is decided upon, and the rails are tenoned dry and levelled off. The framing can then be separated and finally glued up when fixing.

Glueing up Framing in long lengths is accomplished by improvised cramps composed of scantlings, with pieces fixed at either end; folding wedges are inserted at one end, and when tightened, effect the necessary pressure. This method is only resorted to where cramps with lengthening bars are not available. All sections or pieces of framing should have the stiles carried right through, and the bottom rails are made wider to provide fixing for the skirting. The projecting horns on stiles are easily scribed to floor line, and the open spaces under the rail should be made up at intervals with blocks fixed to the wall. For simple skirting it is only necessary to make up a surface line of framing, but skirting of a

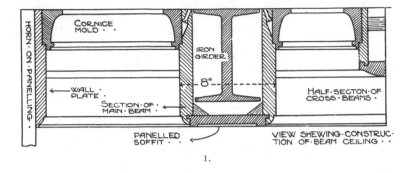

I.

heavier type, tongued together as illustrated in f. 2, demands shouldered bracket pieces, seen in diagram. The dado moulding can generally be arranged as illustrated in f. 1 on opposite page, so concealing the pocket screwing used at top of framing.

Pelleting.—Painted work does not demand the more expensive methods of fixing as detailed above. Screws may be sunk into the surface of the work, and the holes stopped by glueing pellets into them, see chapter on "Workshop Practice" for detailed description. Although this is essentially a device for painted work, it is also resorted to in polished fixtures, when other methods are impracticable.

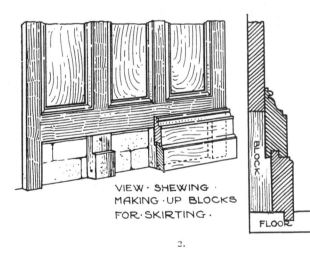

VIEW · SHEWING ·
MAKING ·UP BLOCKS ·
FOR· SKIRTING ·

2.

Building up and Fixing Cornices.—The constructions illustrated on p. 285 show the arrangement of these details. Built-up cornices are mostly used in French decorative interior work, especially the "bracket" and "coved" varieties; a good example of the first named is illustrated in the reproduction on Plate XLVI. of the Marie Antoinette boudoir at Versailles. It is only possible here to illustrate one particular type of French panelling which embraces some common constructional details. The example shown on p. 294 is mortised and tenoned together with long and short shouldered joints, the dotted line indicating the shape of the rails before glueing up the work; the curves are then cut to the inside line, and the rails are rebated to receive the mouldings. Carving in French work is a special feature, and is generally cut out and glued on to the surface before being carved up.

Arrangement and Details of Panelling.—The panelling of each period has some peculiar and characteristic detail. Thus in Gothic woodwork we find the "mason's mitre," described in Chapter IV.; in Tudor and Elizabethan panelling, the bevelled or splayed bottom edge on the rails, see photo on this page, as distinct from Jacobean framing, which is mitred all round the openings; and with French work there is "Sloper nose" moulding. There is, indeed, an endless variety, but space forbids a larger treatment of them.

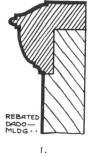

REBATED
DADO—
MLDG..

1.

Fig. 2 is a photograph of panelling of the Henry VIII. period, sometimes called "Holbein" panelling, and represents a type of work done at the commence-

2. An Example of Panelling from an Old House at Waltham Abbey.
Now in the Victoria and Albert Museum.

ment of the English Renaissance, which was further developed in the Elizabethan and Jacobean periods. The portcullis, Tudor rose, and heraldic centres to the medallions, and the scroll-like ornament, are but steps to the decorative details of a later date.

Marking for Fixing.—Each section of panelling is marked in alphabetical order with a stencil or crayon to correspond with the similarly marked scale drawings and designs; its position is then understood—an important detail when the fixing is conducted by labour engaged locally.

ELIZABETHAN AND JACOBEAN DETAIL.

Both the above periods were marked by details in turning, strapwork, low relief carving, and mouldings.   Some are shown in the five panelled

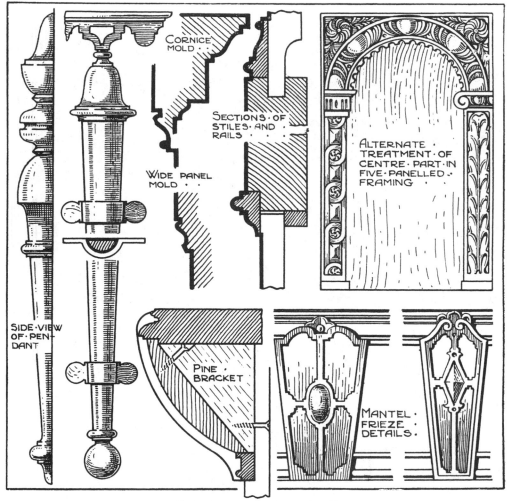

Elizabethan and Jacobean Details.

framing on the opposite page, the centre panels being either rectangular, square, diamond, elliptic, or circular in shape.   The carved decoration shown

CARVED · DECORATION · IN · FRIEZES · AND · RAILS ·

SCALE · FOR · EN-LARGED · DETAILS ·

1 FOOT ·

INCHES ·

PILASTER · AND · RAIL · DETAILS · ·

AN · ELIZABETHAN · TREATMENT · 6 FT · HIGH ·

TYPES OF ELIZABETHAN AND JACOBEAN PANELLING.

JACOBEAN · · PANELLING · · ·

in the right-hand corner of the page, is termed " Nulling," and was much used in frieze rails of panelling and furniture. Strapwork detail with rose centres taken from pilasters, constantly recurs in modern Elizabethan work. The semi-headed panel centre shown on p. 282 is another peculiar feature of this period, either with strapwork pilaster or moulded and carved leaf decoration. The split turning and mouldings shown are taken from Jacobean work. Reference to p. 288 will indicate additional detail of this period.

FITMENT—COLONIAL GEORGIAN (Plate XLIV.).

The adaptation of Colonial Georgian interiors to drawing and bed rooms is an effective treatment when finished to a white colour, and also with silk wall panels, which contrast excellently with the rich tones of eighteenth-century furniture. The finely curved mouldings with fretwork traceries, the fluted

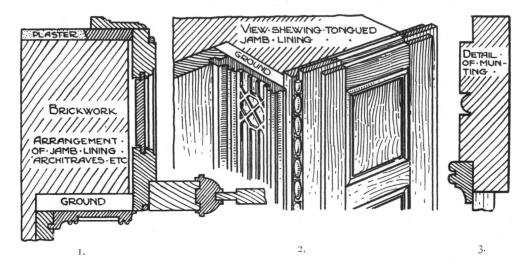

I.   2.   3.

fascias, frieze overlays, and turned decoration on corners and muntings, project delicately graded shadows upon the groundworks. On p. 285 the enlarged details show the method of building up a "coved" cornice; this is rebated over the panelled framing, and screwed through the beaded moulding covering the screw heads; the small projection obtained by housing this moulding is, as shown, an additional advantage, and does not accentuate the union of panelling and cornice. Blocks or brackets are fixed at intervals in the corner of the room to which the top piece of the cove is screwed, and the top member is then mitred round and fixed to the cornice. The lower part of panelling or "dadoing" is made with long and short shoulder mortise and tenon joints, with a moulding mitred round, see f. 3. Muntings are grooved before glueing up the frames, and the split turning "bead and reel" is glued in. The enlarged detail shows the construction of top frames, the moulding forming a rebate to receive the panes. Fluted decoration is worked by machining 6-ft.

INCHES

SCALE·FOR·ELEVATION·
AND·PLAN

3

PORTION·OF·A·DRAWING·
OR·BEDROOM·FITMENT·
EXECUTED·IN·MAHOGANY·
AND·ENAMELLED·WHITE·

THE·DESIGN·BASED·
ON·COLONIAL·
· ·GEORGIAN·

PART·PLAN·ABOVE· ·
INDICATES·FLOOR·LINE

PLATE XLIVA. DESIGN FOR SIDE OF "COLONIAL GEORGIAN" ROOM

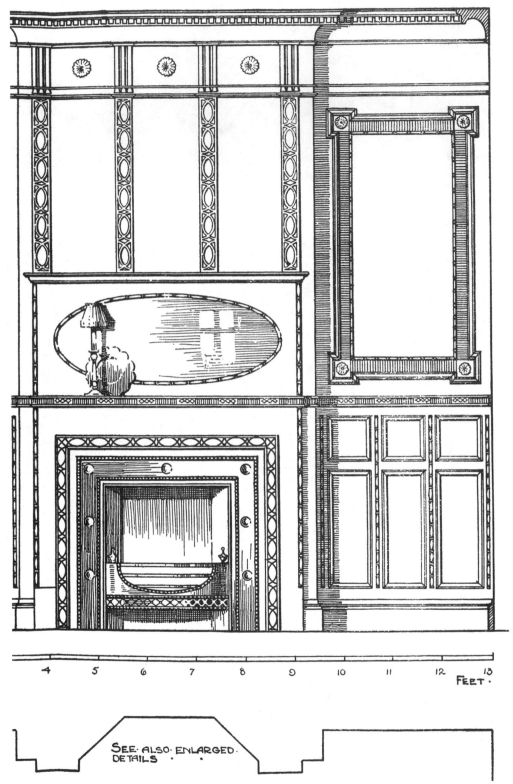

4   5   6   7   8   9   10   11   12   13 FEET.

SEE ALSO ENLARGED
DETAILS

PLATE XLIVB. DESIGN FOR SIDE OF "COLONIAL GEORGIAN" ROOM

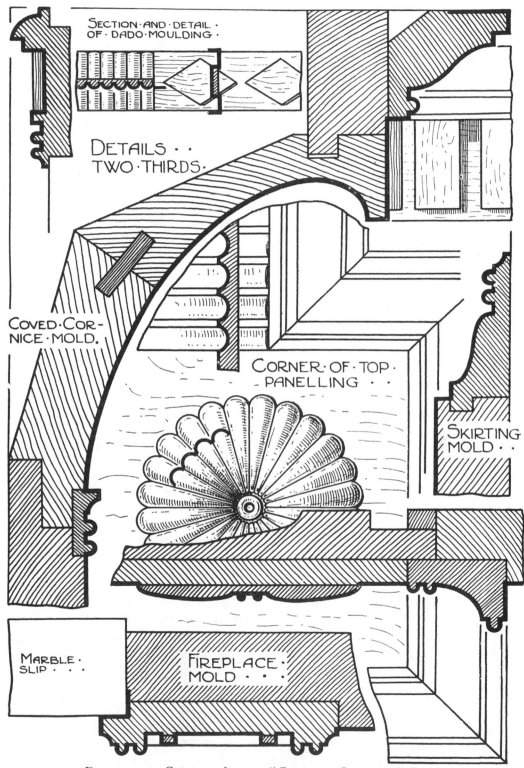

SECTION·AND·DETAIL·
OF·DADO·MOULDING·

DETAILS · ·
TWO·THIRDS·

COVED·COR-
NICE·MOLD.

CORNER·OF·TOP·
PANELLING · ·

SKIRTING
MOLD · ·

MARBLE·
SLIP · · ·

FIREPLACE
MOLD · · ·

DETAILS FOR CORNICE, &c., IN "COLONIAL GEORGIAN" ROOM.

lengths, about 1 ft. wide, and cutting to the width required ; this joints up flush with the corner blocks glued in corners ; turning is then mitred round the inside angles. "Ply" panels are an advantage with such constructive detail, and obviate the necessity of providing for panel shrinkage. The skirting is

Section of the Mansfield-Robinson Patent Panelling.

scribed and fixed to the horns of the framing, and finished by fixing the top moulding. Patterns at the corners are turned to the section shown, and carved to the drawing. Practically all the fixing is effected by screwing under the mouldings, and this should be borne in mind when setting out such panelling.

Door framings to harmonise with the decorative scheme are necessary in such work. With thick walls, panelled jamb linings and "soffit" or head linings are necessary. The soffit is fixed in position, being previously grooved to receive the jamb linings, see view on p. 284. The fronts of linings are made flush with grounds, and the architraves are fixed in the position shown in f. 1 and 2, p. 284, covering the joints. It is not unusual to make the outside of the door and jamb linings correspond with a decorative treatment in the corridor. The door is then faced up on one side with a suitable wood.

GOTHIC PANELLING, &C.

A portion of this type of panelling is shown opposite, which is suitable for dadoing, and can easily be extended to any height. Numerous antique examples about the country reach a height of four or five panels. The dado moulding is characteristic Gothic, as also is the centre sunk moulding in muntings, stopped against the rails. The rounded inside corners of framing are also essentially Gothic, and are a variation of the "mason's mitre," a very common detail in woodwork of this period. To execute such work, it is first necessary to mould the muntings before glueing up, but all mouldings on stiles and rails are stopped, and completed as shown after the framing is levelled off ; this is best effected with carving gouges. Some masons' mitres are finished exactly the same as a plain mitre, with the mitre line quite straight. Pinned tenons are also a pleasing and strengthening feature of this work, similar to the Elizabethan. Linen-fold or parchment panels are also illustrated, and they are so-called because of their resemblance to these materials when folded. There is a paucity of information pertaining to these panels, but the enlarged details of English and Flemish origin, shown herewith, are excellent examples, and provide a sufficient basis for their production. To execute them, the panels are first moulded to the section shown, and carved to the design. As the ultimate effect depends largely upon the moulded section, it will be found a good plan to make a model of pine, moulded and carved until the required "feeling" is obtained, or modelled up in clay, either being used as a pattern when executing the wooden

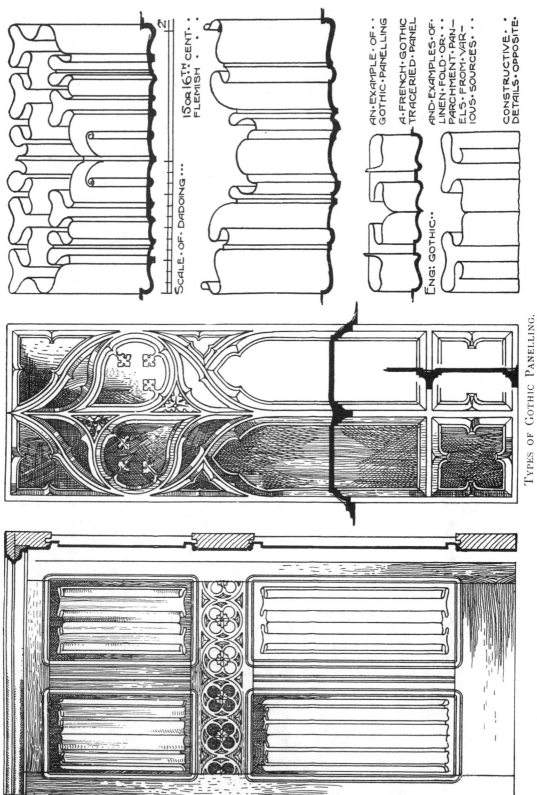

15 or 16th cent.
Flemish

Scale of Dadoing...

An example of Gothic panelling

A French Gothic traceried panel

And examples of linen fold or parchment panels from various sources

Eng: Gothic..

Constructive details opposite.

Types of Gothic Panelling.

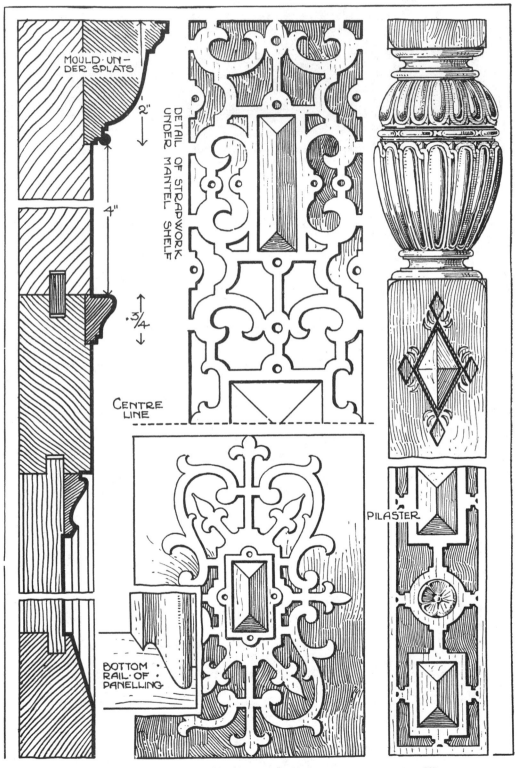

Mould under splats

2"

4"

.3/4

Detail of Strapwork under Mantel Shelf

Centre Line

Bottom Rail of Panelling

Pilaster

Strapwork Turning and Recessed Detail in Elizabethan Work.

panels. A traceried rail is also shown in the panelling, which, in old work, was usually carved out of the solid, but modern conditions demand more economical methods, and it is usual to groove the rail to receive the fretted and carved overlay. The shapes are first cut upon a fret saw and "regulated" with files; mouldings are worked upon a "spindle" machine, and the tracery is completed after being glued down to the groundwork. This method of procedure would also be followed in executing the traceried panel illustrated—an example of French Gothic work. Skirtings are not usual in Gothic panelling, and the fixing is best obtained by slot screwing to wall, a method previously dealt with in this chapter. An additional fixing would also be obtained by screwing through the rebate for dado moulding. The method of rebating dado moulding into the framing and using the top member to cover the joints is also utilised in other periods of panelling, and is a very effective constructive detail, for in addition to hiding the fixing, it economises material. An alternate method is to rebate the dado moulding, fitting it into a rebate as shown. Scribing is used for angle connections of the above, and is fully described in chapter on "Workshop Practice."

Panelling is regarded as a fixture in a house, but a patent method which allows of its easy removal with other furniture was shown in a model cottage at the Franco-British Exhibition. It is known as the "Mansfield Robinson" panelling, after its inventor; and although specially designed for small houses, it is being largely used in banks and other public buildings. The diagram, p. 286, shows a section of it, and illustrates the practical but simple method of fixing. A, B, and C are pine battens rebated on each edge, and screwed to a plugged wall. The stiles are grooved to drop over the rebate, and to take the tongue of the rails; the panel, shown darker, also drops into the groove formed by the rebate. The whole is built up from the floor, and fixed by the top moulding as shown.

A SHERATON FIREPLACE (see next page).

The drawings on the next page illustrate a typically modern example of a fireplace with Sheraton details which includes two china cupboards and a mirror above the shelf. Various broad constructive principles are illustrated, notably in the framed-up groundwork. A half-front elevation is shown of this, and dotted lines indicate the connecting lines of the "facings." Two parts are necessary, and after the groundwork of $1\frac{1}{4}$-in. pine is glued up, and centre space cut, $\frac{1}{2}$-in. facings must be mitred and glued to the groundwork, projecting $\frac{3}{8}$ in. beyond the opening as a provision for the mirror. It should here be observed that all fireplace work must be screwed from the back wherever possible. This applies both to the mouldings and the "facings." An enlarged detail of the cupboard illustrates this portion, and the construction is indicated in the sectional details. The ends run right through, with bottom lap dovetailed up, and a false top slip dovetailed between. The outside ends fit over the back as indicated in the plan, and the cupboards are screwed from behind. Bottom

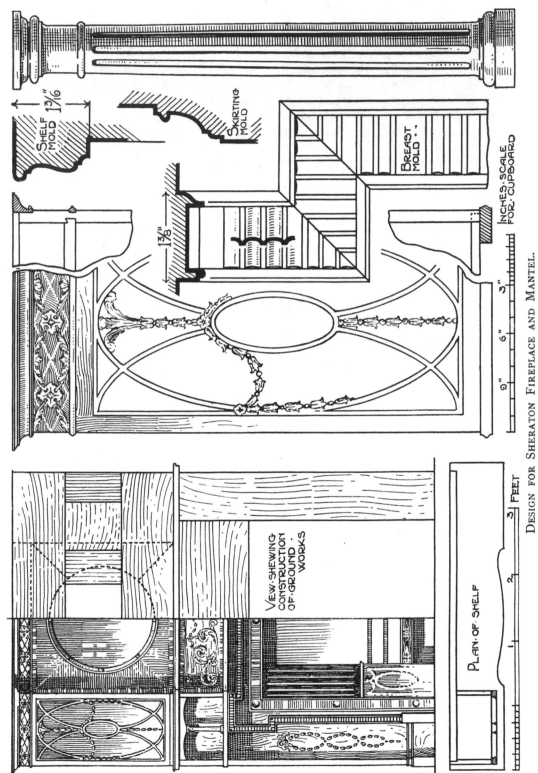

DESIGN FOR SHERATON FIREPLACE AND MANTEL.

parts should be made, whenever possible, in the solid. Marquetry panels are, however, frequently used, necessitating the use of veneer, but this practice is not recommended. The better plan is to introduce carving for decoration, and although this is a departure from the accepted detail of Sheraton work, it is certainly justified when the use of veneer is bad construction, owing to the action of adjacent heat. Methods of fixing are previously dealt with in this chapter.

The sketch alongside illustrates an ordinary "mantel" of the Adam type, above which in the eighteenth century a wall mirror, or to use its present-day name "overmantel," was fixed, delicately carved in low relief and gilt—a considerable variation of the term now applied almost indiscriminately to the cheap "glass," "pillar," and "shelf" variety.

HALF·ELEVATION·OF·A·
MANTEL·IN·PAINTED·PINE

A GEORGIAN FIREPLACE (see next page).

A modernised fireplace, designed on the lines of those produced during the latter part of the seventeenth century, is illustrated on next page, showing some characteristic proportions and details. The fireplaces of this period were of an architectural character, and this will be seen in the consoles, pedimental shelf, modillion cornice, and moulded details. Some of the finest examples produced during the latter half of the seventeenth century, and upon which the later Georgian work was based, were carved by the famous Grinling Gibbons, who worked for Sir Christopher Wren. His work is noted for its extremely natural detail, and superb execution. The carvings were chiefly executed in limewood, a material which lent itself admirably to a vigorous yet delicate treatment of strictly natural designs, such as birds, flowers, and cherubs, arranged in swags, festoons, and pendants. Fireplaces such as this example are used in conjunction with panelled interiors, with large panels in the framing, surrounded by wide carved mouldings. The construction of the lower part of the fireplace is of a straightforward character: a groundwork is framed together, and the pilasters and consoles are added, also the "tablet" at centre with the "egg and tongue" moulding mitred round, and completed by the addition of marble breast linings or "slips." The upper part embraces features not previously described in this chapter, and reference to the enlarged scale sectional view shows the side panels made with a wide top rail, tongued panel, and loose moulding. The wide rail at the top is made the full width, with a narrow bottom rail as shown in figure, connecting the sides together and thus forming a groundwork to receive the panelled breast. The breast extends from the frieze moulding to shelf line, framed together, and panelled

SCALE·FOR
ELEVATION·

1

2

3

4

12" SCALE·
FOR··
11" DETAILS

10"

9"

8"

7"

6"

1 FOOT·

MANTEL·BOARD
MOULDING····

TWO·THIRDS

CENTRE·
FRAME

HALF·ELEVATION
OF·A·GEORGIAN·
FIREPLACE····

DESIGN AND DETAILS OF "GEORGIAN" FIREPLACE AND MANTEL,
By Mr J. Hooper,

VIEW·SHEWING·PROPORTION·OF·PANEL —
LING·AND·ARRANGEMENT·OF·BRACKET·CORNICE

IN JACOBEAN·ROOM· V & A. MUSEUM.

DATE·CIRCA·1696

INCHES · ·

PLATE XLVA. PANELLING AND DETAILS OF JACOBEAN ROOM AT THE VICTORIA AND ALBERT MUSEUM (CONTINUED OVERLEAF).

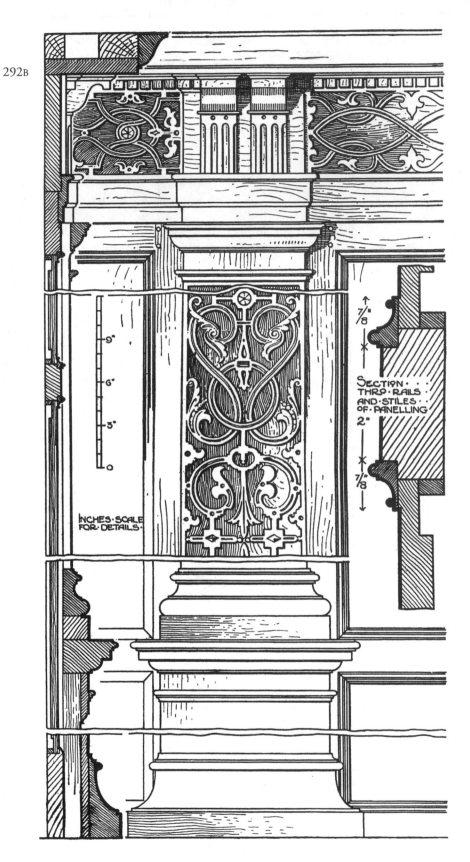

9"

6"

3"

0

INCHES · SCALE
FOR · DETAILS ·

7/8"

SECTION ·
THRO · RAILS ·
AND · STILES ·
OF · PANELLING
2"

7/8"

PLATE XLVB. PANELLING AND DETAILS OF JACOBEAN ROOM AT THE VICTORIA AND ALBERT
MUSEUM.

with a carved moulding glued to the frame with broken corners at the bottom. Numerous devices are resorted to for attaching the moulded frame surrounding an oil painting. The section shows the sketching frame for canvas, screwed to a moulded frame previously mitred and keyed together, inserted as a whole from the front, and readily removed if required. Another treatment is to screw the canvas frame on to the groundwork from the front, with a rebated frame made separately, fitting over the picture and screwed to breast. The painted decoration of this style of work is usually executed in white, contrasting admirably with richly coloured pictures introduced into the fireplace, and in some cases in the form of medallions attached to the panelling. Old ex-

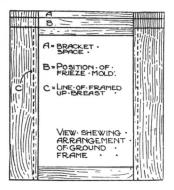

amples of this period were usually painted a cold green colour, relieved at intervals by the application of gold leaf on the details.

A JACOBEAN ROOM.

This example of panelling, said to be one of the finest productions of the seventeenth century, is in the Victoria and Albert Museum, removed there from the "Old Palace" of Bromley-by-Bow, which was built in 1606. The panelling is of a later date. The proportions displayed in the panels, frieze, and pilasters are very fine, with delicate strapwork detail. The pilaster is much better than the frieze, the latter suffering somewhat in the unfortunate "butted" finish of the strapwork against the bracket plates. A curious feature of the framing in the original example is the panel mouldings; these were worked upon the solid and not rebated into the framing as illustrated. Whilst the character and details of this room have been copied and preserved in the drawings, the construction introduced differs from the example, and is such as would be employed in executing a similar room at the present day. The section view shows construction of the bracket cornice. A pine block is fixed round the angles formed by the ceiling and wall, to receive the "soffit." This has another block glued level with front edge, and the fixing is obtained by screwing at back and front, which is concealed by the "frieze board" or "wall plate," and also by the cornice moulding at front. The panelling frames are next placed in position, slot screwed to the wall at intervals in the back to prevent possible sagging, and finally secured by screwing under the frieze moulding and pilasters. The strapwork pilasters occur at intervals round the room, and the framing is made in sections, arranged with wide stiles, so that a fixing for the pilasters can be obtained. No skirting is introduced with this example, and to prevent an unsightly space occurring under the bottom rail, due to shrinkage, a tongue should be left upon the framing and cut into the floor. This is effected by temporarily fixing a long strip of wood in the angles of the room, using this as a fence or guide for a

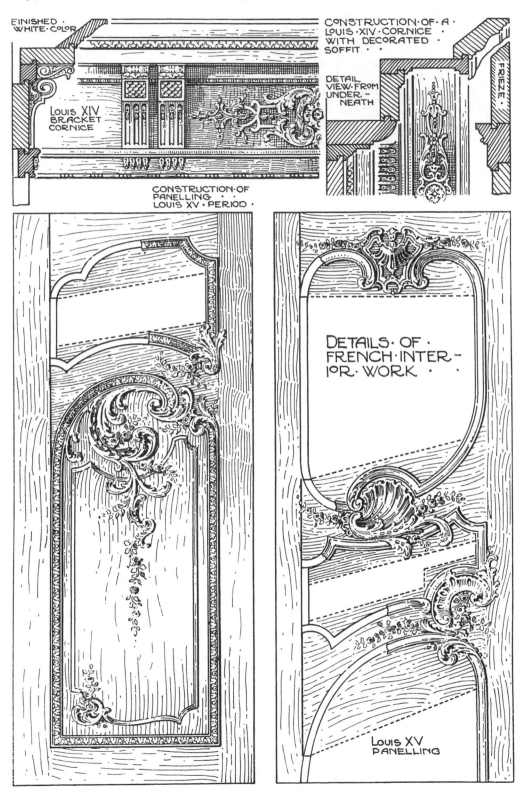

FINISHED · WHITE · COLOR

CONSTRUCTION · OF · A · LOUIS · XIV · CORNICE WITH · DECORATED · SOFFIT ·

DETAIL VIEW · FROM UNDER — NEATH

FRIEZE ·

LOUIS XIV BRACKET CORNICE

CONSTRUCTION · OF PANELLING · · LOUIS XV · PERIOD ·

DETAILS · OF · FRENCH · INTER — IOR · WORK · ·

LOUIS XV PANELLING

TYPES OF FRENCH PANELLING.

PLATE XLVI.

294A

BOUDOIR OF MARIE ANTOINETTE AT VERSAILLES.

PLATE XLVII.

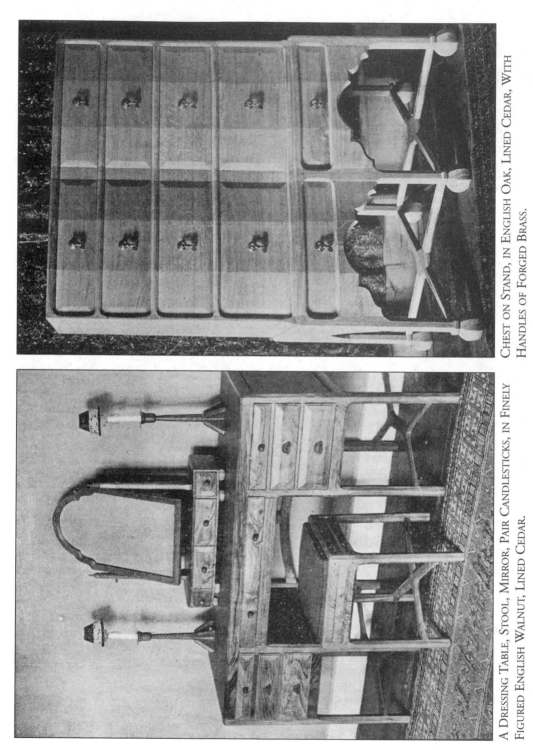

CHEST ON STAND, IN ENGLISH OAK, LINED CEDAR, WITH HANDLES OF FORGED BRASS.

A DRESSING TABLE, STOOL, MIRROR, PAIR CANDLESTICKS, IN FINELY FIGURED ENGLISH WALNUT, LINED CEDAR.

DESIGNED BY GORDON RUSSELL AND MADE BY RUSSELL & SONS, BROADWAY.

"block" saw, and cutting down $\frac{5}{16}$ in. deep. This piece is removed and another piece $\frac{3}{8}$ in. wider is fixed, the $\frac{3}{8}$ in. difference in width corresponding to the tongue in panelling; when cut to desired depth the fence is again removed, and the core removed with a chisel. The sketch illustrates this process. The bracket plates would be added after the framing is fixed up, and completed by the addition of "soffit," "dentil mouldings," and brackets. Pilaster pedestals and shafts would follow next, slot screwed to the framing stiles, and the room completed by scribing round the frieze mouldings. An account of "scribing" and its application is given in chapter on "Workshop Practice." The "pinned" tenons are bored through close to the shoulders after glueing the framing up, and levelling it off to the face surface. An alternate and effective finish can also be obtained by allowing them to project slightly beyond the surface, and in rounding them off. This necessitates their use after the framing is finished off.

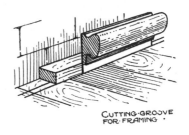

CUTTING-GROOVE
FOR·FRAMING·

CHAPTER XV.

SPECIAL FURNITURE FOR SHOPS, OFFICES, AND MUSEUMS.

Office Cabinets with Filing Drawers and Automatic Locking Action—Library Table with Reading Racks—Bedroom Furniture for the King's Sanatorium with special Hygienic Construction—Museum Show Case on Stand with Dust-proof Joints—Centre Case for Museum with Drawers—Cash Desk with Friction Roller Drawers—Office Cabinet with Sliding Doors—Office Stools and Chairs—Enclosed Washstand—Pedestal Print Stand for Museums with Practical Details of Construction, Movements, and Fittings.

INTRODUCTION.

THE subject of this chapter is a large one, and is dealt with in as practical a manner as the limited space will allow. It is therefore confined to such articles of furniture as embrace special features in this class of work. The examples given in the following pages chiefly illustrate fittings for public buildings, but the application of air-tight joints to furniture is a very necessary part of cabinet-work, and they are commonly used when dust-proof interiors are required. It is a debatable point whether an air-tight interior is best for the preservation of books. Some authorities favour the theory that a free access of air to the bindings acts as a preservative, and even insist on air holes being bored at frequent intervals in the backs. But air-proof interiors are executed in cases for the display of plate and valuable china. Dust-proof joints and their application to carcase work is dealt with in Chapter IV. Various office fittings are included in this chapter, involving special practice and actions. American roll-top desks are perhaps the most used of all office fittings, but they are almost exclusively of American production, the only special constructive feature being the tambour, illustrated in Chapter XII.

The drawing opposite illustrates a suite of furniture designed by Messrs Heal & Son, for the King's Sanatorium at Midhurst. This class of furniture is specially designed for hospitals and sanatoria, and for hygienic reasons mouldings are of the simplest character, projections which would hold dust are avoided, and all corners and angles are rounded to facilitate cleansing. Washstand tops and backs are of white opaque and clear glass respectively, and are so arranged as to be easily detached for cleaning. These principles are extended also to rooms and wards, the angles between floor, walls, and ceiling being rounded.

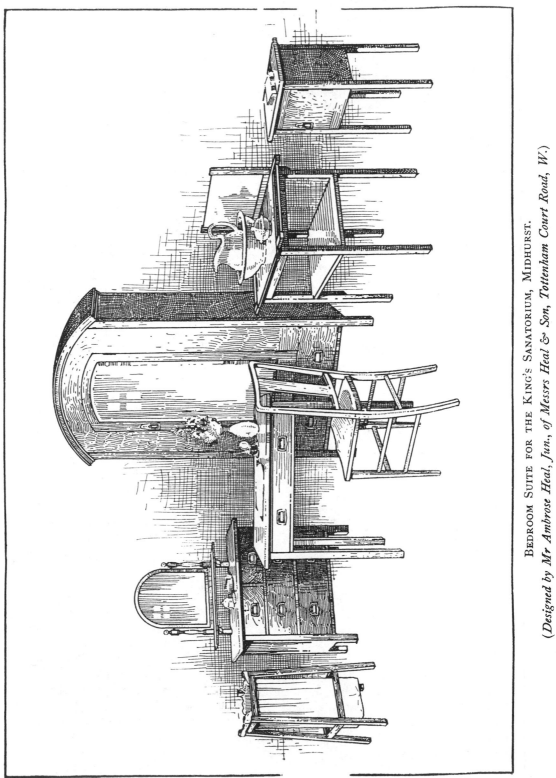

BEDROOM SUITE FOR THE KING'S SANATORIUM, MIDHURST.

(Designed by Mr Ambrose Heal, Jun., of Messrs Heal & Son, Tottenham Court Road, W.)

AN OFFICE CABINET (see opposite).

These drawings are introduced to illustrate mechanical locking actions, a special feature in office filing cabinets, which is also applied to writing tables, print cabinets, &c. The simplest method of locking drawers in dwarf cabinets is by means of a hinged pilaster, locked into the carcase top, or, as it is done in many cases, at both ends. A sectional view of the pilaster and position of hinge are shown below. When the pilaster is opened, a free passage is allowed for all drawers. An enlarged detail of the locking apparatus is shown on this page, the sectional view opposite showing its application to an office cabinet, and it acts simultaneously on thirty drawers, each side of the centre part. One side of the cabinet is fitted with files with a patent attachment, manufactured by the "Shannon" Company, of Ropemaker Street, E.C., see diagrams, and drawers are used in the other part. This, however, does not affect the locking action, all plates being fixed to fit the clips. Reference to the detail below shows the wooden bar A fixed to the carcase top and bottom division and grooved to receive an iron bar. This iron bar is slotted at intervals, and screwed to the wooden part so that it can rise or fall freely to the full extent of the slots. To

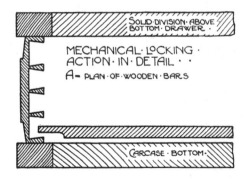

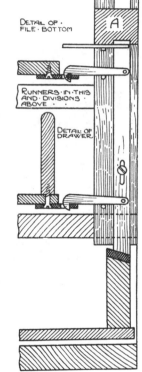

open the three tiers of drawers, the long drawer at bottom is drawn forward about $\frac{1}{4}$ inch, and the A bar then falls and causes the clips to bear upon the pins shown, thus raising the front part. The drawers contained in the cabinet are locked by pushing home the bottom drawer, and locking the same, thus forcing the bar up and allowing the clips to drop. If some drawers have been inadvertently left open, it is not necessary to re-open the bottom drawers, but they should be pushed in, the plate coming into contact with the rounded front of clip effecting a raising action, and the clip falls down into the hole provided on the plates. A plate need not be made the whole length of the bottom drawer back, three short pieces of iron about $2\frac{1}{2}$ in. long, screwed under each falling bar, being sufficient.

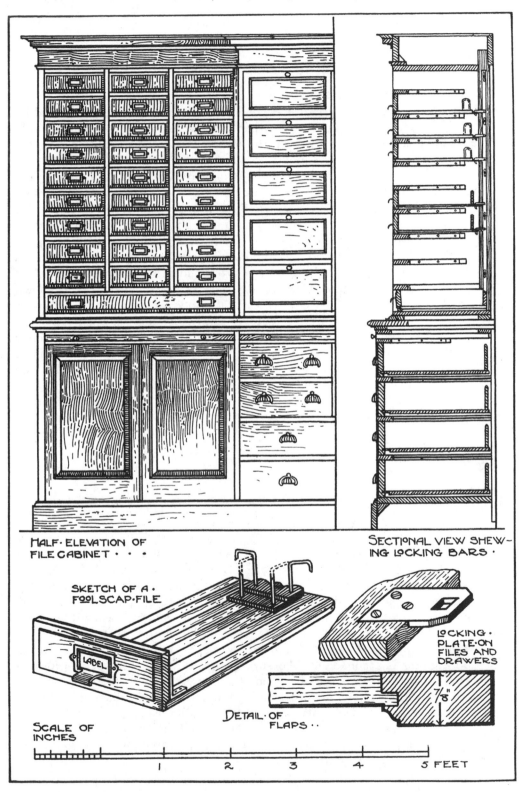

HALF·ELEVATION OF
FILE CABINET · · ·

SECTIONAL VIEW SHEW-
ING LOCKING BARS ·

SKETCH OF A ·
FOOLSCAP·FILE

LABEL

LOCKING·
PLATE·ON
FILES AND
DRAWERS

DETAIL·OF
FLAPS ··

$\frac{7"}{8}$

SCALE OF
INCHES

1   2   3   4   5 FEET

AN OFFICE CABINET.

A LIBRARY TABLE (see opposite).

A reading table suitable for a public museum or library is shown in the drawing. It is arranged to seat four, but this capacity could be increased by extending the length, introducing the pedestals at intervals. It is built up in three distinct sections, explained in the order they take in building up the work—viz., (1) Supporting pedestals with cross bars ; (2) Framed up and lined table part ; (3) Cupboard with falling flaps carrying horsed reading stands. The sectional view shows the construction of framed-up pedestals, and also indicates the framed-up table part. Owing to its width and the necessity for a perfectly rigid top, an under-framing is constructed with moulded lining-up pieces mitred round the edges, and both frames are screwed together. The cross-bearers are cut into the pedestals and bolted down, and the table part can then be fixed, and bolted as shown in section. The construction of cupboard part is also indicated in the sectional view with a centre division between the flaps. Fronts are panelled and a bottom frame is fixed with a set screw to the flap, allowing it to rotate if required, and also to move backwards and forwards in a slot (see sectional plan). The enlarged detail shows the book support frame hinged up, with the shape shown in sectional plan view. A brass fitting is shown, forming a rest for the book, which is folded up when not required for use. The support is made with the stiles continuing below the bottom rail with brass shoes as shown above, fitting into a brass rack (see also enlarged detail).

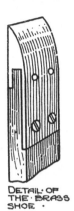

DETAIL·OF
THE·BRASS
SHOE·

A MUSEUM CASE (see p. 303).

The drawings illustrate a glass case upon a stand for the display of jewellery and objects of art. The table part is of simple construction, with rails as shown in plan, the legs being of an octagonal shape. The sloping top part is made with a removable frame for access to the case, and the construction employed is shown in the enlarged details. This frame is secured at both sides with special locks (see section), the dust bead at bottom acting as an air-proof joint, and also keying the frame to the case at the bottom. The top framing is tenoned into the surface moulding, and the rebate formed by mitreing a rebated piece between the uprights. A loose bottom is shown lined with suitable material, and an inner stand is made by glueing the columns into the shelf, fitting into the bottom with $\frac{3}{4}$ in. turned pins underneath a square base (see enlarged detail of columns). This type of showcase is not so fragile as the circular bar kind, and the plate glass can be beaded in as shown in the section.

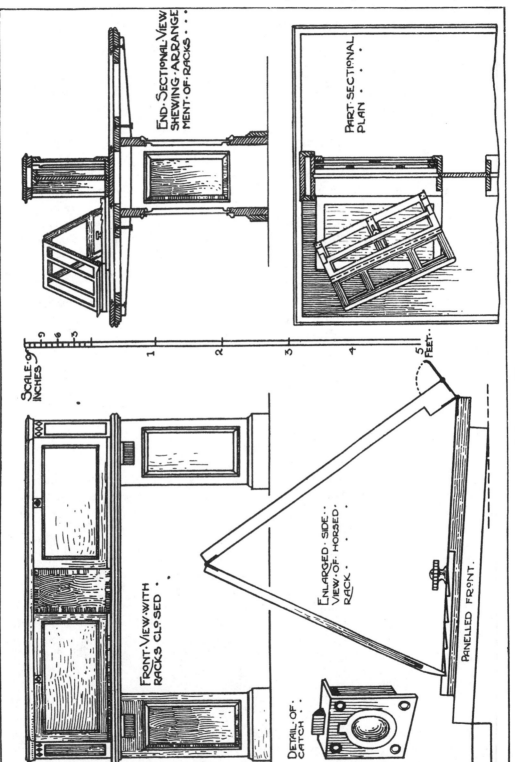

End·Sectional·View· Shewing·Arrangement·of·Racks·. .

Part·Sectional· Plan·. .

Scale·9· inches·. .

Front·View·with· Racks·Closed·. .

Enlarged·Side·. . View·of·Horsed· Rack·. .

Detail·of· Catch·. .

Panelled·Front.

A Library Table.

A MUSEUM FLOOR CASE (Plate XLVIII.).

This double-fronted case is intended for the display of specimens in the upper cases, the bottom part being utilised for storage purposes. Hinged covers are fixed upon the sloping top, and are raised when viewing the specimens ; these are necessary with certain natural history specimens, as a protection from a strong light. This case is made in three distinct parts : (1) The narrow top case ; (2) The sloping part above drawers ; (3) The main part or bottom case with drawers. The sectional plan through bottom case shows the method of framing up inside and outside ends. Their attachment to the main carcase is effected by screwing under the pilasters, the drawer rails are slip dovetailed into the ends, and runners grooved and fixed previously, thus making inner carcases fixed between the outside framing. A view under the top case A in plan shows the end frames connected to wide stiles ; centre stiles are also introduced, and top and bottom rails are tenoned between. The skirting is mitred round, and projects sufficiently to receive the pilaster bases. After fixing the inside carcases, a wide top and bottom rail is dovetailed and screwed down (see plan), thus serving

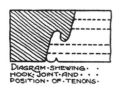

DIAGRAM ·SHEWING· · ·
HOOK· JOINT·AND· · ·
POSITION· OF ·TENONS·

as an additional brace, and strengthening the whole carcase. The construction of the sloping case is shown in enlarged details, the end frames being rebated to receive glass. The bottom rail is tenoned between the short stiles, the upright is tenoned down to bottom rail, and the sloping rails tenoned between short stiles and centre upright. Solid stuff must be used for the front rails, and their connection with end frames is illustrated in enlarged detail, a sectional plan, from which it will be seen that a short stub tenon is used, and the front part mitred. Centre division rails divide the sloping case into four parts which are dovetailed between the rails. A framed-up bottom is used, and this should be rebated into the framing as shown in the enlarged detail. Part sectional plan of case A shows a rail dovetailed down to receive the hingeing piece for the glazed top. The frames are made in four parts meeting upon the division rail, which has the tongued piece glued on in order to render the joints air-proof; the connection above the front rail is also shown with dust bead attached. The thumb moulding is mitred round two sides of each frame only, and upon the ends of hingeing piece fixed at the centre. The lower doors are hinged with a dust-proof shutting joint, and it is advisable, though not indispensable in this case, to use a " hook " or **S** joint for meeting stiles of doors (see above). These are worked with special planes, and necessitate the use of double tenons in making the doors ; they are indicated by dotted lines in diagram.

A CASH DESK (Plate XLIX.).

This cash desk is designed to meet general requirements in a business house, with pedestals, sloping desk, and cash drawer. Similar desks and

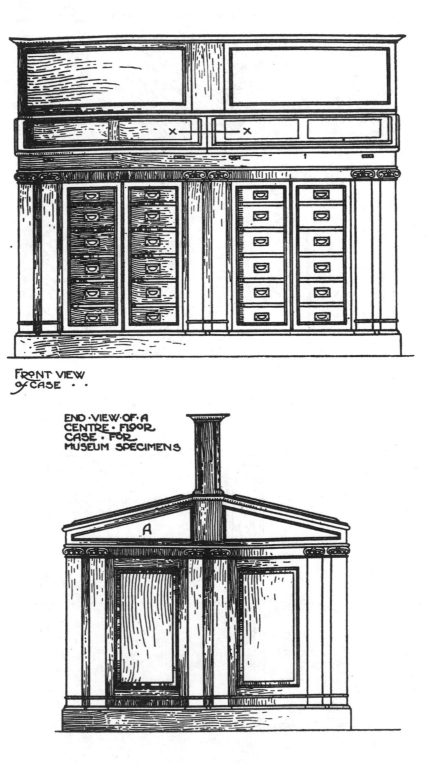

FRONT VIEW
of CASE · ·

END · VIEW · OF · A
CENTRE · FLOOR
CASE · FOR
MUSEUM SPECIMENS

A

PLATE XLVIIIA. A CENTER FLOOR CASE FOR MUSEUMS (CONTINUED OVERLEAF).

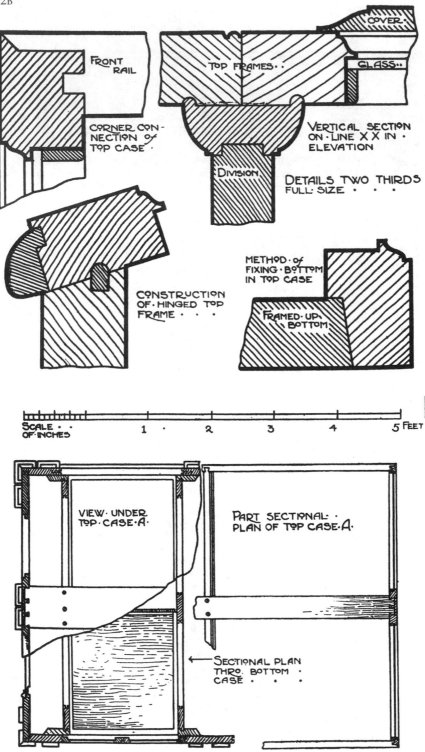

FRONT RAIL

CORNER CON-
NECTION OF
TOP CASE.

TOP FRAMES.

COVER.

GLASS.

VERTICAL SECTION
ON LINE X X IN
ELEVATION

DIVISION

DETAILS TWO THIRDS
FULL SIZE · · ·

CONSTRUCTION
OF HINGED TOP
FRAME · · ·

METHOD OF
FIXING BOTTOM
IN TOP CASE

FRAMED UP
BOTTOM

SCALE · ·
OF INCHES

1 · 2 · 3 · 4 · 5 FEET

VIEW UNDER
TOP CASE A

PART SECTIONAL
PLAN OF TOP CASE A

SECTIONAL PLAN
THRO. BOTTOM
CASE · · ·

PLATE XLVIIIB.   A CENTER FLOOR CASE FOR MUSEUMS.

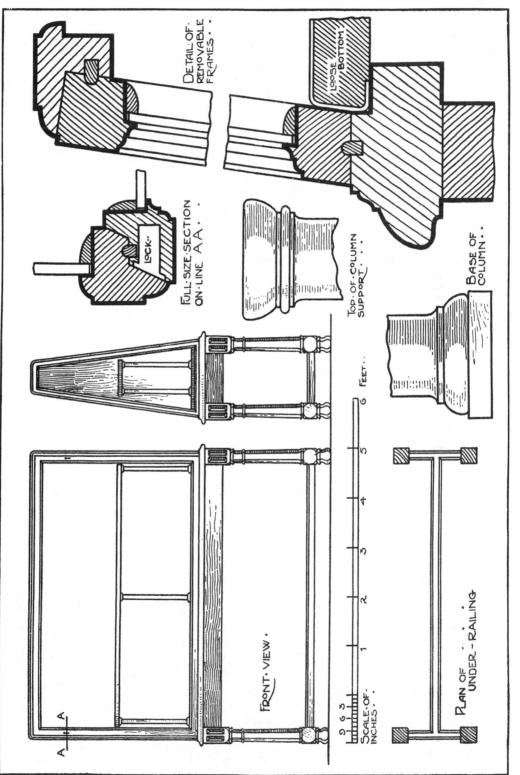

DETAIL OF REMOVABLE FRAMES.

LOOSE BOTTOM

FULL SIZE SECTION ON LINE A.A.

LOCK.

TOP OF COLUMN SUPPORT.

BASE OF COLUMN.

FRONT VIEW.

SCALE OF INCHES.

FEET.

PLAN OF UNDER RAILING.

A MUSEUM CASE.

counters are suitable for banks and offices, differences occurring only in the arrangement and accommodation.   The main idea is to have pedestals containing a requisite storage capacity for books, &c., with sloping desk and counter top supports upon the centre cupboard ; the general and subsidiary counters butting against the desk.   The sectional view shows construction of panelled framing, and the stiles should be allowed to run right through to the floor ; it is unnecessary to carry the bottom rail full width, as, for example, when the fixing for skirting is obtained on the stiles.   The pedestals should be made quite separately, as shown in plans, and screwed to the panelling ; the centre cupboard is constructed by making a frame with centre munting (see back elevation), doors are fitted to the openings, and when the pedestals are in position, the framing is screwed and blocked to the main pedestals.   The sloping desk and cash drawer are also put together in one carcase, and fitted and fixed above the cupboard.   The whole job, when fitted and set true, is completed by the addition of a counter top, framed as shown below.   The inside edge is left square to receive the lift-up desk lid, and side rails are necessary with this to allow the lid to clear mouldings.   A view of

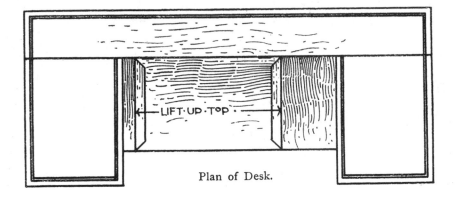

LIFT·UP·TOP·

Plan of Desk.

the cash drawer is shown, with a brass friction roller fixed towards the back. This runs upon brass plates let flush into the drawer runners, and a plate is also let into the drawer with a corresponding roller fixed on the runner at the front. This prevents the wearing away of the drawer fittings, which, otherwise, in a short time would be quite an appreciable amount, and prevent smooth running. The grill is fixed to the top of the cash desk by bolts through the pillars screwed into the surface plates, which are let into the top.   Brass terminals are screwed in the top rail to hide the fixing, and the wooden collar at bottom also prevents the surface plate from showing.   S brackets are necessary to ensure rigidity in any length of grill above 4 ft.   An alternate method of fixing the grill is to bolt from underneath the top into holes previously drilled and tapped in the standards, or with a screw brazed into the standard and bolted from underneath. The overhang of the cash desk top is about 5 in., and prevents the framing being bruised and kicked.   The general counter front is framed together with posts and cross bearers supporting the top, but arrangements at the back are, of course, decided by the nature of the business, whether by racks, shelves, drawers, or cupboards.   Where drawers are introduced, the sides should not be less than

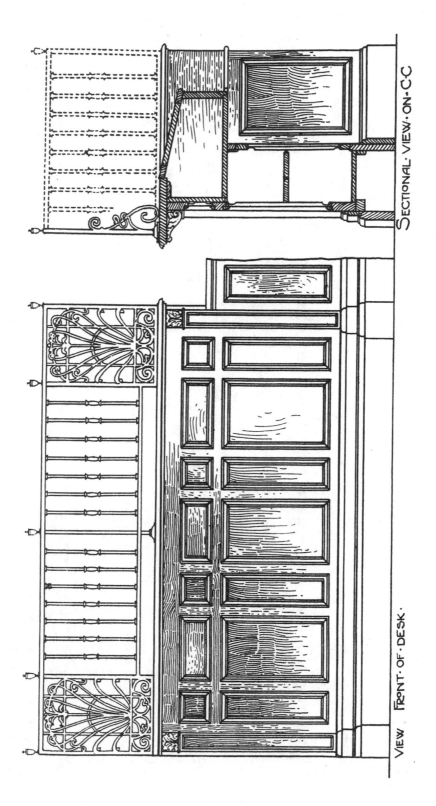

SECTIONAL·VIEW·ON·C-C

VIEW·FRONT·OF·DESK·

PLATE XLIX. A CASH DESK WITH CONSTRUCTIVE DETAILS.

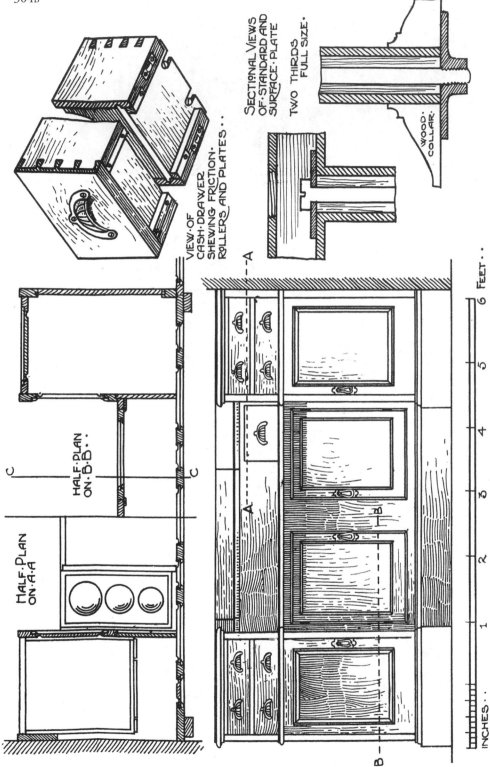

VIEW·OF CASH·DRAWER SHEWING FRICTION· ROLLERS AND PLATES··

SECTIONAL·VIEWS OF·STANDARD·AND SURFACE·PLATE

TWO·THIRDS FULL·SIZE·

WOOD· COLLAR·

HALF·PLAN ON·B·B··

HALF·PLAN ON·A·A

INCHES·· 6 FEET··

PLATE XLIX, PAGE 304B. A CASH DESK WITH CONSTRUCTIVE DETAILS.

$\frac{5}{8}$ in. thick. Bottoms are grooved into the ends as with cash drawers, and are strengthened by glueing blocks to the sides only ; this will allow freedom for the bottoms when shrinking.

AN OFFICE CABINET (see next page).

This type of office fitment has for its main feature a series of rising flaps sliding into grooves, which has the advantage of presenting a level front when any of the compartments are opened. The bottom part is encased by sliding doors, and the interior is divided up for ledgers as required (see plan next page and f. 4 on this page). Sliding tops are introduced under the main top, a useful provision

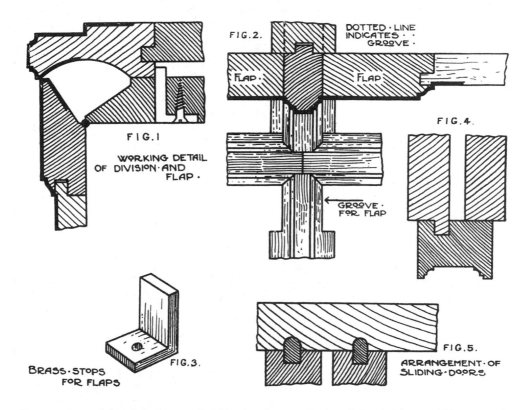

for papers and books when referring to the contents of the cabinet. The actual carcase work does not depart from usual procedure ; and the method of connection between the two top carcases is shown in f. 4. The working detail in f. 2 shows the division edges grooved to receive a moulding, which, when glued in position, makes a rebate to receive the flaps when down. The horizontal divisions must be set back as shown in f. 1, and the moulded and rebated fronts are tongued as shown before slip dovetailing between the vertical divisions. This necessitates a butt joint in front elevation shown in f. 2. All vertical divisions are also grooved to receive the flap, the detail of which is shown in f. 1. The method of

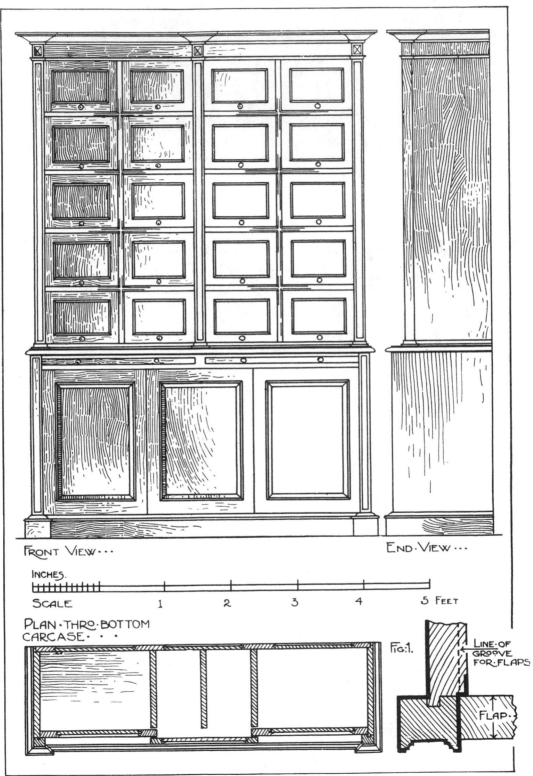

FRONT VIEW···

END·VIEW···

INCHES.

SCALE   1   2   3   4   5 FEET

PLAN·THRO·BOTTOM
CARCASE· · ·

FIG:1.

LINE·OF
GROOVE
FOR·FLAPS

FLAP·

AN OFFICE CABINET.

stopping them against the moulded facings is also illustrated. Fig. 1 on page opposite shows the grooved pilaster and end, the dotted line indicating groove and the rebate provided for the flap. As previously mentioned, the horizontal divisions are fixed between the vertical divisions first with short moulded lengths grooved into the carcase fitted between them—mitre joints could be used—but a more economical way is to scribe the pieces between. The flaps are flush at the back, and are mortised and tenoned together with the panel inserted previous to glueing up. Ordinary butt-joint hinges are used for the flap joints, and small catches are sunk into the bottom edge.

ENCLOSED WASHSTANDS (see p. 308).

These enclosed washstands are used in private offices, &c., where washing accommodation is required in a limited space. The first type illustrated

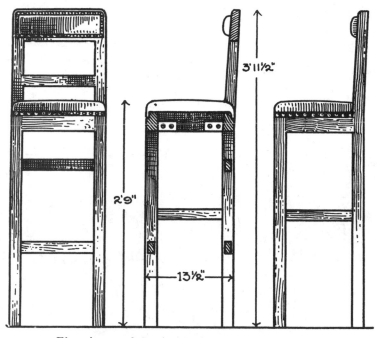

Elevations and Sectional View of an Office Chair.

has the washstand top dovetail housed between the ends, with the bottom lap dovetailed to the carcase ends. A wide front rail is grooved between the ends to enclose the cistern, and a hingeing strip and top are fixed above for access to it. The sloping top is also attached to a hingeing strip slip dovetailed between the ends. A lead cistern fits into the space provided, and the cubical contents of this should equal the contents of water-waste pan placed in the cupboard. A sectional view shows a method of fixing

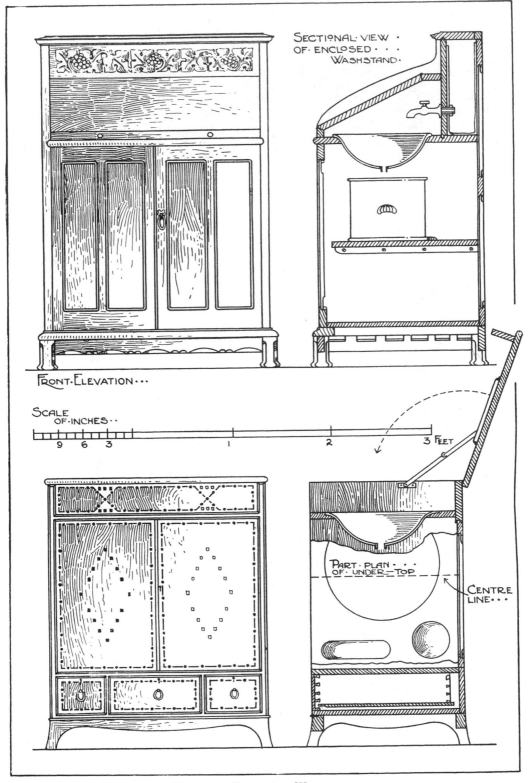

SECTIONAL· VIEW ·
OF· ENCLOSED · · ·
WASHSTAND.

FRONT·ELEVATION···

SCALE
OF·INCHES··

9 6 3   1   2   3 FEET

PART· PLAN · · ·
OF· UNDER—TOP

CENTRE
LINE···

TYPES OF ENCLOSED WASHSTANDS.

the tap and also the bowl cut into the top. Fillets are screwed to the shelf to ensure the water-waste pan fitting directly under the plug. Space is provided in the cupboard at bottom for towels and other accessories.

The second type illustrated is for uses similar to the above but the supply of water must be provided for by a separate receptacle in the cupboard. A basin, soap and brush dishes are sunk flush into the top with the plug and water-waste pan as in previous example. A light-moulded frame containing a looking glass is screwed to the underneath of the lift-up top. This can be hinged,

Details of Museum Print Stand (see next page).

if desired, with a small brass rack for tilting it, with a cabin hook or button to secure it when top is closed. Brass knuckle joint stays are used for supporting the top, the fixing of which is described in chapter on " Brasswork."

An Office Chair (see p. 307).

The drawings represent in elevations and section an office chair with upholstered seat and back rail. Its use demands strength rather than good appearance, and no decoration is introduced. American leather is used for the seat and back with an edging of nails. Angle blocks are keyed and screwed to the rails in the corners to strengthen the frame. Contrary to the general rule in chair work, the seat does not diminish towards the back. Office stools are similar to the chair, but are without the back.

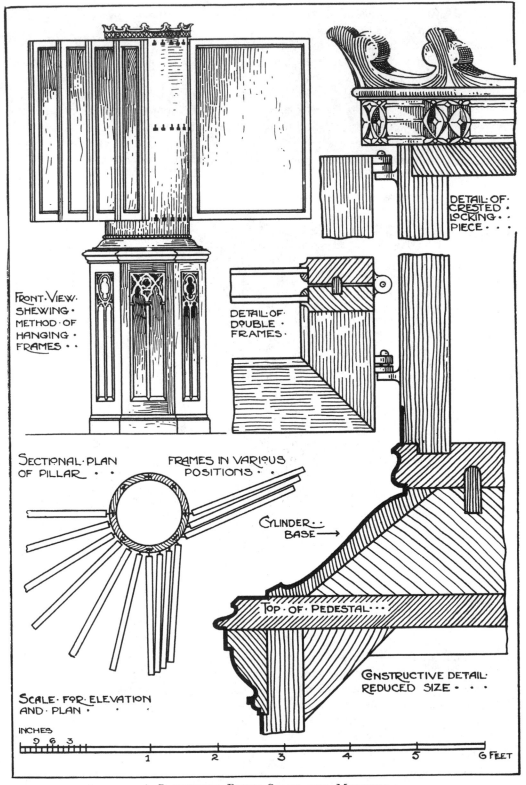

DETAIL· OF·
CRESTED·
LOCKING·
PIECE· · ·

FRONT·VIEW·
SHEWING·
METHOD·OF·
HANGING·
FRAMES· ·

DETAIL·OF·
DOUBLE·
FRAMES·

SECTIONAL·PLAN
OF·PILLAR· · ·

FRAMES·IN·VARIOUS·
POSITIONS· ·

CYLINDER·
BASE ➔

TOP·OF·PEDESTAL· · ·

CONSTRUCTIVE·DETAIL·
REDUCED·SIZE· · · ·

SCALE·FOR·ELEVATION
AND·PLAN· · ·

INCHES
9 6 3   1   2   3   4   5   6 FEET

A REVOLVING PRINT STAND FOR MUSEUMS.

A MUSEUM PRINT STAND (see opposite).

This is a pedestal stand designed to exhibit collections of drawings, embroideries, or prints, and is fitted with twenty-four pairs of double frames showing forty-eight faces. These frames are hinged and fold somewhat in the form of a book. With slight alteration this stand can be made shaped to half the plan and fixed to a wall. The bottom pedestal, octagonal in shape, is made as illustrated in detail (see sketch, p. 309), tongued together at the angles with skirting mitred round; strong bearers are dovetailed across the pedestal to support the upper part and top. The detail on opposite page shows the moulded base ; a softwood groundwork is made to octagonal shape, and the moulding stuff is jointed round the splayed faces, the grain running from top to bottom, and then turned to the section. The upper part is jointed as a cylinder or drum glued into the bottom board,

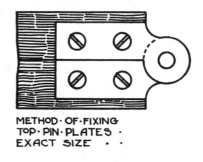

METHOD·OF·FIXING
TOP·PIN·PLATES ·
EXACT SIZE · ·

and the top is rebated and screwed. A carved crested locking piece projects beyond the cylinder, and the frames are thereby secured and cannot be taken off. The frames are connected in pairs back to back with pianoforte hinges on the outside edges. One method of securing the frames is to fix the plates shown above on each frame, and the pin passing through both centres forms an effective lock. Rounded dowels are inserted between the closing stiles of the frames, and ensure them closing into the correct position. The frame fittings are of gun-metal with steel pins ; the centre and bottom set being made to fix with surface plates let into the edge. The top plates, as in the pin plates above, are sunk flush and screwed into the cylinder as illustrated.

CHAPTER XVI.

CHAIRMAKING.

Classification—Introduction of Chairs and Stools—Primitive Examples—Identification of Chairs—Necessity of Studying Historic Examples—Diagrams showing Characteristics of Period Chairs—Chronological Chart giving Names, Periods, Dates, Characteristics, and General Proportions of Chairs and Seats in Various Styles, including " Cavalier," "Charles II. High Back," "Spoon Backs," "Grandfather," "Riband," "Wheatsheaf," "Lattice," "Heart," "Shield," "Oval," "Ladder Back," "Stuff-over Chairs," "Adjustable Settees," "Bed," "Drawing," and "Dining" Room Chairs, &c. **Workshop Practice**—Subdivision of Industry—Special Tools used in Chair Work, Frame Saws, Leg Vice, Routers, Scraper Spokeshaves, Special Cramps, Iron Band Cramps—Use of same—Templates, Material for—Shaping and Moulding Legs and Arms Connecting Segments—Bevelled Mortising—Use of Saddle—Drawing and Dining Room Chairs, Designs for—Methods of Construction—Pierced Splads—Cabriole Leg Detail, Construction of—Bracing Chair Frames, Alternate Types—Loose Seats in Dining Chairs, Construction of—Loose Seat for Settle—Stuff-over Arm-Chair—Arrangement of Rails for Upholstery—General Rules for same—Measured Drawing and Detail of Child's Chair—Chesterfield Settee—Elevations and Sectional Views—Enlarged Detail of Wood and Iron Ratchet Movements—Construction of Framing—Knole Settees—William and Mary Arm-Chair—Development from Earlier Styles—Methods and Process Involved in Inclined Legs—Arrangement for Upholstery—Curved Arms, Method of Working, Moulding same—Finishing a Scroll Terminal—Measured Drawings and Details of a Hall Seat.

INTRODUCTION.

THE craft of chairmaking, embracing, as it now does, settees, couches, divans, and numerous small and arm chairs, is most comprehensive, and is usually practised as a distinct craft. It is divided into sections, such as stuff-over frame work, arm and small chairs. Many cabinet shops, however, still require the cabinetmaker to be skilled also in chair work, which is then practically confined to the reproduction of old examples, seats, and framing, occurring in domestic and ship fitments.

The history of chairs dates back to the earliest times, but it was not until the fifteenth century that they became an accepted type of furniture. To enumerate all the kinds of chairs and seats, ranging from the rude forms of primitive

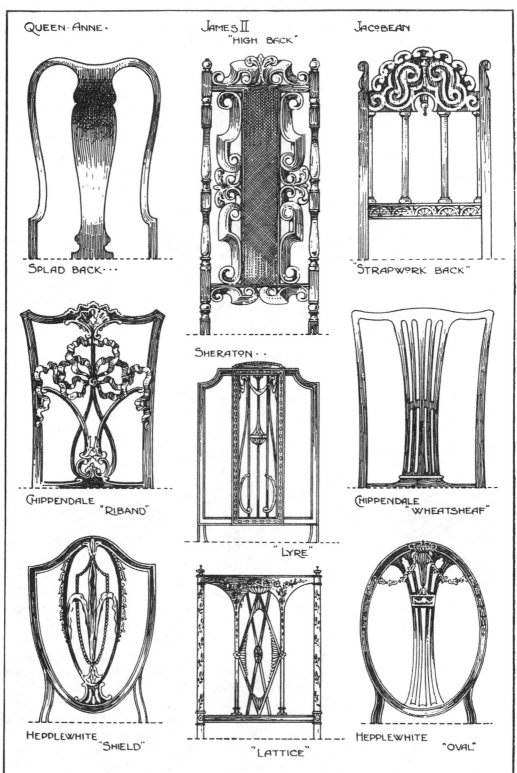

QUEEN·ANNE·

SPLAD BACK···

JAMES II "HIGH BACK"

SHERATON··

"LYRE"

JACOBEAN

"STRAPWORK BACK"

CHIPPENDALE "RIBAND"

CHIPPENDALE "WHEATSHEAF"

HEPPLEWHITE "SHIELD"

"LATTICE"

HEPPLEWHITE "OVAL"

TYPES OF CHAIR BACKS.

stools to the elaborate settees, divans, and chairs of the present date, and even including thrones and chairs of state, would be a long task, but the chronological list given in this chapter (Plate L.) may be consulted for general reference.

Identification of Chairs.—To recognise the development of form and detail in chairs, a study of historic examples is, of course, necessary, and it should prove a rich source of information as to their respective styles. Certain typical shapes, generally the outcome of changing conditions in social life, custom, or dress, are always characteristic of the period. The diagrams given on p. 313 will be found of some assistance in determining dates and styles of chairs produced under the best masters.

Cutting Sweep on Bench.

The Jacobean chair back with lunette-shaped top rail and acorn pendant is typical of that period. Frequently the backs were of solid stuff carved with semicircular headed panels, and also with spindles or pillars as illustrated. James II. high back chairs with cane seats and backs are a further development of Charles II. chairs, a period which marks the introduction of scroll form carvings and twisted turnings. Queen Anne chairs and settees have "centre splads" in the back. This is the most prolific period for chairs of singular beauty and proportion, and is essentially an English style. Queen Anne or Georgian types have also been aptly described as "of great purity." Chippendale brought about the next important development in chairs, and the evolution of the Queen Anne splad is clearly shown in his examples. The introduction of mahogany proved superior to those woods previously used, and elaborate carved "open work splads" (see riband back) were possible. Chippendale chairs always have the splad or centre part connected to the seat rail, part of which is visible

Class.	Style.	Period.	Name.	Back.	Wood.
Stool - -	Tudor - -	1500–1603	Joint - -	...	Oak
Settle - -	Jacobean - -	1603–1649	High back -	Panelled	,,
Child's Chair -	,, - -	,,	Child's arm -	Carved	,,
Dining ,, -	Cromwellian -	1649–1660	High back -	,,	
,, ,, -	Charles II. -	1660–1685	Cane ,, -	Cane	Oak or beech with rush seat
Arm ,, -	William and Mary	1689–1702	High ,, -	Carved	
Dining ,, -	Queen Anne -	1702–1714	Spoon ,, -	Splad	Walnut
Settee - -	,, ,, -	,,	Splad ,, -	Double splad	,,
Arm Chair -	,, ,, -	,,	Grandfather -	Stuff-over	,,
,, ,, -	Early Georgian -	1714–1727	Spoon back -	Splad	,,
Dining ,, -	Chippendale -	1740–1764	Riband ,, -	Carved	Mahogany
,, ,, -	,, -	,,	Ladder ,, -	,,	,,
Arm ,, -	,, -	,,	Riband ,, -	,,	,,
,, ,, -	,, -	,,	Wheatsheaf -	,,	,,
Drawing ,, -	Adam - -	1758–1785	Oval back -	,,	,,
,, ,, -	Hepplewhite -	1780–1800	Heart shape -	,,	,,
,, ,, -	,, -	,,	Shield ,, -	,,	,,
Dining ,, -	,, -	,,	Oval ,, -	,,	,,
,, ,, -	,, -	,,	Wheatsheaf -	,,	,,
Drawing ,, -	Sheraton - -	1780–1810	Lyre shape -	,,	Satinwood
Arm ,, -	,, - -	,,	Lattice - -	Moulded	,,
Lady's Arm-chair	Modern - -	...	Stuff-over -		
Gent.'s ,, -	,, - -	...	,, -		
,, ,, -	,, - -	...	Wing stuff-over		
Chesterfield -	,, - -	...	Stuff-over with adjustable ends	Beech or birch frames, with legs, &c., of various hardwoods - - -
Box, Chesterfield	,, - -	...			
Grecian Settee -	,, - -	...	Stuff-over -		
Canterbury Settee	,, - -	...	,, - -		
Bedroom - -	,, - -	...	Rush-seat -		
Music Stool -	,, - -	...	Box - -		
,, ,, -	,, - -	...	Revolving -	- - - - -

PLATE L. A CHRONOLOGICAL CHART GIVING NAMES, PERIODS, DATES, GENERAL CHARACTERISTICS, AND PROPORTIONS OF CHAIRS AND SEATS IN VARIOUS STYLES (CONTINUED OVERLEAF).

Class.	Style.	Finish.	Legs.	Width at Front.		Width at Back.		Total Height.		Seat Height.		Front to Back.	
				Ft.	In.	Ft.	In.	Ft.	In.	Ft.	In.	Ft.	In.
Stool	Tudor	Waxed	Square	1	9	1	9	1	8	1	8	1	2
Settle	Jacobean	„	Turned	4	6	4	6	4	0	1	4	1	10
Child's Chair	„	„	„	1	1½	1	0½	3	3	2	2	1	0
Dining „	Cromwellian	„	"S" scroll and twisted	1	7	1	4½	4	4	1	3	1	5
„ „	Charles II.	„		1	7	1	4½	3	9	1	4½	1	3½
Arm „	William and Mary	„	Turned	2	1½	1	10½	4	0	1	7	1	9
Dining „	Queen Anne	Polished		1	9	1	5	3	4	1	7	1	5½
Settee	„ „	„	Cabriole with "claw and ball" or "hoof" feet	3	5	2	11	3	6	1	6	1	9½
Arm Chair	„ „	„		2	1	1	11	3	6½	1	4½	2	1½
„ „	Early Georgian	„		1	9	1	5	3	4	1	7	1	5½
Dining „	Chippendale	„		1	9	1	4½	3	2	1	7	1	6
„ „	„	„	"Claw and ball" "club" foot, pierced and tapered legs	1	8	1	3½	3	1	1	6½	1	5½
Arm „	„	„		2	0	1	7	3	3	1	7	1	6½
„ „	„	„		2	2	1	10½	3	8	1	5	1	11½
Drawing „	Adam	Gilt	Turned	1	6	1	2½	3	2½	1	6	1	3½
„ „	Hepplewhite	Polished	"Turned and reeded," also with decorated fluting	1	9	1	2	3	2	1	7	1	6
„ „	„	„											
Dining „	„	„											
„ „	„	„		1	6½	1	3	3	1	1	6½	1	4½
Drawing „	Sheraton	„	Turned and tapered	1	8	1	3	3	0	1	6	1	4½
Arm „	„	„		1	6	1	3	2	11	1	6	1	4
Lady's Arm-chair	Modern			2	1	1	10	3	2	1	4	1	10½
Gent.'s „	„			2	1½	1	11	3	9	1	4½	2	1
„ „	„			2	0	2	0	3	8	1	4	2	1½
Chesterfield	„		Various, including turned, thurmed, cabriole, and tapered	5	6	5	6	3	3	1	5½	2	0
Box, Chesterfield	„	Polished		6	0	6	0	3	0	1	6	2	0
Grecian Settee	„			6	0	6	0	2	5	1	5	2	0
Canterbury Settee	„			6	0	6	0	2	3	1	7	2	3½
Bedroom	„			1	4	1	2	3	0	1	6	1	5
Music Stool	„			2	0	2	0	1	7½	1	7½	1	4½
„ „	„	-	- - -	-	-	Minimum height =				1	6	...	

PLATE L. A CHRONOLOGICAL CHART GIVING NAMES, PERIODS, DATES, GENERAL CHARACTERISTICS, AND PROPORTIONS OF CHAIRS AND SEATS IN VARIOUS STYLES (CONTINUED FROM PREV. PAGE).

above the seat (see also wheatsheaf pattern). Hepplewhite introduced curved backs of heart, shield, and oval forms, with tapering and spade toe legs. Sheraton reverted to a style of design more chaste and refined than the ornate types of Chippendale, and, incidentally, more suitable for the satin-

1. Shaping Chair Leg in Chair Vice.

wood he chiefly worked upon. Many of his chairs are rectangular in outline, and there is nearly always a distinguishing feature in the bottom rail of the back, placed about 2 in. above the seat (see "lyre" and "lattice").

PRACTICE OF CHAIR WORK.

Chairmaking, practised as a separate craft, requires long experience to become an adept, a position generally accomplished by close specialisation in particular branches. The best chair work was undoubtedly executed during the eighteenth century, and with but slight modification and additions, the examples made during that period decide present-day proportions, as well as being the basis of modern chair-work design. For

2. A Scraper Spokeshave.

economic reasons, chiefly speedy production, division of branches in chair-making has been brought about, although the principles and practice of each branch vary but slightly. Tools, appliances, and methods are general. The special tools required in a chairmaker's kit are frame saws of various sizes used for ripping out stuff, straight or curved arms, legs, and segments. The saw is worked by fixing the material flat on the bench, and manipulating it as shown on p. 314. A leg vice is also necessary for holding curved arms and sweeps (see p. 315) during the processes of shaping, filing, and moulding. Loose wooden jaws are fitted over the vice heads to prevent the iron surface bruising the stuff (f. 1 opposite). **Routers** of various shapes for scratching mouldings round framing arms, &c., with a variety of spokeshaves and scraper spokeshaves (see f. 2, p. 315), are important items of equipment. With efficient mastery, this last-mentioned tool will act quicker and cleaner than the ordinary type. It consists of a piece of thin steel, bevelled and sharpened with a scraper edge, fixed between two pieces of stuff, secured by screwing, an escapement being cut as shown in diagram to dispose of the shavings. Special cramps are also necessary in chair work, types of which are illustrated in f. 1, 2, 3, with the jaws made longer than the cabinetmaker's patterns, *e.g.*, an iron tee cramp and wooden cramps. The use of a chairmaker's cramp is obvious in cramping curved work where the additional jaw space allows the cramp to fit over curved rails. Band cramps are also illustrated. Fig. 1 alongside is used for cramping oval or circular seats, and consists of a flexible iron band fixed on two wooden horns, which, when cramped together as shown, effects an equal distribution of pressure round the seat. Another pattern is shown in f. 2, a more simple kind, used only for horseshoe-shaped seats. In this case cramping blocks are fixed to an iron board and a stout wooden bar is placed at the front, the extra length serving as a grip when cramping up. Both cramps are required for this, as shown in diagram, and the pressure is applied by screwing them up simultaneously. A more expensive and effective band cramp is shown in f. 1, the wooden bar of which is interchangeable and made to fit any size seat, the screws being bored through this piece and pressure applied by turning the handle.

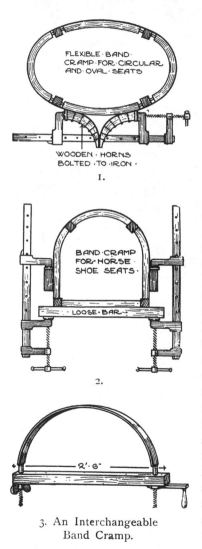

FLEXIBLE·BAND·CRAMP·FOR·CIRCULAR·AND·OVAL·SEATS

WOODEN·HORNS BOLTED·TO·IRON·

1.

BAND·CRAMP FOR·HORSE SHOE·SEATS·

· LOOSE·BAR·

2.

2'·6"

3. An Interchangeable Band Cramp.

Templates.—The method of making templates, an important feature in chair work, is described in Chapter X.; this procedure holds good in chair as in furniture making, but cardboard templates are the general rule, wooden templates only being used for repetition work.

Shaping and Moulding.—The shaping of frames for stuff-over work is straightforward, but in the more complex and highly finished forms such as Chippendale and Sheraton arm-chairs in hardwood it is more difficult in character, and, generally speaking, can only be successfully accomplished by experimenting with softwood models or when copied from a given pattern. The preliminary processes of marking and cutting out the stuff is proceeded with, the segments are roughly shaped, then dowelled or mortised together and carefully spokeshaved and fixed to obtain the necessary "feeling." A working drawing cannot adequately show this, and the senses of sight and touch must be relied upon.

Connecting Segments.—Particular shapes or curves of segments, with the direction of grain, determines the best method of fixing together. Dowelling is effective where the piece is fairly straight-grained. "Dowel screws" are also used in "butt joints." Although dowelling has almost superseded the old-fashioned but better method of mortising and tenoning the frames together, the latter is largely used in better class work where great strength and trueness are required. Bevelled and curved work where mortised is supported in a saddle (see f. 1 above), which provides a firm "bed" when conducting this operation.

1. Mortising Leg on Saddle.

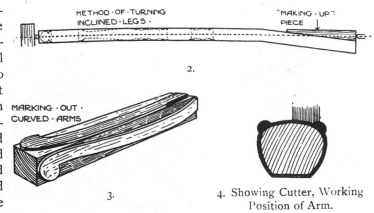

2.

METHOD·OF·TURNING INCLINED·LEGS·

"MAKING·UP" PIECE

MARKING·OUT· CURVED·ARMS

3.

4. Showing Cutter, Working Position of Arm.

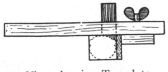

5. View showing Template.

A William and Mary Arm-Chair.

The construction employed in this type is straightforward, the chair parts being either mortised and tenoned or dowelled together. A sectional view of the

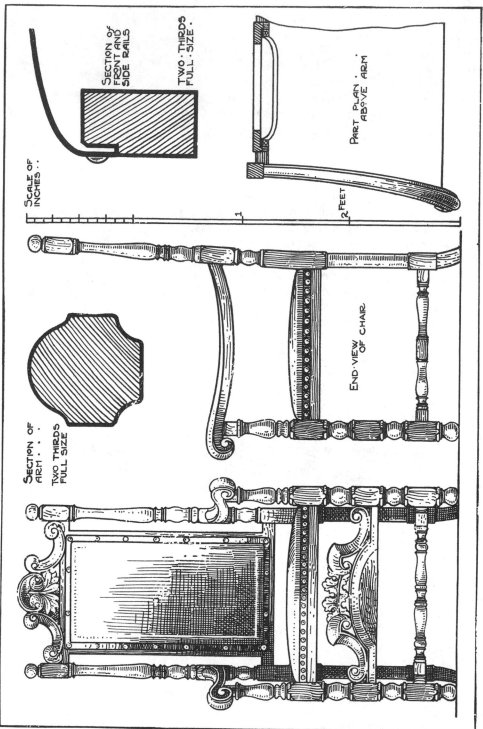

An Arm-Chair with Late Seventeenth Century Details.

rail shows the rebate to receive the covering, finished with rail borders.   Designs in this and the transitory periods frequently show the back legs sloping from the seat upwards, occasionally at a very decided angle.   If this is sufficient to weaken the leg the top part should be made separately with a strong 1-in. dowel into the bottom part.   This type of leg occurs also in work of a later period, and the turning is executed by cramping a block at one end to receive the lathe pivot, see f. 1, p. 317, reversing the process to complete the bottom portion. The sectional plan shows vertical rails mortised between the horizontal rails and rebated for upholstery.   Rebates are carried right through the vertical rails, and the horizontals are stop-rebated to complete the rectangle.   The workshop practice involved in executing the arms is also frequently met with in chair work.   Two templates are required for marking out, shaped to elevation and plan respectively ; they are applied to material as shown in f. 3, when the outline is pencilled and the arm band-sawn to shape.   After cutting, the arms should be " regulated " with files before proceeding to scratch the mouldings.   Fig. 4 shows a section of the moulded arm, and, as indicated in plan, the section is smaller at the back.   Scratching the moulding must therefore proceed in stages.   The first step

1. View showing Construction   2. Loose Seat for a Queen Anne Settee.
   with Dowelled Joints.

is to prepare a piece of wood to the true side view of the arm, with the back end $\frac{3}{16}$ in. thicker than front, this measure representing the difference in the size of bead at front and back ; fix this making-up piece temporarily to one side of the arm and work a half section as shown in f. 5, repeat with the other side of arm and complete the section as indicated by working V shape for bead from top side, finishing the section with spokeshave and scraper.   The scroll part at the front is finished with carving gouges.

DRAWING AND DINING ROOM CHAIRS.

A reference to the chronological chart in this chapter gives details of pro-portions and sizes of the above-named chairs in various periods.   A drawing-room chair is illustrated with a strapwork splad tenoned between the top and seat rails. The piercing should be executed after glueing up.   The section is illustrated in enlarged detail, the straight portions being worked on the face side with a scratch stock, and the back is rounded with rasps and files.   An interesting detail is shown on the plan of the seat.   It will be seen from the elevation that the moulded

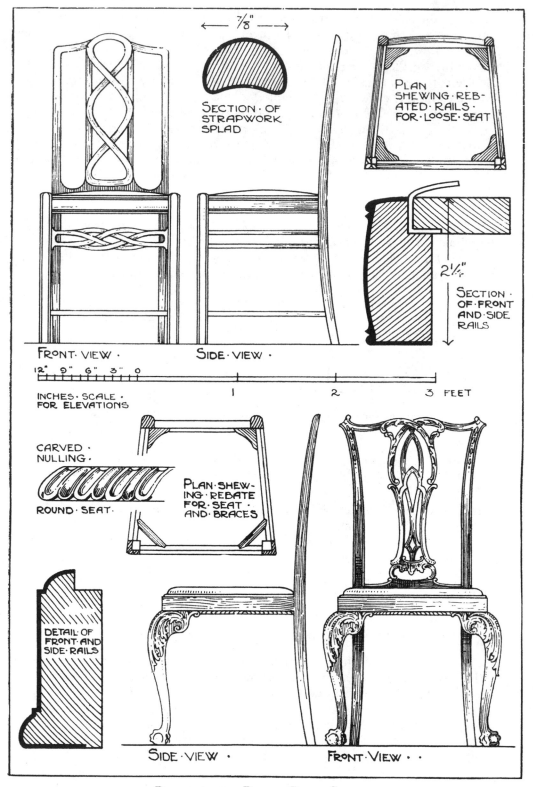

7/8"

SECTION · OF
STRAPWORK
SPLAD

PLAN · ·
SHEWING · REB-
ATED · RAILS ·
FOR · LOOSE · SEAT

2 1/4"

SECTION ·
OF · FRONT
AND · SIDE
RAILS

FRONT · VIEW ·

SIDE · VIEW ·

12" 9" 6" 3" 0

1   2   3 FEET

INCHES · SCALE ·
FOR ELEVATIONS

CARVED ·
NULLING ·

ROUND · SEAT ·

PLAN · SHEW-
ING · REBATE
FOR · SEAT ·
AND · BRACES

DETAIL · OF
FRONT · AND
SIDE · RAILS

SIDE · VIEW ·

FRONT · VIEW · ·

DRAWING AND DINING ROOM CHAIRS.

legs project slightly above the rails, and an effective finish is obtained by making the beads converge to the centre of the leg in the form of a leaf carved rather flatter than the bead moulding. The Chippendale dining-chair also has the splad, "banister," or "baluster," as it is variously called, tenoned into cross-rails or "slats," which are fretted and carved after glueing up. The cabriole leg detail in this chair embodies the usual constructive features of this design, and is cut from 3-in. stuff, with rails tenoned between the knee parts, the scroll-like terminations under the knees being added in the form of a small bracket, tenoned into the legs, and glued to the rails after the frame is glued. These are then levelled down to the leg profiles and carved up. Two methods of "bracing" a chair frame are shown in plan, the front braces are "cogged" into the rails and

A Queen Anne Settee.

screwed, whereas the back types are planed to fit the angle, then glued and firmly screwed : these materially strengthen the frame and ensure rigidity, which is very necessary in frames with loose seats. The plan also shows the knee part of leg cut to coincide with rebated rails. Loose seats are also an especial feature of dining-room chairs of the Chippendale period, and are occasionally used in settees of the Queen Anne period (see p. 319). Fig. 1 (p. 319) represents a view of a loose seat for a dining-chair, made from $\frac{7}{8}$-in. birch dowelled together. Fig. 2, the plan of seat for the settee mentioned above; webbing is fixed to the underside, and the stuffing of horsehair, &c., laid above it. These loose frames should be made smaller than the rebate to allow for the covering materials which are tacked to the underside ; $\frac{1}{8}$ in. is the usual allowance.

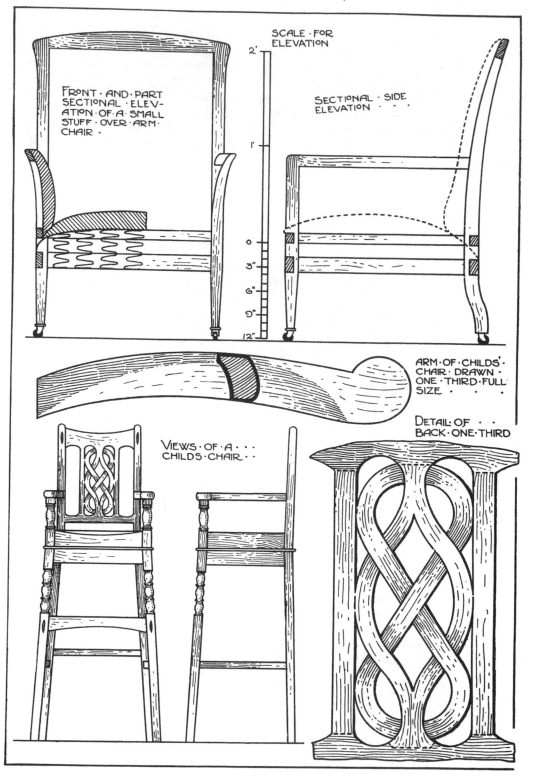

SCALE · FOR
ELEVATION

FRONT · AND · PART
SECTIONAL · ELEV-
ATION · OF · A · SMALL
STUFF · OVER · ARM ·
CHAIR ·

SECTIONAL · SIDE
ELEVATION · · ·

2'

1'

0

3"

6"

9"

12"

ARM · OF · CHILDS ·
CHAIR · DRAWN ·
ONE · THIRD · FULL ·
SIZE · · ·

DETAIL · OF · · ·
BACK · ONE · THIRD

VIEWS · OF · A · · ·
CHILDS · CHAIR · ·

A STUFF-OVER CHAIR AND CHILD'S HIGH CHAIR.

A STUFF-OVER CHAIR (see opposite).

This class of work is so called from the upholstery almost completely covering the framings, another example of which is illustrated in the Chesterfield settee in this chapter. The lines of the frame are determined by the design, and in the majority of cases, closely follow it. The bottom rails of the frame are 2 by $1\frac{3}{8}$ in., and to these are fixed the webbings and also the finished materials of seat (see elevations); the second rail serves as a fixing for the wing or arm coverings and also for the back covering (see dotted lines in side elevation). This arrangement of rails holds good in all stuff-over work. The wood used for chair frames is generally birch, this having superseded the use of beech, which was particularly susceptible to attack by worms and dry-rot. Dowelling is used in fitting up the frame illustrated ; and for repeat work, zinc templates for marking are an advantage, as described in "Dowelling" (Workshop Practice and Construction). When glued up, the frames are levelled by planing and spokeshaving, slightly rounding all edges, and end grains should be well rubbed with thin glue, which acts as a strengthening agent, and prevents the wood splintering when tacking on the covers. The sketch (p. 321) represents a Queen Anne settee with loose seat, the construction of which is described on p. 321. The framing is rebated to receive this seat, and the construction of the curved part is best effected by building up in segments and veneering the surface, forking the legs up into the frame, the moulding being glued into a rebate to receive the seat. This type of frame is, however, frequently made with rails cut from the solid and dowelled up to the legs.

A measured drawing of a child's chair is also shown opposite, with enlarged detail of back, the dotted lines representing shoulder lines on the pierced splad, which is tenoned into the rails. This chair is made in two parts with a bead between the joints under the seat which is pocket screwed from underneath.

A CHESTERFIELD SETTEE (see next page).

The drawings on p. 324 deal with mechanical features of Chesterfield and Knole settees, and also further illustrate the general constructive principles of stuff-over framework previously dealt with in a Sheraton arm-chair. The bed or seat frame is illustrated in plan, the inside end rails being necessary to secure the upholstery work, and leave a space at each end for the mechanical actions (see also dotted line indicating upholstery in sectional elevation). A perspective sketch shows the construction of each corner, the bracket F being dowelled and screwed to the framing at each end with the rail G butted in between. Reference to the enlarged detail of the mechanical action on the next page will more clearly show the necessity for this bracket, which, it will be observed, provides a firm seating for the drop end when lowered to its full extent, and when used in this position it has the greatest strain exerted upon it. The wooden action is illustrated

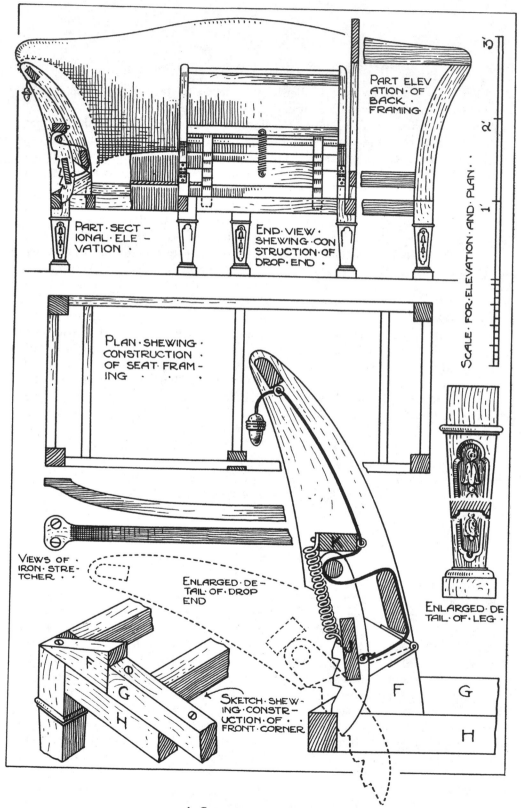

PART ELEV
ATION · OF
BACK ·
FRAMING

PART · SECT -
IONAL · ELE -
VATION ·

END · VIEW ·
SHEWING · CON
STRUCTION · OF
DROP · END ·

SCALE · FOR · ELEVATION · AND · PLAN ·

PLAN · SHEWING ·
CONSTRUCTION ·
OF · SEAT · FRAM-
ING · · · ·

VIEWS · OF ·
IRON · STRE-
TCHER · · ·

ENLARGED · DE -
TAIL · OF · DROP
END

ENLARGED · DE -
TAIL · OF · LEG ·

SKETCH · SHEW-
ING · CONSTR -
UCTION · OF · ·
FRONT · CORNER

F   G

F

G

H

H

A CHESTERFIELD SETTEE.

opposite, and is operated by pulling the cord, thus releasing the ratchet and allowing the end to drop. The rail J is mortised between the ratchets, and when the cord is arranged, as shown, round the rails and drawn upwards, it draws the ratchet from its position on the rail. The spring is attached to two rails pressing against the circular rod, as shown, and pulls the ratchet close to the rail again when the cord is released. Rail K rests upon the ratchet ends, and acts as a strengthening agent when the end is lowered, in addition to providing the requisite fixing for the spring. A part elevation is shown of the back frame, which is dowelled together with a centre rail not shown in the drawing, the outline in this case closely following the finished line of upholstery. The distance between the ends can be extended according to requirements ; the usual practice when dispensing with the centre leg is to use the iron stretcher illustrated, fixed across the rails, and this has the added advantage in its use of following the under line of the stuffing.

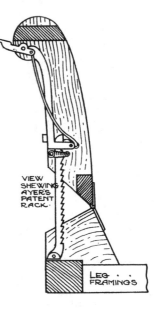

"Knole" settees closely follow the above type in shape and construction, an especial feature being the wide top rail on the frame, which acts as a seating for the springs ; the back also has this wide rail and does not curve. The detail on this page illustrates "Ayer's" patent fitting for these settees, operated by pressing the thumb piece, and raising or lowering when the pressure on it is removed ; the spring acting upon a clip effects a stop on the ratchet. This mechanical action is suitable for both types of settee, as is also the wooden action described above, but the iron attachment has obvious advantages, involving, as it does, a simplification of construction, and also the omission of a perishable cord.

The chart on Plate L. has been drawn up as a reference to the general shapes and dimensions of the various types of chairs. The sizes have been measured from actual examples, but they may vary in different designs and according to the special use for which a chair has been made.

CHAPTER XVII.

ENGLISH, FOREIGN, AND COLONIAL WOODS.

Trees—Botanical Divisions—Growth and Structure—Hard and Soft Woods—Section of
Tree and Names of Parts—Defects and Diseases—Conversion, Seasoning, Shrinkage
and Warpage—Commercial Sizes and Terms—Detailed Description of Woods—
Geographical Distribution—Ports of Shipment—Sizes of Logs—Market Prices and
Uses—Special Section on Colonial Timbers.

A CLOSE knowledge of timber is important to the cabinetmaker from two
points of view. He should know how and where to use it for the best results
in construction, and be able to appreciate its beauties in colour and figure for
decorative purposes. Added to this he should know how to buy and convert
to the best advantage, and select his wood for its special purpose with care
and forethought. All this can only come with experience in handling the wood
itself, but the value of such practical knowledge is increased if backed up by a
close study of the growth and structure of timber in the living tree. It would
not be possible here to refer at any great length to this important side of the
question, but to note only the essentials as they apply in a general or particular
way.

Trees which produce timber are classed by the botanist as " **Exogenous**,"
or, as the word implies, of outside growth. The class opposite to this is " **Endogenous**," signifying an inside growth, such as the palm tree, known to us
as " partridge " and " porcupine " wood, and used only for inlaying. Bamboos
also belong to this class, but are scarcely important enough for notice in spite
of their unfortunate introduction into the furniture trade.

The exogenous trees are again divided into two distinct classes, viz.,
" broad leaf " and " needle leaf." The oak, walnut, mahogany, &c., are broad
leaf trees, and produce timber which is largely made up of real vessels or pores,
and in a general way they are termed " hardwoods," although some of them, such
as whitewood, willow, and poplar, are comparatively soft. They are also deciduous with exceptions in the holm oak, holly, &c. On the other hand needle
leaf trees produce timber without such pores, except in small quantities near
the heart, the woody substance being chiefly composed of what are known as
" tracheïdes," and " parenchyma," or tissue. The difference in the two structures
is easily recognised by examining the end grains of a piece of oak and yellow
deal. The pores are plainly visible in the oak, whilst the deal appears to be
made up of spongy fibres. These needle leaf trees are the conifers, such as
the pines, firs, yews, cedars, and larch, and with some exceptions (the larch is
one) are evergreen. They are called the " soft " and " resinous " woods. Other

points of difference may be noted by reference to the diagram, f. 1, which shows the section of a hardwood tree slightly exaggerated for purposes of illustration. The centre spot represents the pith, heart, or medulla; the rings shown light and dark are the "annual rings," the light one known as the "spring," and the dark the "autumn" ring. As a rule they are the result of one year's growth, formed by the upward or downward movement of the sap and wood-forming substances. They vary in width in different trees. In the conifers they are, as a rule, strongly marked, and also in the oak (see f. 2, a section of English oak full size); in mahogany and walnut a little less, and in ebony they are hardly visible. The outside thick dark ring is the bark, rind, or cortex, in some trees thick and furrowed, as the oak, ash, and chestnut; in others thin and scaly, as in the beech, birch, and plane. Between the bark and the last ring is a thin layer known

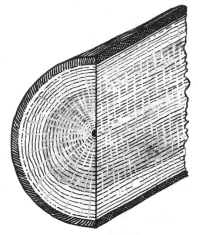

1. Section of Half a Tree, showing Heart, Sap, Rays, and Rings.

as the "cambium," which contains the active wood-forming substances and generative tissue. The shaded portion is the real or heartwood known as the "duramen," whilst the lighter outside rings are known as the "alburnum" or sapwood. This sapwood varies in width, and is usually lighter in colour than the heart, although in some trees, the ash for one, the difference is hardly recognisable. In nearly all woods the sap should not be used as it rots quickly, but the ash is looked upon as an exception to the rule. The lines which radiate from the centre are the "medullary" or "pith" rays which are present in all woods, but are practically invisible in nearly all the "soft" woods, and many of the hard, such as teak, walnut, ash, and

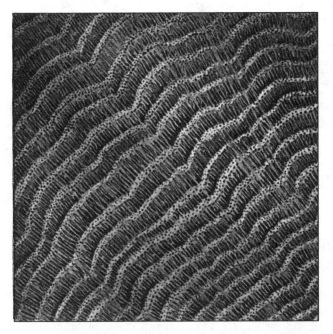

2. Section of English Oak, full size.

mahogany, but are very plain in oak, plane, and beech. In oak they make the "figure" or "silver grain," also known as "clash" and "felt," and give the name to "lacewood," which is figured plane.   These rays are thin plates of cellular tissue running right through the tree, and act as ducts to carry moisture from the sap to the heart.   There are long and short rays, generally known as "primary" and "secondary."

DEFECTS AND DISEASES IN TIMBER.

Defects.—Most woods are liable, more or less, to some defect or disease, either in the standing tree or converted logs.   The most common to the tree are the "Heart," "Star," and "Cup" or "Ring" shakes.   The "Heart Shake," f. 1, affects nearly all timber trees, but amongst the least affected are Sabicu, Cuba mahogany, and English elm.   The diagram shows the shake in a log of oak.   It is said to be due to incipient decay when the heartwood begins to shrink up.

"**Star Shake**," f. 2, is a decided cleavage along the line of the rays, and widening towards the outer rings as the log dries.   This shake may also be

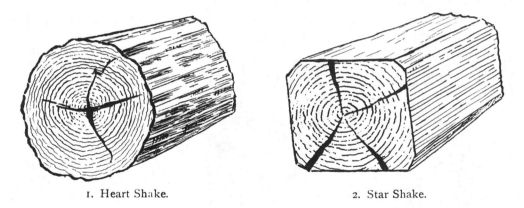

1. Heart Shake.   2. Star Shake.

due to some decay, sudden heat or frost.   The "Cup" or "Ring" Shake, f. 1, next page, clearly shows a separation of the rings due to an absence of cohesive qualities between the layers, caused either by high winds, frost, or insect ravages, and in some cases by all three.   These diagrams have been drawn from actual logs.   "**Rifty**" and "**Shelly**" are terms applied to similar shakes on the surface, whilst "**Thunder Shake**" or "**Upsett**," is caused by sudden fall or violent concussion which crushes the fibres into each other. This shake is usually recognised by a dark broken line across the board shown in the diagram, f. 2, next page.   "**Sun Shakes**" are due to sudden drying when timber is exposed to the sun.   They will be few or numerous according to the time of exposure, and they run in lines parallel to the rays and sometimes along the rings.   The heart of a tree sometimes "wanders" through irregular growth, and the "fibre" or grain is "twisty" through strain when exposed to high winds.

In addition to the above named there must always be numerous shakes and defects in timber which cannot be explained or classified, and it must be noted that the names change in different localities.

Diseases.—"Wet Rot" attacks a standing or newly felled tree, and is caused by excess of moisture, which, having no vent, brings on decomposition, and discolours and rots the wood. It is discovered in boards by the brownish colour and powder similar to touchwood. "Dry Rot" is set up in unseasoned timber or in situations where the ventilation is defective, as in the floor of a house. The first indications of the rot are a fusty smell and a covering of white mildew, together with discoloration of the wood, which powders and crumbles away. "Doatiness" is a term given to a form of decay which produces a stain of a whitish grey colour with dark specks, and reduces the wood to powder.

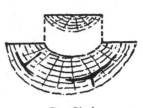

1. Cup Shake.

"Foxiness" is also a form of decay which discolours the wood as in "Brown" and "Pollard oak." "**Druxiness**" is an early state of decomposition recognised by white or yellowish streaks running with the grain. A "**Druxy**" knot is soft and rotten, as against the "**Live**" knot which is hard and well set. "**Rind Gall**" is caused by a bruise in the bark, or by the breaking of a branch leaving a wound which does not heal properly. Trees in full leaf

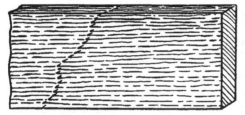

2. Thunder Shake.

are attacked by insects which produce growths known as "galls," of which the "apple" and "artichoke" on the oak are common examples, whilst other trees are ravaged by their own particular pest of fungus. "Burrs" are the result of a defect or malformed growth, and appear as great swellings on the side of the tree. Wood-boring beetles and worms destroy converted and made-up timber, both indoors and out, as well as living trees. The Goat Moth, Wood Wasp, and Pine Beetle are among the largest, whilst the smaller worms are well known as the furniture pests. An attack may be arrested by soaking the part in strong chemical solutions, such as bichloride of mercury, or copper sulphate, but the safest way is to cut out all affected parts, as some of these creatures will migrate to other articles in the same room.

SHRINKAGE AND WARPAGE.

Newly felled timber contains about 40 per cent. of water, which in drying, is reduced to about 12 per cent., so that a considerable contraction in bulk and weight takes place during the drying or seasoning process. The direction of shrinkage is nearly always circumferential, and f. 1 shows it in half a round, and f. 2 in quartered logs. As there is most moisture in the sap, the greatest contraction takes place in the outside rings, which accounts for the distorted

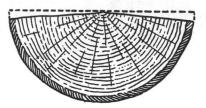

1. Shrinkage in Half-round Log.

2. Shrinkage in Quartered Logs.

square when the opposite corners seem to draw nearer each other. In like manner boards or planks will shrink, and consequently warp, as shown in f. 3,

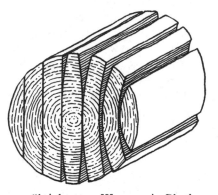

3. Shrinkage or Warpage in Planks or Board.

the part of the board near the heart, or driest wood, remaining practically fixed, whilst each end of the board curls away from the heart, only the centre or heart board contracting equally on both sides. This is an important point to note in using wide stuff for ends or tops, so that the least amount of warpage or "pull" takes place when the stuff is fixed, or allowance is made for it in fixing. Even a well-dried board may warp when planed up and the pores are opened to the air, and boards which are badly warped will return to their right flatness if laid on the damped floor, hollow side down. The degree of warpage depends on the way the board has been cut, the maximum when sawn as in the last diagram, and the minimum when cut on the quarter or parallel to the rays.

SEASONING.

Seasoning is a process whereby the moisture in the wood evaporates or dries up, whilst the wood itself and all it contains gets set or seasoned. The best and surest method, though not the quickest, is known as "natural" seasoning. Logs and planks are stacked in covered sheds with open sides, where they are kept dry but get plenty of air. In the stacking a space is left between each plank to form an air passage, and the layers are put at right angles to each other to allow for this, and to tie the stack together. Planks of hardwood are sometimes stacked on edge in racks, but deals are piled in parallel rows with an air passage between each one. Boards are piled in stacks as they are cut from the log, but with slips of similar wood, all of the same thickness, between each one, for the air passage as in sketch below. These slips are put at intervals of 1 to 4 ft. apart, according to the thickness of the stuff, and strips of wood, or lengths of hoop iron, are nailed over the ends to prevent splitting. The stain sometimes left in a board by the slip is due to its not being moved along in the course of drying. This omission often spoils a whole log of good boards. The period in which the log is drying is known as "First Seasoning," and Mr Thomas Laslett, the great expert on timber, has given eighteen months as the required time for a log of oak from 16 to 20 in. square to season, and nine months for a fir of the same dimensions. The "Second Seasoning" occurs when the log has been converted into planks or boards, and the latter require at least two years on the stacks, and always more if possible before they are taken into the shops for use. Even then it is safer to rough it up and let it stand for a time before working it. In small shops, boards are laid on the beams under the roof, and get well seasoned.

Hot Air Seasoning, or Desiccation.—This process is quicker and is often adopted as a second seasoning. The timber is placed in a chamber in which the air is kept at a temperature of 200 degs. Fahr. The disadvantage of this method is that it bleaches the wood, and also tends to make it brittle, especially mahogany and ash. The price for desiccation varies according to thickness, 1-in. stuff being charged at 5s. per 100 ft. super.

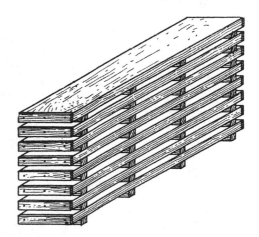

Stacking Boards for Seasoning.

Wet Seasoning for logs is done by immersion in running water, which forces out the sap if the butt end meets the stream. This takes from fourteen to twenty days, and the log must then be stacked for natural and slow drying. Water seasoning is most suitable for logs used in damp situations, such as piles. Other methods are by "steaming" or "boiling," "charring," "oiling," and "smoking," but for all general purposes the natural method is acknowledged to be the best. Rare and fine woods require special processes. Ebony is totally immersed in water for about a year, and then carefully covered for slow drying. Holly is sometimes boiled, and then wrapped up to dry. In all cases it must be the nature of the wood and its uses which determine the process.

CONVERSION.

The methods of conversion vary according to the timber and market requirements. The simplest one is by the "tangent" or "bastard" cut right through the round log, as in f. 1, next page. This produces boards or planks

with "waney" edges.   Pine and fir logs are cut as in f. 2 below, the inner planks
11 by 3 in. and the outer 7 by 2½ in., or as the size of the log allows, f. 3,
being an alternative cut.   Fig. 4 shows the cut in a pitch pine log to obtain the
figure for panel boards.   In oak there are various cuts to obtain the best
figure with the least waste.   Fig. 5 shows four methods, and where the
boards are cut in a line with the rays, the finest clash is obtained.   In the
top right quarter, wide and narrow boards are cut and the pieces left are
used for tile laths, &c.   The other quarters produce both plain and figured
boards in cutting.   In the Riga and Austrian oak the logs are "flitched" as
in f. 6.   The two planks cut from the centre produce "**Wainscot**" boards,
but this term is applied to figured oak generally when it is cut in this way.
The word is of Dutch origin, "Wagen-schot," wooden partition, or wall covering,

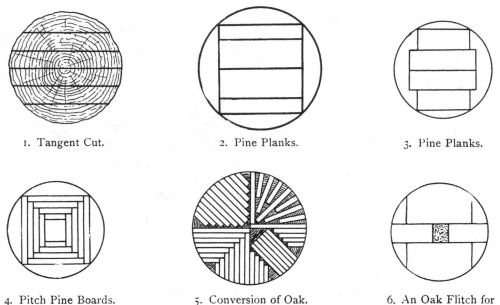

1. Tangent Cut.   2. Pine Planks.   3. Pine Planks.

4. Pitch Pine Boards.   5. Conversion of Oak.   6. An Oak Flitch for
                                                                                    Wainscot.

in which the best oak was used, hence the best boards cut from a log are
"wainscot" wood.   The heart end of the planks are cut off when necessary.
"**Stave Oak**" for coopers is shipped in small balks from 3 to 6 ft. long,
6 in. wide, and 3 and 4 in. thick.   Soft woods are mostly imported in planks
and deals of uniform width and thickness.   A pine plank is usually 11 in.
wide and 3 in. thick in varying lengths.   When cut down the thickness it
produces thin 1½-in. boards which are known as "one cut pine"; two cuts
produce three boards under 1 in. known as "two cut pine," and so on up
to "nine cut" for thin picture backing.   All imported boards of hard
wood are under nominal thickness, and if a board is required to finish 1 in.
it would have to be worked from 1¼-in. stuff, or cut specially from the plank.
Sawing down the width is called "deeping," and through the thickness
"flatting."   These cuts are charged at rates according to depth and length

from 2½d. per dozen. Imported boards are "square edged" or cut from square sawn or quartered logs, whilst home converted logs produce boards with hewn or waney edges if by bastard cut, or one square edge if cut from squared stuff or flitches.

COMMERCIAL SIZES AND TERMS.

Log.—The tree trunk felled and roughly hewn.

Balk.—The log squared for shipment and saw mill.

Plank.—Usually 11 by 3 in. and any length in soft woods; they may be over, but not under 9 by 1¾ in. in hard or soft woods.

Deal.—Usually a small plank 9 in. wide and over 2 in. thick. The term is applied to spruce, viz., white deal, and Baltic fir known as yellow and red deal according to locality.

Boards.—Any length, width over 5 in., and thickness under 2 in.

Batten.—From 7 to 9 in. wide, and between 1 and 2 in. thick, but wall battens are 2, 3, and 4 in. wide.

Quartering.—The stuff produced by sawing or "flatting" a plank into lengths 4 by 3 in. or 3 by 2 in. thickness, also known as "solids."

Scantling.—Any sawn lengths of odd dimensions; "stuff" is a general term.

Square.—100 super ft.

Standard.—Equal to 120 deals, each 12 ft. by 9 by 3 in. or 270 cub. ft. This is the London standard which differs slightly from that in use on the Baltic, viz., 120 deals 6 ft. by 11 by 3 in. equals 165 cub. ft.

Three Ply.—Thin boards made up of layers of veneer crossing each other to a thickness of $\frac{3}{16}$ or ¼ in., can be obtained up to 4 ft. square, and are used for panels, drawer bottoms, &c.

Matched Boards.—Usually imported in white and yellow deal 5 or 7 in. wide, and sold by the square at 5s. or 7s. Soft woods are usually sold by the "load" (50 cub. ft.), "hundred" (120 deals), standard, or in smaller quantities by plank or deal at per foot "run" in the lengths. Hard woods in the log by cubic, and planks and boards by super feet in the inch. Special woods, like rosewood and ebony, which are imported in "billets," and box, which comes in "sticks," are sold by weight. At present there are no means of classifying or testing any new timbers which are introduced, although the authorities at Kew Gardens are always willing to identify or verify a specimen. A name is often given to a wood from its port of shipment, although the same timber may be shipped from two or more places. In the following list alternative names are given when they occur, as they differ even in England sometimes. As far as possible, correct prices and usual sizes are given, but it must be remembered that they fluctuate and vary considerably. This is also true of colour and texture, a fact which makes it inadvisable to lay down hard and fast rules.

HARD WOODS.

Probably the hardest wood known is the ironwood of India, which is practically unworkable. Next come lignum vitæ and the ebonies, whilst the softest are the poplars used for paper pulp.

Oak, English (*Quercus robur*).—Two varieties, the "peduncled" with long stalks to its acorns, and the "sessiled," with short ones, but long stalks to its leaves. The wood of the first named is said to be the strongest and most durable, but as so much depends on soil and situation a doubt always exists. The woods are so much alike in appearance that it is also difficult to verify them. A third variety, "intermedia," with short stalks to acorns and leaves, the latter downy underneath, is uncommon, and is said to yield a much inferior wood. English is the most durable of all oaks, specially under water. The writer has examined and worked old beams over five hundred years old when the wood has been as hard as boards of five years' seasoning. In colour, various shades of light brown, sap yellowish, rings distinct and sometimes wavy (see p. 327), rays distinct and numerous in both kinds, producing the "silver grain," "clash," "figure," or "felt," when cut on the quarter. Grain rather coarse and open, difficult to work, warps and splits in drying, but always repays working up. Darkens with age or in contact with water. Used for church work, shipbuilding (the twisty growth providing good "knees" or "ribs"), cleaving, waggon, and railway work. It is difficult to get, and is but rarely used in cabinetwork.

Brown Oak is a variety of English, or the timber of a tree which has lost its vitality, a form of decay known as "foxiness." The strong acid in the wood turns it into a warm brown colour, but does not destroy its texture. Used chiefly in veneers and dining-room furniture.

Pollard Oak.—The timber of trees which have been "polled" and stunted in their growth. The wood is dark brown with a wavy grain and variable figure. Stumps and gnarls also produce finely figured veneers, very hard and tough, and difficult to lay.

Bog or **Black Oak.**—Any oak will turn black if left in a damp place, but to blacken it right through it should be laid in a pond or bog. The name originated from the trunks of trees dug up out of Irish bogs. The wood is liable to split, and is only suitable for turnery, inlaying, veneer, and fancy articles.

Baltic or **European Oaks.**—These constitute the chief oaks of commerce, and take their names from the ports of shipment. Most of them are *Quercus robur*.

Riga Oak.—The product of Russian forests, and shipped at Riga. Also known as "Riga wainscot" from the numerous rays which produce boards of unusually fine figure. For this reason the logs are sawn and shipped in the shape shown in f. 6, p. 332, known as a "flitch." The wood is moderately hard, light brown in colour, rings and rays distinct, sap narrow and whitish, open in the grain, but takes polish and fume well. Logs and half logs from 18 to 25 ft. long, and 10 to 16 in. wide, and are sold at 10d. to 1s. per foot in the inch. Riga oak is looked upon as the finest in quality of the Baltic oaks, but like all others it varies. The logs are sorted and marked or "bracked" according to the soundness or straight growth of the wood. The best logs are described as "crown," and are given a special mark, W, whilst the second, or twisty, coarse ones are also stamped WW, to show their inferiority. By these marks merchants can easily distinguish the qualities.

Dantzig Oak.—Although taking its name from the port, this oak comes from the Polish forests, and is also shipped at Memel and Stettin. It is similar in colour and texture to the Riga quality, but is not so finely figured. Imported in logs 18 to 30 ft. long, 10 to 16 in. square, and planks from 2 to 6 in. thick. **Staves** are also shipped for cask work. They vary in size, but are usually 3 or 6 ft. long, 6 in. wide, and 3 in. thick. These odd timbers have given it the name of stave oak ; sold at 9d. and 10d. a foot in inch.

Odessa Oak is also a Polish forest tree, but instead of being rafted down the rivers it is taken overland to the Black Sea and shipped at Odessa, the long journey partly seasoning it. In consequence of this it fetches a higher price on the English market.

Austrian or **Adriatic Oak**.—This oak is the product of the great forests of Austria-Hungary, and is perhaps the most useful of the European hardwoods, owing to its even growth, good figure, and easy working. As a rule it is lighter in colour than the others, and has a small silvery figure somewhat resembling the English oak. It is fairly straight in the grain, rays and rings distinct, sapwood a greyish white, and does not twist in working. It is shipped from Trieste and Fiume in logs from 12 to 20 in. square, and sells at about 9d. per foot. It is largely used for furniture, takes fume and polish well, and makes up well for dados and panelling.

Spanish Oak is rather dark, soft, and liable to shrink. The logs are small and curved, and they are imported chiefly for ship work.

Italian Oak is very hard, and heavier than the English wood. It is darkish brown in colour, close in the grain, and difficult to work. In shipyards it is preferred to English oak for framings, but is unsuitable for board work.

French Oak, from Brittany and Normandy, is very similar to English both in colour and texture but smaller in growth. It also shrinks and splits less in seasoning.

Turkey Oak, the "**Mossy Cupped Oak**," has a broad sapwood and a reddish brown heart. It varies in hardness, but its numerous rays give it a very showy figure.

AMERICAN OAKS.

A great quantity of oak comes from America, but it is all inferior to the European wood. Most of it is coarse in the grain, liable to shrink, and does not take fume well, but it is used in considerable quantities for cheap furniture, and owing to its great elasticity can be bent easily.

American White Oak (*Quercus alba*).—Known as "Quebec" and "Baltimore," from Canada and North America.   Light reddish brown with white sap, rays numerous and distinct, rings close and wavy ; heavy, hard, and fairly straight in the grain ; liable to shrink, but less than other American oaks.   When quartered produces finely figured boards.   Shipped from Quebec in logs from 20 to 30 ft. long, and 11 to 20 in. square.   Also planks and " square-edged " boards ; 5d. to 7d. in the inch according to width.   A similar name is given to the **White Oak** of the Western and Southern States.

American Red Oak (*Quercus rubra*).—Canada and North-East America. Commonly named " American " or " Canadian " " Red." Reddish brown and pinkish, open grain and very porous, white sapwood, sometimes heavy and tough and often soft and brittle, inferior to White oak, liable to shrink and warp. Imported in logs, planks, and boards similar to above, and sells from 5d. a foot upwards.   There are many other varieties of oak in America, among which is the Bur oak, very similar to the White and classed with it.   It is a common forest tree from Manitoba to Texas.

The Live Oak from the Southern States, a darkish brown wood, hard and tough, and said to be the toughest and strongest of American oaks ; and the **Yellow Oak** from the Eastern States, which is often sold as White oak but is inferior to it.

African Oak (*Oldfieldia africana*).—West Tropical Africa, shipped from Sierra Leone.   A dark reddish wood, very hard, close grained and extremely durable, and shrinks and warps but little.   Sometimes called **African Teak**.

African Oak (*Lophira alata*).—From the Gold Coast, Lagos.   Intensively hard, deep red in colour, coarse open grain, rays invisible.   Both these woods are known on the London market, and are used for purposes where durable timber is necessary.   The latter is often confused with African mahogany. The **Zeen Oak** from North-West Africa is a real oak of a rosy-yellow colour and very heavy.   Oak grows plentifully in India, and is usually harder and heavier than European wood.

Colonial " oaks " are described in the pages devoted to timbers of the various Colonies.

Mahoganies.

Mahogany was first introduced at the close of the sixteenth century, but did not come into general use for cabinetmakers until the middle of the eighteenth, when Chippendale made his name famous with it.   Real mahogany (*Swietenia mahagoni*) is now getting scarce, and many bastard woods are sold under the same name.   Central America, Mexico, and the West Indian Islands form the main sources of supply of the real woods, whilst immense logs of inferior timber are shipped from Gambia, Lagos, and Benin, and sold as " African mahogany."   Mahogany takes its place as the premier furniture wood from its warm rich colour, variety of fine figure, and good constructional qualities.   It shrinks and warps less than most hardwoods, is generally proof against insect attack, and improves with age.

Cuba Mahogany (*Swietenia*).—Sometimes called **Spanish** from the fact that the Spaniards once held possession of the West Indies.   All the islands, Hayti,

Cuba, Nassau, Jamaica, and Trinidad, supplied mahogany. The wood is a dark reddish brown, hard, heavy, close and straight in the grain, sapwood narrow, rings distinct, and rays just visible with flecks of lime in the pores. The quality and figure vary, and when cut near a branch the tree produces the best " curls " and " feathers " for veneers. Very small and choice logs are shipped from St Domingo, the port of Hayti, and they are seldom over 10 ft. long or 12 in. square. Smaller logs, rarely over 5 ft. in length and from 6 to 10 in. square, come from Nassau, whilst the larger Cuba wood yields logs of varying size from 15 to 25 ft. long, and 12 to 20 in. square. Good Cuba fetches 10d. to 1s. 6d. per foot, according to width, and the veneers from 6d. to 2s. according to figure.

Honduras Mahogany (*Swietenia*).—From Central America. Lighter in colour and weight than Cuba, varies considerably in quality; good wood is clean, crisp, and uniform in grain and colour, easy to work and does not cast; inferior wood is pale brown, soft and spongy, coarse grained and woolly. The plain stuff was sometimes called " Baywood," but much of it is well figured and produces the " Fiddle Back " for veneers. Honduras is the best wood for interior work, drawers, panels, and as a reliable ground for veneering. It shrinks but little, and is consequently used with pine for pattern making. Logs 20 to 30 ft. long, and 12 to 24 in. wide, price from 6d. per foot upwards. A supply of mahogany also comes from Guatemala and Nicaragua; often called **Laguna** wood, but it is similar to Honduras and is sometimes sold as such.

Mexican Mahogany.—This timber, though inferior to Honduras in many respects, is a good substitute for it, and is usually of much larger dimensions, yielding logs from 15 to 36 in. square, especially from the district of Minatitlan. The wood is generally a good colour, but varies considerably in quality. Much of it is soft and spongy near the heart, and so liable to shakes and inclined to be brittle. The best is known as **Tabasco** wood, and quantities of similar timber come from the districts of Santa Ana and Tonala. Much of the Tabasco quality has a good roe figure, which, though difficult to clean up, shows well in the polish. The exceptional width of Mexican mahogany makes it suitable for counter and fascia boards. The price is similar to Honduras, and increases with the width. " **Caoba** " is the Spanish name for this wood.

African Mahogany, " *Dubini.*"—Said to be *Khayu senegalencis*, but, as in the case of Mexican, there appears to be some doubt as to its natural order. It is shipped from the Gold Coast, Benin, and Lagos, and is also known as " Gambia," " Niger," and " Lagos," although these names only specify the district. The best quality, from Lagos, is hard, fairly close in the grain, and sometimes a good colour, but as a rule the wood is pale as though bleached, and coarse as well as soft and woolly. A few logs are found to be well figured, but though it varies in quality, the general texture of the wood is not suitable for good cabinetwork. Imported in logs up to 3 ft. wide, and 12, 15, and 20 ft. long; price from 6d. per foot.

The following timbers resembling mahogany are sometimes used as such :—

Toon or **Indian Mahogany** (*Cedrela toona*).—Or Moulmien Cedar, from Bengal and Burmah. Fairly hard, pale red, straight grained and fragrant, but liable to shakes ; suitable for cabinetwork.

Padouk, or **Andaman Redwood** (*Pterocarpus indicus*).—From Burmah and Andaman Islands. Dark red, heavier than mahogany, hard, close grained, slightly fragrant, with variety in figure.

Sabicu, or **Savicu.**—From the West Indies, especially Cuba. Dark reddish brown, hard, heavy, close in the grain, and sometimes wavy; does not split or shrink much in drying. Altogether a good substitute for mahogany.

Angelique.—From Brazil and British Guiana. Reddish brown, fairly hard, free from knots. Wavy figure and unpleasant smell in working, said to be extremely durable.

Mora.—From Trinidad and Guiana. Reddish brown, fine curly figure, hard, and close grained, takes good polish, and is a good substitute for Cuba mahogany.

Satiné.—Guiana. Deep reddish brown, sometimes well figured and lustrous, hard, and close grained, works up well and takes good polish, quite a good cabinet wood.

Santa Maria.—Honduras and Central America. Pale red, fairly hard, does not shrink or warp much. Very similar to Mexican mahogany and often mistaken for it.

Australian or "Colonial" mahoganies are described under "Colonial Woods."

Walnuts.

English Walnut (*Juglans regia*) is but rarely used in furniture and is difficult to get. It varies in quality according to growth. Usually pale greyish brown in colour, but sometimes marked with dark veins; fairly hard but easy to work. It was largely used for Queen Anne furniture, but has been found to be a prey to worms. Used chiefly for gun stocks.

Italian Walnut (*J. regia*).—Southern Europe generally. Good quality wood, is light brown in colour with darker stripes, and is chiefly cut into veneers for the "herring bone" panels and borders used in furniture of the Queen Anne style. The wood is fairly hard, even grained, and usually easy to work. There is a wide sapwood and considerable waste in boards, consequently it is an expensive wood and is only used in the best work as well as for piano cases. It is shipped from Italy in planks 4 and 6 in. thick, 4 to 12 ft. long, and from 12 to 24 in. wide. Good stuff fetches 1s. a foot in the inch. The "Burrs" are cut into veneers for pianos and fancy tables.

Black Sea or **Circassian Walnut** is a finely figured wood with an open grain quite distinct from the Italian wood. It is largely used in veneers which show a dark wavy figure, but rarely found in cabinet woods. Though inferior to Italian walnut in texture, it is usually classed with it and sold under similar conditions. It is imported in short logs 6 to 10 ft. long and 9 to 18 in. square.

French Walnut is similar to Italian but inferior in colour and figure, much of it being quite plain.

American Black Walnut (*Juglans nigra*).—Eastern North America, but most abundant in the Central States. Dark purplish brown with narrow sapwood. Hard, rather coarse in the grain, but the best wood is fairly easy to work, with not much figure; more durable than European walnut. It stands well and shrinks but little. Shipped from New York in logs from 10 to 20 ft. long and 12 to 25 in. square; also in planks and square edge boards, which are sold from 6d. a foot upwards.

African or **Golden Walnut.**—From West Africa, introduced by Sir Alfred Jones; is a bastard Cedrela, golden brown in colour, hard, coarse grain, good figure, works up well, and is now being used for bedroom suites in place of black walnut.

Satin Walnut or **Sweet Gum** (*Liquidambar styraciflua*).—Eastern States. A reddish brown wood with darker veins, works up with a satiny surface, hence its name, soft and easy to work, but warps and twists considerably. Imported in planks and boards, and used for the cheapest furniture. The **White Walnut** or **Butternut** is a somewhat similar wood, but little used in England.

Satinwoods.

East Indian Satinwood (*Chloroxylon swietenia*).—Ceylon and Central and Southern India. Light or darkish yellow, sapwood greyish, heavy, hard, and close in the grain, durable, from its oily nature. Some wood quite plain but generally with a beautiful figure of striped and zigzag markings. Used chiefly in veneers both knife and saw cut, and sold from 6d. to 2s. 6d. per foot. The curls and feathers are usually very fine in this wood. It is shipped from Singapore in logs 12 ft. long and up to 2 ft. wide.

West Indian Satinwood (*Zanthoxylon*).—From the West Indian Islands, Nassau, Bahamas, and Dominica. An old gold colour, darker than the East Indian and closer in the grain. Produces a fine flowery and mottled fiddle-back figure. Veneers fetch a high price, and the logs are smaller than those from the East Indies. The "yellow woods" of Australia are also known by the same name.

Rosewoods.

Rosewood, South American (*Dalbergia nigra*).—From Brazil, Rio, and Bahia ports, and varieties from the West Indies, Honduras, and Ceylon. Dark reddish brown in varying tints, with almost black or darker brown stripes and markings, works up with a fragrant smell from which it takes its name. Some wood straight in the grain, and much, which is cut into veneers, with a showy spreading figure. The rings are often irregular and wavy, and the wood is heavy and hard. The logs are usually rotten at the heart or shattered with heart shake, which necessitates a conversion to "half rounds" or flitches; and owing to the difficulties of measurement, the wood is sold by weight at prices varying from £10 to £30 per ton.

Indian Rosewood or **Blackwood** (*Dalbergia latifolia*).—A purplish black wood, and, as a rule, fragrant; close in the grain and mostly without figure, works up closely and is usually very tough. Exported from Bombay and sold by weight. Bastard rosewoods are non-fragrant, and are usually of a sickly, purplish colour, and coarse grained. One known as "Borneo Rosewood" produces wide veneers but with little figure.

Ebonies.

Ebony (natural order *Ebenaceæ*) varies in colour from yellowish white, red, brown, green, to jet black, which is the heartwood. It is one of the heaviest and hardest woods known, and it grows chiefly in India, whilst varieties come from the West Indies and Tropical and South Africa.

Black Ebony.—Southern India, Ceylon, Burmah, also from South Africa, known as "Cape Ebony," usually jet black. The best black is said to come from Mauritius.

Brown Ebony.—Also from India, Burmah, and West Indies. Brown, with darker blackish stripes, and not quite so dense as the black.

Green Ebony or **Cocus Wood.**—India and the West Indies. Varies in colour, sometimes greenish black or brown. Used in veneers and for musical instruments, such as flutes. A variety with a reddish tint is known as **Red Ebony**, and comes from Mauritius.

Coromandel Wood or **Bombay Ebony**, from the Coromandel Coast, is generally black with yellowish mottles or thin yellow stripes, a feature which makes it an extremely beautiful and expensive wood, the veneers fetching from 2s. 6d. per foot.

Calamander Wood.—From Ceylon. A dark brown, densely hard wood, black stripes and figure. Very scarce.

Marblewood.—From Andaman Islands. Alternate bands of black or brown, and grey or yellow, going right through the wood. There are quite a number of bastard ebonies, and the "German ebony" of commerce used for backs of brushes, knife handles, &c., is pearwood or sycamore stained. Ebony does not yield very large timber. The sap is usually wide and yellowish, the heart producing the real ebony, or black wood, scarcely ever reaching over 10 in. wide. It is imported in "billets" and small logs which fetch from £5 to £10 per ton, and they are generally converted into veneer, or used for turnery and mathematical instruments.

Small Fancy Woods.

Snakewood, or **Leopard Wood.**—From British Guiana. Dark chestnut brown with darker mottled bands running from the heart at right angles and less distinct near the sap. The wood is hard but generally shaky. Used for walking sticks, violin bows, veneering and inlaying. The sap resembles boxwood, and is sometimes 4 or 5 in. wide as well as being intensely hard. Sold by weight.

Kingwood, or **Violetwood.**—From Tropical America and Guiana. Dark purple with darker streaks, hard and close grained. Imported in small "sticks," seldom exceeding 5 in. wide, and cut into veneers for bandings and inlaying.

Purplewood, or **Purpleheart.**—From Brazil and Guiana. Good quality wood is an even-toned purple which darkens on exposure. Close grained, no figure, hard but fairly easy to work. Veneers 12 to 15 in. wide.

Amboyna.—From Amboyna and Ceram in the Molucca Islands. Shipped from Singapore. Known chiefly from its burrs, which are chestnut or reddish brown, and beautifully spotted, mottled, and figured with a variety of markings, of which the close spotted is the choicest. Sold in slabs by weight, and cut into veneers. A slab of plain wood at Kew is over 6 ft. wide.

Thuya.—A burr from Morocco and Algeria, said to be the "citron" wood of the Romans. Bright chestnut brown with groups of spots which are generally holes, and a wild curly figure resembling burr yew. Distinguished from Amboyna by fewer spots, and which are separated into groups of six or nine. The wood is also harder. Sold in parcels or leaves of veneer.

Burr Yew (*English*).—At one time a choice wood for knife boxes and tea caddies. A reddish brown with wavy figure and dark spots, intensely hard, and showy when polished, but difficult to work. The straight wood of the yew is hard and durable, but fairly easy to work. It has been proved to be almost indestructible under ground. It is sometimes used for chairmaking, but is always difficult to get.

Tulipwood (*Brazil*).—A fleshy red or rose-coloured wood with stripes of yellow or grey. The name is taken from its resemblance to the English tulip. Hard and close grained. Used for veneers and bandings.

Zebrawood.—From Brazil and Guiana. Reddish brown with dark stripes, hence its name. Used for bandings and inlaying.

Porcupine Wood.—A palm tree or coco-nut from India and the Tropics. Being a palm the fibres resemble the black and white quills of the porcupine, which also appear as spots on the cross section. Used for inlaying and walking sticks. The brown variety is known as **Pheasant** or **Partridge** wood, but the same name is given to other woods with similar figure which are not real palms.

Olive Wood.—The Mediterranean, Italy, and Spain. Light brown with dark wavy mottles and veins, fairly hard, easy to work or carve. Used in veneers, and thin boards for boxes, frames, &c.

Lignum Vitæ.—British Guiana and West Indies. Intensely hard, dark brown or greenish black, with yellow sap, which is said to be as durable and hard as the heartwood. Used for cogs, plumbers' tools, and ship blocks.

Box.—Central and Southern Europe. Light yellow, very dense, hard, and difficult to split. Imported in sticks of varying thickness from Circassia and Turkey, and sold by weight.

Harewood or **Mousewood** and **Greywood.**—Stained sycamore, which when fresh has a blue-grey tint. After exposure this turns to a brownish grey, giving the name of harewood. It is found on old French and eighteenth century cabinets, used in veneers, but ¼-in. stuff can now be stained right through.

Holly (*Ilex aquifolium*).—Central Europe and an American variety. Trees in England grow to a girth of 20 in., but they rarely get into the timber yards. The wood is an ivory or greenish white, hard, close in grain, and even in texture, inferior wood coarse. Used for printers' blocks, engraving, inlaying, and stained for imitation ebony.

Cherry.—Europe and North Asia, America, and Australia. Yellowish brown and sometimes a pinkish red, hard, and varying in texture, both close grained and coarse. English wood has a reddish tinge, but there are many varieties. The American and Australian cherry woods are usually a good colour, easy to work, and are useful for inlaying and small interior work.

Pearwood.—Europe and West Asia. A pinkish red centre with yellowish white sapwood. Hard, close-grained even texture easily worked with a satiny surface. English trees vary both in quality and colour. Australian produce good figured wood. Used chiefly for drawing instruments, engraving, inlaying, and stained for ebony.

Apple.—English wood is very hard and heavy, reddish brown with white sapwood, warps badly, and is sometimes extremely brittle. Good for mallet heads, turnery, tool handles, &c.

ENGLISH AND OTHER HARD WOODS AND BROAD-LEAF SOFT WOODS.

Ash (*Fraxinus excelsior*).—Great Britain, Central and Northern Europe, and America. English wood a brownish white, rings distinct, rays almost invisible, sapwood very wide and difficult to distinguish from heartwood, and unlike most woods the two can be used together. The wood is best known for its toughness and elasticity, hence is used for shafts, cooperage, and coach building.

American White Ash.—The wood is much whiter than the English or European, and the sapwood is more distinct. It is imported in logs 12 to 25 ft. long, and 12 to 18 in. square, and also in planks and square-edged boards. It is the ash known in the bedroom furniture trade, and sells from 6d. per foot in the inch.

Canadian or **Quebec Ash.**—Similar to the American, but darker in colour.

Hungarian Ash.—The name given to the finely figured wood from Austria, Hungary, and the Pyrenees. The wood is a whitish yellow, and the wavy figure and mottle known as "ram's horn" makes it a showy wood for panels, hence it is usually sold in veneers.

Beech (*Fagus sylvatica*).—Common to Great Britain, Europe generally, and America. English beech is usually a dull white with a reddish tinge, but the colour varies with the soil. Rings clearly marked, and rays numerous and distinct. The wood is hard, heavy, and tough, and durable under water. In furniture it was used largely for "stuff-over" frames of chairs and couches, and in this respect is often attacked by worms. With elm and ash it is used in the manufacture of small chairs, and is often stained for mahogany. The qualities in beech are divided into red and white, and the red is generally accepted as the best. Beech is plentiful in France, Germany, and Austria, where it is also used as fuel. It is the staple wood for benches, tool handles, mallets, and engineering purposes, and is imported from Germany in large quantities both in log and plank.

American Beech.—Known as "red" and "white," from the United States and Canada. Imported from St John's and New Brunswick, and used for similar purposes to the European beech, but generally inferior in quality.

Birch (*Betula alba*).—Common to Great Britain and Europe generally. Light reddish brown in colour with fine silvery streaks in the grain. Fairly hard and even grained, easy to work, but not very durable, and liable to worm attack. Often used as a substitute for beech in chairmaking. European wood from Prussia, Germany, and Sweden is usually imported with the bark on.

American Birch.—Eastern United States and Canada. Also known as "cherry birch," "mahogany birch," and "mountain mahogany." A red-brown wood which darkens on exposure, hard and strong, and often finely figured near the edges with wide flashes of darker wood. Sometimes stained and described as "**Colonial Mahogany**," and at one time largely used for bedroom furniture. Shipped from Quebec in logs 12 to 18 ft. long, and 12 to 20 in. square, and also in planks, and sold at 5d. and 6d. per foot in the inch.

Chestnut, Sweet or Spanish (*Castanea vesca*).—England, especially southern counties, and Southern Europe and America. Light brown in colour, similar to oak, but no medullary rays showing, and a white sapwood. Grain rather coarse and open, softer than oak, and liable to warp. Sometimes used for dados and panelling in place of oak where a dull, even tone with no figure is desired, but otherwise in little use, whilst the wood of the **Horse Chestnut** is coarse, and only suitable for fences and farming work.

Maple (*Acer campestre*).—Common to England, Central Europe, and America. Yellowish white, and good stuff almost white, hard, tough, and working up with a silky surface. The rays are very fine but distinct, and some wood produces good curly or mottled figure. Used for turnery and knife handles, and the figured wood as veneers for interior finishings for boxes and jewel cabinets.

American or **Bird's Eye Maple.**—Known officially in America as "**Sugar Maple.**" Eastern States of North America. Sapwood whitish, heartwood yellowish brown, fairly hard, close grained, and working up with fine smooth surface. The figure known as "bird's eye" appears in the form of small spots, or pits, at varying intervals, and they are linked up with wavy lines in the grain. The "blister" figure is produced by the rotary lathe cutting spirally, and other figures are the "curly" and "fiddle back" produced by a certain growth and accentuated by methods of cutting. The wood and veneers are imported from St John's and Quebec, and are chiefly used for ships' cabins, trams, railway carriage, and office work. Maple is but seldom used for furniture.

Sycamore (*Acer pseudo-platanus*).—Allied to the Maple but known as the Plane in Scotland. White, hard, and tough, and liable to warp. Rays fine and numerous, which give a lustrous surface. Used chiefly for turnery, coach panels, rollers for washing machines, and veneers for cabinetwork, which are stained all colours as well as black for Ebony. It is common to England, Europe, and America, but the supply is limited. The original Sycamore was used to make Egyptian mummy cases.

Plane Tree.—Two well-divided timbers, one the Eastern (*Platanus orientalis*) of Europe and North Africa, and the other the Western (*Platanus occidentalis*) of North America, also known as "buttonwood" and "lacewood." Reddish brown resembling the red beech, heavy, hard, and tough, cross grained and liable to warp. Often used as a substitute for birch or beech in chair frames. The rays are broad and darker than the wood, and when cut radially produce the figure which gives it the name of "lacewood" as sold in fretwork boards. The well-known tree in the London streets which sheds its bark in flakes is the Eastern plane.

Poplar.—"Black," "white," "Lombardy," and "trembling" or aspen tree, all producing soft whitish woods of little use except for rough fencing and farm work.

Teak (*Tectona grandis*).—Central and Southern India, Burma, and Ceylon. Dark brown, fairly hard, and straight in the grain, and, as a rule, easy to work; darkens on exposure, and is sometimes finely figured. It contains an oily resin which throws off an unpleasant odour in working, and when hardened in the pores easily blunts the tool. This resin makes teak a valuable and durable wood for civil engineering and railway and shipbuilding. It is often used in shop and public office work for dados, flooring, table and counter tops. Imported from Moulmein and Rangoon in logs 12 to 30 ft. long and squaring 12 to 20 in., and sold from 7d. per foot upwards according to width.

Bastard Teak produces a finely figured wood sold in veneers as "Pheasant wood." It is dark brown with old gold and darker markings, and makes a good showy wood for bandings and centres. Also known as "Granite Wood."

Greenheart, from South America and West Indies, is a brownish green wood, extremely durable and insect-proof under water. Imported in logs for piles and shipbuilding.

Hickory.—Closely allied to the walnuts of North America. A reddish white wood, hard, tough, elastic, and coarse in the grain; specially suitable and used for carriage building and handles for tools.

Hornbeam.—A common forest tree in England and Central Europe, and imported from France. Yellowish white in colour, hard, close grained and very tough, with little or no sap. Used for tool handles, cogs, and printers' rollers.

Elm.—English, known as "Common" and "Wych Elm," a tree also distributed over Europe. The wood is light brown in colour with yellowish sap; hard, tough, coarse grained, and liable to twist and warp. Very durable under ground or water, and formerly used for water pipes. Used for coach building, seats for Windsor chairs, naves for wheels, coffin boards, and pulley blocks.

Canadian Rock Elm, from Eastern United States, is also a very tough, durable wood but easier to work than the English elm. Straighter and closer in the grain, but somewhat similar in appearance except when seen in the board, when it does not show such a wild twisty texture. Shipped in logs 12 to 25 ft. long and squaring from 12 to 18 in. Used for similar purposes to English elm and selling 4d. per foot.

Orham Wood, from Canada, is a species of elm but is much coarser than English wood, and is often sold as Rock elm. The name is taken from the French *orme* = elm.

Lancewood.—From Honduras, Cuba, Jamaica. Yellowish white, sap and heart alike, grain very close, hard as box, tough and elastic. Used for turnery, shafts, and imported in small spars.

Lime, or **Linden** (*Tilia parvifolia*).—Common to England and Europe generally. Light yellow, sometimes with a reddish tinge, soft, light, easy to work, and close grained. Much prized by carvers and used by Grinling Gibbons for much of his work. Imported from Europe, the Baltic principally, and also used for turnery and interior piano work.

Basswood, or **American Lime** (*Tilia americana*).—Eastern United States and Canada. Whitish to lemon colour, soft, close grained, and sometimes stringy and tough. Called Bass from the inner bark or "bast," and often confused with and sold as whitewood. The wood shrinks considerably and is not very durable. The tree produces wide boards free from knots, and it is used extensively for cheap furniture, turnery, toys, and paper pulp. As a rule it is distinguished from whitewood by its deeper lemon colour and close grain. Imported in planks and boards and sold at about 4d. per foot.

Whitewood, or **Tulip Tree**.—Also known as **Yellow Poplar** and **Canary Wood**. This is the wood of a large forest tree known as the Tulip Tree (*Liriodendron tulipifera*), abundant in the Central and Southern States of North America, and shipped from New York and Baltimore. The tree grows to an immense size, often to a diameter of from 3 to 6 ft., with a clear stem up to 70 ft. The heartwood is a lemon colour but varies, and the sapwood is whitish with grey or bluish streaks. The texture varies from an even, straight grain to a coarse one, and the qualities sold on the market are known as "prime" and "sap." As a rule it is easy to work, is liable to shrink and warp, takes stain and polish well, and it is free from knots. Occasionally some finely figured mottled veneers are cut, but it is most used in the solid. Imported in planks and square edged boards of varying widths, and used largely for cheap furniture, and as a substitute for pine. Price according to width from 3d. per foot in the inch, planed wood extra.

American Poplar is often sold as whitewood, but it is whiter, softer, and stringy. It is used as "three ply" for drawing boards, and is also known as "cottonwood," one of the softest of pulp woods for paper making.

Willow.—Various species of Salix, the most important being the white willow, common to England and Europe generally. Its chief virtue is in being soft, light, and non-splitting, even when badly bruised, hence its use for cricket bats. It is also in demand for water wheels and steamboat paddles, but is not a cabinet wood, though occasionally made up into chairs.

Alder is another soft wood which does not warp or split. White when freshly cut, it turns to a fleshy red. It is durable under water, and is imported from the Baltic for the bobbin and charcoal trade.

NEEDLE-LEAFED, CONIFEROUS TREES, AND SOFT WOODS.

Yellow Pine (*Pinus strobus*).—A forest tree of North America from Quebec to the Southern States, and known there as White Pine. It was planted in England by Lord Weymouth, and is sometimes named after him. Usually of a straw colour with bluish grey sapwood, soft, easy to work, light, and straight grained, it is the softest but most reliable of the pine woods, but getting scarce. It warps and shrinks but little, and the "first" quality is free from resin and

knots, although the wood is sometimes subject to cup and heart shake. It makes
a good ground for veneering upon, and is clean and suitable for interior work,
and a quantity of wood is used up in the making of drawing boards. Logs
from 12 to 30 ft. long and 12 to 24 in. wide are shipped from Quebec and
St John's, but it is imported chiefly in planks 11 by 3 in. and upwards,
which are sold in selected "firsts" or "prime," "seconds," and "thirds" in
quality, the best fetching 1s. per foot run in 11 by 3 in. planking. The
commonest is usually cut into very thin stuff for picture backing.

Yellow Deal (*Pinus sylvestris*).—Known as Northern Pine, Scotch, Danzig,
Riga, and Baltic Fir, as well as Red Deal. Europe and North Asia, the names
above indicating the ports of shipment. The colour of the wood varies from
yellow to reddish brown, which tends to darken in drying, leaving the sap
whitish with a red tint. It is resinous, and the rings are clearly marked and
close, and knots appear at irregular intervals. The best wood, which comes
from the Baltic, usually Danzig, works up clean and silky in planing, and is the
selected stuff for good house building. It is remarkable for its durability in wet
or dry situations, and although not a cabinetmaker's wood, it is not an uncommon thing to find it used as a carcase wood in Queen Anne furniture and as
a veneer ground. Logs are shipped at the Baltic ports from the forests of
Russia, Poland, 18 to 40 ft. long and 11 to 18 in. square, and also in planks and
deals. It is also imported from Archangel, and Sweden and Norway in various
qualities, the Swedish ranking lowest. The home-grown wood is inferior, and
is generally used up for pit wood. Good planks 3 by 11 in. fetch 1s. per foot
run, but large quantities are bought by the "standard."

White Deal, or **Spruce** (*Picea excelsa*).—"White Fir," "Norway Spruce," and
White Deal in commerce. Sweden, Norway, Denmark, and "Prussia," once
named Pruce, from which it takes its name. The slender stems are shipped
whole for spars and scaffold poles. The larger wood comes in deals and planks.
It is yellowish or straw-white, tough, and springy. The small knots are brittle,
and the wood warps and shrinks moderately, and is not very resinous. It is
used for kitchen dressers and tables, steps, packing-cases, and pulp, and is considerably cheaper than yellow deal.

American or **Black Spruce** is a similar wood, but with small black loose
knots, and is shipped from St John's and Nova Scotia.

Pitch Pine (*Pinus australis*), with varieties.—Southern States of North
America, Georgia, Florida, and Carolina. Very heavy and resinous, autumn
rings broad and dark brown, general appearance of wood an orange-yellow.
Some wood with wavy and showy figure, known as panel wood. Difficult to
work and season owing to resin, and liable to shrink considerably. Extremely
durable, and used chiefly for ship work, piles, and for church and school
furniture. Shipped from Savannah, Pensacola, and Darien in logs 12 to 18 in.
square and from 20 to 30 ft. long, and also in planks. Pitch pine produces the
turpentine of commerce.

Oregon Pine, or **Douglas Fir**.—North-Western America. The wood
varies, but is usually a reddish white with a narrow yellow sap. It is rather
heavy, hard, and tough. The knots are distributed in small clusters as in larch,
and the wood does not warp much, and is fairly straight grained. It is a clean

wood for interior work, but is chiefly used for shipbuilding and carpentry, and especially for ships' masts. The flagstaff at Kew Gardens is a well-known specimen 159 ft. high, and the logs or "spars" vary from 30 to 100 ft. in length, and from 10 to 40 in. in diameter.

Sequoia, or **Californian Redwood.**—A very soft, reddish brown wood, not strong, brittle, easily split, and with a spongy texture. Used for interior work, panels, backs, drawers, &c.

Carolina or **Columbian Pine.**—British Columbia and North Carolina, known in the trade as "Carolina." Dark yellow in colour with lighter strips, light and soft, easy to work, but coarse in texture, fragrant, and does not warp much ; used for interior work. Imported in logs, planks, and boards from 12 to 20 ft. long, and from 12 in. upwards in width.

Canadian Red Pine is a whitish wood tinged with yellow, and works up with a silky surface somewhat similar to the best yellow deal. It is tough, and does not shrink very much though resinous.

Swiss Pine, the wood of the silver fir, is imported from Switzerland, chiefly as sounding boards for pianos. It is also the wood used by the natives for toys and carvings.

Larch (*Larix europæa*).—A native of the European Alps and Northern Europe generally, and well known among the conifers of the United Kingdom. Mostly used for building purposes, scaffold poles, and fencing ; very durable but shrinks badly. Venice is said to have been built on larch piles, and the tree produces the Venice turpentine of commerce. **American Larch** or Tamarack, from Canada and North-Eastern States, is a similar wood used for much the same purposes.

Cedar.—Out of some thirty named varieties, the two best known to commerce are the **Pencil** or **American Cedar** and the **West Indian.** The former (*Juniperous virginiana*) is the well-known pencil wood, very fragrant, soft, easy to work, but brittle. Brownish red in colour, with rather wide, whitish sapwood. Used chiefly for interior work, drawers, pigeon holes, and workboxes. It comes from the Southern States. The **West Indian** "Honduras" or "Mexican" cedar is the reddish wood resembling mahogany. It is fragrant, sometimes figured, and varies in colour, the light wood being used for cigar boxes. The chief supplies come from the West Indian Islands, Central and Tropical America, but there are many bastard woods of good and bad quality. The **Indian Cedars** are reddish woods, fragrant and durable, with some resemblance to mahogany, one being known as "Indian Mahogany," or "Toon." **White Cedar**, really a cypress, is not quite white, but lighter than the above, and is used for canoe building. **Lebanon**, the true cedar, a tree well known and prized on English lawns, and introduced towards the end of the seventeenth century, is but little known for its wood, which is reddish brown, fragrant, very soft and spongy.

Cypress is a reddish brown wood of varying tints and qualities, and a native of Greece and Persia. It is very durable, and was the wood used for mummy cases, but is now but little known. The **American Cypress**, or white cedar of the Southern States, is a deciduous tree, and produces a reddish or whiter wood, according to situation of growth, and is used chiefly in America. The **Cypress**

Pine of North and East Australia, of several varieties, has a strong fragrance, something like camphor, and is sometimes called camphor wood, but cypress is but little known or used in England.

Woods Producing Dyes.

Logwood.—From Central America and Jamaica. Dark brownish red, and very hard. Imported in short logs 3 to 4 ft. long, and sold in chips which produce red or black dyes.

Fustic.—A yellow wood from Tropical America, producing a well-known yellow dye.

Red Sanders Wood.—From India and Ceylon. A hard, deep red wood, soluble in alcohol, and a variety, which is a purplish red soluble in water, known as red sandalwood, from India and Tropical America.

Brazilwood.—From Tropical America, also used for its red dye, and one from India of the same species, known as Sappanwood.

Sandalwood of India is one of many fragrant smelling woods with a similar name, used in Indian work, but known for its sweet scented oil, which is an important commercial product.

Camwood, from West Africa, is also imported, and distilled into a red dye for cottons, whilst **Camphor Wood,** from India, China, and Japan, is a soft yellowish brown wood, imported specially for entomological cases for its strong fragrance.

Sumach, also known as wild olive, a dark yellow wood, is imported from Greece as a dye for leather and woollen stuffs.

Cabinet Woods from the Colonies.

New Zealand, Tasmania, Australia, New South Wales, Victoria, Queensland, South Africa.

The following details of Colonial woods are taken from official handbooks kindly lent for the purpose by the Agents-General for the Colonies named. Many of the specimens described have also been tested and used by the authors, or verified in the Timber Museum at Kew Gardens.

New Zealand.

The official list names eighty-six timber trees, but of these only a few are known to the English trade, or as commercial woods. Foremost among them is the **Kauri Pine** (*Agathis australis*), also known as "Cowdie" or New Zealand Pine. It is a conifer and grows to large dimensions. Light reddish brown in colour, rays and rings partly visible, wide whitish sap, easy to work with a silky surface, close and straight in grain, fairly hard for pine, takes stain and polish well. The coarse stuff inclined to warp and twist, but best boards usually free from blemish, knot, or shake. Used largely for vat-making, and successfully in church work, dados, panelling, &c. Imported in logs and planks from 1 to 3 and 4 ft. wide, and up to 20 ft. long. Price according to width about 4d. per foot super in inch. There are over a dozen varieties, the chief being known as "Mottled Kauri," which is highly ornamental and is cut into veneers for cabinetwork. The mottling is caused by the indentation of the bark in the growth, and takes the form of dark elongated markings in the lighter wood.

Rimu, or **Red Pine** (*Dacrydium cupressinum*).—A conifer not so well known as Kauri. Deep red in colour, figured with dark or light streaks, works up well and takes good polish, wide sap rays invisible, shrinks laterally. Suitable for bank and office work, ships' panels, &c. Burrs produce finely figured veneers. Logs and planks from 1 to 2 ft. wide, 12 to 20 ft. long. Not much known in England.

Honeysuckle or **Rewa** (*Knightia excelsa*).—Two varieties, one reddish brown and the other a "light silver hue," but both with figure similar to "lace-wood" or plane tree when cut radially. The wood is fine and close in the grain, rays and rings distinct. Suitable for panels and cabinetwork generally.

Black Pine, or **Matai** (*Podocarpus spicata*).—Reddish brown or bright cinnamon colour, smooth and silky texture, fine and even grain, strong, fairly hard and durable, rays and rings visible, does not shrink much in drying. A variety called **Miro** is finely figured. Used for cabinet and building work, and yields timber 2 to 4 ft. wide and log length.

Totara, or **New Zealand Yew** (*Podocarpus totara*).—A rich rosy red in colour, sapwood whitish, heavy, fairly hard, close grained, rays and rings visible, does not warp much, said to be a good substitute for mahogany, and resembles pencil cedar, though darker in colour. Produces fine burrs, and is used for ship and office fittings.

Rata is another hard, red wood used in building railway, ship, and wheel-wrights' work.

Black Maire, an olive tree, produces wood of a similar character, hard and durable, sometimes beautifully figured and suitable for cabinetwork.

Red Birch (*Fagus fusca*).—Really a beech, and said to be superior to all others. The wood is reddish brown, with lighter sap rings clearly defined but rays indistinct, tough, straight, and even grained and durable, easy to work, and takes good polish, produces wide boards and said to be a good wood for furniture construction.

Puriri, or **New Zealand Teak** (*Vitex littoralis*).—Dark brown, yellow sap, very hard, heavy, and durable. Rings and rays indistinct. Used for ship-building, railway, and engineering work.

White Pine (*Podocarpus dacrydioides*).—Yellowish white, similar to pale whitewood, rather hard and tough, brittle, works easily, sapwood wide, rings indistinct, rays visible, free from knots, liable to warp, not very durable; suitable for cheap furniture and purposes similar to uses of white deal, but not so strong. Yields wide planks and boards, sold at 3d. in the inch. **Silver Pine,** a white wood with a satiny surface, like good deal, and stronger and tougher than white pine, is sometimes mottled and used for cabinetwork. Although New Zealand timbers are not so well known at present, it is probable that rimu and honeysuckle may become popular as "furniture woods" before many years, especially as the supply of other hardwoods diminishes.

Tasmania.

Tasmania, like Australia, produces many species of the eucalyptus trees, commonly known as gum trees. Such are the "Swamp," "Red," "Blue," "Cider," "Weeping," and "White" Gums. Other eucalypti are the "Stringy" and "Iron Bark," and the Peppermint Tree. These are mostly hard, heavy, dense, and durable woods, in a few cases suitable for furniture, but mostly fit for railway, agricultural, and building purposes, or wood paving. Possible furniture woods are the **Beech** (*Fagus Cunninghami*), known as **Myrtle**, a greyish brown wood with a satiny surface and feathered figure. A pink variety is much prized for cabinetwork. A furniture wood known in England is the "**Blackwood**," or *Acacia melanoxylon*, the latter word meaning blackwood. It resembles walnut, and in some varieties is beautifully figured, though it varies in colour. A similar wood with the same name comes from Australia. The "**Black**" and **Silver** "**Wattles**" are also acacias, the former a yellowish brown wood with a fine figure, and the latter, darker, harder, and heavier. Among the conifers the **Huon Pine** is the best known. The wood is almost a bright yellow with darker spots and wavy markings, but as it contains an oil which oxidises, the yellow turns to a "smoky brown" with age. It also has an unpleasant odour. The oil makes it almost rot proof. It is tough and heavy for pine, but easy to work, takes a good polish, and is suitable for panels and dados. A fine specimen can be seen at Kew. "**Celery Top**," "**Oyster Bay**," and "**King William**" are other pines, while **Sassafras** is also a light-coloured wood said to be good for carving and interior cabinetwork. The **He** and **She Oaks** are well-figured ornamental woods, and the "**Native Cherry**" and the "**Musk**" are used for furniture and joinery. The official handbook names fifty trees, specimens of which can be examined at the Kew Museum. Those named appear to be the chief cabinet woods, some of which are on the London market, viz., Huon pine, blackwood, and sassafras.

Western Australia.

The timbers of this colony appear to be most suitable for railway, engineering, and agricultural purposes, and are confined largely to the products of the eucalyptus trees. Such are Jarrah, Karri, Blackbutt, Wandoo, Tuart, Red, White, and York Gums, all of which are hard, dense, strong, and durable timbers, well known as paving woods, but not yet acceptable as timbers in the furniture trade. Sandalwood is exported to the East, and many of the trees have been successfully acclimatised in South Africa.

PLATE LI.   350A

CHINA CABINET MADE OF AUSTRALIAN BLACK BEAN, EXHIBITED IN THE PANELED ROOM
SHOWN ON PLATE LII, OVERLEAF.

PANELED ROOM AND FURNITURE MADE OF AUSTRALIAN WOODS EXHIBITED AT THE FRANCO-
BRITISH EXHIBITION BY THE GOVERNMENT OF NEW SOUTH WALES.
DESIGNED BY MR. ARNOLD MITCHELL, F.R.I.B.A., AND CONSTRUCTED BY MESSRS GEO.
TROLLOPE & SONS, AND COLL & SONS, LTD.

Victoria.

In this State the principal timbers are also the product of eucalyptus trees. **Red Iron, Bark, Blue Gum, Grey Box, Stringy Barks, Messmate,** and **Blackbutt** are known for similar purposes to those already described. **Blackwood** (*Acacia*) is used for furniture, billiard tables, chairmaking, and general cabinetwork, as well as for railway and boat building. It is often well figured and mottled, is similar to the blackwood of Tasmania. **Evergreen Beech** is also used for furniture and is a good carver's wood, whilst **Satin Box, Pencilwood**, and "**Olive**" are small trees supplying ornamental woods for veneers and turnery.

New South Wales.

New South Wales possesses a vast forest area which produces a great variety of trees, including many of the eucalyptus type, such as the **Iron Barks, Stringy Barks,** the **Gums—White, Spotted, Grey,** and **Red—Blackbutt, Woolybutt, Tallow-wood,** and **White** and **Red "Mahogany,"** all of which, like similar trees in the sister colonies, are strong, hard, and durable timbers, used for paving, railway work, van building, and builder work generally. The colony also produces some interesting furniture woods, chief of which are the **Black Bean,** a dark brown wood rather like walnut but more strongly marked in the grain. Most suitable for heavy furniture and framed work as panelling, dados, general joinery, and gun stocks.

White Beech.—A yellowish or pinkish white wood similar in texture to English lime. It is moderately hard, close in grain, and even in texture, and is highly recommended for carvers. It shrinks but very little, and is also used for ordinary carpentry purposes.

Silky Oak.—Lightish brown in colour with darker figure caused by the ray as in plane tree (lacewood). Quite suitable for small furniture. The **Red Silky Oak** is darker with a reddish tinge.

Rosewood.—A dark reddish coloured wood, fragrant, and with a rich figure. Used as a substitute for Honduras mahogany in furniture and general cabinetmaking, and suitable for all indoor work and show cases.

Spotted Gum is a pale yellowish brown wood with straight grain, tough, and bends well when cold. It is recommended for flooring, and builders' work, whilst its bending properties make it suitable for coach and carriage building.

The room illustrated on Plate LII., opposite, was exhibited at the Franco-British Exhibition by the New South Wales Government. It was designed by Mr Arnold Mitchell, F.R.I.B.A., and made by Messrs G. Trollope & Sons and Colls & Sons, Ltd., by whose kind permission the photographs are reproduced. The panelling and all the furniture and carving was made of New South Wales wood. The panelling of black bean, the carving of white beech, and the parquet flooring of spotted gum. The fine china cabinet on Plate LI., as well as the sideboard, tall-boy chest, and bureau, shown in the room, were made of the black bean. The octagon table and chairs, which looked like mahogany, were made of the rosewood. In all cases the woods were well chosen and suited the designs, the warm brown of the black bean being particularly successful in the panelling and larger furniture. The white beech is well spoken of by West End carvers, and there can be no doubt of the suitability of silky oak for small fancy things. The timbers were shipped by Messrs T. Gabriel & Sons, Lambeth.

The Red Bean.—A dark red wood, of a different natural order to black bean. Sometimes sold as bastard cedar. A good furniture wood with fine figure, takes good polish and looks well made up.

Onion Wood (from its odour) is also a kind of bastard cedar, and is used for similar purposes. **Myall** (*Acacia*) is a dark violet-brown wood, intensely hard, heavy, figured, and fragrant. Used for turnery, chessmen, pipes, and fancy goods, and lately selected by the Ordnance Department for spokes of gun carriages. Varieties of myall are the **Yarran, Brigalow, True** and **Bastard Myall.**

She Oaks (*Casuarina*).—These woods such as **She, He,** and **Silky Oaks** are not real oaks, and they vary in colour from red to light brown. The wood is generally hard and heavy and well figured. In veneers it is valuable for ship and cabinet work, and in the solid for tools, spokes, and turnery. Numerous local names are given to these woods, such as "**Swamp**," "**Scrub**," "**Stunted**," "**Shingle**," "**Silvery**," "**Forest**," and "**Bull**" **Oak**, as well as "**Red Ash**" and **Beefwood.** Other New South Wales woods are **Tulipwood**, resembling olive, and beautifully figured and largely used for cabinetwork; **Blackwood** (*Acacia*); **Muskwood**, similar to bird's-eye maple; **Cudgerie**, and **Native Teak**; **Blueberry Ash**, a whitish, tough wood, suitable for bedroom furniture; **Maiden's Blush**, a rosy coloured wood which fades into brown when cut; **Saxifrage** and **Cork**, or **Coachwood**, which is extremely valuable for coach and carriage building; **Moreton Bay Pine**, the principal soft wood of New South Wales; and **Cypress Pine**, a strong smelling, camphoraceous wood, somewhat like sandalwood, but possessing a fine showy figure in some varieties; **Red** and **White Honeysuckle**, and **Needlewood**, used for pipes; and **Red Cedar**, a real cedar which is said to be equal to mahogany for a furniture wood both in figure and texture, though softer.

Queensland.

Most of the Queensland timbers are also found in New South Wales, and are mentioned above. They are Spotted Gum, Grey Iron Back, Sassafras, Moreton Bay and Cypress Pine, Blue Gum, Yellowwood, and White Cedar.

Flindosa is a very hard wood, and used as a substitute for beech. **Bunya-bunya** is a beautifully figured wood, said to be suitable for furniture; and **Bloodwood** is another name for the rosewood referred to.

South Africa.

Stinkwood.—Also known as **Cape Walnut**. A dark brown, hard, close grained wood with a bright silky surface, but liable to warp ; used for cabinet-making and waggon work. When fresh cut has an unpleasant smell which is lost in seasoning.

Sneezewood.—An extremely durable wood, equal in rank to greenheart. The smell of the dust causes sneezing, hence its name. Light reddish brown in colour, darkening with exposure. Used for furniture, bridges, and engineering.

Yellowwood.—A light yellow, soft wood, even grain, but liable to warp, strong and elastic, used for furniture, &c.

Kamassi.—Also known as **Cape Box**. Light yellow, hard, close grained, suitable for tools, and used for furniture.

Saffronwood.—Reddish yellow in colour, close grain, hard and durable, fine figure, used for cabinetwork and waggon building.

Cape Box, similar to ordinary boxwood, and **Cape Cedar** are both suitable for turnery and cabinetwork. **Cape Ebony** is a jet black, real ebony, and other cabinet woods are **Rock Ash, Cape Ash**, and **Guar**, a dark brown finely figured timber. The South African **Ironwoods**, black and white, are intensely hard, and similar to lignum vitæ.

Canadian, Gold Coast, and Nigerian timbers are described in the Mahoganies, Oaks, and Pines, &c.

India.

Some very useful and well-figured timbers suitable for woodwork and furniture are now (1922) being imported from India. A good selection may be inspected at Messrs Howard's yard, Stanhope Street, W. The following are a few of the best known :—

Silver Grey Wood.—Varies from a uniform grey with a tinge of green in it, to darker figured wood. Works up well and the " grey " is quite permanent.

Laurel Wood.—Very like Italian walnut, but varies considerably in figure and colour. Makes excellent panelling.

Padauk.—The Andaman wood is a rich red with fine figure. The Burma variety is duller in colour.

Haldu.—A dark satinwood colour, said to be suitable for chair work.

White Mahogany.—A light coloured wood suitable for interior parts : a substitute for Whitewood.

Other woods are Koko, Gurgan, Pyenkado, Pyinma, and White Bombwe.

Books of reference on Timbers are included in the list at the end of the book.

A Simple Dresser and Shelves, English Oak.
Designed by Mr. Gordon Russell and made by Russell & Sons, Broadway,
Worcestershire.

A DRESSER OF ENGLISH WALNUT, INLAID WITH BOG OAK AND YEW TREE, AND WITH HAND-WROUGHT BRASS HANDLES.
DESIGNED BY MR. GORDON RUSSELL AND MADE BY RUSSELL & SONS, BROADWAY, WORCESTERSHIRE.

GLOSSARY

A

ABACUS.—The uppermost member of the capital of a column supporting the architrave and entablature.

ACANTHUS.—A leaf ornament based upon the foliage of the *Acanthus spinosa*, and used upon the capitals, friezes, and cornices of the Corinthian and Composite orders of architecture.

ACORN TURNING.—A term applied to turned ornaments resembling the acorn, and largely used in Jacobean work, chiefly on the backs of chairs.

ANNULETS.—Encircling bands or fillets upon the lower part of the Doric capital.

ANTHEMION.—A Greek ornament based upon the foliage of the chamomile.

APRON PIECE.—A term sometimes applied to wide curved rails in furniture, which are fixed at a less height than 3 ft. from the floor line.

ARCHIMEDEAN.—Based upon the principles of Archimede's screw, as in an Archimedean drill which is operated with a spiral thread.

ARCHITRAVE.—The bottom member of the cornice or entablature in architecture ; also a moulding surrounding a door or window opening.

ARMOIRE.—From the French, an old press or wardrobe. See p. 3.

ARRIS.—The sharp edge or line formed by two plain surfaces in any material.

ASTRAGAL.—A half-round moulding worked on the edge ; it is known as a bead.

AUGER.—An instrument for boring holes. Usually made with a long stem, and operated with a wooden handle fixed at right angles.

AUMBRY.—A recess or small cupboard in a wall, sometimes called "Aumrie."

B

BADGER.—A term applied to a wide rebate plane ; length about 18 in. with an iron 2 in. in width, and upwards. Made with a skew mouth, and used for wide rebate and sunk bevels. See p. 8.

BALK.—A roughly squared log of timber. Cuba mahogany is imported in this form.

BALTIC TIMBER.—The term "Baltic" embraces all kinds of timber shipped from ports on the Baltic Sea, including Russian, Prussian, Polish, Swedish, and Norwegian shipments.

BALUSTER.—A small pillar or shaped upright used to support handrailing.

BALUSTER TURNING.—Characteristic of the Elizabethan and Jacobean periods. An example of the former type is illustrated on p. 282.

BALUSTRADE.—A row of turned pillars supporting a rail.

BANDING.—A strip or band of veneer in a panel or round a drawer front, as in "cross" or straight banding.

BANISTER.—A corruption of the term "Baluster." The name is also given to the uprights in a chair back.

BAREFACED TENON.—A tenon shouldered on one side only.

BAREFACED TONGUE.—Similar to the above.

BARRED DOOR.—A framed-up door with traceried patterns made up with mouldings and "slats" called "bars." Introduced during the Chippendale and Sheraton periods.

BASE.—The bottom of an object, such as the base moulding of a column ; also the plinth in carcase work.

BASIL.—The angle to which the cutting edge of a plane, iron, or chisel is ground.

BAY.—Applied to windows, the term indicates a projection from the wall, forming a recess in the room. See also ORIEL WINDOW.

BEAD.—A small semicircular moulding, one of the group of nine classical mouldings. See ASTRAGAL.

BEAD AND BUTT.—A term applied to the finish of flush panels in framing. The sides of panels are separated from the stiles or muntings with a "bead," and the ends butt against the rails ; also applied to drawer slips. See p. 82.

BEAD AND FLUSH.—When the bead is worked and let in all round the panel.

BEAD AND REEL.—Ornamental turning resembling these objects strung together alternately, and frequently fixed in an angle or corner.

BEAM COMPASS.—An instrument consisting of a long rod or lath with two sliding heads attached, one fitted with a point, and the other with a pencil. It is used for describing large circles or arcs.

BEARER.—The drawer rail in a carcase or table, bearing the drawer.

BED MOULDING.—Any moulding placed under a "corona" or "drip" moulding of a cornice.

BED POST.—The legs of a bedstead, also applied to turned shafts or pillars supporting the canopy of a bedstead, see p. 188. Characteristic of Chippendale, Elizabethan, and Hepplewhite four-poster bedsteads, which were often reeded and carved.

BEDSTEAD BOLT.—An iron bolt and nut used for connecting the side rails of French wooden bedsteads to the posts. See p. 186.

BELLY.—The protruding portion of a piece of work, also "bellied" ; applied to panelling that has buckled owing to dampness.

BENCH END.—The upright end to a pew or church seat·

BEVEL.—A kind of chamfer ; also an adjustable tool similar to a square, used for marking out "bevelled" work.

BEZEL.—The metal ring surrounding a clock face glass, usually hinged.

BIDET.—A small stand fitted with a pan for bedroom use.

BIRD'S-BEAK LOCK.—Used on piano falls, cylinder tables, and tambours, the bolt, when thrust out, resembling a bird's beak.

BLOCK PLANE.—An iron plane, with an exceptionally low pitch to the iron, especially intended for use upon a mitre block, and also with a shooting board.

BLOCK SAW.—For use upon a mitre block. See pp. 68 and 295.

BODYING IN.—A term applied to a process in French polishing executed before the finishing stage ; literally, filling in the grain of the wood.

BOLECTION.—A rebated moulding, fitting over the edges of parts of framing, and raised above the surface.

BOLE.—The trunk or stem of a tree.

BOMBÉ.—A convex or arched surface, a feature in the construction of tables and commodes in the Louis XV. period.

BOSS.—A projecting ornament used at the intersection of angles in the mouldings of a ceiling.

BOTTLE TURNING.—A detail of Dutch origin, so-called because of its resemblance to a bottle. A characteristic of the William and Mary period.

BRACKET CORNICE.—A feature of the Elizabethan, Jacobean, and French François I. and Louis XIV. periods, consisting of a cornice moulding, supported by brackets fixed to the frieze part.

BRANCH WOOD.—An inferior quality timber, not generally used for cabinet and joinery work owing to its extreme tendency to twist.

BRASS FOIL.—A Dutch production, consisting of thin sheet brass beaten out to a foil thickness.

BREAK.—The projection on a cornice, carcase, or plinth when it stands forward or when the line is broken.

BRIDLE.—A woodwork joint, an open tenon. See chapter on "Joints."

BUFFET.—A sideboard or cupboard for the display of china, plate, &c. A French term.

BUHL or BOULE WORK.—A style of decoration comprising inlays of brass, tortoise-shell, ivory, silver, &c., invented by André Charles Boule. See chapter on "Veneering."

BULBOUS.—A knobby or protuberant style of turnery of Dutch origin, and characteristic of turned work executed in the Queen Anne period.

BULKHEAD.—A division or partition in shipwork, the sides of a cabin or saloon.

BULL-NOSE.—A small plane with the mouth fixed close to the fore part of the stock. Used for planing close up to a projecting part.

BUREAU (plural BUREAUX).—A writing desk or chest for holding papers. See p. 146.

BURR.—A growth or excrescence on the bole of a tree; also the arris or cutting edge of a scraper, chisel, &c.

BUSH.—A lined metal collar or connection.

BUTT HINGE.—Used for hanging doors. See p. 260.

BUTT JOINT.—A joint between the end grains of two pieces of timber when there is no shoulder. See p. 47.

C

CABINET.—Originally a small room, a private room for consultations, but now applied to a form of cupboard enclosed by doors, and used for the display of china, plate, &c.

CABIN HOOK.—A small hook and eye, chiefly used in cabin doors, and also applied to flaps and doors in cabinet and joinery work.

CABRIOLE.—A name given to a curved leg with a projecting knee part, curved shaft, and shaped toe, originating in legs resembling animal forms. Largely used during the Queen Anne and Chippendale periods. See p. 321.

CAMBER.—The convexity of a surface or arch. The convex deck line from port to starboard in shipwork.

CAMP BEDSTEAD.—Portable, consisting of a light framework, with legs folding underneath when closed.

CANDLE BOARD.—A characteristic of Sheraton work, consisting of a small ledge or shelf fitting underneath a table top, for the reception of a candlestick. Now almost obsolete.

CANOPY.—A fixture over a throne or bedstead; also an ornamental Gothic projection over an arch, niche, or doorway, &c.

CANT.—An inclination or form of chamfer, as "canted" or bevelled edge.

CANTEEN.—A case containing cutlery and table accessories.

CANTERBURY.—A seat with a "well" to contain music, made specially for use at the piano.

CAPITAL.—The carved or moulded projecting member at the head of a shaft or column; also called "Cap" (an abbreviation) and formerly chapiter.

CARCASE.—The body part of a box-like piece of furniture, without ornament or doors and fittings. See Wardrobe carcase on p. 75; also "Wing" carcase, occurring in large furniture, and placed at the side of the main carcase, and "bottom" carcase, as in the bottom part of a bookcase or tall-boy chest of drawers.

CARCASE WORK.—Pertaining to carcases as distinguished from table work, i.e., framed-up rails and legs.

CARD TABLE.—Specially designed for card playing. See illustrations on p. 133.

CARTOON PAPER.—Large-sized roll paper intended for full-size drawings and fresco designs.

CARTOUCHE.—A form of ornament resembling a tablet or scroll unrolled—a feature of the French François I. style of decoration.

CARYATIDE.—A conventional female figure supporting an architectural arch or entablature.

CASEMENT.—A French form of window, hinged and opening outwards, either singly or in pairs.

CASEMENT STAYS.—A pivoted and drilled bar attached to sill and casement to fix the window when adjusted to the desired angle of opening.

CAST.—The term applied to timber means twisted, and is generally used with reference to lengthwise twisting.

CAUL.—A piece of wood or zinc plate used to impart the necessary heat and to distribute the pressure obtained by clamps and hand-screws evenly over the veneer surface. See chapter on "Veneering."

CAVETTO.—One of the classic mouldings generally described as, and synonymous with, "Hollow."

CELLARET.—A deep drawer or tray in a sideboard for bottles.

CELLULOID.—A chemically formed substitute for ivory, obtainable in thin sheets for marquetry, and also in lines for inlaying. It consists of gun-cotton and camphor, and is highly inflammable.

CHASING.—A decorative finish applied to metal mounts, effected by incising patterns.

CHECK.—A northern term identical with "Rebate."

CHEQUER.—Decoration in the form of squares, differently shaded or coloured alternately, as in a draught-board.

CHEST.—See Chapter I.

CHESTERFIELD.—The name given to a stuffed-over couch with double ends.

CHEVAL GLASS.—A large glass or mirror swinging between framed-up supports.

CINQUEFOIL.—Gothic foliation having five cusps or foils. See p. 240.

CLAMP.—To fix or render firm, to prevent wood from casting ; also mortise and tenon clamping, mitred clamping, and dowelled clamping ; *tee iron* clamps used for strengthening wide panels, and also to prevent them buckling. See chapter on "Joints."

CLASH.—The figure in oak ; the other words used are "felt" and "silver grain."

CLASSICAL.—Applied to the Greek and Roman orders of architecture.

CLAW AND BALL.—A carved detail of ancient origin, resembling a bird's claw clasped round a ball ; a characteristic detail at the bottom of Queen Anne and Georgian legs. See p. 322.

CLEAT.—A form of clamp, a batten nailed on to carpentry and joinery work for strengthening purposes.

CLEFT.—Meaning "split," stronger than sawn or "cut" stuff, and used for hand-screws, &c.

CLUB FOOT.—Used in early Queen Anne and Chippendale work, usually in conjunction with a straight type of "cabriole" leg.

CLUSTERED COLUMNS.—A Gothic detail, consisting of columns placed together in clusters of three and upwards, extensively used in the Chippendale period.

COCKED BEAD.—Semicircular and projecting beyond an edge or surface, used round drawers, especially in work of the eighteenth century makers ; when sunk below the surface, the term "sunk bead" is used, and when separated by a narrow sunk fillet or bead, it is called a "quirked" bead. A STAFF BEAD is worked upon the edge of angles, and it is also termed a "return" bead. See chapter on "Mouldings."

COLONIAL GEORGIAN.—A style of furniture and decoration based upon the work of British settlers in the United States, and having an eighteenth century influence.

COMMODE.—A small cabinet or pedestal fitted with pan for bedroom use. The name was also given to a chest of drawers.

COMPASS PLANE.—A plane with a curved or flexible sole to fit circular forms and curved shapes.

COMPO.—An abbreviation of the term "composition," a substitute for wood carving ; also called "stucco," introduced into English interior decoration by the brothers R. and J. Adam. The chief constituents are whiting, glue, and resin ; the patterns are cast from a mould carved in hard wood.

COMPOSITE.—The fifth order of architecture, a combination of Ionic and Corinthian.

CONCAVE.—A hollow curved line or surface.

CONFIDANTE.—A sofa with seats at each end.

CONIFEROUS.—A term applied to cone-bearing trees, such as the fir, cypress, pine, and yew.

CONSOLE.—A large projecting bracket, usually of a scroll form, applied indiscriminately in furniture to "console" or bracket support tables and to large brackets under beams, &c.

CONTOUR.—The profile or section of a moulding.

CONVOLUTE.—Material rolled in the form of a scroll.

COOPERED JOINTS.—They are used in curved work, and resemble those made by coopers in barrels and tubs.

CORE.—An internal mould used for castings; the term is also frequently applied to internal parts of furniture, such as the inside of a pillar; also to remove the core, *i.e.*, waste material between saw cuts in grooves and housed joints and in mortises.

CORINTHIAN.—The third order of Grecian architecture which possesses the most elaborate capital.

CORK RUBBER.—A flat piece of cork about 4 in. by 2½ in. by 1 in., used with glass-paper for finishing work. Cork carpet glued to a piece of wood answers the same purpose. Rubbers are also shaped to fit the contour of mouldings, &c.

CORNICE.—The crowning or finishing part of a capital or column, the top member of an entablature, or the projecting connection between the wall and ceiling of the room. See also BRACKET CORNICE.

CORONA.—One of the classic mouldings, usually a large flat projection in a cornice moulding. Also called a "drip" moulding, from the original use of this member, *i.e.*, in preventing "capillary attraction"; this was effected by throating or undercutting the projection (see p. 274), and rain water then could not "soak" under the "soffit."

COUNTERSINK.—A tool to form a conical depression or cavity in a piece of wood or metal to receive a screw head.

COURT CUPBOARD.—An Elizabethan form of cabinet; a chest on legs with a recessed cupboard above.

COVE.—A large hollow. This term usually refers to rooms; applied to furniture, it denotes a large hollow cornice, and is also synonymous with "niche," a curved recess which often contains a statuette.

CRAMP.—An iron or wooden instrument serving to force or bring together joints in woodwork. For chair-maker's cramp, see p. 316.

CREDENCE.—A Gothic name for a side or re-table.

CURL.—An arrangement of natural figure in the grain of wood, in the form of a feather, cut at the intersection of a large bough with the tree trunk. See chapter on "Veneering."

CURTAIN PIECE.—Refers to shaped rails, properly called "span rails," when placed above the eye-line.

CUSP.—A Gothic ornamental detail, consisting of a point or knob which is frequently carved, projecting from the intersection of two curves, a feature of trefoiled, quatrefoiled, and cinquefoiled arches. See p. 241.

CYLINDER.—In furniture this term is applied to the "fall" of a writing table in the shape of a quadrant or arc of a circle.

CYMA RECTA.—(Cyma = a wave.) A classic moulding commonly termed an "ogee" moulding. See p. 273.

CYMA REVERSA.—One of the classic mouldings, meaning a "reversed ogee" moulding. See p. 273.

D

DADO.—Dadoing, consisting of a decorated portion of a wall; also the wooden framing fixed round a room up to about 5 ft. high.

DAIS.—The raised portion of the floor at the end of a large dining-room or hall, of ancient usage, and upon which the "high table" was placed.

DEEPING.—This refers to machine saw-cuts through the deepest part of a plant. See also p. 332.

DENTILS.—An ornamental detail, consisting of small rectangular blocks with spaces between them, usually placed in a cornice moulding, and probably originating from the projecting ends of horizontal roof timbers; also used in inlaid work, the pattern being made with veneers of contrasting colours.

DESICCATING.—Drying timber in a hot-air chamber. See chapter on "Timber."

DIAGONAL.—A line joining two not adjacent angles in a four or more sided figure ; thus the cross rails in a rectangular table, called "diagonal rails."

DIAMETER.—A line through the centre of a circle or cylindrical object.

DIAPER.—A regular and systematic decorative arrangement of a repeating pattern in marquetry, inlay, painting, gesso, woven materials, and low relief carving, much used in the decorative marquetry treatment of Louis XVI. furniture.

DOG-TOOTH.—An ornamental detail characteristic of Early English work, consisting of a small pyramidal repeat ornament, used chiefly as a member in mouldings.

DOLPHIN HINGE.—So called because of its resemblance to the creature of that name, used in conjunction with quadrant stays to secretaires. See chapter on " Brasswork."

DONKEY.—A marquetry cutter's implement. See illustration on p. 221.

DONKEY EAR SHOOT.—See p. 68.

DORIC.—The first order of Grecian architecture, from the Dorian race in Ancient Greece.

DOVETAIL.—A joint so named because of its resemblance to the tail of a dove. See examples on Plate IX.

DOWEL PLATE.—An iron plate about ¼ in. thick, used to reduce dowels to any required diameter. See also p. 65.

DRAUGHTSMAN.—One who prepares plans and drawings. See also chapter on "Foremen's Work."

DRAWER LOCK CHISEL.—An instrument used chiefly for making small mortises in confined positions, generally in connection with the bolts of drawer locks.

DRAWER SLIP.—The grooved slip or strip to take the drawer bottom.

DRIFT.—The direction taken by a saw away from the right line when improperly set ; also the slanting direction of a nail when badly driven.

DRIP MOULDING.—See CORONA.

DROP ORNAMENT.—A split turned ornament used in Jacobean wood and stone work ; also a decorative detail resembling a "husk" used in eighteenth century decoration.

DUMB WAITER.—A form of dinner waggon, illustrated in chapter on " Miscellaneous Furniture."

DUST BOARD.—A horizontal division between drawers, introduced to prevent tampering with their contents, and also as a preventive against dust deposits.

E

EBENISTE.—A French term for cabinetmaker.

EBENISTERIE.—French for cabinetwork.

EBONISE.—To impart to wood by means of staining and polishing a finish resembling the real ebony wood.

ECHINUS.—A Grecian moulding with carved eggs and darts as a decorative feature.

EDGE ROLL.—A Gothic moulding detail, somewhat resembling a "staff bead."

EDGING.—The small solid square let in on the edge of a top when the face is veneered, as a protection to the veneer.

EGG AND TONGUE MOULDING.—Used largely in architectural mouldings of a classical character ; also used in Georgian furniture and decoration.

ELIZABETHAN.—Relating to the Renaissance style of architecture and woodwork prevailing during the reign of Queen Elizabeth. See also p. 251.

ELLIPSE.—An oval figure produced by cutting a cone right across in a direction not parallel to the base without touching the base. See OVAL.

EMPIRE.—A French style of decoration based upon ancient Grecian and Egyptian forms and details. " English Empire" style, a term occasionally heard, is also an interpretation of Greek forms.

ENAMEL.—A finish for furniture prepared by coating the wood with whiting and size ; this is rubbed down level and then finished off with a transparent French polish ; also a fusible substance of the nature of glass, usually nearly opaque occasionally used in the decoration of furniture mounts.

ENDIVE SCROLL.—A detail in carving belonging to the Louis XIV. and XV. styles and also the Chippendale period, the detail being derived from a species of leaf.

ENDOGENOUS.—See chapter on "Timber."

ENGRAVING.—A term applied to the decoration of marquetry, by which a "relief" effect is produced by engraving fine lines on the veneers, the lines afterwards rubbed with a black composition to render them visible.

ENRICHMENT.—A term applied to ornamental detail, usually in a continuous run such as an "enriched" moulding, &c., meaning decorated with carving, inlaying, or painting.

ENTABLATURE.—An architectural term applied to the members above the column, composed of frieze or architrave moulding and cornice moulding. Used with reference to furniture the term is synonymous with a "cornice."

ENTASIS.—The swell or slight curve in a "column" to correct the hollow effect caused by an optical illusion if quite straight.

ESCRITOIRE.—A writing desk or bureau.

ESCUTCHEON.—A heraldic term, meaning a shield charged with armorial bearings or bearing other devices; also a brass fitting for a keyhole, such as "rim escutcheon," "overlay escutcheon," and "inlaid escutcheon" cut from mother of pearl, ivory, veneer, or metal.

ETAGÈRE.—A French name given to a series of shelves supported by columns. Similar to a "What Not."

EXOGENOUS.—See chapter on "Timber."

EXTERIOR ANGLE.—A projecting or "salient" angle.

EXTRADOS.—The outside curve of an arch.

F

FAÇADE.—The front view or elevation of a building.

FACE MARK.—A mark to indicate the prepared and tested face of a piece of wood.

FACING.—Applied to furniture construction it means a thin covering of wood upon a ground-work, used for economical reasons, such as a white wood drawer rail "faced up" with Cuba mahogany.

FAIENCE.—A general term applied to glazed pottery and porcelain.

FALDSTOOL.—A portable folding seat similar to a camp stool.

FALL.—The term applied to the falling fronts of bureaux, secretaires, writing desks, and pianos.

FASCIA.—One of the classic mouldings, consisting of a broad fillet or band, a member of a moulding; also a name-plate or board above a shop front.

FAULTY.—Shaky, unsound, applied to timber.

FAUN.—A legendary demi-god, represented by a half goat and half man, used largely as a decorative detail in work of the Adam period.

FAVAS.—Diaper detail, resembling the cells in a honeycomb. Used in Louis XVI. decoration.

FEATHER EDGE.—Planing off to a point or fine edge, feathering.

FESTOON.—A decoration in the form of a wreath or garland, or flowers arranged in a curved form.

FIDDLE BACK.—Is applied to figured veneer, resembling the finely marked sycamore used in violin backs.

FIDDLE BOARD.—A term used in shipwork to designate a board cut out to receive the stems of glasses.

FILIGREE.—Ornamental work done in gold or silver wire.

FILLET.—A small "slip" or ledge used for supporting shelves; also a classic moulding, consisting of a small "band" or "fascia," used as a connecting member.

FINGER JOINT.—Composed of five tongues or fingers interlocking, used on table brackets. See p. 52.

FINIAL.—This term was originally applied to a foliated knob at the extremity of a Gothic pinnacle; it is, however, also used to denote a "finishing point," such as the carving above a newel post.

FISH SKIN.—A material prepared from fish skin, usually dressed and dyed to a delicate green colour. Used for covering caskets and clock cases, and especially suitable in combination with silver mounts and fittings. The surface presents a coarse "egg shell" appearance.

FITMENT.—Any article made and fixed to a wall or room, including panelling, chimney-pieces, and "fitted furniture."

FITTING UP.—The final process of finishing a piece of furniture after it is polished, consisting of fixing fittings, glass, &c.

FELT.—See CLASH.

FENCE.—A piece of wood fixed on a plane as a guide in planing or grooving.

FIELDED.—Applied to a panel which is moulded, sunk, or raised, or broken up into smaller panels.

FIXATIVE.—A preparation of white shellac and methylated spirit or spirits of wine, used for "fixing" or rendering permanent pencil sketches and charcoal drawings, and applied by means of a spray.

FLASH.—A timber term denoting large patches or "flashes" of brightly shaded figure.

FLATTING.—A process connected with "veneering," necessary when using buckled veneers. See p. 215. Also saw-cutting through the thickness of planks, called "flatting."

FLEUR-DE-LIS.—The royal insignia of France, supposed to represent a lily or iris.

FLOAT.—An instrument resembling a file. The cutting action is caused by a series of saw-like serrations. See p. 64.

FLUSH.—Signifies level or even with an adjoining surface

FLUTING.—A decorative detail, consisting of a series of semicircular furrows or channels round a column, shaft, or leg, or on a pilaster or frieze.

FLY RAIL.—Side rail of a flap table, which opens to support the flap.

FOIL.—Denotes the point formed by the intersection of two circular arcs ; a Gothic detail used in the "trefoil," "quatrefoil," "cinquefoil," &c.

FOLIATED.—Pertaining to the use of "foils" ; decorated ornaments enriched with leaves.

FRAMED WORK.—Indicating work "framed" together ; also "grounds" for fixing. See p. 279.

FRANÇOIS PREMIER.—A French style of furniture of the time of Francis I., noted for its delicate work and "cartouche" carving.

FRESCO.—A term applied to the *al fresco* painting upon a wet ground ; generally employed upon walls or ceilings.

FRET.—A geometric detail largely used in the Chinese and Chippendale styles, formed by cutting or piercing thin wood or metal ; also "Fretwork," and "Fretting."

FRIEZE.—That part of a "cornice" or entablature between the frieze or "architrave" moulding and the cornice moulding.

G

GADROON.—A form of "nulling" decoration characteristic of Elizabethan and Jacobean woodwork, resembling large reeds or inverted flutes on friezes and turning.

GALLERY.—A decorated wood or metal ledge round a table top or case.

GEORGIAN.—Pertaining to work executed during the reigns of the Georges, a period reaching from 1714 to 1820, but usually applied to the earlier years ; other styles being in vogue after about the middle of the eighteenth century. See p. 252.

GIRANDOLE.—A carved chandelier or wall candle bracket, a feature of the eighteenth century interior decoration.

GOBELINS.—A name given to the tapestry made in France ; after Jean Gobelin, who introduced it into that country in the fifteenth century.

GOTHIC.—A term used to describe the architecture and woodwork of the Middle Ages following on the Romanesque period ; it may be subdivided into styles as follows : twelfth century ; thirteenth century, Early English or Lancet ; fourteenth century, Decorated ; and fifteenth century, Perpendicular.

GRIFFIN.—A legendary animal, composed of a lion's body and an eagle's head and wings ; largely used in carvings belonging to the French and Italian Renaissance.

GROIN OR GROINING.—The line or rib made by or applied to the intersecting of surfaces of a vaulted roof.

GROUND.—The rough framing fixed to brickwork previous to fixing a fitment or panelling ; also the core or "groundwork" of veneered objects.

GROUNDING OUT.—A process connected with carved work. The outline is cut down with gauges, and the surplus wood removed, leaving the design projecting above the "ground" or "groundwork."

GROTESQUE.—A term usually applied to monstrous or comic figures or heads, used as ornament in wood or stone work.

GUILLOCHE.—A type of ornament composed of curved and interlacing lines, usually composing circular forms. It may be in one or more rows.

H

HANGING STILE.—The stile of a door upon which the hinges or pivots are fixed.

HARLEQUIN.—An automatic table, invented by Sheraton, the centre part rising when flaps are raised.

HATCHING.—Diagonal lines to show a section, which has been reduced in width.

HAUNCH.—The projecting part of a tenon.

HEAD.—The upper member or rail of a door, also the top part of framing. As in "semi-head," indicating a "semicircular" head.

HERRING BONING.—A veneered detail of Queen Anne work, consisting of two narrow bands of striped veneer, cut obliquely and placed together, resembling herring-bone patterns in half-timbered work.

HONE.—A stone of very fine grit, used for sharpening instruments and tools.

HOOK JOINT.—A dust-proof joint for doors of show-cases. See p. 302.

HOPPER.—A kind of trough, diminished towards the bottom, used by millers, &c. The term is generally applied to cabinet and joinery work which resembles a "hopper."

HOUSING.—The process of recessing or grooving one piece of wood into another ; also diminished housing and "stopped housing." See chapter on "Joints," pp. 43, 44.

HUSKS.—A form of drop ornament used on eighteenth century work. See pier table top, p. 131, and piano, Plate XXXVI.

HUTCH.—See CHEST.

I

IMPOST.—The capital of a column or pilaster which marks the springing of an arch ; also the part of a pillar upon which arches rest.

INCISED ORNAMENT.—Meaning to cut in or engrave ; a feature of some sixteenth century cabinetwork, the incessions being afterwards filled in with a coloured composition.

INGLE NOOK.—A recessed chimney-piece with seats on either side.

INLAYING.—A general term applied to a decorative process, in which lines, strings, and bands or flowers are grooved or cut into a groundwork. See p. 222. Refer also to INTARSIA and MARQUETRY.

INTARSIA.—Meaning to insert or to inlay. A general term applied to inlaid decorative work where the design is cut out and fitted into corresponding cavities in a ground, whereas "Marquetry" is cut through several thicknesses of veneer and built up into a sheet before glueing to the groundwork.

IN THE WHITE.—A trade term applied to cabinetwork in any wood before it is polished.

INTRADOS.—The under or inside of a curved arch.

IONIC.—The second order of Grecian architecture, the name derived from Ionia in Greece.

ISOMETRIC PROJECTION.—See p. 32.

IVORY BLACK.—Made from charred bones or ivory ; a black substance used for staining.

J

JACOBEAN.—The style of woodwork immediately following the Elizabethan period, from James I., 1603. Applied to work of early Renaissance type.

JAMB.—The side of a wall opening. The upright portion of a fireplace.

JAPANNING.—See LACQUER.

JARDINIERE.—A box or pedestal specially designed to take flowers. See p. 173.

JIGGER.—A light treadle fret saw, used for frets and general shape cutting.

JOINT STOOL.—Belonging to early Tudor times. See Chair Chart, Plate L.

JOYNER.—The original term applied to mediæval craftsmen before the separation into "cabinet-maker," one who made furniture, and "joiner," whose work was restricted to that of a fixed or architectural character. See Chapter I.

K

KERF.—The cut made by a saw.

KEYING.—A method of strengthening mitre joints, &c. Illustrated on p. 45.

KEYSTONE.—A wedge-shaped stone placed at the centre of an arch, serving to bind it together ; a detail imitating this form was occasionally used in Elizabethan woodwork.

KIDNEY TABLE.—Resembling a kidney shape in plan, introduced by Sheraton in pedestal writing tables. See p. 111.

KNEE-PART.—The upper portion of a leg into which the rails tenoned.

KNUCKLE JOINT.—Resembling a finger joint. See p. 52.

L

LACQUER.—Also the French term "Lacque," resembling japanning ; applied to furniture, it refers to Japanese lacquer work and the French Vernis Martin process, used chiefly in commodes and cabinets of the Louis XV. and Chippendale periods.

LADDER BACK.—A term applied in the late seventeenth century to chair backs, the slats or rails of which resemble the rungs of a ladder. Chippendale also used them.

LAMBREQUIN.—The centre piece of drapery in a valance.

LAMINATE.—To build up in layers ; also known as "three-ply," "five-ply," &c.

LANCET.—A pointed arch of thirteenth century Gothic. See GOTHIC.

LANDSCAPE PANEL.—A panel placed with the grain horizontal.

LATTICE.—Resembling network. "Lattice Back" refers to a Sheraton chair. See p. 313. He also used brass lattice work in bookcase doors, with pleated silk behind. Also "Lattice Pattern," inlay work of the Louis XVI. period.

LECTERN.—An ecclesiastical reading-desk, usually made of wood, and also in brass and stone.

LINEN-FOLD PANELS.—A Tudor detail. See examples on p. 287.

LINING UP.—A term synonymous with thickening up ; a moulded frame screwed underneath a top to strengthen it, and also to increase the thickness.

LISTEL.—An alternative term for "fillet," a flat moulding member. See FILLET.

LIVERY CUPBOARD.—A name given to cupboards in which bread was kept for distribution to the poor. There are some still in use in St Albans Abbey.

LOCKING STILE.—That stile of a door upon which the lock is fixed ; also called in the case of double doors a "meeting stile."

LOOSE SEAT.—A stuffed frame let into the framing of a chair but not fixed.

LOO TABLES.—Oval tables made for the old game of loo.

LOPER.—The "sliders" supporting a bureau fall, and also the "sliders" of an extending dining-table.

LOTUS.—Egyptian decorative detail resembling a water-flower.

LOUVRED LIGHT.—A frame with bevelled slats, designed for ventilation purposes, and used in shipwork, &c.

LOW RELIEF.—Applied to "carving" or "gesso work," the ornamental detail of which does not project far from the groundwork, as, for instance, carved panel centres and ceiling decorations of the "Adam" period.

LOZENGE.—Resembling a "diamond shape," a feature of Elizabethan work in overlays, and in "lozenge shaped" panels of "Adam" period.

LUNETTE.—A crescent or semicircular space or window.

M

MANTELPIECE.—The shelf above a fireplace.

MARQUETRY.—A form of inlaid work. See chapter on "Veneering," pp. 209 *et seq*. See also INTARSIA and INLAYING.

MEDALLION.—A plaque or medal, with figures or heads in low relief, a classic detail largely used by the brothers R. and J. Adam.

MITRE.—The intersection of a moulding; an angle of 45 degrees equals a "right mitre."

MITRE BLOCK.—A tool used for planing mitres (see p. 17); also "Mitre Shooting Board" (see p. 68), and "Mitre Cut" (see p. 67), a prepared block for cutting the mitre angles.

MODILLIONS.—Enriched brackets placed under the cornice in the Corinthian and Composite styles of architecture; also a term applied to small brackets used as "dentils" under a cornice moulding.

MODULE.—The tenth part of the semi-diameter of a column in Classic architecture, forming a unit of measure by which other proportions are decided.

MORTISE.—A cavity cut into a piece of timber to receive a projection upon another piece called a "tenon."

MOSAIC.—Decoration composed of very small pieces of wood or stone; in woodwork also known as "Tonbridge ware" and mosaic bandings.

MOTHER-OF-PEARL.—The hard and brilliantly coloured internal layer of shells, chiefly those of pearl oysters. "Japanese" and "Blue Pearl" are similar substances characterised by richer markings and colour.

MOTTLED.—Meaning a speckled or variegated grain in veneer, giving a spotty effect.

MOULDING.—A projecting band shaped in section, used to break the continuity of surfaces, and for decorative effect. See pp. 273, 274.

MOUNT.—A general term applied to metalwork or "ormolu," used for decorating furniture; sometimes finely sculptured and chased, as in historical French furniture.

MULLET.—A grooved piece of wood used for testing panel edges and drawer bottoms.

MUNTING or MULLION.—The inside vertical divisions of doors and framing.

N

NECKING.—Any small band or moulding near the top of a shaft or column.

NEEDLE POINT.—The pointed end of a needle, used for fixing light and delicate overlays and mouldings.

NEWEL.—A large post supporting a handrail.

NICHE.—A semicircular recess in a wall or cabinet to receive a bust or statuette.

NESTED TABLES.—See chapter on "Tables," p. 121.

NULLING.—Turned or carved detail, quadrant shaped in section, used on friezes and mouldings in Jacobean work.

O

OBLIQUE PROJECTION.—A method of graphically presenting an object in three dimensions, viz., height, breadth, and thickness. See p. 32.

OGEE.—A waved moulding, Classic term "Cyma Recta." A "broken ogee" consists of an "ogee" moulding with the continuity of its sections broken by a square or "fillet." See p. 273.

OLD WOMAN'S TOOTH.—A tool with a projecting tooth or iron ; a router. See p. 9.

ORIEL.—A projecting window, frequently semi-octagonal in shape, and supported by corbels not going right down to the ground ; first used as a Gothic feature.

ORMOLU.—A composition of brass and zinc made to resemble gold, the material chiefly used for casting furniture mounts ; often richly chased and "water gilt."

OTTOMAN.—A seat without a back, of Turkish origin. In a box ottoman the seat is hinged.

OVAL.—A term incorrectly applied to an ellipse, really a form composed of two semi-ellipses egg-shaped.

OVERMANTEL.—The upper portion of a chimney-piece.

OVER-DOOR.—A pedimental form fixed above a doorway.

OVOLO.—A Classic moulding. See p. 273.

OXIDISING.—A finish imparted to metalwork by treatment with acids upon a brass surface.

OYSTER SHELL.—Veneering. See p. 224.

P

PARCHMENT PANEL.—An alternative term for a linen-fold panel. See example on p. 287.

PARQUETRY.—A process of inlaying or building up a floor of wood in the form of mosaic. See also chapter on "Veneering."

PATERÆ.—Small circular or elliptic carved ornaments applied to friezes, pediments, chair legs, &c.

PEDESTAL.—The part underneath the column in architecture ; also a stand for statuettes, &c. (see p. 205) ; also a rectangular form with a cupboard or drawers supporting the frieze and top of sideboards and various tables : hence the term "pedestal table," &c.

PEDIMENT.—A triangular or curved gable over a portico door or window ; also a similar form placed above the cornice in various types of furniture.

PEITRA DURA.—A form of inlaying in marble.

PELLETS.—Small wooden plugs or studs used for concealing screw-heads. See p. 74.

PEMBROKE TABLE.—A table with a fixed frame and flaps on each side, supported with brackets.

PENDANT.—A hanging ornament on ceilings and roofs, or to parts of furniture.

PERPENDICULAR STYLE.—The last of the Gothic periods, fifteenth and sixteenth centuries. The name refers to the upright and rectilinear forms of its tracery, &c.

PIE-CRUST TABLE.—Small circular tables with the edge curved, and raised above the surface, as in Chippendale tables.

PIER GLASS.—A wall mirror hanging between windows, usually above a semicircular or "pier table."

PIGEON HOLES.—The divisions or compartments in a stationery case for the reception of papers, &c.

PILASTER.—A rectangular shaped column fixed close to a wall or similar surface, and projecting about one-fourth of its width.

PILLAR.—An alternative term for, and synonymous with, "column" or shaft.

PILLAR AND CLAW.—Applied to circular tables of the eighteenth and nineteenth centuries made with a centre pillar and claw feet.

PITCH.—Applied to the angle or "pitch" of a plane iron.

PLANTED.—Applied to mouldings, means those mitred and fixed separately from the framing or groundwork, not stuck on the solid.

PLAQUE.—A circular or elliptic medallion of porcelain, Sevres, or Wedgwood, used in the decoration of furniture.

PLINTH.—The framed-up base or bottom part of carcase work.

PLUGGING.—Consists of driving pieces of wood into the joints of brick walls for purposes of fixing framing. See p. 277.

POCKETING.—A method of preparing parts of work for the reception of screws. See p. 51.

POLLARD.—A tree that has had the boughs and top "polled" or "lopped off," causing a peculiar growth at the top, which yields finely figured veneers.

POUNCE.—A coloured powdery substance, used by marquetry cutters to copy and mark out designs, which they do with a pounce box.

PRESS.—A dwarf cupboard or wardrobe, used for linen.

PRIME COST ESTIMATE.—Refer to ESTIMATE.

PROFILE.—The outline or contour of an object.

PROJECTION.—A term given to the overhang of a top cornice or moulding. See also ISOMETRIC and OBLIQUE PROJECTION.

Q

QUADRANT STAY.—A metal support used for supporting flaps, falls, and secretaire fronts. See p. 264.

QUARTERED OAK.—The method of cutting a log into four quarters, and then parallel to the "medullary rays" or "silver grain," synonymous with "wainscot oak." See description on p. 240.

QUATREFOIL.—A Gothic detail consisting of four foils within a circle. See p. 240.

QUIRK.—The narrow groove or "sunk fillet" at the side of a bead.

R

RADIAL BAR.—A wooden bar to which a point and pencil are attached in order to strike large curves.

RAKING.—Pitched up, out of horizontal.

RATCHET BRACE.—A brace or stock with a wheel and tooth attachment, which enables it to be used in corners close to a wall or floor.

REBATE.—A rectangular channel on the edge of a piece of wood or framing worked with a rebate plane.

RECESS.—An alcove in a room, or a niche shape in a wall.

RECESSING.—Refers to a machine process, by which an effect is obtained similar to overlaid fretwork, a feature of Chippendale work.

REEDING.—Semicircular moulded projections, similar to inverted flutes on turned shafts and pillars.

RENAISSANCE.—Meaning literally, New Birth. A style of architecture and decoration which originated in Italy in the fifteenth century.

REP.—A material used in upholstery work, of a fine cord-like texture.

REREDOS.—The back of an altar ; an altar piece or screen.

RETURN.—This term indicates a repeat or continuation of two adjoining faces.

RIBAND DECORATION.—Carved or inlaid ornament resembling ribbon, a feature of various eighteenth century styles.

"RIBAND BACK."—A characteristic Chippendale chair back, p. 313.

RIBBON AND STICK.—Ornamental detail resembling ribbon wound upon a stick, Louis XVI. detail.

RIFFLER.—A curved file or rasp.

RIM.—An edge or projection round tray and table tops, also the circular shape underneath the tops of shaped tables.

ROCOCO.—French ornament of the Louis XIV. and XV. period, resembling shell forms and dripping water, sometimes referred to as "pebble and splash."

ROE.—Pertaining to the peculiar markingsof figured veneer, a spotty arrangement or fish roe appearance.

ROSETTE.—An ornament or patera resemblig a rose.

ROTTEN STONE.—A soft stone used in combination with oil in polishing "Buhl," pearl, and metal work.

RULE JOINT.—See chapter on "Joints."

RUN OUT.—Applied to a moulding which runs out to a point as in old work, before mitres were used.

S

SAND BAG.—An arrangement used for curved veneering. See p. 214.

SAG.—The curvature effected by the action of a weight or load, as in thin shelves in a bookcase.

SALIENT ANGLE.—An outside or projectin angle or corner.

SCALLOP.—Carved detail resembling an "escallop shell."

SCOTIA.—A classic moulding. See p. 273.

SCRIBING.—See description on p. 69.

SCRIBING PIECE.—A piece of stuff screwed on to the back of a carcase, and under the projection of the top, for the purpose of being scribed over the skirting.

SCROLL ORNAMENT.—An architectural detail of convolute form, i.e., rolled together.

SCRUTOIRE or SCRIPTOIRE.—An old name given to enclosed writing cabinets or tables, from Escritoire.

SECRETAIRE.—A piece of furniture with falling front used for writing purposes, an escritoire ; usually applied to the deep drawer which pulls forward and has a hinged front.

SECTION.—A representation of any object as if cut through on a line, which is indicated in plans and working drawings by blue section lines.

SERPENTINE.—A term applied to various articles of furniture, such as "serpentine sideboard," in which the front lines in plan consist of a serpentine or curved shape.

SETTEE.—A light seat with low back and arms, sometimes stuffed.

SETTING OUT.—The process of preparing rods and working drawings.

SETTLE.—An old form of seat with ends and a back.

SHADED MARQUETRY.—A process of shading, effected with hot sand. See chapter on "Veneering."

SHOW WOOD.—Applied to stuffed chairs with parts of the frame showing.

SKIVER.—An inferior kind of leather used for lining table tops, and made from split sheepskin.

SLATS.—Horizontal rails in a chair back.

SLIDERS.—Flaps or shelves, which pull or slide out of a carcase. See also LOPERS.

SLOT SCREWING.—A method of fixing whereby the screw heads are not seen. See p. 277.

SOCLE.—A plain block acting as a plinth or pedestal to a statuette.

SOFA TABLE.—A table with flaps at the ends, designed by Sheraton.

SOFFIT.—The under side of an opening, i.e., head lining in a wall ; also the under side of wide "corona" mouldings.

SOLE.—The bottom or face of a plane.

SPADE TOE.—A characteristic finish at the bottom of tapered legs in the eighteenth century styles, the outline resembling a spade in shape.

SPANDREL or SPANDRIL.—The triangular space left between one side of the curve of an arch and the sides of a rectangle enclosing it. Span-rail, a perversion of the above, is a term applied to a curved rail between two uprights. See Dresser on p. 97.

SPECIFICATION.—A written statement giving a minute description and particulars of work to be executed.

SPINDLE.—A small turned pillar used in galleries ; also applied to a moulding machine.

SPINET.—An early form of piano.

SPIRAL TURNING.—A special process of turned work on the principle of Archimedes' screw, characteristic of chair and table legs of the seventeenth century.

SPLAT or SPLAD.—The upright and wide rail in a chair back, usually applied to chairs of the Queen Anne period; also called "Banister" when narrow.

SPLAY.—A slope, or bevel, of unequal depth or width.

SPLIT HANDLES.—Brass drop handles of the Queen Anne period, resembling "split" turning, and usually cast hollow.

SPRUNG MOULDING.—A term applied to a curved moulding ; also a thin moulded piece of wood used for cornices, and attached to blocks or brackets fixed to the cornice frame.

SPOON BACK.—A term applied to Queen Anne chair backs, which, when viewed from the side, resemble the curve in a spoon, and fit into the figure.

SQUAB.—A loose cushion seat for a chair or couch.

STACKING.—Refers to seasoning of timber ; the planks or balks are "stacked" with spaces in between to allow the free access of air.

STAFF BEAD.—Synonymous with return bead, worked upon a salient angle with a quirk upon each side.

STALL.—The seat for an ecclesiastical dignitary in a church ; also the choir stalls.

STANDARD.—Applied to furniture, means the upright supports of a toilet glass frame. For timber, see p. 333.

STEAM CHEST.—An iron contrivance or box containing steam for purposes of heating glue, cauls for veneering, and bending wood.

STILE.—The outside vertical members of a door or piece of framing.

STRAPWORK.—Carved detail derived from bands frequently interlacing, used in the decoration of furniture, especially in the Elizabethan and Jacobean periods.

STUB TENON.—A short tenon.

STUCCO.—A fine plaster-like substance used for internal decorations, chiefly of the Adam period.

STUCK MOULDING.—Any moulding worked upon the solid, i.e., stiles and rails of a door.

STUD.—A small metal object, with projecting head part, used for supporting adjustable shelves See p. 143.

STUFF-OVER.—Applied to chairs stuffed all over.

STYLE.—Applied to furniture and decoration, means "period" work, or the delineation of certain characteristic proportions and forms in vogue during a specific period, or the manner of a certain master or designer, i.e., Sheraton and Adam styles.

SUNK PANEL.—A recessed form, used in pilasters.

SURBASE.—In architecture the group of mouldings at the top of the pedestal ; in furniture, a moulded part between the cornice and plinth, such as the table part.

SWAG.—A form of swinging or suspended ornament, usually drapery or festoons of flowers, characteristic of many styles.

SWAN-NECK.—Applied to the curved pediments on Chippendale cabinets.

SWEEP.—An alternative term for curve, usually applied to a symmetrical freehand curve.

SWIVEL HOOK.—A reversible pivoted hook fixed in wardrobes.

T

TALL-BOY.—A double chest of drawers, one carcase above another.

TAMBOUR.—A flexible shutter or fall, made by glueing thin strips of wood to a linen backing.

TANG.—The end of a chisel or tool which enters the handle.

TAPER.—A diminishing form characteristic of the eighteenth century legs, usually with a "spade toe."

TEMPLATE.—A pattern made of thin wood or metal.

TERMINAL.—The finish to a newel or standard.

TERN FEET.—Tern meaning three, applied to Chippendale and Louis XV. work. Feet consisting of a three scroll arrangement.

TESTER.—The flat covering at the top of a bed, in the form of a canopy supported by posts;
when only at the head it is a half tester.

THICKNESSING UP.—The process of apparently increasing the thickness of a top by glueing a
narrow margin of wood on the under side.

THREE-PLY.—See LAMINATE.

THUMB PLANE.—Small planes.

THURMING.—A process of turning by which a square moulded effect is obtained. See p. 272.

TOAT.—A plane handle.

TOOTHING.—Effected with a toothing plane, to assist the cohesion of two surfaces. See
descriptions on p. 212.

TORTOISE SHELL.—Used in "Buhl" work and inlaying; a gilt or vermilion groundwork is
prepared to add lustre to the shell.

TORUS.—A Classic moulding, resembling a large bead.

TRACERY.—Ornamental geometrical divisions and overlays in Gothic work, also synonymous
fretwork in Chippendale work, also pierced brass and metal lattice work in Sheraton
doors used in combination with silk backing.

TRAMMEL.—An instrument used for describing ellipses. See illustration on p. 28.

TRANSVERSE SECTION.—A cross section horizontal, a sectional plan.

TRAVERSING.—The process of cross planing wide surfaces. See p. 60.

TREFOIL.—A Gothic detail consisting of three foils, "trefoliated." See p. 240.

TREILLAGE.—A form of trellis work, made with laths of wood, and used for floral decoration.

TRENCHING.—Grooving.

TRESTLE TABLE.—The original form of table, consisting of boards placed upon trestles; now
used for portable purposes.

TRIPTYCH.—An altar piece made of three parts—a centre, and two side compartments
folding over the centre.

TROCHILUS.—A classic moulding, consisting of a complex hollow curve.

TUDOR ROSE.—A conventional carved rendering of a rose characteristic of early Tudor work.
See example on p. 281.

TUSCAN.—One of the five architectural orders, a variety of the "Doric."

U

UNDER-CUT.—A term applied to mouldings of the Louis XIV. and XV. periods; also termed
"Sloper Nose"; also under-cut carving; a feature of Grinling Gibbons' work; leaving
portions of the work separate from the ground.

UPSETT FIBRE.—Caused by unskilled felling, whereby the fibres are crushed. See chapter
on "Timber."

URN.—A vase-shaped vessel, used as turned detail or ornaments; also urns and knife cases
standing upon a pedestal and characteristic of the Adam period.

V

VALANCE.—A fringe of drapery hanging from a cornice or bed rail.

VAULTING.—Arched work in roofs and ceilings.

VENEER.—Thin sheets of wood, the thickness ranging from $\frac{1}{32}$ to $\frac{1}{16}$ of an inch, termed
"knife" and "saw cut."

VERNIS MARTIN.—A French process of "Lacquer" or "Lacque" work invented by Vernis
Martin, born in 1706.

VESTIBULE.—An antechamber between the hall and outer doors.

VIGNETTE.—Gothic detail, running ornament of fine leaves and tendrils.

VOLUTE.—A spiral scroll used in Ionic, Corinthian, and Composite capitals.

VOIDER.— An old name for a butler's tray.

W

WAINSCOT.—Applied to timber, means oak cut specially to show the "silver grain." "Wain-scoting" is synonymous with "Dadoing"; the panelling about five feet high round a room. See chapter on "Timber," p. 332.

WARPING.—The effect produced on timber due to unequal shrinkage ; also termed "winding."

WATER GILDING.—The gilding of ormolu mounts by covering them with a thin deposit of gold and mercury, the latter being then volatilised.

WATER LEAF.—An ornamental detail resembling an elongated laurel leaf used chiefly in Hepplewhite and Sheraton work.

WAVE MOULDING.—Resembling a wave in outline, executed chiefly in ebony and ivory, or stained sycamore. See examples on p. 224.

WAX INLAYING.—A species of incised work, filled in with coloured wax substances.

WORKING DRAWING.—A full-sized representation of an object with sections. Plans indicated by red section lines, and vertical sections with blue.

WROUGHT (abbreviated form, "Wrot").—A term used by architects, synonymous with "worked" or "planed."

WHAT-NOT.—A tier of shelves supported by turned posts. See ETAGERE.

Y

YORKSHIRE DRESSER.—A form of dresser with a low back, made in oak or deal, and peculiar to Yorkshire.

Terms applied to timber, tools, and construction will be found in the chapters dealing with those subjects.

INDEX

A

P

Q

R